# The Japanese Shakespeare

I0593018

Offering the first book-length study in English on Tsubouchi and Shakespeare, Gallimore offers an overview of the theory and practice of Tsubouchi's Shakespeare translation and argues for Tsubouchi's place as "the Japanese Shakespeare."

Shakespeare translation is one of the achievements of modern Japanese culture, and no one is more associated with that achievement than the writer and scholar Tsubouchi Shōyō (1859–1935). This book looks at how Tsubouchi received Shakespeare in the context of his native literature and his strategies for bridging the gaps between Shakespeare's rhetoric and his developing language. Offering a significant contribution to the field of global Shakespeare and literary translation, Gallimore explores dominant stylistic features of the early twentieth-century Shakespeare translations of Tsubouchi and analyses the translations within larger linguistic, historical, and cultural traditions in local Japanese, universal Chinese, and spiritual Western elements.

This book will appeal to any student, researcher, or scholar of literary translation, particularly those interested in the complexities of Shakespeare in translation and Japanese language, culture, and society.

**Daniel Gallimore** is a professor in the School of Humanities at Kwansei Gakuin University, Japan. He completed his DPhil in Oriental Studies at Oxford University, UK.

# Routledge Advances in Translation and Interpreting Studies

**The Sociology of Translation and the Politics of Sustainability**
Explorations Across Cultures and Natures
*Edited by John Ødemark, Åmund Norum Resløkken, Ida Lillehagen
and Eivind Engebretsen*

**Relevance and Text-on-Screen in Audiovisual Translation**
The Pragmatics of Creative Subtitling
*Ryoko Sasamoto*

**Critical Approaches to Institutional Translation and Interpreting**
Challenging Epistemologies
*Edited by Esther Monzó-Nebot and María Lomeña-Galiano*

**Towards Inclusion and Social Justice in Institutional Translation and Interpreting**
Revealing Hidden Practices of Exclusion
*Edited by Esther Monzó-Nebot and María Lomeña-Galiano*

**Agencies in Feminist Translator Studies**
Barbara Godard and the Crossroads of Literature in Canada
*Elena Castellano-Ortolà*

**Collaborative Poetry Translation**
Processes, Priorities and Relationships in the PoetTrio Method
*W.N. Herbert, Francis Jones and Fiona Sampson*

**The Japanese Shakespeare**
Language and Context in the Translations of Tsubouchi Shōyō
*Daniel Gallimore*

For more information about this series, please visit: www.routledge.com/Routledge-Advances-in-Translation-and-Interpreting-Studies/book-series/RTS

# The Japanese Shakespeare

Language and Context in the
Translations of Tsubouchi Shōyō

**Daniel Gallimore**

Routledge
Taylor & Francis Group
LONDON AND NEW YORK

First published 2025
by Routledge
4 Park Square, Milton Park, Abingdon, Oxon OX14 4RN

and by Routledge
605 Third Avenue, New York, NY 10158

*Routledge is an imprint of the Taylor & Francis Group, an informa business*

*British Library Cataloguing-in-Publication Data*
A catalogue record for this book is available from the British Library

ISBN: 978-1-032-27700-4 (hbk)
ISBN: 978-1-032-27701-1 (pbk)
ISBN: 978-1-003-29377-4 (ebk)

DOI: 10.4324/9781003293774

The Open Access version of chapters 2 and 3 were funded by Daniel Gallimore.

This book is dedicated in grateful memory of my parents, John and Primrose Gallimore.

# Contents

**4   Staging Shōyō**                                                          149

# Preface

This monograph on the early twentieth-century Japanese Shakespeare translator Tsubouchi Shōyō (known generally in Japan and here by his pen name Shōyō) has grown out of my two previous published books: the first my doctoral thesis on the treatment of prosody in Japanese translations of *A Midsummer Night's Dream* (2012) and the second a study of an experimental musical drama by Shōyō (2016) that deepened my interest in his ideas and rich cultural background. As the centenary of the completion of his translation of Shakespeare's Complete Works in 1928 approaches, I have wanted to produce a longer and more comprehensive introduction to his translations and individual reception of Shakespeare, and having taught Shakespeare's plays to my students in Japan over the last two decades, I hope too that this monograph will make a valid contribution to the field of global Shakespeare. Shōyō's fascination with reality and illusion, with the art and craft of writing, and with linguistic and cultural difference, not to mention the way that Shakespeare affected his view of his native culture, all seem to me relevant to our contemporary situation. My analyses in Chapters 3 and 4 focus mainly on Shōyō's translations of *Hamlet*, *King Lear*, *Macbeth*, and *Othello*, together with *The Merchant of Venice* and *The Tempest*, and a further nine of his Shakespeare translations are discussed within the book.

Since this book is intended for readers both with and without Japanese reading ability, a concern in Chapters 3 and 4 has been the presentation of excerpts from Shōyō's translations. The beauty of Sino-Japanese *kanji* characters and native *kana* phonetic symbols was certainly important to Shōyō, and (like most Japanese writers) he exploits visual relationships between characters and symbols to enhance the poetics of his translations. Most of the excerpts in Chapter 3 on Shōyō's translating style include the original text as it was printed in the prewar Japanese script that is substantially the same as modern-day usage, but I have chosen not to include Japanese script for the excerpts in Chapter 4, which are focussed mainly on stage directions and the organisation of speeches for which the visual impact is less significant. All the examples include romanised transliterations, and I have also sometimes included phrase-by-phrase back translations where stylistic points cannot be adequately explained by glosses alone. It should also be noted that, with the exception of a few well-known words such as "Tokyo," I have followed the standard practice of macronising double *a*, *u*, and *o* vowels in Japanese words (e.g., *ōkii*, "big") and some consecutive *o* and *u* combinations (e.g., "Shōyō" for "Shouyou," pronounced "Shoh-yoh," but not *omou*, "think"). Japanese names are given with the family name first (e.g., Tsubouchi Shōyō), and I use Edo and Tokugawa interchangeably to refer to the era in which Shōyō was born, which lasted from 1603 to the Meiji Restoration of 1868. Translations of quotations from Japanese texts are my own translation unless indicated otherwise.

Perhaps as a reflection of Shōyō's singlemindedness, the research and writing of this book has been more of a solo effort than it might have been, but I have been helped along the way by numerous individuals and institutions, starting with my colleagues and students at Kwansei Gakuin University. A lecture I gave to the university's Society of English and American Literature in September 2019 was particularly helpful in formulating the book's general direction.

That lecture was given just after I had returned from a year's sabbatical leave kindly granted by Kwansei Gakuin, the first ten months of which were spent as a Visiting Fellow at the Northrop Frye Centre, Victoria College, Toronto, where the bulk of my research was carried out. I am indebted to the College's principal, Angela Esterhammer, for her generosity and kindness before, during, and since my stay in Toronto, and to the Centre's director, Bob Davidson, who invited me to present my initial findings to the Centre in November 2018.

In 2021, I was honoured to be invited by Fuyuki Hiromi and Motoyama Tetsuhito of Waseda University to participate in their ongoing collaborative research project, "A Brave New World for Japanese Shakespeare Adaptations: Rethinking Shakespeare Studies through Adaptations" (MEXT/JSPS KAKENHI Grant Number JP22H00648), which has further enabled me to develop my Shōyō studies. I have also greatly appreciated assistance given by the staff of the University of Toronto Libraries and of the Kwansei Gakuin University Library, and by Ishibuchi Rieko at the Tsubouchi Memorial Theatre Museum Library, Waseda.

Editors Katie Peace and Khin Thazin at Routledge's Singapore office have offered unwavering support, and I am grateful to two long-time friends, Brian Powell (my initial doctoral supervisor at Oxford) and Aragorn Quinn of the University of Wisconsin-Milwaukee, for their expert comments on my chapters.

Among others who have encouraged me directly and indirectly in my Shōyō studies, I would like to mention Ashizu Kaori; Mari Boyd; Leo Tak-hung Chan; Jessica Chiba; Mika Eglinton; Andrew Gerstle; John Gillespie; Jonathan Hart; Hayashi Kazutoshi; Graham Holderness; Ishiguro Tarō; Kawachi Yoshiko; Kawai Shōichirō; Nely Keinänen; Lee Hyonu and the Shakespeare Association of Korea; Morita Masaya; Cody Poulton; Jonah Salz; Suematsu Michiko; Glynne Walley; Alex Watson; and Laurence Williams. My greatest debt remains to my wife Miho, who kept me going with countless cups of *kanpo* herbal tea as I got the thing done.

# Acknowledgements

I am grateful to the editors of the journals named here for permission to reproduce revised versions of sections of my published articles:

*Critical Survey* 33, no. 1 (Spring 2021): 8–22; Society of Humanities, Kwansei Gakuin University, *Jinbun Ronkyū* 72, no. 3 (December 2022): 65–90; Department of English and American Literature, Kwansei Gakuin University, *Journal of the Society of English and American Literature* 61 (March 2017): 1–19, and *Journal of the Society of English and American Literature* 65 (March 2021): 1–20; British Shakespeare Association, *Shakespeare* 9, no. 4 (July 2013): 428–47.

# 1    In Search of Shōyō

## Shōyō's Reputation

Tsubouchi Shōyō is one of those Shakespeare translators, like Voltaire in eighteenth-century France and Boris Pasternak in Soviet Russia, who was also a significant literary figure in his own right. In modern translation studies, it is generally accepted that the translator is something more than an invisible mediator: that the voices of translators are demonstrably present in their translations, whose appreciation can depend on an understanding as much of translators' lives and cultural contexts as of the original source texts.[1] Shōyō's voice is distinctly audible in the sonorities and theatrical mannerisms of his Shakespeare translations, and he was also an intellectual whose prolific ideas and creative works made an influential contribution to the formation of a modern culture in late nineteenth- and early twentieth-century Japan. His ideas on Shakespeare were especially central to his agenda of cultural reform as it was articulated through numerous books and articles published between the 1880s and his death in 1935. Shōyō's reputation reached its height in the years following the completion of his translation of Shakespeare's Complete Works in 1928, and while it has been overshadowed by contemporaries such as Futabatei Shimei and Natsume Sōseki, he is still known as the "father" not only of Japanese Shakespeare studies but also of the modern Japanese novel and comparative literature in Japan: the first person to raise the basic questions of what his native tradition could learn from Western drama and literature and to establish norms of Shakespeare translation. This monograph attempts to assimilate a stylistic analysis of Shōyō's Shakespeare translations with an analysis of his view of Shakespeare and of Shakespeare's various meanings in modern Japan.

Shōyō's reputation has been kept alive in his own country through the steady stream of biographies and critical studies mentioned here, through the two works that made his name at the age of twenty-six – his theoretical polemic *Shōsetsu shinzui* (The Essence of the Novel, 1885–6) and novel *Tōsei shosei katagi* (Characters of Modern Day Students, 1885–6), which have remained continually in print – through his play *Kiri hitoha* (A Single Paulownia Leaf, 1894–5), which was reckoned the best kabuki play of the Meiji era and is still occasionally performed,[2] and through the Tsubouchi Memorial Theatre Museum which he was instrumental in founding at Waseda University; it was formally opened on 27 October 1928, and named to commemorate the

DOI: 10.4324/9781003293774-1

completion of Shōyō's translation of Shakespeare's Complete Works the same year. To the left of the museum's façade, which is modelled on the Elizabethan Fortune Playhouse, a bust of Shōyō oversees the daily exits and entrances, looking professorial and perhaps a little like a samurai hero from his beloved kabuki.

Since Shōyō's Shakespeare translations were replaced by more modern ones as standard versions for reading and performance in the 1960s and '70s,[3] his more lasting legacy lies in the continued vibrancy of the Japanese theatre and Shakespeare performance and studies in Japan. Outside Japan, Shōyō has been the subject of only a couple of book-length studies in English,[4] but he appears frequently in studies of modern Japanese literature and drama and Shakespeare's reception in Japan and Asia. The growth of the latter as a field of Shakespeare studies in the last three decades offers an opportunity for a longer study of Shōyō's Shakespeare, but even in the Japanese literature these have usually been considered in the context of his other achievements without a single book being devoted solely to the translations. Moreover, Shōyō's landmark 1891 essay on *Macbeth* (discussed later in this chapter) is usually read as a contribution to his debate with Mori Ōgai on the role of "hidden ideals" in literature (*botsurisō ronsō*) rather than for what it says about Shakespeare.

While not an explicitly political writer, Shōyō courted controversy throughout his career as he sought to work out his points of view and keep the spirit of drama alive in modern Japan. Since he always asserted the utilitarian goal of stimulating reform of his native drama by translating Shakespeare, one can suppose that his arguments are correspondingly stimulated by his engagement with the dialectic of Shakespearean drama. Shōyō is concerned with positioning Shakespeare in relation to his native drama and establishing reasons for translating and staging Shakespeare in Japan, and he frequently rues his own inadequacy and that of his modernising language to do justice to the diversity and wealth of Shakespeare's language.

Shōyō's most complete statement comes in "Jibun no honyaku ni tsuite" (On My Shakespeare Translations), originally composed in 1918 and included at the end of his *Shēkusupia kenkyū shiori*, the introduction to Shakespeare studies that formed the final, fortieth volume in his series of Shakespeare translations (and is a testament to the breadth of his scholarship). In this essay, Shōyō outlines the evolution of his translating style from his initial *jōruri* (i.e. classical recitative) adaptation of *Julius Caesar* in 1884 through periods of scholarly literalism and theatrical experimentation as he directed a number of his translations for performance by the Bungei Kyōkai (Literary Arts Association), Japan's first modern acting company, which he helped to found in 1905. Shōyō's point of reference is kabuki, and he describes his controversial *Hamlet* translation of 1909 as having been "touched inevitably by kabuki and the seven-five syllabic meter of Japanese poetics."[5] Inspired by Lafcadio Hearn's advice to render Shakespeare in his colloquial language,[6] after the company was dissolved in 1913 he adopted a version of contemporary colloquial Japanese for the rest of the plays as he translated them over the next fifteen years, and then revised all his translations in the last seven years of his life to make them more suited for theatrical performance. The three poles of Shōyō's evolution as a translator are his debt to – and initial distance from – his native drama and literature; his accumulating knowledge of Shakespeare and the Western critical and performance traditions; and the rapid modernisation of the language during his lifetime, in particular the integration of the classical written and colloquial forms (*genbun itchi*) accomplished during the second half of the Meiji era. Shōyō is guided throughout his five stages by the touchstones of Shakespeare's realism and what he calls "the unchanging naturalness of Shakespeare's language."[7] Chapter 2 of this monograph explores this remarkable literary and academic hinterland, and Chapter 3 considers the extent to which this hinterland is present in his style of translating individual Shakespeare plays.

Born in 1859, eight years before the Meiji Restoration, Shōyō straddles the two trajectories of Edo culture and modernisation that by the time of his death had lifted Japan to the status of a global power, but while engrossed in his Shakespeare studies he never quite embraced modernity with the passion of his younger contemporaries.[8] Shōyō's conservatism can be rationalised in terms of his scholarly integrity and his influential literary theories that, though radical in his youth, aged in the new century against challenges posed by new trends such as Nietzschean philosophy.[9] While biographers such as his Waseda pupils Kawatake Shigetoshi and Yanagida Izumi (1939) have tended to place his Shakespeare translations within the context of his intellectual development,[10] not to mention the drama of his life story,[11] Shōyō's debt to kabuki in particular has been problematic for critics with less enthusiasm for his ideas. The most serious criticism made during his lifetime of what he was attempting to do with Shakespeare came in a review by Natsume Sōseki of Shōyō's production of *Hamlet* for the Bungei Kyōkai in 1911: serious because, in addition to being the most highly regarded writer of his generation, Sōseki knew his Shakespeare almost as well as his senior and appeared to doubt whether Shōyō's translation had any literary or dramatic merits at all.

At the heart of Sōseki's critique is the suggestion that Shōyō's belief in Shakespearean realism misses the point about "a poetic beauty" that is achieved "in compensation for Shakespeare's distance from reality."[12] The difference between the two is that whereas Sōseki insists that readers may "through years of study gradually become aware of the natural state that lies behind" Shakespeare's poetic language,[13] in Shōyō's theory, that "natural state" remains hidden, known only to Shakespeare, and what matters for Shōyō is more the power of the language to provoke an audience's awareness of its own lived reality. Sōseki does not mention kabuki in his review, but a view which is sometimes voiced that Shōyō's Shakespeares sound too much like kabuki is in effect the view that kabuki stylisation is a poor substitute for what Sōseki calls Shakespeare's "extraordinary poetic world"; in failing to use "a single word or phrase that might appeal to Japanese psychology or customs,"[14] Shōyō had missed his opportunity to introduce the Meiji public to Shakespeare's actual genius. In the more ideological context of modern Japanese drama (*shingeki*), a similar objection was expressed in 1937 by the Brechtian stage director Senda Koreya:

The theatrical system known as kabuki comprises an artificial if compelling assortment of songs, dances, impersonations, and reverie, which when imposed on Shakespeare soon reveals its true colours. The Shakespeare of Dr. Tsubouchi smells to us too strongly of the kabuki with its poses, conventions and contrived rhythms.[15]

For Senda, kabuki's artificiality got in the way of Shakespeare's ideas, and Japanese actors from the last fifty years have also found Shōyō's style to be somewhat of a mouthful. Yet Shōyō's *Hamlet* had plenty of admirers at the time, and Shōyō admitted its limitations, since after 1913 he toned down the kabuki mannerisms in the colloquial style in which he was to translate the majority of the plays. In recent times, drama critic and Shakespeare translator Ōba Kenji has admired the stylistic mixing of Shōyō's experimental translations from the 1900s for a charm that is not necessarily relevant to kabuki drama,[16] while Shakespearean Arai Yoshio maintained that Shōyō's translations are demonstrably less "old-fashioned" and reliant on kabuki than has been supposed.[17] The debate is inherently ideological, related to Shōyō's aesthetic of Shakespeare reception and his normative role as a pioneer of Shakespeare translation, but rather than coming down on either side of the debate, this monograph attempts first of all to get inside his translations and analyse his various techniques as practical strategies. Chapter 3 surveys a cross-section of examples from his translations and attempts to account for the limitations that Shōyō's critics (and himself) found in them, while Chapter 4 looks at how his translations have been staged in the modern Japanese theatre.

Shōyō's significance as a Shakespeare translator has been recognised in book chapters by Japanese drama historian Brian Powell (1998) on the 1911 *Hamlet* and by Shakespeare scholars Kishi Tetsuo and Graham Bradshaw (2005) in their discussion of the discrepancies Shōyō experienced with his native drama when he first translated Shakespeare in the 1880s.[18] Leith Morton (2009), from a literary rather than theatrical perspective, also offers a sympathetic treatment, observing that Shōyō's translations enabled Japanese audiences "literally [to] see and hear a new mode of expression of their humanity that was alien to Japanese tradition."[19] Morton refers to Nakamura Kan (1986), who suggests that by the 1910s, having engaged superficially with Shakespeare's dramaturgy and rhetoric in mid-Meiji, Shōyō was better able to appreciate the inner psychological effects of that rhetoric (the dark as well as consoling side), and relates that change to a parallel development in modern Japanese literature.[20] Friederike von Schwerin-High (2005) details tropes in Shōyō's 1915 translation of *The Tempest* that support his attempt to render Shakespeare as modern realist drama,[21] and among previous studies of translations of single plays, Niki Hisae (1974) notes the importance of Shōyō's early *Julius Caesar* adaptation in determining his rejection of didacticism in literature, while David Rycroft (1999) illustrates the poetic strengths of the 1909 *Hamlet*.[22]

Within Japan, Shōyō's problematic relationship with his native culture has led him to be labelled both a Hamlet and a Don Quixote:[23] Hamlet for his condemnation of such icons of Tokugawa literature as novelist Takizawa Bakin, and Don Quixote for his tilting at the windmills of theatrical tradition. His call in the 1890s for more literary and coherent playscripts did not, as he might have hoped, lead to a string of "Japanese Shakespeares" (except for the couple in his own hand), and his disparagement of kabuki period plays (*jidaimono*) overlooks the immense generic differences with Shakespeare. His attacks on Tokugawa fiction have proven even more controversial, leading to radical reassessments by Atsuko Ueda (2007) and others. Ueda suggests that Shōyō's preference for aesthetic detachment (in other words, for writers of Shakespeare's genius who were apparently able to conceal their personal beliefs within their art) and his distaste for the alleged didacticism of Bakin's fiction was itself profoundly ideological,[24] because he started to attack Bakin in the 1880s at just the time he came under the patronage of the liberal states-man and founder of Waseda University, Ōkuma Shigenobu. Ōkuma supported the creation of the Diet in 1889 but sided with the Meiji oligarchy in its opposition to demands of the popular Freedom and People's Rights Movement for a more total democracy that threatened the oligarchy's authority. Bakin's novels, with their somewhat uncomplicated moral values and privileging of local identities, were popular texts for communal reading among the Movement's members, but to the young Shōyō they seemed unsophisticated in the light of what he had been learning from his English literary studies about the nature of literary art.

Shōyō's conflation of literary authorship with political authority is a familiar one that relates to a critique by Karatani Kōjin (1980) of Shōyō's tendency to conflate differing historical timeframes.[25] Aragorn Quinn in his account of the 1884 *Julius Caesar* adaptation (2011) asserts that Shōyō's sympathies "stand in contrast" to both the radical democrats and the oligarchy.[26] One can see how in his anxiety to preserve Shakespeare's detachment and his own academic integrity he may, for pedagogical as well as dramatic purposes, have absorbed Shakespeare's conflations of the historical and contemporary, and his response to the anti-bardolatry of Tolstoy and Shaw is instinctively anti-socialist.[27] Shōyō clung to his conviction that art's "proper objective" was (in Nanette Twine's translation) "to arouse in the beholder by its sublime beauty emotions so profound that [the] spirit seems involuntarily to soar,"[28] and he passed this on to pupils such as Hasegawa Tenkei, who recalled how listening to his teacher lecturing on *King Lear* he seemed "to lose all sense of time passing."[29] It would be naïve to deny the political dimension of Shōyō's aesthetics, even a diminution of the "true" Shōyō and his desire for release from inner contradictions. One solution to the impasse may be to detach Shōyō from the ideological ferment of the modern Japanese theatre and to place him in his broader East Asian context, which is the focus of the short concluding Chapter 5.

Beauty was important to Shōyō, the beauty of kabuki dance and woodblock prints as much as of Shakespearean verse, and his aesthetic idealism raises the inevitable question as to wherein lies the beauty of his Shakespeare translations. Sōseki claimed to have found in Shōyō's *Hamlet* not "a single word or phrase that might appeal to Japanese psychology or customs," but the poet (and pupil of Shōyō) Hattori Yoshika expressed "surprise first of all" at

> the wealth of Dr. Tsubouchi's vocabulary, and at the same time surprise at the subtlety with which he deploys that vocabulary. Of course, Shōyō's language is Shakespeare's language, and the nuances of his style are Shakespeare's

as well. That alone is remarkable enough, but to Shakespeare Dr. Tsubouchi
adds a degree of sophistication and tenderness.[30]

It is such additions that this monograph explores. Shōyō was a man of ideas and
a strong personality in an era of strong personalities, and gifted with a voice that
he was unafraid to use.[31] These features stand apart from Shakespeare but are
also defined and shaped through his six decades' engagement with Shakespeare.
Shōyō's life is a life lived through Shakespeare.

## A Life in Shakespeare

Tsuno Kaitarō reproduces three memorable photographs of Shōyō in his award-
winning biography (2002).[32] The first shows the twenty-five-year-old writer of
*Tōsei shosei katagi* sitting Japanese-style on the floor, in Japanese dress and at his
desk, shaven, dreamy eyed, a man of tender years. The second photograph is from
1917, and shows Shōyō with the bell and white tunic of En, the mountain hermit of medieval legend and subject of his sensational modern drama *En no gyōja*
(Hermit En, 1917). Despite the solemn countenance, one can only smile at this
image, knowing that it is Shōyō and that the ascetic's motives are benign. A third
photograph that is discussed by Tsuno shows the sixty-nine-year-old Shakespeare
translator dressed to the nines for his final lecture at Waseda, in a hat, collar and

*Figure 1.1*  Shōyō at 25

*Figure 1.2* Shōyō in 1917, dressed as Hermit En

tie and holding a briefcase and walking cane. The white bristles of his luxuriant moustache betray his age,[33] but a quizzical, even comical expression gives him a certain youthful appearance, as if he has been made young by decades of acquaintance with Shakespeare's youthful pen. This discrepancy and the cane and hat recall Charlie Chaplin, who by 1928 was well known in Japan and was to visit the country in 1933.

As Chaplin, Shōyō fits Tsuno's thesis of the "comic giant" (*kokkeina kyojin*) of his book's title, the man who popularised the Japanese generic term for comedy (*kigeki*) and in translating Shakespeare's seventeen comedies introduced to Japan a genre that had basically been lacking in his native tradition.[34] Another way of

*Figure 1.3* Shōyō in 1928

perceiving the three images is to relate them to the three principles of *wa* (Japan), *kan* (China), and *yō* (the West), whose harmonisation was a theme of Shōyō's thought:[35] the localism of *wa* is represented by his position close to the ground and in Japanese dress, the universality of *kan* by the omniscience of Hermit En, and the dual tradition and vitality of *yō* in a man who appears both old and youthful.

For Japanese people, Shōyō is perhaps most readily associated with the images of *okina*,[36] the "old man" of Noh drama whom Origuchi Shinobu found "meddle-some" (*oshitsukegamashii*)[37] and his close friend Takata Sanae "excessively naïve" (*junjō sugiru*),[38] and that of *sensei* (teacher), not only because he was a teacher but because by being in the right place at the right time, he was one of the first to seize on the basic questions about modern literature and drama that have interested Japa-nese writers and intellectuals ever since. Finally, Donald Richie described him to me as *nidaime*, a kabuki actor who lacks the honed good looks of a lead actor and so specialises in supporting roles. These characteristics would support a stereotypi-cal view of Shōyō the translator: a writer with the necessary skill and diligence to write but lacking the temperament required for true originality, although the role in which Shōyō would most likely have cast himself is that of the "Oriental" sage who has achieved the authority of wisdom through his studies and is comically able to accept his destiny.

The first thirty years of Shōyō's life seem essential to understanding the person he became. To start with, he seems to have been almost born to play the role of mediator or translator, and like Shakespeare was a country boy who made his career in the capital and lived through an era of great social change. He was the third son of a samurai of the Owari domain in the town of Ōta Minō on the banks of the Kiso river, fifty miles upstream of the city of Nagoya in what is now Gifu prefecture. Owari was one of a number of domains under the direct control of the family of the Tokugawa shogun rather than being governed by semi-autonomous local lords, and in that sense Shōyō's father was positioned between his community and the central government, besides being a mediator in local affairs. Heinoshin was a meticulous official who ensured his sons received the Confucian education of a samurai. By memorising the Confucian classics and learning the thousands of Chinese characters required to read them, Shōyō came to enjoy *gesakubon*, the novels of Tokugawa writers such as Bakin and Ihara Saikaku, which while moralistic on the surface and affirming the rules of Tokugawa society, stirred his imagination with their tales of adventure, romance, and the supernatural. A travelling library would visit once a year, and Shōyō would also accompany his mother Michi on regular trips to see the kabuki in Nagoya. Nagoya itself occupied a historically neutral position between the ancient capital of Kyoto in the west and the shogun's seat at Edo in the east, renamed Tokyo after the Meiji Restoration, when Heinoshin was pensioned off and moved the family to Nagoya.

Enrolled at the Aichi English school at the age of thirteen,[39] Shōyō excelled at his studies and made full use of Nagoya's Daisō, the largest library of its kind in late Tokugawa Japan. At school he was introduced to the works of Shakespeare by an American teacher, J. A. MacLellan, who once surprised his charges by reciting Hamlet's "To be, or not to be" soliloquy with the aid of a pocket knife.[40] At seventeen, Shōyō was awarded a scholarship to study at the Kaisei Gakkō, the preparatory school of what was to become the Imperial University (later University of Tokyo); majoring in political science, he was introduced to a rigorous modern curriculum taught mainly by foreign professors such as William Houghton, another American. He was encouraged in his literary interests by Takata (a native Edoite), and while he never acquired the English conversational skills of contemporaries such as Okakura Tenshin,[41] he read widely in English literature at this time, including works by Shakespeare, Spenser, and Milton. In 1880, at the end of his third year, he was failed by Houghton for writing a moralistic assessment of the character of *Hamlet*'s Gertrude,[42] lost his scholarship, and had to repeat the year, supporting himself by running his own English school. This setback scotched any hopes he might have had of securing preferment for overseas study, and he was never once in his life to leave Japan.

Shōyō's literary knowledge was acquired from his extensive lifelong reading, and although he also gained considerable theatrical experience from his work with the Bungei Kyōkai, he was known primarily as an academic, even bookish translator, whose authority rested on his knowledge of the texts and criticism. Shōyō, for his part, aimed to produce translations that were both scholarly and performable. Staying in Tokyo also enabled him to develop his characteristically nativist literary responses, taking issue with the Platonism of art historian Ernest Fenollosa,[43] and Shōyō started to contribute regular articles on literary topics to Japan's burgeoning newspaper trade.[44] After his previous disappointments, Shōyō was receiving a due and thorough training in the writer's profession; the volume of his ensuing output is remarkable by any standard.[45]

First his father in 1880 and then his mother two years later died of illness, and Shōyō took on the burden of the family debts. As his career as a writer took off, Shōyō was soon earning more than any of his brothers (who were employed in the bureaucracy), and since he and his wife were unable to have children of their own, they adopted two sons named Shikō and Daizō by elder brothers of Shōyō and a daughter, Kuni, of family friends, which was common practice at the time. Shōyō's relationship with Shikō was not always easy, but in the Taishō era Shikō was to become arguably his most important disciple, studying Western drama at Harvard and in London (where he corresponded with Edward Gordon Craig), acting the quintessential Hamlet of his generation on his return, and developing his father's ideas on dance and musical drama though his work as executive director of the Takarazuka Revue. In the role of paterfamilias, it is hard to believe that Shōyō had once lived a hedonistic lifestyle that would not have been out of place in a kabuki *sewamono*: at university he was nicknamed *goraku tonbo*, or "pleasure dragonfly." At the Imperial University, he frequented the nearby Nezu pleasure district, where in 1884 he met an indentured prostitute named Ugai Sen. The two fell in love, and having bought her freedom he married her in 1886.[46] Shōyō was unusual among his generation in marrying for love, even more for marrying a prostitute, and readily preached the notions of romantic love he had picked up from Shakespeare and the Western tradition.[47]

At university, Shōyō was a member of a literary and political discussion circle started by Takata Sanae, the Banseikai, and while still students the two collaborated on translations of the first part of Sir Walter Scott's *The Bride of Lammermoor* and the whole of *The Lady of the Lake*.[48] Shōyō's rapid entry into the Meiji *bundan* (literary establishment) was due partly to Takata's friendship. In 1884, the two were recruited by Ōkuma to teach at his newly established Tokyo Senmon Gakkō (renamed Waseda University in 1902). The ethos of Ōkuma's college was ambitious and patriotic, but at one remove from that of the Imperial University or language of the 1889 Meiji Constitution, which legalised the myths of Imperial power.[49] Shōyō's first literary effort upon graduating in 1882 was a series of newspaper columns that satirised the new breed of political opportunists, and at Tokyo Senmon Gakkō he was hired initially to teach English constitutional history. Yet Great Britain was famously a nation without a written constitution, one whose ideals were "hidden" within layers of tradition and precedent, and from Bagehot it was a relatively short step to Shakespeare and Shōyō's respect for the hidden ideals of great literature.[50]

Tsuno states that Shōyō's position with regard to the Meiji Constitution was that of a *kokuwakuha* ("structuralist"), in other words someone who valued it as a framework for social progress rather than an end in itself,[51] and Hayashi Kyōhei described him to me as *kōnan* (literally "hard and soft"), or someone who combined samurai Stoicism with the Epicureanism of the merchant class.[52] The *kōnan* character, although only six of one and half a dozen of the other, is strongest in times of rapid change and uncertainly, such as in mid-Meiji Japan,[53] and attracted to hybrid, ambiguous modes of experience, such as Shakespearean tragicomedy and indeed the multifarious characterisation of a Shakespeare play. Unable to offer political or philosophical assurances, the voice of *kōnan* is pragmatic, psychological, and above all realistic, accepting life "as it is" (*ari no mama*) without defining that reality as a single entity.[54] Shōyō was a rhetorician, not a philosopher: his task was to get inside the structures of Western literature, above all Shakespeare's dramaturgy, and by applying it to his own drama and literature to tap new sources of realism. As the political establishment solidified (or "hardened") in the 1890s, Shōyō struggled to find his footing and was at odds with the liberal, "softer" climate of the 1920s.

Shōyō's utilitarian motives correspond with Ōkuma's liberalism, and also owe something to the Social Darwinism he acquired at the Imperial University under the leadership of Katō Hiroyuki.[55] He was probably not, however, influenced by the tolerance of Christian teaching in Meiji Japan, for example by the proselytising of Uchimura Kanzō, who even translated a little Shakespeare. With the introduction of Western ideologies to fill the vacuum left by Tokugawa feudalism, Herbert Spencer's philosophy of social evolution was attractive to Meiji intellectuals seeking personal and national advancement and, as Suzuki Sadami (1998) suggests, meshed with Shōyō's "thinking on human instinctive desire."[56] Although Shōyō became thoroughly acquainted with Christian teaching through his Shakespeare studies, his concept of human nature (*ninjō*) came from Buddhist doctrine and aesthetics, for example the 108 passions (*hyakuhachi bonnō*) that he expounds upon in *Shōsetsu shinzui*.[57] For Shōyō, the purpose of literature was not so much to censure human desires, as a Christian author might, but to manifest them convincingly through the gamut of literary devices – characterisation, structure, trope, and so on – as a means of enabling readers better to appreciate their lived reality or, as he puts it in his Buddhist terminology, "the mysteries of destiny" (*inga no himitsu*).[58] What surprised Shōyō about Shakespeare, therefore, was how the writer's instinctive understanding of human behaviour seemed to agree so totally with what he had learned from his native tradition.

At the same time, Shōyō insisted that literature should not serve to promote immorality, referring to the erotic, sometimes pornographic aspect of Edo fiction,[59] and as Suzuki explains, "he differed from Spencer in that he saw no connection between the unfettered play of 'human desires' and the betterment of society."[60] Human beings acted on their desires as they had always done, not necessarily to make themselves better people; for Shōyō, therefore, the function of literary and dramatic structures was to contain this play of human desires. He writes of the power of drama to "console" weary audiences,[61] but this was not to let things get out of hand. Shakespeare also had a libidinous dimension, but it was contained within coherent dramaturgies that he found lacking in the episodic, spectacular kabuki genre.

Shōyō's contribution to the activities of the Engeki Kairyō Kai (Theatre Reform Society), founded by Suematsu Kenchō in 1886, benefited from the first flourish of his Shakespeare studies. In "Waga kuni no shigeki" (Historical Drama in Japan, 1893–4), he called for better scriptwriting, more coherent and thematically structured plots, and above all the treatment of drama as literature.[62] Shakespeare's plays were written mainly in metrical verse, with minimal stage directions and relatively slight variations between the Victorian editions he consulted, whereas texts in the kabuki tradition were largely subordinate to the conventions that covered every aspect of performance from acting to makeup, the quality of writing was uneven, and there was no editorial tradition as such. Shōyō's debt to Victorian scholars such as Edward Dowden is discussed in Chapter 2, and since his main point of comparison was with the historical genre of kabuki *jidaimono*, his reading at this time of the German Shakespearean Hermann Ulrici (and the Episcopalian clergyman Henry Norman Hudson) was also helpful in formulating his ideas on poetry and history. Following Ulrici, Shōyō maintained that dramatic poetry was subordinate to historical truth, serving to manifest that truth rather than as an end in itself, and he thus demanded greater historical verisimilitude in *jidaimono*.[63] This argument is reflected obliquely in the famous thesis of his *Shōsetsu shinzui*, that "The abiding concern of the novel is human nature. Social conditions and mores are secondary" (*Shōsetsu no shunō wa ninjō nari, setai fūzoku kore ni tsugu*).[64] What mattered about both genres was the sense of lived human experience. Shakespeare's histories also had their fantastical dimension, the final ghost scene in *Richard III* for example, but the plots hang together like the stories in a history book, and for this reason Shōyō called them "straight history" (*seishi*).[65]

Shōyō's call for better writing was driven not only by envy at Shakespeare's genius, but by his awareness that

> Long ago, the superficiality of human nature meant that all a man's feelings showed in his face, so that there were often unusual things to be seen, which was very convenient for the stage. Cultural development put an end to eccentricity, however, and many things can no longer be dealt with by [facial expressions] alone.[66]

As civilisations advanced, human beings knew more about the world and had more reason for protecting their feelings behind the mask of language. The psychological naivety of traditional drama was why, in Shōyō's view, "the theatre ha[d] gradually lost ground to the novel,"[67] but as he was to discover, Shakespeare was the writer par excellence whose language created character, meaning, and situation. He also realises at this time that better playwriting advanced the role of the actor as the person physically and emotionally responsible for speaking the lines.[68] These realisations had profound implications for the way that Shōyō would translate Shakespeare.

Drama generally contained fewer words than the novel with which to comment on the state of the world, but as a physical medium was blessed with an immediacy that the other genres lacked. Drama was also, therefore, at a greater remove from social realities than the other genres, and this position of detachment suited Shōyō as he sought to promote his university as a centre of theatrical teaching and research. Waseda in the 1880s was a rural village surrounded by rice fields a few miles from the metropolitan centre. The literary disputes (*ronsō*) in which Shōyō engaged in his early and later career were essentially with the new establishment: with Fenollosa at the Imperial University in the mid-1880s, with Imperial Army doctor Mori Ōgai in the early 1890s, with nationalist critic Takayama Chogyū at the end of that decade, and more discretely as I have mentioned with the former Imperial University lecturer (and Ministry of Education scholar) Natsume Sōseki in 1911. With their proximity to the poiesis of the Meiji Constitution, these prominent writers each in their different ways asserted a subjective idealism that was ideologically at odds with Shōyō's objective realism. Yet drama had a remarkable potential to speak with the illusory voice of universality, and Shakespearean drama gave Shōyō a model for developing that voice.

Shōyō's philosophy of Shakespeare is stated in his short essay "'*Makubesu* hyōshaku' no shogen" (Preface to a Commentary on *Macbeth*, 1891), in which he also indicates something of the reach of his Shakespeare studies by this time:

> The works of Shakespeare are like a mirror reflecting the faces, that is to say the ideals of all their many hundreds of readers. Gervinus found his philosophy in Shakespeare's works, as did Bräker, Bucknill, Moulton, Hudson, and Dowden in more recent times; they all have been stunned by the realisation that it is Shakespeare alone who is without ideals. There has never been as great a poet as Shakespeare, neither before nor since. No one approaches Shakespeare's creativity, which is as broad and deep as the ocean itself, a bottomless lake. It is truly remarkable how many readers have found their own ideals reflected in Shakespeare's works, and surely this is because they never seem to manifest any single big idea.[69]

Later in the essay he mentions Shakespeare editors Nicholas Rowe, Samuel Johnson, Alexander Pope, and William Warburton from the neo-classical tradition; the Germans Goethe, Gotthold Lessing, and the concordance compiler Alexander Schmidt; Romantic critics Samuel Taylor Coleridge and William Hazlitt; and the theologian Edwin Abbott Abbott, whose *Shakespearian Grammar* had been published in 1870. Most of these names will recur frequently in his writings on Shakespeare.

The essay was written as an introduction to an annotated translation he was contemplating of the first act of *Macbeth*, included in the first issue of *Waseda Bungaku*, the journal he established to promote the Waseda school of literary and theatrical research. In the essay, he explains that there are two types of Shakespeare commentary, the "critical" or textual commentary, which explains "the meanings of words and grammar" in order to elucidate "the author's intentions and his ideas as they are revealed in the original texts," and "the interpretive," which "can be a highly profound and profitable method for more perceptive readers, but for the less perceptive a little learning can be a dangerous thing, and for the inattentive can lead to undesirable errors."[70] Shōyō opts for the first type of textual commentary, and elaborates on this choice to argue it is impossible to tell what Shakespeare means or intends by his works. It is in the nature of Shakespeare's genius for the writer's ideals (his personal beliefs and opinions) to remain "hidden" and unknowable in the texts. Shakespeare's art works to provoke an individual (rather than uniform) response from his readers, and although that art could be rationalised by the kind of textual commentary that he proposed, there were clear dangers of readers confusing their individual responses with whatever Shakespeare intended. Shōyō writes of the "bottomless lake" of Shakespeare's genius with the implication that those who venture too deep into that lake risk being drowned.[71]

Shōyō's own response is twofold. First, his Shakespeare studies raise the potential of transferring Shakespeare's dramaturgy and rhetoric to his native drama: not perhaps the blank verse (which is infeasible in Japanese phonology) but the Shakespearean devices of rhythm, repetition, metaphor, structure, and his characteristic verbal fluency. Secondly, it sent him back to his native tradition as the basis of his individual response. He writes that "Shakespeare's works may be compared to 'the face that launched a thousand ships,' that is to say to the essence of creativity,"[72] and with this essay Shōyō launches the first few in a line of comparisons with his culture that will continue throughout his career. His register is strikingly Buddhist. Calling Shakespeare a "very jewel of nature,"[73] he recognises in Shakespearean drama a dual capacity to provoke instinctive feelings of satisfaction and remorse, and thus to motivate readers to live more virtuous lives. At the same time, Shakespeare's art cannot be priced or quantified, is as free to be enjoyed as nature itself, and in Shōyō's view is almost in itself a natural process producing a natural response like the flow of blood to the brain: "Creativity fulfils itself in an empty heart. Shakespeare's plays are very close to this meaning of creativity."[74]

There is a question as to whether Shōyō was merely repeating what Western scholars such as Dowden had told him about Shakespeare, although in the essay he seems to be saying little more than that a writer such as Shakespeare will always elicit some kind of response. In 1891, the opposition comes from another contemporary, the mentor of Japanese Romanticism Mori Ōgai, who insisted that literature did express discernible ideas that could and should be cited in social debate.[75] Shōyō's essay became the opening shot in a dispute with Ōgai conducted mainly through the new literary journals of the day: the "hidden ideals" dispute. Ōgai was influenced by the German idealist philosopher Eduard von Hartmann,[76] and having studied in Berlin in the 1880s was certainly more in tune with the European Zeitgeist than his literary rival. The Romanticism of Coleridge and Hazlitt is important to the formation of Shōyō's views, but in Japan he is known first and foremost as a realist: someone for whom the beauty of reality was sufficient in itself.

Shōyō retired from his full-time position at Waseda in 1915 when Takata was appointed Minister of Education in a new administration led by the seventy-seven-year-old Ōkuma, and so resigned as the university's president to be replaced by the economist Amano Tameyuki, who instituted unpopular reforms. Shōyō had always kept his distance from political, if not literary controversy, and by stepping down from his hectic teaching schedule gave himself more time in which to pursue his research and writing. As an emeritus professor, Shōyō continued to spend much of his time at Waseda, and to keep his house at Ōkubo not far from the university,[77] but in 1920 moved permanently with his wife to the seaside hot spring resort of Atami, some sixty miles to the west of Tokyo. Atami had become fashionable in the 1890s as a resort for the Tokyo business and literary elite,[78] and the Tsubouchis had honeymooned there in 1886. Thirty years later, Shōyō had the money to buy land in Atami overlooking the Pacific Ocean, and personally designed a retirement villa with a three-storied tower in the garden in the shape of a Buddhist pagoda that he used as his study. The first floor, being closest to the ground, represented Japanese *wa* 和 in his tripartite way of thinking that I mentioned earlier, the second floor Chinese *kan* 漢, and the third floor the Western world of *yō* 洋 with its ethereal philosophies. The castellation at the top was inscribed on the inside with a quotation from *King Lear*: "Fortune, good night. Smile once more; turn thy wheel" (2.2.188), spoken by the banished Kent, and a likely reference to Tsubouchi's sixtieth birthday in 1919, his *kanreki*, or completion of the sixty-year cycle in the lunar calendar, which is celebrated as a rite of passage in Chinese, Japanese, and Korean society.

It was in the tower at Sōshisha that Shōyō translated the seventeen or so Shakespeare plays he had not already translated in Tokyo, together with the Sonnets and Poems, and kept up to date with modern Shakespeare criticism and editions from the likes of T. S. Eliot and John Dover Wilson.[79] There were as usual numerous distractions, including the Great Kantō Earthquake on 1 September 1923, which he experienced as he happened to be at the university on that day, and he had to rush to complete his translations in time for his official retirement from Waseda in 1928. In 1916, he was invited to contribute an essay on Shakespeare in Japan in a tome edited by Sir Israel Gollancz of King's College, London, in commemoration of the tercentenary of Shakespeare's death. While he was no longer influential in the literary scene, his translations were widely read in the new universities and beyond, and a public lecture he gave in 1927 attracted an audience of 1,600. Following the dissolution of the Bungei Kyōkai in 1913, a further fifteen of his translations were staged during his lifetime, including *Macbeth* in 1916, *Othello* in 1917 with kabuki actor Matsumoto Kōshirō in the title role, and *A Midsummer Night's Dream* at the Imperial Theatre in 1928. Shōyō was not actively involved with these productions, but was happy to offer advice and attend performances.

Shōyō's relative detachment from Taishō and early Shōwa society reflects his view of Shakespeare's political detachment, although his adopted son Shikō was not alone in feeling that it made for a style of translation that could seem self-indulgent and out of touch with the modern world.[80] Shōyō's published diaries give away little about what Shakespeare meant personally to the translator, although its information on the books he was reading, the visitors he was receiving at Sōshisha, and the pace at which he translated individual plays may offer useful hints.[81] The prefaces to the translations and other essays, written in the familiar tone of the Meiji intellectual, offer a more complete insight into how Shōyō had internalised Shakespeare. In an essay accompanying the Bungei Kyōkai's production of *Julius Caesar* in 1913, he makes a surprising comparison of Marcus Brutus' idealism with that of General Nogi Maresuke, the hero of the Russo-Japanese War who had committed suicide the previous September in ritual atonement for the Emperor Meiji's death.[82]

Shōyō's three most important plays, *Kiri hitoha* and *Maki no kata* (The Lady Maki, 1896) from the 1890s, and *En no gyōja* from 1917, each contain strong Shakespearean interests. Shōyō described the first of these as "putting the new wine of Shakespeare into the old bottles of kabuki,"[83] with the protagonist Katagiri corresponding with Hamlet and the killing of the innocent Chinpaku with Hamlet's accidental killing of Polonius. The Lady Maki resembles Lady Macbeth in character as well as name, and about *En no gyōja* J. Thomas Rimer observes that "the play is, more than anything else, a disguised autobiography," suggesting that its use "of Western dramatic materials to aid in the construction of the narrative and the contours of the characters" recalls "Prospero with all his magic."[84] Shōyō's appropriation of Shakespeare's dramaturgy in his playwriting demands careful analysis, but where he most seems to internalise Shakespeare is in the aspect of character. In 1928, he writes that

> those famous old words which can be difficult even for English people to understand, expressed in complex, sometimes fearfully concise archaisms, richly metaphorical and bound up in old grammar, move me mysteriously and speak directly to my heart, and I believe that in the mouth of a Portia or Cleopatra, a Stephano or Bottom, a Macbeth or Lady Macbeth, they are to be heard in the Japan of today.[85]

Shakespeare's language is difficult, and Shōyō is wary of assuming that Shakespeare's ideas are his own, but he never seems to doubt that the characters can come alive in modern Japan.

Where we need to exercise caution is with regard to a tendency of Shōyō to conflate or neglect the reader-writer relationship. While he is critical of Romantic subjectivism, at the same time his respect for interiority recalls the value the Romantics give to creativity as a mysterious force that could not be rationalised. Shōyō conceives of creativity as a continuous, even organic process that elicits the reader's ideals, but one that does not appear to stimulate much in the way of a dialogue that might unsettle either the reader or Shakespeare. As a pioneer of his field, Shōyō lacks a *sensei* of his own with whom to touch base against the critics,[86] and, like the Edo culture into which he was born, can seem isolationist in his dogged profession of Shakespeare's genius.

### Shōyō's "Five Stages"

Shōyō divides the stylistic development of his translations into five stages.[87] The first stage is the classical style of his 1884 *Julius Caesar* translation, which was the dominant dramatic style before *genbun itchi*. In the 1890s, as his knowledge of Shakespeare deepens, Shōyō swings in the other direction, translating the first acts only of *Hamlet* and *Macbeth* in a style that was "as literal as possible."[88] This stage has a historical context, but what he notices is that his "vocabulary was cramped, losing the warmth and style of the original poetry, and even as plain writing" it sounded "quite peculiar."[89] He was translating Shakespeare as an extension of his literary theories, and – apart from a couple of outings to the Gaiety Theatre in Yokohama to see Shakespeare done in English by the Miln touring company – had little sense of how Shakespeare's characters might live and breathe upon a Japanese stage.

Shōyō realised his limitation almost immediately with the formation of a play reading group at Waseda in 1890.[90] Through reading original Shakespeare and kabuki plays with this group and his own theatrical ventures (*Kiri no hitoha* in 1898 and *Shinkyoku Urashima* in 1904), he had acquired the confidence to stage Shakespeare, and with the formation of the Bungei Kyōkai in 1905, he staged the trial scene of *The Merchant of Venice* and two scenes only of *Hamlet* in his own translations before directing *Hamlet* in full in 1911. Shōyō's utilitarian goal in staging Shakespeare had been the reform of Japanese drama rather than the service of Shakespeare, and thus he may have underestimated the difficulty of his task. In an article in 1907, he gives a hint of what was to come:

> For Japanese actors to portray Westerners on stage, and not just Westerners but English people, and not just English people but the English of Elizabethan times, and not just Elizabethans but those of Shakespeare's *Hamlet*, and to portray such unique and yet diverse characters as Hamlet, Claudius, and Polonius, each with their own authentic history, is without question intellectually infeasible, and yet quite apart from what Shakespeare scholars might say, if we are to grasp the bull by the horns and assert that human feelings are fundamentally alike, we should be able to find some ways of portraying these roles.[91]

In 1911, Shōyō did grasp the bull by the horns, but later admits that as he started "to direct *Hamlet* a powerful awareness of what Shakespeare meant gradually dawned on me. It was with only a rather vague idea of what lay ahead that I started to translate the play."[92] In Sōseki's judgement he failed, and even in his own he knew that he had failed to find a new dramatic language, perhaps by being a few years too early: "Things are different now. I could not have hoped for the rise of *shinpa* [a proto-modern theatrical genre originating in the 1880s] and the free and natural rhetoric of the *shingeki*."[93] Having criticised Kawakami Otojirō's *shinpa Othello* in 1903 for inauthenticity,[94] Shōyō was no doubt pushed into a corner as he struggled to produce *Hamlet* in a style that was both novel and faithful. According to Kobayashi Kaori, he had been influenced by the English productions he saw in Yokohama in 1894, which were done in an old-fashioned declamatory style that he became convinced best approximated the classicism of Shakespeare.[95]

For Shōyō, the issue becomes one of "following the original in its blend of formal poetry, poetic prose and colloquial language" so as "to convey its warmth and rhythm," but as he admits, this approach was haphazard and formulaic, relying more "on guesswork" than on a thorough knowledge of the text and Western theatrical practices.[96] His later translations for the Bungei Kyōkai were in this mixed literary and colloquial style,[97] and it "could produce some interesting results" that are worth unpacking: his fourth stage.[98]

Shōyō's final translation in this mixed style was that of *Julius Caesar* for the Bungei Kyōkai's production at the Imperial Theatre in 1913, but with the company's dissolution later that year he entered his fifth stage in which the remaining plays were translated, starting with those that were of greatest personal interest: *The Merchant of Venice* in 1914; *The Tempest, Antony and Cleopatra* and *A Midsummer Night's Dream* in 1915; *Macbeth* in 1916; *Measure for Measure, The Winter's Tale* and *Richard III* in 1918; the two parts of *Henry IV* in 1919; and *As You Like It* and *The Taming of the Shrew* in 1920. Shōyō makes the no doubt painful realisation that a coordination of literary and colloquial Japanese is an unrealistic analogy of Shakespeare's own "blend of formal poetry, poetic prose and colloquial language."[99] He regards his contemporary Japanese as "impoverished," observing sardonically that translation into the newly emerging Tokyo dialect made "Ophelia and Juliet sound like bar girls and students,"[100] but insists that only colloquial usage was able "to capture the remarkable creativity of Shakespeare's language."[101] Just as Shakespeare's creativity was exercised through repeated acts of communication, there was potential for modern Japanese to become a more creative and versatile language through repeated acts of communication between its users. Yet Shōyō recognises from the start that he will have to intersperse his colloquial register with literary, even classical usage, to the extent that the translations of his fifth period may not necessarily sound very different from what had come before, writing that

> Shakespeare uses archaisms, foreign words, slang, and dialect as the situation demands, and the translator should do likewise. The literary and spoken styles of long ago, the language of Confucianism and the Chinese classics, of the Tōhoku and Kyushu dialects, of Akinari, Bakin, Saikaku, and Chikamatsu, these should all be exploited in an approximation of Shakespeare's dually refined and popular language. Unless one does this, one cannot hope to capture even one ten-thousandth of the plays' original spirit.[102]

The likely departure of the fifth stage is that Shōyō abandons his misleading equivalence of Shakespearean with Japanese classicism, and so becomes more pragmatic in his usage of classical style. In contrast to the more formulaic approach of his earlier periods, Shōyō envisages a rather fluid movement between the contemporary and the classical, which he contrasts with official attempts of the time to standardise usage through the system of textbook authorisation.[103] Above all, he is motivated by what he calls the "warmth" (*jōmi*) and "rhythm" (*chōshi*) of Shakespeare's language, which therefore become the two poles of his translating style and take priority over alternative stylistic norms: *jōmi* refers to the rhetorical appeal of a text and *chōshi* to musical qualities such as pitch and tone as well as rhythm.[104]

What Shōyō apparently likes about the contemporary language is that it enables him to write translations that are "strikingly rhythmical."[105] This point says something of the achievements of *genbun itchi* over the previous forty years, not to mention free verse poets such as Hagiwara Sakutarō, in developing a fluent modern style. Where a literary style is more appropriate is in order "to prevent the language from sounding grammatically awkward,"[106] which is not presumably the fault of *genbun itchi*. These tensions between the contemporary and classical, and between Shakespeare's "warmth" and "rhythm" and native cultural norms, are played out in the numerous personal and professional relationships that surround his life in Shakespeare, which can also be categorised according to the five stages of his stylistic development.

During his first period in the 1880s, Shōyō was one of a group of young men who had received a typical Confucianist education under the Tokugawa hierarchy and became the "rising generation" of the Meiji state. As I have mentioned, Takata Sanae was important in nurturing Shōyō's literary interests, when he might have entered the bureaucracy, and Takata's review in 1886 of *Tōsei shosei katagi* enabled his friend to make the transition from fiction to Shakespeare.[107] Shōyō was going to be happier with a broad panoply of characters that suited his ambition to portray society in its totality, but since his talent up to that point had been for parody, he was going to struggle with the level of psychological detail he had demanded of the modern novel in *Shōsetsu shinzui*.

Shōyō's position at that time can be compared to the *gidayū* narrator in the *jōruri* format he adopted for his *Julius Caesar* adaptation, giving him time to develop the interests that would eventually feed into his Shakespeare translations of the 1900s and beyond and to tell the story that others beside himself would enact. Nakamura Kan distinguishes three types of novels that emerge after *Shōsetsu shinzui*.[108] The most successful are Futabatei's *Ukigumo* (The Drifting Cloud, 1887) and Ōgai's *Maihime* (The Dancing Girl, 1890), which focus on the depiction of *ninjō* (human feelings). The Kenyūsha group led by Ozaki Kōyō and Yamada Bimyō thrive on *share* (wordplay, but more generally verbal ingenuity), and the novelists connected with the Meiroku society are good at character. These three aspects of emotion, rhetoric, and character are the ingredients of Shakespearean drama, which he did not feel ready to translate in full for another twenty years.[109]

Shōyō is also at one remove from the long-running debate on prosody that interested his star pupil at Waseda, Shimamura Hōgetsu, and has little time for the experiments in Japanese blank verse initiated by Toyama Masakazu and Yatabe Ryōkichi at the Imperial University in their pioneering anthology of translations of Western poetry, *Shintaishishō* (Selection of New Poetry, 1882), and developed by Bimyō in the 1890s.[110] Outside Shakespeare, Shōyō's main interest of this time was in kabuki and historical drama, where his kabuki mentor was the outstanding dramatist of nineteenth-century kabuki, Kawatake Mokuami, who died in 1893. Mokuami himself wrote a now-lost *Hamlet* adaptation, and a grandson of his by marriage, Kawatake Shigetoshi, was to study at Waseda under Shōyō and later serve as a long-running director of the Tsubouchi Memorial Theatre Museum between 1934 and 1960.

Shōyō's two forays into Shakespeare translation in the 1890s are reflected in his debate on "hidden ideals" with Ōgai in 1891 and then on historical drama with Takayama Chogyū in 1896. A subtext of the first of these is the commentary Shōyō was writing for his *Macbeth* translation, since Macbeth is a character famously lacking in ideals and Shōyō was implicitly attacking those among his contemporaries who waded into the depths of world literature with little idea of what they were doing. The debate with Chogyū is a variation on the same theme, with Chogyū's Romantic preference for individual character criticism playing a kind of Hamlet to Shōyō's academic values (for example, his interest in dramatic structure).[111] As I have noted, Shōyō felt that the vocabulary of these two partial translations was "cramped" and lacking in the "warmth and style of the original poetry." His point of comparison, therefore, was with Shakespeare, but he cannot have been helped either by the rise of "pure literature" (*junbungaku*) in the 1890s led by such writers as Kitamura Tōkoku and Shimazaki Tōson (who translated *Venus and Adonis* in 1892).[112] His academic purism – for example, the demand for commentary rather than interpretation in the *Macbeth* essay – no doubt cramps his style, but he is saved by his awareness that group reading and performing Shakespeare with the Bungei Kyōkai (his third stage) are themselves academic exercises. In the 1900s, the Imperial University graduates Tozawa Koya and Asano Hyōkyo translate nine of the plays in the style of *junbungaku*,[113] but it is Shōyō's theatrical experiments that offer the way forward.

Shōyō's lasting persona may (as I have suggested) be that of the "Oriental" sage in his tower at Atami, but he is always at the centre of his communities, including Atami,[114] and values the diversity of voices that he finds in the community of Shakespearean drama:

> The particular strength of Shakespeare's writing is the way that through its unique qualities and rhythms the reader directly experiences the feeling and personality of the characters. What a translator must convey above all else is the lofty flavour of the words, the distinction between high and low, the interactions of intelligent minds, the reality of good and evil, and sense of urgency. One has to translate for the stage – and without any additional explanation – the folly and solemnity, the negative capability and the chivalry, the politeness and candour, the passionate and the cool, the long and the short, the tender and the blatant, city and country.[115]

Within the Bungei Kyōkai, Shōyō gathered around him a diverse group of individuals, most of them Waseda graduates from provincial backgrounds, and he made their careers: his Hamlet in the 1911 production, Doi Shunsho from Kumamoto; the court musician Tōgi Tetteki (from Tokyo); the Naturalist critic and Ibsen translator Hōgetsu, from Shimane prefecture; and Shōyō's Ophelia, Matsui Sumako, a housewife from Nagano. It was the scandal of Hōgetsu's affair with Sumako that led to the company's dissolution, but Shōyō was genuinely remorseful when Hōgetsu died from Spanish flu in November 1918 and Sumako took her life shortly after.

Sōseki's critique had pinpointed Shōyō's own difficulties in coordinating the literary and colloquial, which was a managerial as well as a stylistic problem. In particular, the sheer amateurishness of the company's activities suggests an underlying failure to realise that Shakespeare is undemocratic as well as magnanimous. Shōyō's retreat to his study and embrace of the contemporary is in that sense an acceptance that if he is to be true to Shakespeare, he has to set himself above the fray, giving parts to all but never allowing his own position to be undermined. The community of his fifth period therefore comprises those of the younger generation who were prepared to go along with the Doctor: theatre people such as Osanai Kaoru, Ichikawa Sanki at the Imperial University, critic Hasegawa Tenkei, his publishers at Chūō Kōron, and more critically, his adopted son Shikō. He is courteous to the younger generation of translators and to Ōgai, when the latter translated *Macbeth* in 1913,[116] but refrains from quizzing foreign and for the most part Japanese scholars, who might have helped him with the finer points.

While Shōyō owns up to his mistakes, his determination to preserve the purity of his vision has been true to his theories all along. In *Shōsetsu shinzui*, he had prioritised feeling (*ninjō*) above custom (*fūzoku*), which in Shakespeare meant those characters such as Shylock who threatened legal action and the free exchange of romantic feelings. For all its literary failings, the actual achievement of *Tōsei shosei katagi* had been its exploration of male heterosexual experience as a healthy alternative both to prostitution and to the sterile homoerotic relationships that constitute the novel's social background,[117] while – on a rather different tack – Kano Ayako argues critically about the Bungei Kyōkai that the untainted feelings of "the Japanese Shakespeare" that Shōyō endeavoured to promote through the company's activities "idealized a pure, uncommodified, natural interiority" that depended structurally on an external domain of commodified sex.[118] There are plenty of "sex workers" in both Shakespeare and Chikamatsu, but Shōyō has little room for them in modern Japan.

Translation is a creative practice, but for someone who began his career as a parodist and found his metier as a translator, there must always remain some doubt as to whether he does finally have a voice of his own. Shōyō does have a recognisable style, and with his theories and academic knowledge clearly has something to say, but a significant postscript is suggested by Komori Yōichi's characterisation of the narrative style of *Tōsei shosei katagi* as a kind of eavesdropping:

> The characters, who have a limited field of vision within the narrative, peep at and "eavesdrop" on others, but because of certain limitations they cannot reproduce the original meaning of the conversation they listen in on and thus make decisive mistakes.[119]

This is different from a Shakespeare play, where the characters' "field of vision" is enlarged by dramatic means, but it might describe the stylistic borrowings of his final, contemporary period when he was bound to "eavesdrop" on the younger generation who spoke a modern type of Japanese, by which he was probably both repelled and attracted, but which he needed for his translations. An image of the elderly professor in the tram or railway carriage overhearing the excited conversations of uniformed teenagers and young adults comes to mind. Inoue

Miyako (2006) emphasises the importance to older writers of this time of *jogaku-sei* (female students), who were freer than boys from social control and led new fashions:

> As the cultural construct of *jogakusei* became increasingly recognized, objec-tified, and imagined as a metonymy of Japan's modernization, their speech became the object of social imaginaries.[120]

For Shōyō, however, the issue may be not so much one of mishearing conversa-tions on the tram but of misreading Shakespeare's rhetoric and subtexts.

The concerns of Kano and Komori are beyond the scope of this monograph, but they are important subtexts in the way that we read Shōyō's translations. More relevant to my analyses is Satō Miki's observation (2010) that Shōyō stands out from other Meiji translators such as Morita Shiken in his preference for domestica-tion (*dōka*) over foreignisation (*ishitsuka*).[121] The logic of foreignisation was that it allowed Meiji readers to grasp the content and details of a foreign text without compromise, and so to take what they needed. What Shōyō hopes his translations will release from their originals is a creative energy, and what they may obscure are the differences between source and target. Domestication as a strategy for making Shakespeare at home in Japanese culture also supports Shōyō's pioneering role in establishing the norms of Shakespeare's reception in Japan.

In the next chapter, I explore what Shakespeare meant to Shōyō in terms of his native tradition and reading of Shakespeare criticism. One reason for Shōyō to domesticate rather than foreignise Shakespeare in his translations is that, despite his youthful consternation at the state of Tokugawa literature, he realised that Shakespeare had more in common with Chikamatsu in particular than he may have at first thought. Shakespearean drama, like kabuki, was a drama of ideal passion, and Chikamatsu was every bit as rhetorically complex. What Shakespeare repre-sented for Shōyō was a creative force that could not, in his theory, be quantified but could be harnessed qualitatively to the modern trajectory of his native literature. His main theoretical concern, therefore, was not so much the imitation of Western writers but the search for new literary styles. Shakespearean translation was not an end in itself but the vehicle for a lifelong search for a modern style that has its roots in eighteenth-century philology and aesthetics. It is not surprising that Shōyō should sometimes confuse historical perspectives when, from his perspec-tive, Shakespeare's stylistic mixing had already achieved what seventeenth- and eighteenth-century writers such as Chikamatsu and Ueda Akinari were to start to achieve only a few generations after Shakespeare's death. That Shakespeare seemed to Shōyō so much more profound in his realism than the Tokugawa writers was not necessarily because Shakespeare understood the human condition any bet-ter than Japanese writers but because of a rhetorical energy and skill that seemed so much more capable of exploring the range of human characters and situations than his native literature with its more rigid hierarchies. Shakespeare translation gave Shōyō permission to question those hierarchies, and Shakespeare's rhetoric a model for doing so.

There is much that is overblown and contradictory in Shōyō's Shakespeare: his insistence, for example, that Shakespeare is a writer of "hidden ideals" when modernisation in Japan would have been impossible without the embrace of new ideas, and Shōyō's theory is an idea in itself. This monograph, however, attempts to read Shōyō on his own terms by going in search of what he found beautiful (and "natural") in Shakespeare and of how he sought to reproduce that beauty in the language he knew best.

## Notes

1 Translators' subjectivity and agency are apparent in the stylistic choices they make. In the case of Shakespeare translation, I assume that translators' choices can be traced irrespective of whether a translation is a so-called academic version determined by the communication of content or a literary or stage translation determined by aesthetic considerations, since there is inevitably variation among academic translations of the same play and academic translators also subscribe to distinctive cultural fields. Shōyō is significant as a Shakespeare translator who strove for academic authority and was at the same time obsessed with stylistic issues. Literary translations of his era have attracted interest both as agents of linguistic and literary reform and because of their departure from the mechanistic content-based translations of pre-modern and early modern Japan. See Mizuno Akira, "Stylistic Norms in the Early Meiji Period: From Chinese Influences to European Influences," in *Translation and Translation Studies in the Japanese Context*, ed. Nana Sato-Rossberg and Judy Wakabayashi (New York: Continuum, 2012), 92–114.

2 Toyoda Minoru, *Shakespeare in Japan: An Historical Survey* (Tokyo: Iwanami Shoten, 1940), 110. An adaptation was staged at Owl Spot Theatre, Tokyo, by the Hanagumi Shibai company in 2016.

3 The dominant stage translations of the 1960s were those by the director and playwright Fukuda Tsuneari, succeeded by Odashima Yūshi in the 1970s (Kawachi Yoshiko, *Shakespeare and Cultural Exchange* [Tokyo: Seibidō, 1995], 90–100), and more recently by Matsuoka Kazuko. Fukuda translated about half the plays, Odashima and Matsuoka the Complete Works.

4 Marleigh Grayer Ryan, *The Development of Realism in the Fiction of Tsubouchi Shōyō* (Seattle: University of Washington Press, 1975); and Daniel Gallimore, *Tsubouchi Shōyō's "Shinkyoku Urashima" and the Wagnerian Moment in Meiji Japan* (Lewiston, NY: Edwin Mellen Press, 2016).

5 Tsubouchi Shōyō, "Jibun no honyaku ni tsuite" (1928), in *Shōyō senshū*, supp. vol. 5, ed. Shōyō Kyōkai (Tokyo: Daiichi Shobō, 1977), 255.

6 Ibid. Hearn made this suggestion at a lecture at the Imperial University attended by Shōyō in 1896.

7 Ibid., 257.

8 Kawatake Toshio makes this point forcefully in *Nihon no Hamuretto* (Tokyo: Nansōsha), 288.

9 See Gallimore, *Tsubouchi Shōyō's "Shinkyoku Urashima"*, 44–5.

10 Kawatake Shigetoshi and Yanagida Izumi, *Tsubouchi Shōyō* (1939; repr., Tokyo: Daiichi Shobō, 1988). See also Yanagida's account of Shōyō's early years, *Wakaki Tsubouchi Shōyō* (Tokyo: Shunshōsha, 1960).

11 The classic Shōyō narrative is Matsumoto Seichō's novel *Bungō* (Tokyo: Bungei Shunjū, 2000), and Osada Ikue's play *Tōsei goraku katagi* (Tokyo: Note, 2015) also tells the Shōyō story. Kamei Shunsuke, *Eibungakusha Tsubouchi Shōyō* (Tokyo: Shōhakusha, 2021), which is the most recent of book-length studies, follows precedent in limiting the Shakespeare translations to a single chapter alongside Shōyō's other achievements.

12  Natsume Kinnosuke, "Tsubouchi-hakase to *Hamuretto*" (1911), in *Sōseki zenshū*, vol. 16 (Tokyo: Iwanami Shoten, 2019), 397.

13  Ibid., 396.

14  Ibid., 395.

15  Quoted in Arai Yoshio, *Sheikusupia geki jōenron* (Tokyo: Shinjusha, 1972), 289.

16  Ōba Kenji, *Sheikusupia no honyaku* (Tokyo: Kenkyūsha, 2009), 14.

17  Arai Yoshio, "Shōyō no Sheikusupia," in *Tsubouchi Shōyō Kenkyū Shiryō* 5 (1974): 39–52.

18  Brian Powell, "One Man's *Hamlet* in 1911 Japan: The Bungei Kyōkai Production in the Imperial Theatre," in *Shakespeare and the Japanese Stage*, ed. Sasayama Takashi, J. R. Mulryne, and Margaret Shewring (Cambridge: Cambridge University Press, 1998), 38–52; Kishi Tetsuo and Graham Bradshaw, "Shakespeare and Traditional Japanese Theatre: Tsubouchi Shōyō," in *Shakespeare in Japan* (New York: Continuum, 2005), 1–28.

19  Leith Morton, *The Alien Within: Representations of the Exotic in Twentieth-Century Japanese Literature* (Honolulu: University of Hawai'i Press, 2009), 42.

20  Nakamura Kan, *Tsubouchi Shōyō ron – kindai Nihon no monogatari kūkan* (Tokyo: Yūseidō, 1986), 218–20. Nakamura observes a parallel between Shōyō's trajectory and that from the Japanese Romanticism of the 1890s to the political and literary nationalism of the 1920s.

21  Friederike von Schwerin-High, *Shakespeare, Reception and Translation: Germany and Japan* (New York: Continuum, 2004), 180. She suggests that Shōyō's use of techniques such as keywording makes his *Tempest* translation "extremely speaker-bound" (214) and so suppresses the play's non-realist aspects.

22  Niki Hisae, "'*Shīzaru kidan: jiyū no tachi nagori no kireaji* – Shōyō's First Translation of *Julius Caesar*," *Shakespeare Translation* 1 (1974): 53–68; David Rycroft, "Tsubouchi Shōyō's Translation of *Hamlet*," in *Shakespeare in Japan*, ed. Anzai Tetsuo (Lewiston, NY: Edwin Mellen Press, 1999), 187–226. See also Niki's *Shakespeare Translation in Japanese Culture* (Tokyo: Kenseisha, 1984).

23  Tōkawa Shinsuke, *Shinchō Nihon bungaku arubamu – Tsubouchi Shōyō* (Tokyo: Shinchōsha, 1996), 3. The comparison with Don Quixote was made by Shōyō's adopted son Shikō.

24  Atsuko Ueda, *Concealment of Politics, Politics of Concealment: The Production of "Literature" in Meiji Japan* (Stanford, CA: Stanford University Press, 2007), 24.

25  Karatani Kōjin, *Origins of Modern Japanese Literature*, trans. Brett de Bary (Durham, NC: Duke University Press, 1993), 149.

26  Aragorn Quinn, "Political Theatre: 'The Rise and Fall of Rome' and 'The Sword of Freedom,' Two Translations of *Julius Caesar* in Meiji Japan by Kawashima Keizō and Tsubouchi Shōyō," *Asian Theatre Journal* 28, no. 1 (Spring 2011): 176. See also Aragorn Quinn, *Performing the Politics of Translation in Modern Japan* (New York: Routledge, 2020), 19–24. Kawashima's *Julius Caesar* of 1883 was the first complete Japanese translation of a Shakespeare play, preceding Shōyō's version by a year; he also published a translation of *Romeo and Juliet* in 1887.

27  Shōyō was more apolitical than anti-socialist, and in some respects anti-élitist. His 1907 critique of Tolstoy comes at the time that he was working hardest to establish Shakespeare's reputation in the Japanese theatre.

28  Tsubouchi Shōyō, *Shōsetsu shinzui* (1885–6), in *Tsubouchi Shōyō shū*, ed. Inagaki Tatsurō (Tokyo: Chikuma Shobō, 1969), 45, trans. Twine.

29  Hasegawa Tenkei, "Tsubouchi-sensei no *Riya ō* kōgi," *Saō Fukkō* 14 (1934): 21.

30  In Hattori Yoshika and Inagaki Tatsurō, eds., *Tsubouchi Shōyō kenkyū zadankai* (Tokyo: Kindai Bunka Kenkyūsho, 1976), 248.

31  Powell, 41.

32  Tsuno's biography was awarded the Nitta Jirō Literary Award for 2003.

33  Facial hair had been prohibited under the Tokugawa shogunate but became popular during the Meiji era as Western fashions were imitated. Shōyō first grew a moustache after

his marriage in 1886, and by the time he retired from Waseda in 1915 it had acquired the luxuriant shape of the number eight in Japanese (*hachi hige*). Since facial hair became less popular in the 1920s, when the fashionable "modern boys" (*mobo*) were clean shaven, Shōyō's moustache dated him as a man of the 1880s.

34 See Taira Torahiko, "Meiji ki ni okeru kigeki no keifu – sono yakugo to jōen wo megutte," *Engeki Gakuronshū* 27 (1989): 64, and Matsumura Masaie, "Tsubouchi Shōyō to yūmoa ron," *Hikaku Bungaku* 18 (1975): 15–22. Shōyō also expresses a quite Shakespearean view of tragicomedy in *Shōsetsu shinzui*, asserting that "it is the blending of humour and pathos which demands the most careful attention" (*Shōsetsu shinzui*, 47, trans. Twine), even if his main concern is that readers do not get "bored," and his view of modernity is comic to the extent that modernity rejects the "tragic" feudal attitudes he critiques in *Shōsetsu shinzui*.

35 Yanagida Izumi, *Wakaki Tsubouchi Shōyō* (Tokyo: Shunshōsha, 1960), 5.

36 In Japanese culture, notably in Noh drama, *okina* is an auspicious figure signifying the harmony of heaven, earth, and man, in other words the kind of universal wisdom that Shakespearean drama was said to embody (even though Shakespeare wrote most of his plays before his middle age). When Shakespeare was first received in China and then Japan in the nineteenth century, his name was written with the two characters *sa* (or *sha*), meaning "sand," and *ō*, another reading for *okina*, "old man."

37 Quoted in Tsuno Kaitarō, *Kokkeina kyojin: Tsubouchi Shōyō no yume* (Tokyo: Heibonsha, 2002), 193.

38 Ibid., 51.

39 One of seven prefectural schools established by the Japanese government in 1873 to promote Western learning.

40 Tsubouchi Shōyō, "Gakusei jidai no tsuioku" (1925), in *Shōyō senshū*, vol. 12 (1977), 48.

41 Itō Sei, "Pioneers of the New Literature," *Japan Quarterly* 2, no. 2 (1955): 225.

42 Tsubouchi Shōyō, "Kaioku mandan" (1925–6), in *Shōyō senshū*, vol. 12, 345. This famous episode likely triggered his polemic against didacticism in *Shōsetsu shinzui* a few years later.

43 See Kaneda Tamio, "Fenollosa and Tsubouchi Shōyō," in *A History of Modern Japanese Aesthetics*, trans. and ed. Michael F. Marra (Honolulu: University of Hawai'i Press, 2001), 53–67, and Shōyō's essay, "Bi to wa nani zo ya" (1886), in *Modern Japanese Aesthetics: A Reader*, trans. and ed. Michele Marra (Honolulu: University of Hawai'i Press, 2002), 48–64, which was written in response to a lecture he heard Fenollosa giving at the Imperial University. Shōyō's pen name *shōyō*, meaning "rambling" or "peripatetic," refers to Aristotle's Peripatetic School of the fourth century BCE (Seth Jacobowitz, *Writing Technology in Meiji Japan: A Media History of Modern Japanese Literature and Visual Culture* [Boston: Harvard University Asia Center, 2014], 214), whose ideas were based on personal experience in contrast to Plato's theory of forms (or idealism). His birth name was Yūzō. In the 1880s he was known by the literary pen name of Haru no Ya Oboro, but adopted the name Shōyō after turning full-time to literary scholarship.

44 Shōyō wrote mainly for *Yomiuri Shimbun*, founded in 1874 and at that time known as a small literary newspaper rather than the mass circulation daily it has become. Its first chief editor (1887–91) was Takata Sanae, followed by another close university friend and founding Librarian of Waseda University, Ishijima Kenkichi.

45 The standard bibliography is Takita Teiji, *Shōyō shoshi* (1937; repr., Tokyo: Kokusho Kankōkai, 1976). Only about half of Shōyō's complete output is included in *Shōyō senshū*, each of whose seventeen volumes runs to 700–900 pages.

46 Sen, who was from the same Owari domain as her husband, was sold by her father at the age of eighteen to pay off family debts to the famous Dai Hachiman Rō brothel in Nezu, where she had the name of Hanamurasaki. This was common practice in Japan through to the 1930s, but considered bad karma by Shōyō's educated friends, most of whom married women of their own class. That Shōyō spent much of his career accruing

good karma through benevolent activities such as Shakespeare translation was no doubt partly in compensation for his youthful profligacy. In 1900, Sen developed a gynecological infection that prevented intercourse, and although happily married they avoided sexual relations for the rest of their life together. He was devoted to Sen, who struggled to read even a daily newspaper, and did not take a mistress in later life. Sen's story is told in Yatayama Seiko, *Tsubouchi Shōyō no tsuma – Dai Hachiman Rō no koi* (Tokyo: Sakuhinsha, 2004).

47  See Saeki Junko, "From *Iro* (Eros) to *Ai=Love*: The Case of Tsubouchi Shōyō," trans. Indra Levy, *Translation in Modern Japan*, ed. Indra Levy (Abingdon, Oxon: Routledge, 2016), 73–101.

48  For an account of Shōyō and Takata's Scott translations, see my article, "Sir Walter Scott and the Romanticism of Tsubouchi Shōyō," *Poetica* 79 (Spring 2013): 101–13.

49  Shōyō's friend Takata Sanae, as one of Waseda's founding fathers, was influenced by the Victorian model of gentlemen's education and "critical of the examination-centered Meiji state education system, in which middle and higher education were ultimately linked to the recruitment of bureaucrats." Motoyama Yukihiko, "The Spirit of Political Opposition in the Meiji Period: The Academic Style of the Tōkyō Senmon Gakkō," trans. I. J. McMullen, in *Proliferating Talent: Essays on Politics, Thought, and Education in the Meiji Era*, ed. J. S. A. Elisonas and Richard Rubinger (Honolulu: University of Hawai'i Press, 1997), 349.

50  Walter Bagehot's *The English Constitution* (1867) was translated into Japanese in 1883; Shōyō read Bagehot's book and used it as a text in his early lectures. Bagehot was a lesser figure in Meiji thought than other Victorians such as Mill and Spencer, and the Meiji Constitution of 1889 was influenced more by the Prussian rather than the British Westminster model. It was Shōyō's mentor, Ōkuma, who in 1882 had advocated a British style of government with a cabinet responsible to Parliament.

51  Tsuno, 70–2.

52  My – not Hayashi's – gloss.

53  The years of Shōyō's higher education (1876–83) were a period of economic and political turmoil, beginning with the Satsuma Rebellion in 1877 and culminating in the attempted assassination of the leader of the Freedom and People's Movement, Itagaki Taisuke, in Shōyō's home prefecture of Gifu in 1882.

54  For an account of Shōyō's realism, see Tomi Suzuki, *Narrating the Self: Fictions of Japanese Modernity* (Stanford, CA: Stanford University Press, 1997), 19–23.

55  A veteran samurai born in 1836, Katō was Superintendent of the Departments of Law, Science, and Literature at the Imperial University while Shōyō was an undergraduate, and a major influence on Shōyō and his contemporaries as the exponent of Social Darwinism in Meiji Japan.

56  Suzuki Sadami, *The Concept of Literature in Japan*, trans. Royall Tyler (Kyoto: International Research Center for Japanese Studies, 2006), 155.

57  *Shōsetsu shinzui*, 16.

58  Ibid., 7.

59  Ibid., 3.

60  Suzuki Sadami, 155.

61  Tsubouchi Shōyō, "Shingakugekiron" (1904), in *Tsubouchi Shōyō shū*, 347.

62  Tsubouchi Shōyō, "Waga kuni no shigeki" (1893–4), in *Tsubouchi Shōyō shū*, 311–15.

63  Sadoya Shigenobu, *Tsubouchi Shōyō–dentōshugisha no kōzu* (Tokyo: Meiji Shoin, 1983), 90–1.

64  *Shōsetsu shinzui*, 16.

65  In its Chinese etymology, the term *seishi* refers to official dynastic histories.

66  *Shōsetsu shinzui*, 14, trans. Twine.

67  Ibid.

68  Kishi and Bradshaw, 15.

69 Tsubouchi Shōyō, "'*Makubesu* hyōshaku' no shogen" (1891), in *Shōyō senshū*, supp. vol. 3 (1978), 166. Among the authorities Shōyō cites, Hudson was a well-known Shakespeare editor and scholar of the second half of the nineteenth century. Ulrich Bräker was a Swiss autodidact known for his commentary on Shakespeare plays published in 1780, and Sir John Bucknill an English psychiatrist who published an influential study of Shakespeare's medical knowledge in 1860.

70 Ibid., 163.

71 Tsubouchi Shōyō, "Soko shirazu no mizuumi" (1891), in *Tsubouchi Shōyō shū*, 282.

72 "'*Makubesu* hyōshaku' no shogen," 165.

73 Ibid.

74 Ibid., 164.

75 The two were closer than is sometimes supposed, since as Donald Keene explains (*Dawn to the West – A History of Japanese Literature, Vol. 4, Japanese Literature of the Modern Era: Poetry, Drama, Criticism* [New York: Holt, Rinehart and Winston, 1984], 511), Shōyō was insistent that "submergence of ideals" (*botsurisō*) was not the same as "lack of ideals" (*murisō*), of which Shōyō had plenty. Nakamura Kan (259) defines their difference as more temperamental: Ōgai as Apollonian and Shōyō Dionysiac.

76 Richard Bowring, *Mori Ōgai and the Modernisation of Japanese Culture* (Cambridge: Cambridge University Press, 1979), 73–5.

77 Shōyō's spacious residence in what is now the heavily populated Shinjuku district in western Tokyo served as the headquarters and rehearsal space of the Bungei Kyōkai, and escaped the devastation of the 1923 earthquake. Shōyō donated the property to his university in 1928.

78 Atami became nationally known through Ozaki Kōyō's novel *Konjiki yasha* (The Golden Demon), serialised in *Yomiuri Shimbun* between 1897 and 1902. The story contains a famous scene set on the Atami seashore in which the student Kanichi kicks his lover Omiya for having rejected him in favour of a wealthy businessman.

79 Among the early twentieth-century scholars listed in *Shēkusupiya kenkyū shiori*, Shōyō includes R. W. Babcock, Edmund Blunden, A. C. Bradley, G. Wilson Knight, W. W. Lawrence, and Alwin Thaler. Babcock had written on late eighteenth-century Shakespeare criticism (1931), the poet Blunden had lectured on Shakespeare at the Imperial University in the 1920s, Bradley's seminal study of Shakespearean tragedy was published in 1904 and Wilson Knight's mythic study of Shakespearean tragedy in 1930, Lawrence's study of Shakespeare's problem comedies was published in 1931, and Thaler's groundbreaking *Shakespeare's Silences* in 1928: *Shōyō senshū*, supp. vol. 5 (1977), 90–2.

80 Tsubouchi Shikō, *Tsubouchi Shōyō kenkyū* (Tokyo: Waseda University Press, 1953), 176.

81 Shōyō worked quickly, perhaps helped by his tendency for insomnia. In his diary for 4 October 1917, he notes that he has started on *Measure for Measure*, and then working on it every day he finishes the first draft on 15 October: *Shōyō nikki, 1916–19*, ed. Kikuchi Akira (Tokyo: Shōyō Kyōkai, 1999), 110–12.

82 Tsubouchi Shōyō, *Shōyō gekidan* (Tokyo: Tenyūsha, 1919), 368.

83 Kawatake Shigetoshi, *Ningen Tsubouchi Shōyō – kindai gekidan sokumenshi* (Tokyo: Shinjusha, 1959), 92.

84 J. Thomas Rimer, "Shakespeare Meets the Buddha: Tsubouchi Shōyō, Osanai Kaoru, and *The Hermit*," *Kyoto Conference on Japanese Studies* 2 (1994): 290.

85 "Jibun no honyaku ni tsuite," 257.

86 Shōyō's authoritative status was sealed in 1902 by Waseda's award of an honorary doctorate, and he was henceforth usually known as *Tsubouchi-hakase*, "Dr. Tsubouchi."

87 "Jibun no honyaku ni tsuite," 254.

88 Ibid.

89 Ibid., 255.

90 The group was meeting as early as 1890, and came to include key personnel of the Bungei Kyōkai such as Doi Shunsho and Tōgi Tetteki.

91  Tsubouchi Shōyō, "Nihon de enzuru *Hamuretto*" (1907), in *Sheikusupia kenkyū shiryō shūsei*, vol. 2, ed. Sasaki Takashi (Tokyo: Nihon Tosho Centre, 1997), 201.

92  "Jibun no honyaku ni tsuite," 255.

93  Ibid., 258.

94  Tsubouchi Shōyō, "Tsubouchi-hakase no *Osero* dan," *Kabuki* 34 (1903): 1–7.

95  Kobayashi Kaori, "Shakespeare and National Identity: Tsubouchi Shōyō and His 'Authentic' Shakespeare Productions in Japan," *Shakespeare* 2, no. 1 (2006): 69–71.

96  "Jibun no honyaku ni tsuite," 256.

97  Moriya Sasaburō, *Nihon ni okeru Sheikusupia* (Tokyo: Yasshio Shuppan, 1986), 44–5.

98  "Jibun no Shēkusupiya honyaku ni tsuite," 256.

99  Ibid., 257.

100  Ibid., 266.

101  Ibid., 264.

102  Ibid., 263.

103  Ibid., 246.

104  Ibid., 257.

105  Ibid., 256.

106  Ibid.

107  See James R. Reichert, "Tsubouchi Shōyō's *Tōsei shosei katagi* and the Institutionalization of Exclusive Heterosexuality," *Harvard Journal of Asiatic Studies* 63, no. 1 (2003): 72–3, for an overview of the mainstream critical response to the novel.

108  Nakamura, 16–22.

109  Moriya, 19.

110  Kawamoto Kōji, *The Poetics of Japanese Verse: Imagery, Structure, Meter*, trans. Stephen Collington, Kevin Collins, and Gustav Heldt (Tokyo: University of Tokyo Press, 2000), 189.

111  Keene, 526.

112  The notion of "pure literature" may be confusing, especially as Shōyō had been calling for the treatment of drama as serious literature, but given the association of *junbungaku* with new subjective genres such as the I-novel and Naturalist fiction, we can see how purely literary values may have contradicted with the more ragged diversity of dramatic voices Shōyō was finding in Shakespeare.

113  Moriya, 131.

114  In 1923, Shōyō wrote the words for the town's song.

115  "Jibun no honyaku ni tsuite," 258.

116  Shōyō was invited to inspect Ōgai's translation prior to its staging that year by the Kindaigeki Kyōkai.

117  In a departure from the mainstream view of *Tōsei shosei katagi* as second-rate, Reichert (113–14) reevaluates the novel as "a crucial first step in establishing modern Japanese literature as a discursive sphere monopolised by the perspective and experience of the male heterosexual." This sphere can be seen to be explored by Tsubouchi within the "masculine" dimension of Shakespearean drama.

118  Ayako Kano, *Acting Like a Woman in Modern Japan: Theatre, Gender, and Nationalism* (London: Palgrave, 2001), 160.

119  Komori Yōichi, "Translation and Formation of Style in the Modern Japanese Novel," *Trans-Humanities* 6, no. 3 (2013): 119.

120  Miyako Inoue, *Vicarious Language: Gender and Linguistic Modernity in Japan* (Berkeley: University of California Press, 2006), 97.

121  Satō Miki, "Kaidai: Tsubouchi Shōyō, *Jiyū no tachi nagori no kireaji* fugen," in *Nihon no honyaku ron: ansorojī to kaidai*, ed. Yanabu Akira, Naganuma Mikiko, and Mizuno Akira (Tokyo: Hōsei University Press, 2010), 68. Shiken's "careful style" (*shūmitsu buntai*), adopted for his popular translations of Jules Verne, sought a closer hybridity of foreign elements with classical Japanese style than had so far been attempted by Meiji translators.

# References

Arai Yoshio. *Sheikusupia geki jōenron* [Shakespeare Performance Studies]. Tokyo: Shinjusha, 1972.

———. "Shōyō no Sheikusupia" [Shōyō's Shakespeare]. *Tsubouchi Shōyō Kenkyū Shiryō* 5 (May 1974): 39–52.

Bowring, Richard. *Mori Ōgai and the Modernisation of Japanese Culture*. Cambridge: Cambridge University Press, 1979.

Gallimore, Daniel. "Sir Walter Scott and the Romanticism of Tsubouchi Shōyō." *Poetica* 79 (Spring 2013): 101–13.

———. *Tsubouchi Shōyō's "Shinkyoku Urashima" and the Wagnerian Moment in Meiji Japan (with a Translation of "Shinkyoku Urashima")*. Lewiston, NY: Edwin Mellen Press, 2016.

Hasegawa Tenkei. "Tsubouchi-sensei no *Riya ō* kōgi" [Professor Tsubouchi's *Lear* Lectures]. *Saō Fukkō* 14 (November 1934): 17–21.

Hattori Yoshika and Inagaki Tatsurō, eds. *Tsubouchi Shōyō kenkyū zadankai* [Tsubouchi Shōyō Research Symposium]. Tokyo: Kindai Bunka Kenkyūsho, 1976.

Inagaki Tatsurō, ed. *Tsubouchi Shōyō shū* [Works of Tsubouchi Shōyō]. Tokyo: Chikuma Shobō, 1969.

Inoue Miyako. *Vicarious Language: Gender and Linguistic Modernity in Japan*. Berkeley: University of California Press, 2006, https://doi.org/10.1525/9780520939066.

Itō Sei. "Pioneers of the New Literature." *Japan Quarterly* 2, no. 2 (January 1955): 224–34.

Jacobowitz, Seth. *Writing Technology in Meiji Japan: A Media History of Modern Japanese Literature and Visual Culture*. Boston: Harvard University Asia Center, 2014, https://doi.org/10.1163/9781684175628.

Kamei Shunsuke. *Eibungakusha Tsubouchi Shōyō* [Shōyō as an English Literary Scholar]. Tokyo: Shōhakusha, 2021.

Kaneda Tamio. "Fenollosa and Tsubouchi Shōyō." In *A History of Modern Japanese Aesthetics*, translated and edited by Michael F. Marra, 53–67. Honolulu: University of Hawai'i Press, 2001, https://doi.org/10.1515/9780824843625-005.

Kano Ayako. *Acting Like a Woman in Modern Japan: Theater, Gender, and Nationalism*. London: Palgrave, 2001, https://doi.org/10.1007/978-1-349-63315-9.

Karatani Kōjin. *Origins of Modern Japanese Literature*. translated by Brett de Bary. Durham, NC: Duke University Press, 1993. Originally published as *Nihon kindai bungaku no kigen*. Tokyo: Kōdansha, 1980, https://doi.org/10.1215/9780822378440.

Kawachi Yoshiko. *Shakespeare and Cultural Exchange*. Tokyo: Seibidō, 1995.

Kawamoto Kōji. *The Poetics of Japanese Verse: Imagery, Structure, Meter*. translated by Stephen Collington, Kevin Collins, and Gustav Heldt. Tokyo: University of Tokyo Press, 2000. Originally published as *Nihon shika no dentō – shichi to go no shigaku*. Tokyo: Iwanami Shoten, 1991.

Kawatake Shigetoshi. *Ningen Tsubouchi Shōyō – kindai gekidan sokumenshi* [Tsubouchi Shōyō, the Man, and the Modern Japanese Theatre]. Tokyo: Shinjusha, 1959.

Kawatake Shigetoshi and Yanagida Izumi. *Tsubouchi Shōyō* [Tsubouchi Shōyō]. 1939. Reprint, Tokyo: Daiichi Shobō, 1988.

Kawatake Toshio. *Nihon no Hamuretto* [*Hamlet* in Japan]. Tokyo: Nansōsha, 1972.

Keene, Donald. *Dawn to the West: A History of Japanese Literature, Vol. 4, Japanese Literature of the Modern Era: Poetry, Drama, Criticism*. New York: Holt, Rinehart and Winston, 1984.

Kikuchi Akira, ed. *Shōyō nikki, 1916–19* [Diary of Tsubouchi Shōyō]. Tokyo: Shōyō Kyōkai, 1999.

Kishi Tetsuo and Graham Bradshaw. "Shakespeare and Traditional Japanese Theatre: Tsubouchi Shōyō." In *Shakespeare in Japan*, 1–28. New York: Continuum, 2005, https://doi.org/10.5040/9781472555281.ch-001.

Kobayashi Kaori. "Shakespeare and National Identity: Tsubouchi Shōyō and His 'Authentic' Shakespeare Productions in Japan." *Shakespeare* 2, no. 1 (June 2006): 59–76, https://doi.org/10.1080/17450910600662919.

Komori Yōichi. "Translation and Formation of Style in the Modern Japanese Novel." *Trans-Humanities* 6, no. 3 (October 2013): 119–31, https://doi.org/10.1353/trh.2013.0004.

Matsumoto Seichō. *Bungō* [Great Man of Letters]. Tokyo: Bungei Shunjū, 2000.

Matsumura Masaie. "Tsubouchi Shōyō to yūmoa ron" [Tsubouchi Shōyō's Theory of Humour]. *Hikaku Bungaku* 18 (October 1975): 15–22.

Mizuno Akira. "Stylistic Norms in the Early Meiji Period: From Chinese Influences to European Influences." In *Translation and Translation Studies in the Japanese Context*, edited by Nana Sato-Rossberg and Judy Wakabayashi, 92–114. New York: Continuum, 2012.

Moriya Sasaburō. *Nihon ni okeru Sheikusupia* [Shakespeare in Japan]. Tokyo: Yasshio Shuppan, 1986.

Morton, Leith. "Translating the Alien: Tsubouchi Shōyō and Shakespeare." In *The Alien Within: Representations of the Exotic in Twentieth-Century Japanese Literature*, 10–42. Honolulu: University of Hawai'i Press, 2009, https://doi.org/10.21313/haw aii/9780824832926.003.0002.

Motoyama Yukihiko. "The Spirit of Political Opposition in the Meiji Period: The Academic Style of the Tōkyō Senmon Gakkō," In *Proliferating Talent: Essays on Politics, Thought, and Education in the Meiji Era*, edited by J. S. A. Elisonas and Richard Rubinger, translated by I. J. McMullen, 317–53. Honolulu: University of Hawai'i Press, 1997, https://doi.org/10.1515/9780824864033-009.

Nakamura Kan. *Tsubouchi Shōyō ron – kindai Nihon no monogatari kūkan* [Tsubouchi Shōyō and the Space of Modern Japanese Narrative]. Tokyo: Yūseidō, 1986.

Natsume Kinnosuke. "Tsubouchi-hakase to *Hamuretto*" [Dr. Tsubouchi's *Hamlet*]. 1911. In *Sōseki zenshū* [Complete Works of Natsume Sōseki], vol. 16, 393–8. Tokyo: Iwanami Shoten, 2019.

Niki Hisae. *Shakespeare Translation in Japanese Culture*. Tokyo: Kenseisha, 1984.

———. "*Shīzaru kidan: jiyū no tachi nagori no kireaji* – Shōyō's First Translation of *Julius Caesar*." *Shakespeare Translation* 1 (1974): 53–68.

Ōba Kenji. *Sheikusupia no honyaku* [Shakespeare Translation]. Tokyo: Kenkyūsha, 2009.

Osada Ikue. *Tōsei goraku katagi* [Pleasures of Meiji Students]. Tokyo: Note, 2015.

Ozaki Hirotsugu. *Tsubouchi Shōyō – Nihon kindaigeki no sōjishatachi* [Tsubouchi Shōyō, Pioneer of Modern Japanese Drama]. Tokyo: Miraisha, 1965.

Powell, Brian. "One Man's *Hamlet* in 1911 Japan: The Bungei Kyokai Production in the Imperial Theatre." In *Shakespeare and the Japanese Stage*, edited by Sasayama Takashi, J. R. Mulryne, and Margaret Shewring, 38–52. Cambridge: Cambridge University Press, 1998.

Quinn, Aragorn. *Performing the Politics of Translation in Modern Japan*. New York: Routledge, 2020.

———. "Political Theatre: 'The Rise and Fall of Rome' and 'The Sword of Freedom,' Two Translations of *Julius Caesar* in Meiji Japan by Kawashima Keizō and Tsubouchi Shōyō." *Asian Theatre Journal* 28, no. 1 (Spring 2011): 168–83, https://doi.org/10.1353/atj.2011.0004.

Reichert, James R. "Tsubouchi Shōyō's *Tōsei shosei katagi* and the Institutionalization of Exclusive Heterosexuality." *Harvard Journal of Asiatic Studies* 63, vol. 1 (June 2003): 69–114, https://doi.org/10.2307/25066692.

Rimer, J. Thomas. "Shakespeare Meets the Buddha: Tsubouchi Shōyō, Osanai Kaoru, and *The Hermit*." *Kyoto Conference on Japanese Studies* 2 (1994): 284–93.

Ryan, Marleigh Grayer. *The Development of Realism in the Fiction of Tsubouchi Shōyō*. Seattle: University of Washington Press, 1975.

Rycroft, David. "Tsubouchi Shōyō's Translation of *Hamlet*." In *Shakespeare in Japan*, edited by Anzai Tetsuo, 187–226. Lewiston, NY: Edwin Mellen Press, 1999.

Sadoya Shigenobu. *Tsubouchi Shōyō – dentōshugisha no kōzu* [Tsubouchi Shōyō: The Making of a Traditionalist]. Tokyo: Meiji Shoin, 1983.

Saeki Junko. "From *Iro* (Eros) to *Ai=Love*: The Case of Tsubouchi Shōyō." In *Translation in Modern Japan*, edited by Indra Levy, translated by Indra Levy. 73–101. Abingdon, Oxon: Routledge, 2016, https://doi.org/10.4324/9781315084602-5.

Satō Miki. "Kaidai: Tsubouchi Shōyō, *Jiyū no tachi nagori no kireaji* fugen" [Tsubouchi Shōyō's Early *Julius Caesar* Adaptation]. In *Nihon no honyaku ron: ansorojī to kaidai* [An Anthology of Japanese Translation Studies], edited by Yanabu Akira, Naganuma Mikako, and Mizuno Akira, 67–70. Tokyo: Hōsei University Press, 2010.

Schwerin-High, Friederike von. *Shakespeare, Reception and Translation: Germany and Japan*. New York: Continuum, 2004, https://doi.org/10.5040/9781472555489.

Shōyō Kyōkai, ed. *Shōyō senshū* [Selected Works of Tsubouchi Shōyō], 17 vols. (1927–8; reprinted with 5 supplementary volumes). Tokyo: Daiichi Shobō, 1977–8.

Suzuki Sadami. *The Concept of Literature in Japan*. translated by Royall Tyler. Kyoto: International Research Center for Japanese Studies, 2006. Originally published as *Nihon no "bungaku" gainen*. Tokyo: Sakuhinsha, 1998.

Suzuki Tomi. *Narrating the Self: Fictions of Japanese Modernity*. Stanford, CA: Stanford University Press, 1997, https://doi.org/10.1515/9780804764759.

Taira Torahiko. "Meiji ki ni okeru kigeki no keifu – sono yakugo to jōen wo megutte" [The Development of Comedy in the Meiji Era in Translated Words and Theatre Productions]. *Engeki Gakuronshū* 27 (May 1989): 63–73, https://doi.org/10.18935/jjstr.27.0_63.

Takita Teiji. *Shōyō shoshi* [Tsubouchi Shōyō Bibliography]. 1937. Reprint, Tokyo: Kokusho Kankōkai, 1976.

Tōkawa Shinsuke. *Shinchō Nihon bungaku arubamu – Tsubouchi Shōyō* [Illustrated Lives of Japanese Writers: Tsubouchi Shōyō]. Tokyo: Shinchōsha, 1996.

Toyoda Minoru. *Shakespeare in Japan: An Historical Survey*. Tokyo: Iwanami Shoten, 1940.

Tsubouchi Shikō. *Tsubouchi Shōyō kenkyū* [Studies in Tsubouchi Shōyō]. Tokyo: Waseda University Press, 1953.

Tsubouchi Shōyō. "Bi to wa nani zo ya" [What Is Beauty?]. 1886. In *Modern Japanese Aesthetics: A Reader*, translated and edited by Michele Marra, 48–64. Honolulu: University of Hawai'i Press, 2002.

———. "Gakusei jidai no tsuioku" [Memoir of My Student Days]. 1925. In *Shōyō senshū*, vol. 12, 47–51, 1977.

———. "Jibun no honyaku ni tsuite" [About My Shakespeare Translations]. 1928. In *Shōyō senshū*, supplementary vol. 5, 254–77, 1977.

———. "Kaioku mandan" [Reminiscences]. 1925–6. In *Shōyō senshū*, vol. 12, 341–72, 1977.

———. "'*Makubesu* hyōshaku' no shogen" [Preface to a Commentary on *Macbeth*]. 1891. In *Shōyō senshū*, supplementary vol. 3, 161–9, 1978.

———. "Nihon de enzuru *Hamuretto*" [Performing *Hamlet* in Japan]. 1907. In *Sheikusupia kenkyū shiryō shūsei* [Research Materials on the Reception of Shakespeare in Japan], vol. 2, edited by Sasaki Takashi, 196–202. Tokyo: Nihon Tosho Centre, 1997.

———. "*Sheikusupiya kenkyū shiori*" [A Companion to Shakespeare Studies]. 1928. In *Shōyō senshū*, supplementary vol. 5, 1–277, 1977.

———. "Shingakugekiron" [Theory of New Musical Drama]. 1904. In *Tsubouchi Shōyō shū*, 344–52.

———. "*Shōsetsu shinzui*" [The Essence of the Novel]. 1885–6. In *Tsubouchi Shōyō shū*, 3–58. translated by Nanette Twine, *Occasional Papers* 11 (Department of Japanese, University of Queensland, 1981), electronic edition, accessed 23 October 2023, http://archive.nyu.edu/html.2451/14945/shoyo.htm.

———. *Shōyō gekidan* [Essays on Drama]. Tokyo: Tenyūsha, 1919.

———. "Soko shirazu no mizuumi" [The Bottomless Lake]. 1891. In *Tsubouchi Shōyō shū*, 279–82.

———. "*Tsubouchi-hakase no Osero* dan." [Dr. Tsubouchi on *Othello*]. *Kabuki* 34 (October 1903): 1–7.

———. "Waga kuni no shigeki" [Historical Drama of Japan]. 1893–4. In *Tsubouchi Shōyō shū*, 287–315.

Tsuno Kaitarō. *Kokkeina kyojin – Tsubouchi Shōyō no yume* [Comic Giant: The Dream of Tsubouchi Shōyō]. Tokyo: Heibonsha, 2002.

Ueda Atsuko. *Concealment of Politics, Politics of Concealment: The Production of "Literature" in Meiji Japan*. Stanford, CA: Stanford University Press, 2007, https://doi.org/10.1515/9781503626898.

Yanagida Izumi. *Wakaki Tsubouchi Shōyō* [The Young Shōyō]. Tokyo: Shunshōsha, 1960.

Yatayama Seiko. *Tsubouchi Shōyō no tsuma – Dai Hachiman Rō no koi* [The Love of Shōyō's Life]. Tokyo: Sakuhinsha, 2004.

# 2   Shōyō's Shakespeare

## Essential Shōyō

Although he was not a native of Edo, one of Shōyō's reputations is that of an Edo *tsūjin*, or dilettante.[1] Through his education at the Imperial University and friendship with Takata, Shōyō gained an entry into the cultural life of the city that enabled him to pursue such typical *tsū* pastimes as kabuki and haiku, not to mention the pleasure quarters in his youth, and his approach to Shakespeare translation seems tainted by this outlook of the Edo dilettante. In an early essay, Shōyō compares the relationship of a translation to its source to "that of a man with a woman."[2] A comparison in the same essay of foreignisation to the then-novel "use of Western grapes" in Japanese cooking suggests a connoisseur's tastes.[3] Yet coming as he did from the Tōkai region of central Japan, Shōyō's role as an Edo *tsūjin* was inevitably to some extent a reaction to his rural origins, a pose that suited his aspirations in an era of rapid social transition, all the more so when combined with that of *Edokko*, "child" or native of Edo. This is apparent in Shōyō's adult preference for Edo to his native Nagoya and even the modern Tokyo dialect,[4] but since the "spirit of resistance" was a definite trait of the Edo character (and of Edo kabuki),[5] he may also be *Edokko* in his sometimes-brash repudiation of aspects of both his native and foreign cultures.

The *tsū* personality eschews rules and categories in favour of cultivation, and in Shōyō's case gravitates towards his dominant trait of being behind the times (*jidai okure*). A subtext of his Shakespearean polemic is that Shakespeare is as "old" as kabuki and in some respects more "cultivated" than his native Japanese drama; paradoxically, the impulse for assuming so may have originated in native cultural hierarchies such as *tsū*. This was not to discredit the values, Buddhist or otherwise, on which his culture was built, only to assert that Shakespeare's response to cultural memory and lived experience seemed to Shōyō more organised and compelling, even more sophisticated. Shakespearean drama seemed to offer a more integrated worldview than was possible within the kabuki dichotomy of tradition (*sekai*) and innovation (*shukō*), which in always rushing to keep up with the times tended to do too much and so allow the "illogical structures" for which Shōyō criticises kabuki *jidaimono*,

DOI: 10.4324/9781003293774-2

their lack of overarching narrative and the random plot transitions. He adds of Chikamatsu's *jidaimono* that

> The incidents portrayed in these plays are apt to resemble the phantasmago-
> ric transformations of a dream: at times like reality, at times like the past, at
> times with a logical sequence, at times without, at times implausible and at
> other times quite plausible, at times showing human beings as they are not
> and at other times as they are.[6]

Shakespeare, who kept his distance from the modern classicism of the Jacobean theatre, appealed to Shōyō partly because he was "old," the venerable sage or *okina* by which his name was initially known in Japan. Up to 1945 Shakespeare was com-monly known as *Saō* (or *Shaō*), combining a character with the same sound as the first syllable in "Shakespeare" and *ō* (the Sino-Japanese reading of *okina*), and in 1891 Shōyō portrays him as a kind of venerable Buddha who, having gained mas-tery over nature, appears to understand his audience better than they do themselves:

> Shakespeare's genius is a jewel of nature able to liberate the spirit of nature,
> to stir the rustics, the maiden and Benka of old from their apathy, but though
> we may price his jewel as highly as a castle, it is in itself no more than a rare
> stone, worth no more than any passing fad, for it is only human nature to
> inflate the value of the things we admire.[7]

Benka was a historical figure in the ancient Chinese kingdom of Chu who had his left foot cut off when the king refused to believe that a valuable but unpol-ished gemstone he had found in the mountains was real, and then his right foot by the king's successor for the same reason. It was only when Benka polished the stone that its value was recognised, and it was sold in exchange for fifteen castles. Shōyō's conceit relates to the Buddhist doctrine of the ultimate emptiness of nature: only Shakespeare knew the actual emptiness of his words, and in this section of the essay Shōyō suggests that Chikamatsu's "jewel" had similar powers. The maiden, incidentally, knew nothing, having yet to experience true "sadness."[8]

As Tsuno observes, "practical consequences" are always more important for Shōyō than "logical consequences."[9] Since it was going to take some time for Japanese scholars and theatre people to work out a practical, workable response to Shakespeare's genius, his initial reception in the Meiji era runs like a pageant comprising one colourful adaptation after another without the focus of a kabuki *sekai*, although a focus of sorts is provided by *Hamlet* as the play with which the reception begins and ends. Shakespeare's name became widely known in Japan in 1871, when Nakamura Keiu translated Polonius' "To thine own self be true" on the cover page of his bestselling translation of Samuel Smiles' *Self-Help*, and the tragedy remained at centre stage with the translations of Hamlet's fourth solilo-quy by Toyama Masakazu and Yatabe Ryōkichi in their collection of translations of English verse, *Shintaishishō* (Selection of New-Style Poetry), published in 1882. The pageant reaches a denouement with Shōyō's production at the Imperial

Theatre in 1911, which demonstrated that Shakespeare could be translated and staged in the Japanese language.

Shakespeare's *Hamlet* therefore offered Meiji Shakespeareans a view of the world and even *sekai* as, more than any other play, it established the myth of Shakespeare's universality from which future Japanese encounters would proceed. Shōyō's first adult encounter with Shakespeare was with *Hamlet* when he failed Houghton's examination for writing a moralistic assessment of Gertrude's character. This understandable error is redolent of the kind of kabuki narrative where characters are arbitrarily executed for little more than being in the wrong place at the wrong time, but Shōyō took advantage of his momentary alienation by agreeing with Houghton and going the way of anti-didacticism.

Shōyō's transgressive spirit comes from within his native tradition, but his feeling for what was important about Shakespeare was shaped within the ambitious scope of his reading of Western scholarship from the 1880s onwards; this reading challenged and affirmed his existing convictions, opening up an imaginary space between his own subjectivity and Shakespeare's otherness. From Dowden he acquires the idealism that shaped his own realism, and from Moulton the inductivism that rationalises his intense involvement with Shakespeare's texts. Comparativists such as H. M. Possnett and Hippolyte Taine narrow the cultural gap by aligning Japanese tradition with universal historical forces, and Shōyō partakes of the Whiggish teleology of Thomas Babington Macaulay and the Social Darwinism of Herbert Spencer, both of whom are mentioned in *Shōsetsu shinzui*.[10] From Dryden he receives approval for treating translation as literature, while the dichotomy between Johnson's eighteenth-century neoclassicism and Coleridgean imagination frames Shōyō's sense of the moralistic and psychological dimensions of literature.

Shōyō's seminal response to his age of confusion comes in *Shōsetsu shinzui*; although it is about fiction and does not mention Shakespeare, it has straightforward implications for his later Shakespeare studies, especially when read in tandem with his statements on Japanese drama and in the "hidden ideals" debate that were to follow. Shōyō's stance is rhetorical rather than philosophical or even ethical. On the one hand, he seems to add to the confusion by conflating popular Edo genres such as the historical romance (*haishi*) within the single category of popular fiction (*gesaku*) in opposition to his ideal category of the modern novel (*shōsetsu*) or, as Atsuko Ueda comments with regard to the opening passage of the treatise,

> The complex, diverse genre of the *gesaku* is reduced to an entity that becomes the negative precursor to the *shōsetsu*, defined as that which is not the *shōsetsu*.[11]

This conflation is implicit also in his assumption that Shakespeare's characterisations must be so much more diverse than those in the more limited scope of his native literature. For Shōyō, however, the real complexity was to be found less in literary hierarchies than in the breadth and diversity of human behaviour which was the proper subject of fiction, and which the adoption of a single category was meant to rationalise.

At this early stage in his career, Shōyō asserts a current superiority of fiction to drama in exploring what he understands by human nature, but in Shakespeare he will discover a writer who is equally capable of exploring human interiority by dramatic and rhetorical means. This is to say that while his native theatrical conventions may, like the categories of Edo fiction, have tended to conflate cultural practices with individual behaviour and so "expound a warped view of human nature,"[12] the logical movement of Shakespearean drama was towards a sympathy with individual desires and motives. Genres and styles may lose their relevance over time, but Shōyō's conservative view was that human nature remained constant even if its outward manifestations became more (and sometimes less) sophisticated through the accretion of cultural knowledge and experience.

From his upbringing, Shōyō acquired a straightforward Buddhist perception of human nature, which in *Shōsetsu shinzui* he categorises numerically as the 108 "worldly desires,"[13] and thus recognises that a play like *Othello* is about the destructive effects of jealousy, and that Shakespeare's comedies can be read as exercises in the Buddhist virtue of compassion. At the same time, one reason why Shōyō does not pursue a strictly Buddhist approach to Shakespeare is surely his susceptibility to nineteenth-century Victorian "optimism": for example, Macaulay's belief in the inevitability of progress and Taine's positivist assertion of the weight of racial character. Buddhism takes a more pessimistic view of history and society, problematising consciousness[14] – and therefore imagination – in addition to the five senses of sight, sound, smell, taste, and touch as sources of pleasure from which the follower seeks liberation. That the types of romantic love portrayed in both kabuki and Shakespeare, however beautiful or well intentioned, were hindrances to enlightenment hardly needed stating, but in idealising Shakespeare's imagination Shōyō's motive was clearly literary rather than religious. Similarly, his theory of "hidden ideals" that posits the authority of Shakespeare's genius as emanating from beyond the text can be said to refute the idealisation of visible authority figures in Confucianism, while the Buddhist Shōyō appears to favour a version of Christian monotheism as a metaphor for the novelist's potential:

> Fiction exposes the hidden and obscure aspects of life; it assimilates the manifold passions of human beings within its pages, which naturally causes readers to ponder on their own experience. Novelists are similar in my opinion to the Divine as the author of Creation and yet absent from Creation in the way that they strive to create a panoply of characters from whom they too are absent, and to make a realistic portrayal of everyday life. Yet the sheer infinite extent of Creation makes it all the harder for ordinary, uncomplicated folk to grasp the underlying relationships of cause and effect, so that the role of the novelist in my estimation is to identify the essential points and arrange them as materials for the reader's consideration and appraisal. This is asking a huge amount of a writer, but if carried out effectively can achieve something quite out of the ordinary.[15]

What Shōyō in effect proposes is a compromise between a Buddhist culture in which actions are understood to have consequences (and praised or condemned accordingly) and a basically Christian view that asserts the inscrutability of the Divine and ultimately of history as well. Moreover, since human nature in Buddhism was defined as attachment to existence and enlightenment as freedom from such attachments, the novel had the potential to enact the process of enlightenment through its objective depiction of, and therefore distancing from, human attachments, although (as Shōyō would argue) for the process to be convincing the author had to remain invisible; that is where Christian notions of inscrutability come in handy. Literature, in other words, had to be as convincing as history could not fail to be.

Unlike some of his contemporaries, Shōyō was never going to turn Christian himself: his motivation is pragmatic. By opening its doors to the Western world, Japan had exposed itself to infiltration by Western ideologies and religions such as Christianity, and Shōyō was not alone in hoping that Western thought systems could be harnessed to address faults in his own. His belief that Japanese literature and drama needed reform came not only from what he had learnt from his foreign professors at the Imperial University but from a native discourse that dated back to the eighteenth century and beyond. This discourse is central to the thesis of *Shōsetsu shinzui*.

*Shōsetsu shinzui* is divided into two parts, the first part stipulating Shōyō's ideal of fiction and the second discussing stylistic issues. The two parts foreshadow his later views on Shakespeare and Shakespeare translation, for example on lexical choice and plot construction. At the age of twenty-five, Shōyō was already well read in both Japanese and English literature and was a connoisseur of kabuki, and so could reasonably claim (as I have previously quoted) that

> art, different by nature from practical crafts, should never be created with predetermined controls. To arouse in the beholder by its sublime beauty emotions so profound that his spirit seems involuntarily to soar – that is its proper objective, and that is what makes it art.[16]

Towards the end of his life, having been engrossed for many years in Shakespeare's poetic drama, he was to reflect that he felt a kind of "floating" or spiritual elation when he translated Shakespeare.[17] The metaphor of "floating" is familiar from the "floating world" (*ukiyo*) of Edo culture, but in the wake of Japan's encounter with modernity, Shōyō wonders how the reader's spirit can continue to float in a world where old certainties have been challenged, suggesting that the literary mode of realism involves a rhetorical journey into reality that enables the reader to soar above less enlightened states of mind. Reading becomes a recovery of an integrity of outward behaviour and inner thoughts that has been sundered at earlier stages of civilisation.

The recovery of integrity underlies Shōyō's thesis that "the abiding concern of the novel is human nature (*ninjō*). Social conditions and mores (*fūzoku*) are secondary."[18] *Ninjō* and *fūzoku* were intrinsically related, because to understand what society does to people was also to gain insight into human nature. Shōyō does not, therefore, deny the relevance of environment to character, and in his argument with romantic nationalist Takayama Chogyū was to insist that it was environment that formed character against Chogyū's view that it was heredity.[19] For Shōyō, human nature and culture flourished just as well outside the constraints of family, while human nature remained the focus of literary art. His job description of the novelist could just as readily be applied to Shakespeare:

> A writer of novels is like a psychologist. His characters must be psychologically credible. If he ends up creating characters who are incompatible with how people are, or worse still contradict the principles of psychology, those characters will be no more than a figment of his imagination rather than real human beings, and not even a clever or intriguing storyline will be able to make the work into a true novel.[20]

Characters in novels became "psychologically credible" as they intimated a reality that was always greater than themselves rather than being manifestations of reasons that were already known. Shōyō terms the latter tendency "didacticism," and criticises the didactic tendency of Edo novelists such as Tamenaga Shunsui and Bakin, observing of Bakin's epic *Nansō satomi hakkenden* (The Eight Dog Chronicles, 1814–42) that

> As a didactic novel it is unbeatable, but as a record of human nature it falls somewhat short for the simple reason that not only the behaviour but even the inner motives of the eight protagonists remain reasonable and virtuous from beginning to end.[21]

This dichotomy is something like the transition from the English miracle and morality plays, with their stock types, to the illusion of psychological depth and change in Shakespeare's plays.

What Shōyō particularly wishes to avoid is the static dichotomy he finds in Tokugawa fiction between high moral ideals, typically to do with duty and loyalty, and narratives that "luxuriate in sadism and pornography,"[22] which, because they satisfy the suppressed desires of readers – suppressed, in part, by the Tokugawa regime – may actually be more attractive than the ideals that are meant to override them. Shōyō feels that a human impulse to indulge in acts of violence and gratuitous sexuality, however compellingly evoked, is no substitute for nuanced psychological explorations, or (as he would put it) the mysterious processes of cause and effect.

Towards the end of *Shōsetsu shinzui*, Shōyō makes the following critical comparison between what he calls realism and idealism:

> It is easy enough to become a realist writer but rather more challenging to master its secrets. Contrarily, it is a lot harder to join the idealist school, but once in, the way ahead is an easy one.[23]

In other words, it may be easy enough to describe a single situation in realistic detail but far harder to develop that situation into a lucid narrative. The idealist, by contrast, needs to have acquired a high degree of knowledge and self-mastery that is comparable perhaps to a samurai's self-discipline but having done so can assert his ideals with freedom and authority. Having as it were made himself, the idealist has the licence to impose his own fiction on his readers, but against this viewpoint Shōyō insists that no amount of self-mastery can be representative of the total perspective of a readership. The realist's challenge, therefore, is to exclude his or her "own personality traits"[24] so totally from the narrative that characters are manifested as complete individuals irrespective of the author's personal beliefs and prejudices. Realism in this sense was more difficult to achieve than idealism because it shirked a moral compass.

Shōyō's norms are aesthetic rather than moral. As principal of his university's high school at the turn of the century he will espouse an ethical outlook, but according to his argument, good literature is in any case inherently moral:

> Fiction should not be treated as a vehicle for carnal indulgence but aspires instead to entertain readers by appealing to their higher sensibilities. A predisposition for refinement and delicacy of feeling are the noblest of attributes, known only to civilised and culturally advanced peoples. Ignorant barbarians seek only the gratification of their baser desires.[25]

The rhetoric is of its time and place, but what Shōyō proposes in *Shōsetsu shinzui* is not that Prospero teach Caliban his classical language, but that Caliban teach Prospero the colloquial.

For Shōyō, the classical style is unsuited "for the description of passionate emotions. . . . It is lacking in directness and vigour, and appears not to take itself seriously,"[26] whereas

> The colloquial style is natural in its use of everyday language. Vivid and lucid, it has an obvious equivalent in the colloquial style of Chinese and indeed Western fiction.[27]

In the Taishō era, Shōyō will conclude that the naturalness of the contemporary language makes it suited for translating Shakespeare. What he means by classical style is the literary form of Japanese (*bungo*) that dated back to the eighth century and which Shōyō learnt at school and university as the standard for writing the language. *Shōsetsu shinzui* was written in this style, but not the kabuki plays he enjoyed or his own creative works of the Meiji era, which were written in the early modern Japanese of the Edo era that during Shōyō's lifetime evolved into the modern Japanese of today.

Modernisation was achieved mainly by the imposition of the dialect spoken by the Tokyo middle class as the national standard for writing the language, and continued earlier historical processes of phonological change and the rationalisation of grammatical inflexions and orthography, as well as introducing a considerable number of foreign loan words and allowing the coinage of new *kanji* compounds. What Shōyō means by the colloquial in 1885 is essentially the spoken form of Edo Japanese, and what he means by the contemporary in 1928 is the modern colloquial form as it had evolved over forty years of language reform, thus abandoning various Edo archaisms that Shōyō himself may have continued to use and wished to preserve in his translations. The differences between classical and modern Japanese are more extreme than between Chaucer's Middle English and Shakespeare's English, or between Shakespeare's English and the Modern English of the late nineteenth and early twentieth centuries. Shōyō admired Shakespeare's economy of expression, but this was not the same as the emotional restraint he found in classical Japanese and was considered basically unsuited for use in modern novels and Shakespeare translation.

Classical restraint was also different from the suppression of authorial identity that was central to Shōyō's theory of Shakespeare and to the richly emotional texture (the "world of feeling")[28] he found in both Shakespeare and kabuki drama, which was written mainly in Edo or Kamigata dialect. Shōyō's abiding concern as a Shakespeare translator was with Shakespeare's rhythms, and he believed colloquial Japanese (both archaic and modern) to be inherently rhythmical and capable of rendering Shakespeare's rhythmicality and all that it meant.[29] In *Shōsetsu shinzui*, by embracing the colloquial as the appropriate vehicle for psychological realism, Shōyō also reveals why he will never translate Shakespeare in a strictly classical style. Yet neither will he ever fully abandon classical inflexions and archaisms as appropriate for conveying Shakespeare's nuances.

### Edo Literature and the Aesthetics of Human Feelings

For Shōyō and his contemporaries, Shakespeare was the "hometown of the heart" (*kokoro no furusato*) and the hidden unconscious of the Meiji era.[30] As the most mysterious and at the same time representative of Western writers, Shakespeare filled a vacuum left by the native culture as it retreated from itself in the face of Westernisation (or at least up to the promulgation of the Meiji Constitution in 1889). His dramas spoke to this era of change by embodying a spirit of nature and creativity that was believed to be lacking in the native culture. Shōyō compares Shakespeare's works to "the essence of creativity" and maintains that "they are as desirable to ordinary people as the beauties of nature,"[31] but his concept of Shakespearean imagination was meaningless without some organising principle.[32] In the case of the novel, this was provided by its structure, which as an imitation of the Buddhist chain of cause and effect was "open to countless variations" and "impossible to predict."[33] Shakespeare's genius was his ability to organise the material of human feelings and desires into logical structures that were strong enough to withstand Shōyō's personal fears of loss of objectivity and identity by keeping the reader guessing and stimulating the reader into continuous introspection.

Shōyō's nativist viewpoint, although expressed previously in his critique of Fenollosa, can only have been reinforced by his reading of Shakespeare's *Macbeth* in which the protagonist becomes seemingly detached from reality through the power of his soliloquies; the play was a casebook study in the Buddhist logic of cause and effect. Yet, as Suzuki Sadami suggests, Shōyō's reification of human feelings conflated a modern, evolutionary phenomenology of desire with the aesthetics of Edo Japan.[34] Shōyō's debt in particular to the eighteenth-century classicist Motoori Norinaga is essential to understanding the balance Shōyō strikes in his reception of Shakespeare between native thought and Anglo-American scholarship.

In *Shōsetsu shinzui*, Shōyō praises Norinaga's influential critique of *The Tale of Genji* with his view that

> Very few Japanese have read fiction with Norinaga's depth of understanding. My impression of those numerous classical scholars who brazenly insist on interpreting even such a work as *The Tale of Genji* as didactic is that they have been deceived by the little they know.[35]

While Shōyō's academic research was focussed on Shakespeare and drama, Norinaga remains a putative influence on his view of Shakespeare that was highlighted by his pupil Honma Hisao in his 1959 study.[36] Emphasising the detachment of Confucianism from utilitarian motives in Norinaga's thought, Honma argues that Shōyō's utilitarian motive for translating Shakespeare does not originate in Shakespearean drama per se, and implies a connection between Norinaga's aesthetic of *mono no aware* and Matthew Arnold's maxim of the function of criticism as being "to see the object as it really is."[37]

Norinaga asserted the explanatory principle of *mono no aware*, which has been variously translated as an appreciation of the transience of beauty, the innate pathos of things, or simply as a profound awareness of beauty, and which remains a pertinent approach in Shakespeare's reception in Japan. His conviction that "directness of feeling is the essence of humanity and the heart of the Japanese"[38] was also a political response to the dominant Confucianist ideology of a regime that subordinated individual expressions of feeling to the needs of the state. As Suzuki quotes:

> Since Confucianism and Buddhism are dedicated to giving people instruction and guidance, they often issue stern warnings that violate human feelings, considering in many respects that to act in accordance with one's heart is bad and that to pursue practice by suppressing one's feelings is good.[39]

Norinaga sought to bypass Confucianism by returning "to the thoughts and feelings of antiquity"[40] so that not only did *mono no aware* express those feelings that were typically circumscribed by the state – sexual love and love between parent and child being paramount examples – but which found their purest expression in the ancient poetry (*uta*) in which Norinaga was expert.[41] Shakespeare appealed to Meiji writers like Shōyō because his plays also thematised the expression of individual feelings against prescriptive external forces: the love of Romeo and Juliet and of Lear for Cordelia. Shōyō could understand Shakespeare because native writers such as Chikamatsu covered similar territory and were capable of the same rhetorical tricks.

As Shōyō argued in *Shōsetsu shinzui*, the difference between the two sides was mainly one of moral purpose: Shakespeare and George Eliot did not tell their readers what to think; nor was Shakespeare necessarily any more imaginative than the Tokugawa novelists, since as Charles Shiro Inouye comments of *gesaku* fiction, "Anything c[ould] be imagined because everything is justified and/or properly condemned."[42] Bakin, in particular, was a writer whose vivid evocations of the samurai code and immersion in classical poetry allowed his imagination free rein. Shakespeare too may have had moral principles, but in Shōyō's observation it was Shakespeare's success at concealing them that unleashed readers' imaginations and invited them to impose their own ideals (or moral judgements) on Shakespeare's imagined worlds.

At the time of writing *Shōsetsu shinzui*, Shōyō apparently regarded drama as inferior to fiction, or at least to have lost its original purpose of entertaining people with the fantasies (or "enactment of legends") in which their ancestors had believed,[43] and so had been forced into a position of moral didacticism. In other words, the representation of flawed human behaviour on the stage could be tolerated only so long as it was seen to give moral instruction, which was also the position of the Meiji government, as at the same time as Shōyō was writing *Shōsetsu shinzui* it actively sought to reform the kabuki theatre.[44]

Through his encounter with Shakespeare, however, Shōyō comes to believe that drama, or at least Shakespearean drama, is better equipped even than the novel for concealing its ideals:

> I suppose that if Shakespeare had written his tragedies in prose, as novels in other words, they would have been of lesser value, which is because it would have been harder for them to conceal their ideals. The tragedy of *King Lear*, for example, would be seen to have the same moralistic purpose as a Bakin novel, because Shakespeare never gives his own opinion in the play, and so its meaning can be deduced from the surface details of the plot, interpret it as one will. To give an example from one of Bakin's novels, the characters of Mr. and Mrs. Hikiroku are depicted with great vigour and realism, but from the viewpoint of hidden ideals the story has a clear moralistic purpose. The author is clearly visible within the story. Likewise, Bashō's famous "frog" haiku has various interpretations but they all stem from the same author's point of view, and so too *The Tale of Genji*.[45]

What Shōyō means by Bakin's "clear moralistic purpose" is basically that of upholding the value system of the Tokugawa regime, and in the case of *The Tale of Genji* the Buddhist aesthetics of the Heian court. The writer whose name appears most frequently in *Shōsetsu shinzui* is in fact Tamenaga Shunsui, who died only fifteen years before Shōyō was born and is considered the most representative of writers in the genre of *ninjōbon*, or popular love stories. Even if Shunsui's stories centred somewhat predictably on the Edo pleasure quarters, he was less crudely erotic than the humorous *sharebon* of the previous century in his portrayal of strong, compassionate women, and provided Shōyō with a model of popular literary style (*zokubun*) that would feed into his Shakespeare translations, contrasting with the restrained aristocratic style (*gabuntai*) of *The Tale of Genji*. Poet and English literary scholar Yano Hōjin claimed that

> If *The Tale of Genji* gave Shōyō a model of elegant style, then the model of popular directness comes from Tamenaga Shunsui. What Shōyō conceived as the creation of a new literary style derived from the traditional blending of classical and colloquial styles (*gazoku setchū*) is achieved in the ambitious and painstaking efforts of his Shakespeare translations.[46]

What Shōyō sees in Shakespeare is something like this aesthetic ideal of *gazoku setchū*.

All three of these writers (Shakespeare, Murasaki Shikibu, and Shunsui) occupy emotional territories that for Shōyō are broadly defined as the literature of romantic love that flourishes in reaction to official disapproval: for Murasaki the masculine world of the Heian court, for Shakespeare the Puritans, and for Shunsui the officials who towards the end of his life had him manacled and his books burnt. Shōyō's lesser antagonists are the ideologues of a regime that sought to impose uniformity on social and linguistic diversity (for example the linguist Ueda Kazutoshi, who promoted an organic view of national language based on the ideology of *kokutai* or national polity),[47] and in striving for the modern ideal of equal love between men and women he expresses frustration at both the exclusivity of the classical culture and the reductionism of the popular, the sense that nothing was possible outside static hierarchies.

At the same time, as I have mentioned, hierarchies also served to free the imagination and, in the "floating world" of the pleasure quarters stimulated the development of elaborate cultural codes that subverted as well as complied with authority. As Saeki Junko argues, Shōyō's rejection of *iro*, the aesthetic of sexual love personified by the character of Prince Genji, in favour of modern *ai* (romantic love) was also to lose "sight of the rich meanings *iro* had held in the spiritual and cultural history of Japan."[48] Shōyō's puritanism is to a large extent redeemed by Shakespeare, for example the Ovidian poetics of *A Midsummer Night's Dream*, the populism of the Falstaff plays, and the eroticism of Antony and Cleopatra. The exasperation he expresses in *Shōsetsu shinzui* at lowbrow audience tastes is not necessarily disapproval of what he calls "customs" or "mores" (*fūzoku*) but a realist's refusal to essentialise the local as morally ideal and a writer's determination to get to the end of the story.

Another writer who comes close to Shōyō's ideal of stylistic mixing is the late eighteenth-century "man of letters" (*bunjin*) Ueda Akinari, described as a writer who "by writing in a mixture of colloquial and classical styles" was "able to incorporate both poetic atmosphere and emotional intensity to his text."[49] Yet Akinari was not rediscovered until the twentieth century, and the literary model that both sustains and repels Shōyō's imagination even more than Shunsui turns out to be Bakin. As he writes in his memoir,

> I wrote *Shōsetsu shinzui* in order to criticise Bakin's excessive proneness for preaching to readers, but because I had been engrossed in his fiction since I was a child, I could not help myself from imitating his way of writing.[50]

Though he wanted to "embrace" the earlier Genroku style of a century before Bakin,[51] it was nevertheless Bakin's that "prevailed" within him, and which he was naturally gifted at imitating:

> The more I realised Bakin's influence the more I came to dislike my own prose style, and yet despite this antipathy I could not outgrow it. This was a complex with which I had to struggle for many years after.[52]

The central device in *Hakkenden* of the eight dog warriors representing one each of the eight Confucian virtues (*jingi hachigyō*) seemed to the young Shōyō no substitute for the emotional complexity of Shakespeare's characters (and they were only dogs after all). Bakin's achievement was the detail and energy with which he sustained his characterisations over the extraordinary length of the work, but the energy was libidinous and Bakin's style famously opaque, and Shōyō resented the notion that any work of literature could trick him into indulging his own "licentious passions" simply in order to instil lessons about duty and loyalty already learnt in his upbringing. Bakin's opaqueness (*inbi*) might correspond with the illusory depth of a writer like Shakespeare, and have introduced Shōyō to one of the basic pleasures of reading, but in Shōyō's theory it was more of a puzzle to be solved than a stimulus for the reader's personal ideals. The fact, however, that Bakin does retain its grip on Shōyō, even into old age, is surely indicative of Bakin's literary strengths, in particular that his didacticism was as much structural as to do with its message, and that (as Lawrence Marceau argues) *Hakkenden*'s "latent or hidden message" (*inbi*)

> may have to do with the ironic distance between the virtuous heroes and the corrupt world within which they act, or it may deal with the distance between the ideals themselves and how they play through in an imperfect world. For Bakin, the juxtaposition between an overly didactic framework and a more subtle reading provides a tension that makes his work compelling even today.[53]

In other words, *Hakkenden* was not necessarily as closed a work as Shōyō's initial comparison with Shakespeare and Victorian fiction may have led him to believe, and its openness makes Bakin more a writer to be channelled than "cancelled" outright. Different from the utopian "happy ending" of Shakespearean comedy, where Bassanio and Bertram are forgiven their indiscretions, Bakin "consciously positions amorousness as the ideological antipode of benevolence but also illustrates how desire continually resurges from within the sphere of benevolence."[54] This is the psychological flipside of *kanzen chōaku*: the slogan of "virtue rewarded and vice punished" that is frequently cited by Shōyō and that, as Kamei Hideo argued, allowed for a greater range of moral possibilities than conventional historical discourse.[55] *Hakkenden* was a work of remarkable stylistic sophistication, and although Bakin's characters may have been predestined in their roles, that did not stop them from behaving as unpredictably as any other human being; his dialogues also revealed a striking debt to kabuki style.[56] Moreover, Bakin did flout poetic justice, if not exactly in the manner of a Shakespeare, who was criticised in the seventeenth century for his tendency of allowing wicked characters such as Duke Frederick in *As You Like It* to escape punishment by embracing virtue in the course of a play.

### Chikamatsu and the Kabuki World

While it is no wonder that Shōyō keeps coming back to Bakin, he still has many reasons for wanting to get away from him, not the least being Bakin's lengthy sentence structures which, in any case, were rapidly supplanted through the influence of *genbun itchi*.[57] Bakin died just eleven years before Shōyō's birth, and his earnest "dog warriors," while serving as powerful role models for the teenage Shōyō, may have seemed lacking in Shakespearean feeling as he encountered Shakespeare in his twenties. For human feelings (*ninjō*), the model was not the decadent Kasei culture of his grandparents' generation (1804–30), which works such as *Hakkenden* were meant to redress, but the artistic flourishing of the Genroku era (1688–1704), with its basis in *mono no aware* aesthetics. In the 1890s, as Jason Karlin argues, as Westernisation provoked nostalgia for a lost sense of community, Genroku culture in particular became imagined as:

> a liminal moment and space wherein differences in social status were ignored and a sense of *communitas* emerged centred on ideas of equality rather than neo-Confucian notions of hierarchy.[58]

Shōyō contributed to the 1890s Genroku boom through his Chikamatsu studies and, since Shakespeare is Chikamatsu writ large in Shōyō's mind, can even be said to coopt Shakespeare to his detachment from the Meiji establishment; Karlin argues that the Genroku boom was a reaction against the centralising, fracturing trajectory of government-led modernisation.[59] Shōyō, of course, is also a Meiji moderniser (and Shakespeare a foreigner), but his reception of Shakespeare as well as challenging past fantasies places Shakespeare's genius mysteriously beyond the borders of the synchronised time and place that modernisation promoted, and even to promote a democracy of the human spirit.

Like Shakespeare, Chikamatsu often wrote on romantic themes (especially in his *sewamono* domestic tragedies), was capable of totalising dramatic effects in works such as *Kokusenya gassen* (The Battles of Coxinga, 1715), and aspired to a dramaturgy that transcended theatrical and social conventions: his plays are considered less purely theatrical and more unfettered in their level of social awareness, with Andrew Gerstle stressing the "temporal and spatial unity" of his *sewamono*.[60] In an essay written in English for the Shakespeare tercentenary in 1916, Shōyō devotes much of the space to a flattering portrait of the Genroku master:

> Chikamatsu is ingenious in rhetoric, rich in language; possesses both pathos and humour (of course, as compared with Shakespeare's, the magnitude is small and merit is inferior); has suitable talents for a tragedy as well as for a comedy; makes a free and happy passage between realism and romanticism; is gifted with clear common sense, which is a rare thing in a poet; holds a moderate view of life and morality and his attitude as a writer is always objective.... [T]he swan-like gentleness of his disposition can be seen from his style and a kind of tenderness which is the pervading tone of his composition. It appears that he did not attempt to propose a new idea or problem, but that he made it the aim of his art to give a pleasure and an unobtrusive lesson [*sic*]. This is also a position in which he resembles Shakespeare. He seems to have been a wonderfully rapid writer; his works may sometimes be suspected to have been composed half unconsciously and almost in spite of himself, and many defects which come from carelessness are found in them; but there is, as in Shakespeare, some unstudied charm.[61]

Shōyō does not make detailed comparisons of individual Chikamatsu plays with any of Shakespeare's, but as plays on contemporary incidents puts Chikamatsu's *sewamono* on a par with the anonymous *Arden of Faversham* (1592), which dramatised the sensational murder of one Thomas Arden by his wife Alice and her lover.[62] The *sewamono* that Shōyō lists, such as *Shinjū ten no Amijima* (The Love Suicides at Amijima, 1721), which was based on an actual double love suicide that took place in Osaka the preceding year, rely too much on recent events for their dramatic appeal in Shōyō's thinking, and therefore reflect too obviously on the so-called lesser ideals of official morality. Yet *Shinjū ten no Amijima*, which was hailed by Donald Keene as "Chikamatsu's masterpiece,"[63] offers numerous examples of what Shōyō regards as Shakespearean realism, as in the final, third act when in the early hours of the morning the paper merchant Jihei is about to depart for his tryst and love suicide with Koharu, but almost ends up forgetting his dagger:

JIHEI.      I left my dagger behind. You couldn't fetch it for me. You know, Denbei, that's one good thing about being a samurai, because if I were a samurai myself and had forgotten my sword, I'd probably have to kill myself right there!

DENBEI.   I'm sorry I forgot I was holding on to it for you. Here's your knife as well.

CHANTER. He hands Jihei the dagger, who fastens it securely inside his sash.

JIHEI.      Difficult to relax without your dagger. Good night to you!

CHANTER. Jihei exits.

DENBEI.   Come back to Osaka soon! It's always good to have you.

CHANTER. With this hasty exchange Denbei clatters shut the bolt of the door. There is absolute silence, not a sound. Jihei pretends to leave, but then creeps back stealthily inside. He clings to the door of the teahouse, and peeping inside he is startled to see shadows moving in his direction. He conceals himself by the house opposite until the figures pass.[64]

The scene is discernibly realistic in the way that people easily forget things when they are preoccupied with more serious matters such as the prospect of imminent death, and it epitomises the thematic tension between duty (*giri*) and feeling (*ninjō*). Jihei's dagger is both the instrument of his suicide and a symbol of the honour that binds the mercantile society of Osaka which, with trusted friends like Denbei around, he may be reluctant to leave. Jihei is not of the samurai class for whom the wearing of the two swords was mandatory, and (as he jokes) for whom decisions of life and death were relatively straightforward. Yet through his weakness, Jihei has been drawn into an impossible situation in which suicide is the only way he can prove his sincerity to his lover (who must also die), his wife (whom he loves), and his creditors.

What is attractive about Jihei is that while the culture might be considered psychopathic, he is far from being a psychopath himself, and in this final act seems far from certain that he is doing the right thing. His liminal situation is mirrored dramatically in the detail of the shadows "moving in his direction," which soon reveal themselves to be no more than his brother Magoemon with Magoemon's apprentice Sangorō and Jihei's son Kantarō on Sangorō's back. In a few hours the truth will be out, and Kantarō will be in the care of a surrogate father. Jihei could still belong to that world if only he could wait for the light of day and allow the norms to have their way, and Koharu traded in marriage to a man she does not love. Yet the shadows that startle him are as nebulous as his own feelings. He cannot know what the shadows are until they come close enough for him to be seen and to hear their voices. Likewise, he cannot have known what erotic love was until he had experienced it, and cannot know what death is until he has passed that threshold for himself. It is (*pace* Norinaga) such respect for human realities that drives Shōyō's anti-didacticism.

Jihei looks out from the teahouse onto the darkness of a world in which (as Dowden writes of *King Lear*)[65] moral judgement stands apart from sensual desire. There is a moral import insofar as Jihei and Koharu follow the convention of double love suicides by facing west in the direction of the Buddhist paradise, Amida, in which they hope to be united. This is where the sun will set the following evening, by which time their suicide will be news and known all over Osaka. Yet the ensuing dialogue depicts a couple who have condemned themselves to death by their transgressions; the latter can only accumulate further as they abandon their families and kill themselves in the incorrect manner (since Jihei's stabbing of Koharu is clumsily executed, and he then hangs rather than disembowels himself). Where they succeed, however, is as lovers, and just as for Norinaga erotic love and love between parents and children were the sublime examples of human feeling (*ninjō*),[66] the couple become paragons of human feeling that Chikamatsu's audience could not fail to recognise and admire. Their true story is the historical truth that will become the poetic truth of Chikamatsu's drama. Although Chikamatsu lacks the hiddenness of Shakespearean dramaturgy, the couple's love can only be expressed aesthetically as an alternative to the social and moral norms that have destroyed them. Jihei's talk of crows may sound like pathetic fallacy, but the more he talks in this way, the more real he becomes for his audience:

KOHARU.    You must be worried sick about the children.

JIHEI.     I want to start crying again when you mention them. I can almost see them lying peacefully asleep with no idea, the little innocents, that their father is about to kill himself. I can forget about everything else.

CHANTER.  He slumps to the ground with weeping. The cawing of crows departing their nests at dawn drown out his sobs. The thought they might be lamenting his fate makes him weep only more.

JIHEI.     Listen to the crows . . . come to lead us to the world of the dead. You know what they say about whenever someone writes a prayer on the back of a Kumano amulet, then three crows will die on one of the sacred mountains of Kumano. We have always sworn our love for each other in writing each New Year, and often at the start of a new month too, so if each of our oaths has killed three crows, can you imagine how many must have bitten the dust? The crows always sound like they're calling for their lovers, but knowing the terrible thing we are about to do their cry now is "Revenge, revenge!" I have only myself to blame for the painful death you must endure. Forgive me, Koharu!

CHANTER.  He takes her in his arms.

KOHARU.    No, I'm the one to blame![67]

Shōyō tends to avoid systematic comparisons of the two playwrights, because while Shakespearean drama can be reduced to three genres and thirty-seven plays, a Chikamatsu play is inseparable from its traditions of chant, song, dance, and musical accompaniment, and in many cases the two genres of *jōruri* puppetry and kabuki acting; it is, specifically, musical drama. Shakespeare and Chikamatsu for Shōyō are more like the two components of a metaphor. They are unrelated but can be defined in terms of each other to intimate a new meaning, which is the nature of drama. His alleged mistake of conflating the differing contexts of Shakespeare's age with Chikamatsu's Genroku may be related to his Aristotelian view of the universality of drama as containing in itself the particular truth that is history: drama gifts to the future the lived experience of history, the more convincingly the better. His concern of the 1890s was the historical drama and historical novel, but even non-historical plays like *Hamlet* and *A Midsummer Night's Dream* were tasked with preserving lived experience for the future. Thus, when Shōyō compares Chikamatsu with Shakespeare as he does most exhaustively in his essay of 1909,[68] he may be suggesting no more than that since the two writers each manifest a profound understanding of human nature, which constitutes the principal engine of historical change, the historical truths that their plays express are all of a piece, reflecting on a shared human nature. The ages of Chikamatsu and Shakespeare are different in time and place but are driven by similar, even identical principles of cause and effect.

In the same essay, Shōyō lists eighteen "resemblances" between the two writers, namely

(1) they lived in historically similar periods – the early modern mercantilism of Shakespeare's London and Chikamatsu's Osaka in the late seventeenth and early eighteenth centuries created a large urban audience for new theatrical distractions;[69]

(2) the biographical details of their lives are obscure – similar to Shakespeare's so-called "lost years" (between the ages of twenty-one and twenty-eight), relatively little is known about Chikamatsu's early life until his emergence as a playwright in the 1680s at the age of thirty;[70]

(3) they had rather similar careers before achieving fame – both were "staff play-wrights," Shakespeare for the Lord Chamberlain's Men and King's Men and Chikamatsu for the Takemotoza puppet theatre, although unlike Shakespeare he never acted (or worked puppets);[71]

(4) each cultivated "a close acquaintanceship with people of noble birth" – similar to Shakespeare's likely patronage by the 3rd Earl of Southampton, Chikamatsu served a noble Kyoto family as a page after his father lost his position as a samurai for obscure reasons;[72]

(5) they both "became leaders of the dramatic world when it was still somewhat immature" – the modern bunraku puppet theatre began in Osaka in the 1680s, while the first English play written in blank verse was staged in London in 1561;[73]

(6) they borrowed widely from literary and other available sources, such as popular songs – Chikamatsu reworks the structures and plots of classical Noh plays, especially in his historical *jidaimono*, while the sources of only a couple of Shakespeare's plays remain unidentified;[74]

(7) they "both brushed up others' works, or collaborated with others" – Chikamatsu with Takeda Izumo II (one of the writers of *Kanadehon Chūshingura*), and Shakespeare with George Wilkins and others (Shōyō suggests Marlowe);[75]

(8) "both men appeared at a time when the drama was in a primitive state" – this point is certainly true of Shakespeare although less of Chikamatsu, for whom Noh drama had already been flourishing for three hundred years;[76]

(9) they worked in a wide range of dramatic genres – Shakespeare in tragedy, comedy, historical drama, and "problem plays," and Chikamatsu in historical *jidaimono* plays and contemporary *sewamono* domestic dramas (both of which usually have tragic endings);[77]

(10) they benefited from strong creative partnerships (Shakespeare with the actor Richard Burbage and Chikamatsu with the *jōruri* narrator Takemoto Gidayū);[78]

(11) neither were without adversaries; for example, the Blackfriars and Takemoto theatres – with reference to Ben Jonson, Shōyō comments that "their

opponents were not so jealous, deep or subtle; they challenged them fairly or squarely. Theirs was a real fight for art's sake";[79]

(12) they both had their work published while they were still alive – Chikamatsu also had his work published in a Japanese "folio" edition shortly after his death in 1724;[80]

(13) "both of them were praised as the first and probably last of the greatest figures in the literary world";[81]

(14) they have similar literary qualities; for example, their ability "to express more than one sentiment simultaneously" and in "the musical tone of their works" (Shakespeare in the musicality of his prosody);[82]

(15) the two are broadly similar in their dramatic influences, being "neither moralists like Bakin nor such outright revealers of the truth as Ibsen" but wishing simply for their audiences "to enjoy a glorious world, basking in the soft and amorphous ecstasies of life" – Shōyō comments on the similarity of the two writers' artistic views, Chikamatsu's that "Art is something that lies in the slender margin between the real and unreal" and Shakespeare's skill at tempering realism with fantasy (or idealism), and suggests that what Shakespeare understands by aesthetic pleasure is close to Chikamatsu's word "comfort" (nagusameru), which Shōyō also frequently uses;[83]

(16) they are both "equipped with a sound philosophy of life and endowed with ample common sense";[84]

(17) in the late nineteenth century they each became subject to revisionist criticism, Shakespeare by Tolstoy and Shaw and Chikamatsu by the Japanese Naturalists, who found Chikamatsu too idealistic and preferred the grittier realism of his near-contemporary Ihara Saikaku;[85]

(18) and finally, their works "have been arbitrarily adapted for the convenience of the stage," in other words are open to a wide range of theatrical interpretation – Chikamatsu arguably more so than Shakespeare because of the priority of performance over text in kabuki, although Shōyō mentions John Dryden's adaptations of The Tempest and other plays of the Restoration era.[86]

Shōyō's comparison is revealing of both writers and in his elusive hints at the requirements of literary genius, but it obscures the main difference between kabuki and Shakespearean drama, the former being defined by theatrical tradition and the latter by the texts. Chikamatsu comes across as the same kind of self-made man as Shakespeare's name was first known in Japan; that notion is developed by Shōyō's demands for coherent dramaturgy and character formation. Shōyō's tendency to conflate timeframes, while tendentious, is informed by his ear for different historical styles, and this explains his preference for Chikamatsu's kabuki. His 1907 essay on Hamlet in Japan is worth quoting at length in this regard, beginning with his viewpoint that

The Elizabethan age is basically similar to our own Genroku and Kyōhō eras in the way that the latter broke with the Momoyama culture of the previous century, and yet displays some of the qualities of the tenth-century Heian era, being on the one hand extremely aristocratic and feudalistic but at the same time democratic in its openness to the wave of individualism known as the Renaissance.[87]

The Momoyama era (1573–1615) was a period of continual civil war dominated by the austere values of the samurai elite, and therefore in contrast to the mercantile Genroku culture of a century later; Chikamatsu's *Shinjū ten no Amijima* was written in the Kyōhō era (1716–36). Like Elizabethan England, Chikamatsu's Japan was a rigidly hierarchical society that was also amenable to sceptical reflection and acts of individual agency, notably through the emergence of the resilient mercantile culture of the Kamigata region of western Japan which produced Chikamatsu's puppet theatre. Kamigata (the traditional name of both the region and its dialect) was associated especially with the *jōruri* and kabuki drama that emerged in Osaka in the seventeenth century, with a preference for love stories (known as *wagoto*) and plot rather than dance. Shōyō's interest in dance drama aligns him with Edo kabuki, but as a Shakespearean he was also strongly attracted to the literary style and plots of Chikamatsu.

As will be discussed in the next section, the colloquial and narrative style of Chikamatsu *jōruri* is at a radical remove from the formal idiolect of the imperial court and nobility (both Meiji and feudal), not to mention the refinement of classical Japanese poetry. Shōyō asserts that "the fictional monarchs and princes of Shakespeare's plays" such as Hamlet, King Lear, and Macbeth "are of a lower rank than Japanese emperors" and "correspond more with the Tokugawa shoguns" in their agency.[88] As one example, "Hamlet's father sleeps in his orchard unattended by pages and courtiers," which no emperor could have ever done. Shōyō treats the episode as evidence of Shakespeare's "populism" and of why a "candid and unrestrained domestic style might go well with the classical thoughts of Shakespeare's kings and queens." This is the style of Chikamatsu *sewamono*, with Shōyō adding that Hamlet's "antic disposition" "can only be translated by resorting to" the Chikamatsu style and that Meiji Japanese was simply too integrated (and lacking in flavour) for the stylistic jumps that occurred in Shakespeare's tragedy: too laden with emotive classical echoes (and kabuki too stylised and performative) to achieve the "detachment" (*fusoku furi*) Shōyō saw in Hamlet.

Shōyō's equivalence of Shakespeare with Chikamatsu is therefore more than the unqualified pairing of two so-called classical playwrights but based first on his realist agenda and next on his pragmatic reading of Shakespeare's texts. Characters such as Hamlet discuss their states of mind in a way that is foreign to kabuki, where the action evolves more from arbitrary plot developments than individual speech acts, but Shōyō – at least in 1907 – believes that Hamlet can do so in the Kamigata dialect of Chikamatsu *sewamono*. Shakespeare is "unfettered" and kabuki "restricted" by its numerous conventions, but this is not to deny their common interest in the complexity of human relationships,[89] nor that kabuki conventions allow for a tighter dramaturgy than Shōyō cares to admit. They are also based in a calendar that is every bit as seasonal as Shakespeare's imagination, since

Barbara E. Thornbury insists (and more than Shōyō would have perhaps cared to admit) that

> Edo kabuki was not illogical but was based on a performance calendar which provided a controlling context for each play that was produced in the course of it.[90]

The romanticism that absorbs Shōyō in his 1890 studies arises from the two writers' individuality, which in Shakespeare is the inherent desire for freedom and in Chikamatsu the "spirit of resistance,"[91] and their focus on nature as a source of salvation.

Kawatake Mokuami, whom Shōyō esteemed as "an embodiment of centuries of kabuki art" and up to his death in 1893 had been Shōyō's mentor in the exclusive kabuki world,[92] might seem an even apter parallel to Shakespeare, and unlike Chikamatsu Mokuami knew Shakespeare's work. Similar to Chikamatsu's proclivity for word associations (*engo*) and pivot words (*kakekotoba*), Mokuami is considered a master of seven-five syllabic meter, and his skill at onomatopoeia was the kind of detail that Shōyō wanted to imitate. Moreover, while Chikamatsu was superior at *sewamono* (which, for Shōyō, is the closer parallel to Shakespeare than his *jidaimono*), Mokuami was the more skilled at "capturing the vicissitudes of historical change" in his historical dramas.[93] In plays such as *Benten kozō* (Benten the Thief, 1862) he had shown a Shakespearean sympathy for the social outcast that related to Shōyō's understanding of the ethical dimension of dramatic literature. It also contrasted with the more cynical tone of Mokuami's Kasei predecessor, Tsuruya Nanboku.[94]

What Chikamatsu and Mokuami mainly have in common with Shakespeare, as Shōyō asserts in his *Tempest* afterword,[95] is their ability to create dramatic situations. In Mokuami's dance drama *Momijigari* (Maple Viewing, 1887), the transformation of the beautiful Princess Sarashina into a fire-breathing demon to be killed by a divine sword wielded by the warrior Koremochi exemplifies kabuki at its most sensory (and innovative); although it has no narrative equivalent in a Shakespeare play, it is theatrically equivalent to Shakespeare's general fascination with behavioural changes; for example, Othello's jealousy that is inexplicable to all except Iago and – contrary to Sarashina – appears to feminise his character. Like Shakespearean drama, a kabuki masterpiece is also accessible to a range of interpretations, for example that "the forces of rationality, order, and progressive modern world (in the person of Koremochi) stand arrayed against the forces of an older, mysterious, and superstitiously reactionary past."[96] This interpretation by Richard Emmert and Alan Cummings relates *Momijigari* to its Meiji context, and (one might add) to Shakespeare's context where in plays such as *A Midsummer Night's Dream* Shakespeare exploits past superstitions to theatrical effect. Like Shakespeare, Mokuami's achievement stands at the beginning of a new age, and there is a parallel between Shōyō's demand for coherent dramaturgy in the theatrical reform movement and the shift to classicism in Jacobean drama. At the same time, Mokuami's position at the end of the age of classical kabuki and Shakespeare's at the outset of modern

English drama implies a rather different approach to their craft. Shakespeare's alleged capacity for "hiddenness" creates a new kind of drama that is radically different from both classical and medieval models, whereas Mokuami is seeking to improve on two hundred years of kabuki tradition. It is against that tradition that modern notions such as dramatic realism will be judged.

### Shōyō's Prefaces and the Cultural Hinterland

Shōyō provided prefaces to each of his Shakespeare translations as they were published by Waseda University Press between 1909 and 1928. Unlike Dr. Johnson's seminal Prefaces of 1765, Shōyō's can hardly be said to amount to a critical event, but there is a parallel between Johnson's claims for Shakespeare's genius in the wake of neoclassicism, in particular his truth to nature, and Shōyō's more incremental assertions against the modern theatre of ideas with which his translations competed. Johnson's admiration for Shakespeare arises from his comparative study of seventeenth- and eighteenth-century English poets, and is significant for its defence of Shakespearian tragicomedy. Shōyō's comparisons are with his native playwrights and novelists (never poets), and even if the argument about tragicomedy is a European one, the issue of generic mixing is wholly relevant to his context.

Against the ideological integrity of *shingeki* and the artistic traditionalism of kabuki, Shōyō's translations assert repeatedly that "truth to nature" is the big idea and that it does not have to end badly. Johnson and Shōyō share a belief in their critical instincts: their authority as educated men of letters to make balanced judgements. Johnson's are rooted in Enlightenment common sense, Shōyō's in his native aesthetics and the realism he first expounded in the 1880s. Shakespeare, for Shōyō, is true to nature not only because the Anglo-American critics tell him so but because his cumulative reading of the plays makes him aware of all he has known to be true from his native literature. In particular, his reading enables him to get away from single comparisons, and to realise Shakespeare's creativity across the entire canon; Shakespeare's plays are universal for Shōyō only to the extent that they make sense for him in terms of his native culture.

*Titus Andronicus*, for example, whose translation Shōyō completed in July 1926, becomes *chi no higeki*, "a bloody tragedy,"[97] suggesting a number of comparisons to his blood-stained kabuki. The early nineteenth-century dramas of Tsuruya Nanboku have what he calls "an unnatural congeniality" with Shakespeare's early tragedy,[98] unnatural because they both make dramatic art out of onstage gore. He writes that

> The heartless cruelty and sheer bile of a play like *Titus Andronicus* are viewed by a popular audience as one would watch Nanboku's *Ehon gappō ga tsuji* [An Illustrated Picture Book of the Crossroads of Gappō, 1810], his *Tōkaidō Yotsuya kaidan* [Ghost Story of Yotsuya, 1825], or revenge plays like *Kameyama adauchi* [Revenge of Kameyama, 1701] and *Katakiuchi Tengajaya mura* [Revenge at Tengajaya, 1781].[99]

There is a murder in every scene of *Ehon gappō ga tsuji*, but the most obvious parallel is between the horror of Lavinia's mutilation by Demetrius and Chiron and the disfigurement and murder of Oiwa by her villainous husband Iemon in Nanboku's *Yotsuya kaidan*, the most successful of nineteenth-century kabuki plays and the most famous of Japanese ghost stories. Oiwa's face is disfigured by a poisoned facial cream supplied by the family of a rival lover, and she is then accidentally killed in a confrontation with a man sent to rape her so that Iemon can sue for divorce. The final scenes in which Oiwa's ghost appears to haunt Iemon and drive him mad are especially memorable, and for a Japanese audience as sensational as the muted and mutilated Lavinia's incrimination of her assailants with the stumps of her arms.

Just at the time that Shōyō was translating *Titus Andronicus*, T. S. Eliot was to label it "one of the stupidest and most uninspired plays ever written,"[100] but Shōyō asserts its moral and poetic strengths, and if for him Nanboku is more like Thomas Kyd than Shakespeare, then he knows where Shakespeare's early tragedy is coming from.[101] In Shōyō's theory, the point of these comparisons is that if Edo drama and literature depended on sensation to advance its agenda of rewarding virtue and punishing vice, then writers such as Nanboku had developed the theatre of sensation to its highest degree. Yet realising the limitations of his culture Shōyō could understand even more easily why Shakespeare should have graduated to writing of greater psychological depth and stylistic variety. That trajectory would lead Shakespeare eventually to *Macbeth*, coming ten years after *Titus Andronicus*, and one of the eight plays whose translations Shōyō selected for inclusion in Volumes 4 and 5 of his Selected Works.

Shōyō could not have wanted to include all his translations when they were already available in cheap pocket-sized format. His selection offers a compelling overview of what he valued about Shakespeare. To start with, the ordering of the selection across the two volumes manifests a dichotomy between classicism and modernity that runs throughout his career. The five plays selected for Volume 4 – *The Tempest* (translated February 1915), *A Midsummer Night's Dream* (October 1915), *Henry IV*, Parts 1 and 2 (June and July 1919), and *The Taming of the Shrew* (November 1920) – are all Elizabethan plays with the exception of *The Tempest* (for reasons that will become clear), while the three in Volume 5 – *Antony and Cleopatra* (May 1915), *Measure for Measure* (July 1918), and *Macbeth* (February 1916) – are from after 1603.

This periodic shift is reflected in Shōyō's response. The plays in Volume 4 evoke a lighter response rooted in Shōyō's classical instincts, while those in Volume 5 seem to him darker and more modern. In this paradigm, *The Tempest* is the first in line because it was the one Shōyō found easiest to translate, whereas he apparently struggled with *Macbeth*:

> In contrast with the comedies, which even if they are not uniformly carefree and relaxed do feel as if they were written in a spirit of some relaxation, the tragedies – in particular *Hamlet*, *Othello*, *King Lear*, and *Macbeth* – seem a lot more profound and meticulous in their composition, almost like the

apocryphal sculptor of statues of the Buddha who bows three times to the statue before applying his chisel, and for this reason demand three or four times the effort to translate.[102]

This observation indicates the difficulties Shōyō encountered in translating the tragedies, which he did mainly in the 1910s, and even the transition from didacticism to realism must at some point require a serious grappling with the tragic genre. The tragedies were also more likely to be associated with the tragic genre of kabuki *jidaimono*, with the expectation that they should be translated in kabuki-style *shichigochō*. Shōyō's translations of the comedies, completed mainly in the 1920s, are mainly colloquial prose and less reliant on syllabic meter.

In his "Preface to a Commentary on *Macbeth*," Shōyō had praised the Scottish play as Shakespeare's greatest tragedy: the one that most clearly exemplified "the remarkable resemblance of Shakespeare's works to nature itself."[103] Its translation will amount to rather more than the parodies in which he had indulged as a student: something like a translation of "nature" itself. The Romantics may have managed this, but even if Shakespeare had already done most of the work Shōyō was still, in his view, encountering a work greater than any in his own tradition. He writes grandiosely that

> since Shakespeare is a born poet and fortunately not the slave of small ideals, his descriptions follow the Creator's universe, thus moving our intellect and emotions today and – between the lines – foretelling the future.[104]

*Macbeth* may not necessarily – word for word – be a difficult play to translate, but any mistake would feel like a desecration of the original, and Shōyō must wonder whether his translations will achieve anything like the original's rhetorical effect.

In an account of Shōyō's aesthetics, Ishida Tadahiko describes this impasse of theory and practice as the intersection of the limitless horizon of the protagonist's tragic vision with finite reality.[105] Nakamura Kan suggests that Shōyō's initial enthusiasm for the power of Shakespeare's imagination to affirm readers' individual ideals reflected a wider optimism among fin-de-siècle Japanese writers as they embraced nineteenth-century ideologies such as Naturalism, Romanticism, and socialism, but that this confidence had all but evaporated by the 1920s as none of the new movements had succeeded in creating for Japan a true and lasting modernity.[106] In other words, while Shōyō was wary of losing himself in Shakespeare's imagination, his innate caution may not have been enough to prevent himself from being swept along by the rhetoric of the Scottish play, especially when the dramatic impasse Shakespeare himself achieves between limitless imagination and finite reality was apparently beyond the scope of his native tradition. As Nakamura observes, Shōyō's Shakespearean realism (along, of course, with the efforts of such writers as Ōgai and Sōseki) obliquely failed in its intent of making readers "grow up" by facing reality,[107] leaving the nation spiritually "immature" and exposed to the rising militarism of the 1930s.

Nakamura further argues that what Shōyō learnt from *Macbeth* in particular was "the darkness of individuality":[108] that (to apply his quotation) "Macbeth does murder sleep" (2.2.37), since in Nakamura's analogy, Shōyō himself is like Macbeth through his disturbance of the cultural status quo with the agenda of reform he pursued as a young man, and rued his youthful ambition in his later years.[109] Macbeth was clearly the opposite of the "good man" (*yoki hito*) of tradition who, subduing his "passions" in the face of numerous temptations stood at the centre of the social community.[110] Casting himself in that role as an ethically responsible translator, Shōyō had to handle Macbeth's villainy with due care. Moreover, while Shōyō may have been repelled by his subject, any misreading of Macbeth's lines was also to detract from Macbeth's essential individuality. It was this inherent darkness of Macbeth's character, or rather its potential to be released among innocent Japanese readers, that made the act of translation the *yoki hito*'s control of distracting passions, while for Shōyō the tragedy's sheer "naturalness" made it a play that refused to stand still.

At the other end of the literary spectrum, and the first in the series, is *The Tempest*, where the demands made of the translator are less austere. The preface and afterword Shōyō wrote for his *Tempest* translation comprise the longest commentary he wrote on any Shakespeare play. In contrast to the Buddhist respect for nature, Shōyō's *Tempest* is a Confucian play in which the *yoki hito* Prospero takes central position. Shōyō admires the play's poetry and musicality, and the balance Prospero achieves between his inner and outer selves, which is the *yoki hito*'s ability to master his passions. Having previously been puzzled by the loose dramatic structures of Shakespeare's plots, he was pleased to encounter a play that basically adhered to the Aristotelian unities,[111] and so enabled him to get a clearer grip on what he was translating.

At one point in his afterword, Shōyō compares the unities with the role of Confucian ideals in feudal Japan in maintaining the social contract.[112] In *Shōsetsu shinzui*, the problem had not been with Confucianism itself but rather with what he saw as Tokugawa fiction's tendency to present a superficial morality that was undermined by "a distorted view of human experience" and "illogical plots."[113] Shakespeare too was a writer whose works, albeit with greater subtlety, juxtaposed a conservative social order with a subversive strain. Shōyō's challenge as a translator was to get inside that dramaturgy while avoiding any unwanted equivalence with Confucian morality and the neoclassical morality about which Dowden had been uneasy:

> Shakspere introduces into the world no little ethical code. Such a little ethical code would flutter away in tatters across the tempest and the night of Lear's agony. But Shakspere discovers the supreme fact – that the moral world stands in sovereign independence of the world of senses.[114]

That was all very well, and one of those desirably modern traits that appealed to a developing society more interested in Social Darwinism than Christianity, but for a person of Shōyō's generation raised in the years leading up to the abolition of samurai privileges in the 1870s, it must have come as some relief to find the ideals of benevolence and harmony present not only in Prospero's comic revenge but in the unified Aristotelian structure of which Prospero is master.

Shōyō puts Shakespeare's romance comedy on a par with the tragedies but is at pains to find an appropriate rhythm of translation. While noting a transition between *sewa chōshi*, the rhythm of kabuki *sewamono*, and the more sonorous *jidai chōshi* of kabuki period plays,[115] he regrettably does not give any specific examples of how he manifests this balance in his translation, but throughout the play we can see how quieter domestic scenes, such as Prospero's dialogue in 1.2 and the comic banter of Stephano and Trinculo, give way to scenes of epic grandeur engineered by Prospero's magic, such as the wedding masque and inveiglement of Alonso and Antonio. Shōyō conceives the play's internal rhythm as follows:

> It is impossible to translate a play like *The Tempest* without in some way accounting for its delicate transitions from the historical to the contemporary, and likewise its moments of rising strength as the style changes back to the historical. These things are intuitive. Shakespeare's works contain numerous such instances where we feel a living and breathing reality, and these are especially apparent in *The Tempest*.[116]

By "historical," Shōyō presumably means those moments when we become aware of Prospero's past and the classical and biblical mythologies in which he frames his narrative, and by "contemporary" those moments that are focussed on present realities and the immediate future. His preoccupation with style and "a living and breathing reality" takes us back to the realism of *Shōsetsu shinzui*, and compared with other Shakespeare plays he finds rather few equivalents in his native drama, instead making a general comparison between *The Tempest* as a kind of "comic opera" with the sensuality of Chikamatsu and Mokuami (and, intriguingly, Max Reinhardt).[117] Yet since Shōyō follows the current critical fashion of identifying Prospero with Shakespeare himself, and he is Shakespeare's dominant voice in early twentieth-century Japan, then the translator had the potential to contribute to cultural change through the techniques he mentions, such as stylistic mixing. The irony of this analogy is that, to the extent that Prospero's magic is identified with Shakespeare's "hidden" genius, the translator's ability to grasp the essence of Prospero's character diminishes, and Shōyō seems to admit as such when he comments that

> If you translate his speeches in Tokyo dialect, he sounds nouveau riche and cannot relax, and if you translate them in the contemporary colloquial dialect they sound too rough.[118]

Shōyō's Prospero must be greater than both the entrepreneur and the man about town.

Shōyō's comments on *A Midsummer Night's Dream* focus on cultural parallels rather than translation issues, suggesting that the play's mixing of folklore and classical mythology is similar to the mixing of animist Shinto and Buddhist elements in bunraku plays.[119] The localised aspect of Shinto, with its belief in local spirits and deities, corresponds here with the folklore, and Buddhism as a pan-Asian religion with the Greco-Roman mythology, and Shōyō makes a further comparison between Shakespeare's classical allusions and the basis of much of Edo kabuki in medieval Japanese legends and history. The stories of the Kamakura and Ashikaga eras (lasting from the twelfth century through to the sixteenth) provided kabuki with sources of plot and character that were similar, in particular, to the use Shakespeare makes of Ovid's *Metamorphoses*. Shōyō's basic point is that Shakespeare's creativity lies in the use he makes of his sources, and that this is a technique with which Japanese readers must be familiar from their native drama. Yet in comparing the mechanicals' play to the greatest of *jōruri* puppet plays, *Kanadehon Chūshingura* (The Treasury of Loyal Retainers, 1748; adapted later that year for the kabuki stage),[120] where the forty-seven masterless samurai (*rōnin*) are able to hide their revenge motives from the authorities partly by comic foolery, Shōyō is also aware of a subversive potential of generic mixing in both Shakespeare and his native drama.

Shōyō makes a subtle rejoinder that if *A Midsummer Night's Dream* was originally "intended as a dream play then its confusion of historical periods is all the more extreme."[121] Against his earlier unflattering comparison of Chikamatsu's *jidaimono* to the same Shakespeare comedy for their excessive use of fantasy, he makes an alternative point that like Prospero, whose language was apparently not spoken in 1920s Japan, *A Midsummer Night's Dream* might even surpass his native drama in the scope of its dramaturgy, being more clearly focussed on the single motif of the dream. In yet another essay, he was to write that the two areas in which he felt kabuki did exceed Shakespeare were in its depiction of sex and violence; this was a genre in which the female lovers are often professional courtesans rather than Shakespearean virgins, and fathers allowed their young sons to be beheaded to please the whims of a scheming official.[122] In Shakespeare's plays, with exceptions such as *Titus Andronicus*, grotesquely violent or erotic scenes usually occur offstage, for example the murder of Lady Macduff and her children, and the conventionalised sensuality of kabuki has seldom been part of Shakespeare tradition. It is this often-grotesque aesthetic, with the demands made on performers and its ideological function, that Shōyō is least able to deny about kabuki. *A Midsummer Night's Dream* and its tragic counterpart *Romeo and Juliet* are both overtly physical plays, but the coupling of Bottom and Titania is an object of humour and the lovers' quarrel in the woods leads to a comic resolution that eludes the two young lovers. Sex and violence are seldom ends in themselves in Shakespeare, the language with its references to classical mythology being more shocking than what is demanded of the mise-en-scène.

In the final part of his preface, Shōyō devotes a whole five pages to an analysis of Puck, mainly comprising a monologue in the words of a Japanese Puck.[123] This character observes that Japanese folklore also has its tradition of native spirits and goblins, notably the *kappa* who were believed to lure travellers to their deaths in lonely roadside bogs. Shōyō refers to a study of Japanese folklore published six years before his *Dream* translation by his contemporary Yanagita Kunio, considered the "father" of Japanese folkloristics and known for his linguistic theory of centre and periphery: that new words created in cultural centres such as Kyoto do not always have the momentum to replace existing synonyms in outlying areas.[124] This reference makes striking, if oblique sense in the context of *A Midsummer Night's Dream*, where the mechanicals' play in the final act unconsciously satirises the behaviour of the upper-class lovers and where one of Shakespeare's purposes is to harmonise English folklore with the Christian ideal of marriage. For Shōyō too, there is perhaps a comic realisation that ignorance of the folklore and mythology that underlies a work like Shakespeare's *Dream* can itself lead to unfortunate errors; such details are essential for containing the play's imaginative power.

Shōyō praises *Measure for Measure* for its "psychological naturalness,"[125] referring primarily to the integrity of the lovers in contrast to Angelo's hypocrisy and Isabella's pleas for mercy, which he regards as even more dramatic than Portia's in *The Merchant of Venice*.[126] He writes that although the play may be faulted in places for obscurity of plot and "unnatural" characterisation,

> it is, compared with native *jōruri*, *kusasōshi* story books and the popular novels of Bakin, of profound psychological interest, displays its writer's characteristic realism and lightness of touch, especially in its depiction of comic types, and vividly captures the city life of three hundred years ago.[127]

Shōyō draws a parallel between the narrative device of Duke Vincentio's disguise as Friar Lodowick and the Kamakura regent Hōjō Tokiyori, who in 1256 resigned from his position to take the Buddhist tonsure.[128] Shōyō does not elaborate the comparison, but Tokiyori had been known as a reforming administrator, who according to legend travelled the country incognito to inspect the living conditions of the people; one such episode was preserved for posterity in the Noh play *Hachi no ki* (Potted Trees), attributed to Zeami.[129] Unlike Vincentio, Tokiyori's retirement was due to ill health, and he forestalled political chaos by dividing the roles of regent and family head between his cousin Nagatoki, a benevolent administrator who lacked the will to seize absolute power, and his infant son Tokimune, who eventually succeeded to both roles to become one of the most ruthless of Kamakura statesmen. These two figures can be said to combine the two sides of Angelo's character as both repressed and repressive, an unfortunate combination that Shōyō calls *dojingata*, a chauvinist type unsuited to running a big city, since as well as being a type of ceramic figurine *dojingata* can also mean someone who is both uncouth and a stickler for rules.[130] The analogy would also align him with types such as Puck and Caliban who exist only inside their native culture.

What Shōyō does not mention in his preface, although perhaps the comparison was too obvious to need repeating, is that the plot of *Measure for Measure* is strikingly the opposite to a Chikamatsu *sewamono* like *Sonezaki shinjū* (The Love Suicides at Sonezaki, 1703) where the lovers Tokubei and Ohatsu have little choice but to kill themselves in the end, and unlike with Claudio and Juliet there is no possibility of salvation from within the system. For Shōyō, the appeal of *Measure for Measure* is surely that not only does it seek to put the kind of demi-monde associated with *sewamono* in its place but it does so through the inherent interest of the narrative and characterisation, especially of straight characters such as Angelo and Isabella, who are made interesting by the hiddenness of Shakespeare's dramatic genius; his argument with Tokugawa literature is as much with the society that produced the works as with individual writers.

Shōyō's view of *Antony and Cleopatra* is more oblique. He finds it Shakespeare's "most enthralling work,"[131] being enchanted by the image of the mature couple outromancing the forces of reason and propriety:

> If Cleopatra is obviously a human Venus, then Antony on the River Cydnus is like Tannhäuser when he first enters the forest of pleasure [i.e. Venusburg].[132]

Shakespeare's tragedy was as pleasurable as anything in Shōyō's native tradition, and in the person of Cleopatra the pleasure was recognizably "Oriental." Shōyō's experimental musical drama *Shinkyoku Urashima* (1904) had adapted the plot and structure of Richard Wagner's early opera *Tannhäuser* to the folktale of Urashima Tarō, mentioned in the eighth-century *Nihon shoki*, which records the mythological and historical origins of the Imperial line. The parallel between Shakespeare's "demigods"[133] and the poor fisher boy Urashima and Princess Otohime is clearly on a different scale from the realism of Chikamatsu's *sewamono* and the superhuman warriors of kabuki *jidaimono*. It opens up a creative, eroticised space that (in the struggle between the sacred and profane) is at one remove from kabuki's medieval and early modern settings and from Christian history in Shakespeare's case, and more than anything else expresses the power of drama to detach audiences from the passing of time. In his preface, Shōyō also paraphrases Dowden's Wagnerian assessment of the couple as characters who

> insinuate themselves through the senses, trouble the blood, ensnare the imagination, invade our whole being like colour or like music. The figures dilate to proportions greater than human, and are seen through a golden haze of sensuous splendor.[134]

About the two parts of *Henry IV*, Shōyō observes that the power struggles between the king and his barons are similar to those of medieval Japan, and that the tavern scenes with Falstaff and his cronies recall a similar populist vein in Edo culture, but that altogether the plays seemed more modern in sensibility than, for example, the depiction of lowlife characters in the late Tokugawa fiction of his childhood reading.[135] Through Shakespeare's conflation of the early fifteenth century with the Elizabethan present, Henry's usurpation of his cousin, King Richard II, and Prince Hal's final rejection of Falstaff after his coronation could be said to harbour the political realities of the modern age, but for Shōyō the power struggles of medieval Japan must have seemed like more of the same, while – for a more modern parallel – the escapades of the comic duo in Jippensha Ikku's classic *kokkeibon* novel *Tōkaidō Hizakurige* (Shank's Mare, 1802–22) served mainly to affirm the richness and variety of a culture that did not need modernising. Jippensha's comic novel, which Shōyō read in his youth, recounts the journey of two accident-prone male travellers along the main Tōkaidō road from Kyoto in the west to Edo (present-day Tokyo) in the east. Like Shakespeare's plays, it is sympathetic in its characterisa-tion but (for all its literary qualities) was primarily meant to promote domestic tourism, which is a fate that Shōyō desires neither for Shakespeare nor for his native literature.

In his preface to *The Taming of the Shrew*, Shōyō compares the boisterous induc-tion scene, as well as the various crudities that characterise this early Shakespeare comedy, with the genre of popular *niwaka* farce that continues to this day with its clever punch lines, *niwaka* meaning "offhand" or "impromptu."[136] *Niwaka* farces are typically based on scenes from mainstream kabuki plays, and as an Osaka rather than Tokyo tradition situates a character such as Petruchio within the softer mercantile culture of the Kamigata region. Yet Shōyō's comparison also hints at the cultural embeddedness of the play's chauvinism. He translated the play in 1920, shortly after propertied British women over the age of thirty had been given the right to vote. Japanese women were not granted suffrage until 1946, although a suf-frage movement had existed since the nineteenth century, and in 1920 the lives of Japanese women were largely governed by their menfolk, particularly their fathers, in a system that was not very different from that of Elizabethan society.

There were plenty of strong women in kabuki: geisha who sacrifice their lives for their lovers and know exactly what they are doing, loyal wives and jealous mothers-in-law, and so on, but they did so in the context of a strict patriarchy, and it is to such a society that a Japanese Petruchio would have his Kate conform, all the more so in the Kamigata context. Yet through Kate's robust rejection of Petru-chio's advances, Shakespeare's play could also be said to look forward to a world in which a woman's freedom to assert her independence was the accepted norm, with Shōyō commenting that

> it is interesting how this play, which is still regarded . . . as evidence of the chauvinistic instincts of the male psyche, also looks forward to a world in which perfect equality between men and women might be easily achieved.[137]

Shōyō, for his part, supported the advancement of women in the theatre with the admission of actresses such as Matsui Sumako to the Bungei Kyōkai, but the fact that they were forbidden from having relationships with the male members echoes the discipline Petruchio imposes on Kate to tame her shrewish behaviour.

### Shōyō and Modernity

With his reputation for being "behind the times," Shōyō can be expected to have a complex relationship with modernity. He wishes to modernise his native drama and literature, but (as Tsuno Kaitarō argued) his essentially comic vision sets him apart from the tragic individualism of younger contemporaries such as Sōseki and Shimazaki Tōson,[138] and this vision is rooted in his Shakespeare studies. To start with, the coherent structures he finds in Shakespeare are at odds with a modernist sense of life's incompleteness, and whereas the Japanese modernist responds to formlessness and disintegration with new forms and a strong belief in self, it is enough for Shōyō that Shakespeare merely affirms him in his reality. Against the confessional mode of early twentieth-century I-novelists such as Tōson and Shiga Naoya what Shōyō rather likes about Shakespeare is his capacity for hiding his inner feelings, and when Shōyō does talk about himself it is usually in a histrionic mode that comes "after the event," which it therefore congratulates its speakers for having survived. Shōyō also has a greater faith in history than many moderns. In his Aristotelian view, poetry is secondary to history, with little of the urgency of the moment, and his own position as translator comes a somewhat distant third place, as he indicates in a speech he gave in 1928 to mark the completion of his Shakespeare translations that is typically "Meiji" in its florid comparisons with past adventurers:

> this publication has been a perilous undertaking at this ominous time when the publishing world has been threatened by economic recession and, if I may adopt a maritime metaphor, the winds have been fierce and the waves high. Yet not only have the vessels been laden with a cargo of incomparable value, namely the works of William Shakespeare, but they have been Japanese boats, ramshackle rigged vessels of a former age, thirty-five to forty of them, among them the good ships *Hamlet* and *Romeo*. Weathering the storm of this terrible recession has without doubt been a feat of great danger. Taking arms against this sea of troubles was my editor, the redoubtable Shimanaka, whose gallantry recalls the heroic voyage by the merchant Kibun to transport *mikan* fruits to Edo in the early eighteenth century, the illicit exploits of Zeniya Gohei in the last century, and even the greatest of them all, Yamada Nagamasa in the early period of the Tokugawa shogunate. My own role has been that of the ship's carpenter, as it were, and though my worries have been nothing as great as the master carpenter Jūbei in Rohan's story *The Five-Storied Pagoda*, it was at least my responsibility to prepare the boats for voyage, and while the company may never have suffered the hardships of a Pericles or an Alonzo, it was by no means all plain sailing. The fact that we reached harbour without serious incident and on time is surely an achievement that deserves congratulation.[139]

Shōyō's role as translator, therefore, is not even to beautify Shakespeare but to keep the plays "afloat," and in this regard he must also be referring to his efforts to sustain popular interest in Shakespeare during the economic stagnation of the 1920s. Shōyō does not doubt the historical "truth" of his precious cargo: it is the present that is unstable and threatening, while a spirit of adventure is clearly better suited than any modern ideology for steering Shakespeare's "truth" to harbour.

A consequence of Shōyō's anti-ideological stance is that he may on the face of it stand for not very much at all; Tsuno suggests that his commitments can be reduced to the family (*katei*), especially his own, and to education (*kyōiku*).[140] His deepest – because closest – antagonism is toward the Naturalism of Shimamura Hōgetsu. The Japanese Naturalism that emerged at the end of the nineteenth century was based in realism but from the perspective of rigorous subjective observation that for Shōyō was a distraction from the import of Shakespeare's texts; Tsuno contrasts Shōyō's noisy, declamatory teaching style at Waseda with Hōgetsu's quieter classroom at the same university in which students focussed on what they could "honestly" say about a text.[141] A typically Naturalistic response to Shakespeare was made by the novelist Shiga Naoya who, on seeing the Bungei Kyōkai *Hamlet* in 1911, was at once appalled by the frivolity of Doi Shunsho's Hamlet and drawn to the "sensitivity" (*kanjusei*) of Tōgi Tetteki's Claudius, whom Shiga saw as a man whose life had been turned upside down by his brother's death and marriage to his brother's widow;[142] Hamlet, like Shōyō, talked too much.[143] In an earlier intervention, a story by Shimazaki Tōson, Tōson quotes Lorenzo's lines from the final scene of *The Merchant of Venice*, adding the crucial (and italicised) word "perhaps":[144]

*Perhaps* in such a night
Troilus, methinks, mounted the Trojan walls
And sighed his soul toward the Grecian tents
Where Cressida lay that night.

(5.1.3–6)

Tōson cannot tell for sure.

Hōgetsu's Naturalism was a systematic attempt to introduce a modern European literary school into a culture whose traditional aesthetics was based partly on an awareness of seasonal change, but differed from the objectivity of Shōyō's realism and from Norinaga's eighteenth-century aesthetic of the pathos of things. For Sōseki, Naturalism was still too deterministic to allow the kind of radical engagement with Western culture he deemed necessary for the survival of Japanese culture in the modern age, and similarly he refutes Shōyō's assumption that Shakespeare's take on reality is his own. Sōseki is more interested in what happens when modern Japanese people start behaving like Hamlet and Ophelia than in what Shakespeare and even his culture teach him to be "true." This discrepancy (*zure*) is captured in the haiku he wrote summarising the plots of Shakespeare's plays, as in the following for *As You Like It*:

> *yo wo shinobu*
> *otoko sugata ya*
> *hanafubuki*

Renouncing the world in the guise of a man. A cascade of cherry blossom.[145]

The poem is inspired by Rosalind's lines as she prepares to abscond from the cruel world of her uncle Duke Frederick's court disguised as a young man, "I could find in my heart to disgrace my man's/apparel and to cry like a woman" (2.4.4–5), but the image of falling cherry blossom intimates a deeply felt dichotomy of renunciation and eroticism in Sōseki's native context.

Hōgetsu's Naturalism reaches its peak with his theatrical adaptation of Tolstoy's *Resurrection* for the Geijutsuza in 1914. Shōyō admired Shakespeare for his stylistic diversity, but this was not necessarily the same – although Shōyō himself felt it probably *was* the same – as the diversity and differentiation at which Tolstoy excelled, and at which Tolstoy felt Shakespeare was sorely inadequate. For Tolstoy Shakespeare's characters lacked a reason for living (or social purpose), and he memorably lambasts *King Lear*:

> Lear's vacillations between pride, anger, and the hope of his daughters' giving in, would be exceedingly touching if it were not spoilt by the verbose absurdities to which he gives vent, about being ready to divorce himself from Regan's dead mother, should Regan not be glad to receive him, – or about his calling down "fen suck'd frogs" which he invokes, upon the head of his daughter, or about the heavens being obliged to patronise old people because they themselves are old.[146]

In short, "All [Shakespeare's] characters speak, not their own, but always one and the same Shakespearian, pretentious, and unnatural language, in which not only they could not speak, but in which no living man ever has spoken or does speak."[147] For Shōyō the appeal of Shakespeare's tragedy was its lack of obvious "moral purpose," and so it was inevitable that he should respond in kind to Tolstoy's anti-Bardolatry. In the light of Tolstoy's Christian convictions, Shōyō makes pointed reference to the religious origins of both European and Japanese drama, being aware that the primitive purpose of performance to appease the gods has been transferred to the modern purpose of "consoling" (or entertaining) a modern audience, which is a largely upper-class one at that.[148] On Tolstoy's side, Shōyō is also critical of bardolatry, which he sees as no substitute for true religion.[149]

Shōyō is less able to refute the dramatic strengths of George Bernard Shaw, and in 1913 he translated Shaw's play about a high-class brothel madam, *Mrs. Warren's Profession*. Having bought his wife Sen's freedom from a Tokyo brothel in order to marry her, Shōyō had no wish for the licensing of prostitutes in the Edo era to degenerate into the kind of prostitution endemic in nineteenth-century European cities, and he praises Mrs. Warren's daughter Vivie, who finally rejects her mother on account of the latter's lucrative profession, as a paragon of modern womanhood;[150] this is in marked preference to Nora's "selfish" abandonment of her husband and children in Ibsen's *A Doll's House*, which exceeded even *Hamlet* in its influence on the late Meiji and early Taishō theatres. Shōyō argued this point in a lengthy anti-feminist tract entitled *Iwayuru atarashii onna* (The So-Called "New Woman," 1912).[151] Prostitution also flourished in Shakespeare's London, but Vivie rang true against Shakespearean heroines such as Isabella and notably Marina in *Pericles* who, having been sold into the brothel in Mytilene. manages to preserve her virtue by persuading potential clients that they too should preserve theirs. Marina's rhetorical prowess is a striking analogy of what Shōyō knows to be the purpose of Shakespeare's "hiddenness," namely that of preserving Shakespeare's "honour" (and potential for compromise) by keeping his personal ideals hidden from view. Moreover, Shōyō's rhetoric about "ramshackle rigged vessels of a former age" comes to seem less old-fashioned (and more prescient) when set against George Orwell's view that Shakespeare deserves appreciation if only because he has "survived," and that he has done so not because of his ideas (since, as Shōyō knows, he has none) but because of his language;[152] this is a point that Shōyō the translator is in a better position to appreciate than Tolstoy, who never translated Shakespeare. He is more unreserved in his appreciation of the dramaturgy of Ibsen's modern social realism, which (unlike Shakespeare) was a theatre of ideas. Shōyō is always impressed by the rigour of Ibsen's dramaturgy but finds him lacking in "warmth" compared to Shakespeare and Chikamatsu.[153]

## Dowden's "Bottomless Lake" and Victorian Shakespeare

That Shōyō can speak up to the Russian novelist with relative confidence is a reflection of national confidence in the wake of Japan's victory against Russia in the Russo-Japanese war only two years earlier. Just as the Imperial Japanese Navy had been supported by British training and technology, so too is Shōyō supported in his utilitarian viewpoint by over two decades of absorption in the Western critical heritage. In his theory of "hidden ideals," Shakespeare's ability "to reflect the ideals of [his] many hundreds of readers"[154] seemed exactly to fulfil utilitarianism's goal of "the greatest good for the greatest number," while the mainly Victorian scholars Shōyō encountered as he started to study Shakespeare in the 1880s offered alternatives to the exhausted dichotomies of Edo culture. As one example, Richard G. Moulton's statement that "it is the exceptions to the universality of retribution that make the free atmosphere in which alone the highest morality can develop"[155] offers a striking alternative to the dominant revenge motif in kabuki drama. Even if Shōyō could not accept the Christian notion of an external redemptive power as the counter to retribution from his Buddhist perspective, Moulton's understanding of "comedy in Shakespeare" as "story raised to its highest power"[156] did accord with his anti-didacticism. As he argues about fiction in *Shōsetsu shinzui*, for Shōyō the realism of a Shakespeare play is inevitably superior to whatever moral lesson is imparted at the end, even more so with comedy where the narrative potential is not jeopardised by tragic denouements. Shakespearean realism was also conducive to the kind of "free atmosphere" in which moral reflection thrived, and in that sense differed from the typical arbitrariness of kabuki plot construction that supported a tragic, fatalistic view of the universe in which morality was seldom up for discussion, but limited to the lowest common denominator of accepting the arbitrariness of fate and punishing those who believe they can overcome it.

Moulton's rationalism is a breath of fresh air for Shōyō, but the major influence both on his view of Shakespeare and in the "hidden ideals" debate is Anglo-Irish scholar Edward Dowden. Shōyō frequently quotes Dowden and paraphrases his insights into the plays, sometimes without attributing the source. Dowden's popular *Shakspere: A Critical Study of His Mind and Art* (1875) remained at the top of Shōyō's recommended Shakespeare reading in his primer of 1928.[157] Like Shōyō, Dowden's star had shone early, since at only twenty-six he was appointed to the first chair of English literature at Trinity College, Dublin, and having made his name six years later with the publication of *Mind and Art* he remained active as a scholar of mainly Shakespeare and Romanticism, dying in 1913. Dowden's preference for the nascent Protestant work ethic he found in the Elizabethan Shakespeare over the rising Celtic nationalism of Parnell and Yeats connects him with Smiles' *Self-Help* and Shōyō's instinctive conservatism, and his positivism with that of Taine's and Moulton's scientific criticism.

While *Shōsetsu shinzui* was instrumental in shaping Shōyō's view of Shakespeare before he read Dowden,[158] in 1980 the Meiji theatre historian Matsumoto Shinko suggested convincingly[159] that Shōyō's image of the "bottomless lake" as a trope for Shakespeare's creativity was drawn from a passage in Dowden's *Mind and Art*:

> Shakspere, like nature and like the vision of human life itself, if he does not furnish us with a doctrine, has the power to free, arouse, dilate. Again and again we fall back into our little creed or our little theory. Shakspere delivers us; under his influence we come anew into the presence of stupendous mysteries, and, instead of our little piece of comfort, and support, and contentment, we receive the gift of solemn awe, and bow the head in reverential silence. These questions are not stated by Shakespeare as intellectual problems. He states them pregnantly, for the emotions and for the imagination. And it is by very virtue of his very knowledge that he comes face to face with the mystery of the unknown. Because he had sent down his plummet farther into the depths than other men, he knew better than others how fathomless for human thought those depths remain.[160]

What is "fathomless" for Dowden is not so much Shakespeare's creativity as the mystery of human existence, but the point for Shōyō is that Japanese writers who sought to emulate that creativity risked losing themselves in a trajectory that only Shakespeare had mastered and which was both profounder than and separate from their own intellectual and emotional experience. That warning becomes the conclusion of his satirical essay "The Bottomless Lake" (Soko shirazu no mizuumi, 1891), the most rhetorical expression of his theory of hidden ideals, whereas the reference to Matsuo Bashō's "frog" haiku ("An old pond. A frog jumps in. The sound of water.") insinuates a precedent in Japanese culture for the ambitious writers and intellectuals of Meiji to jump right in:

> I see a pond lined with exquisite pines, and there is Bashō's frog on the bank. Someone is jumping in right now, followed by tens of thousands more. The legend has taken its full course, for only a lake with no bottom could hold so many thousands of people. It is a place famous for its remarkable beauty, unusually celebrated in the common mind. People revere this famous place as the lake without bottom; it is unique in history. There have been countless other bottomless lakes but this lake is the most beautiful under heaven. In England there is a great swamp that is comparable, and another such place

in Germany. The swamp in England is called "Shake-sphere," in Germany *Gyōten* [Goethe, the word means "astonishment," denoting Romantic awe]. It is madness to lose yourself in these places. Take heed while you can, and value your independence. We need only look at the people drowning in the lake to see that it is a deadly place.[161]

Shōyō did not know German but places Goethe alongside Shakespeare in his essay, perhaps aware at this time of Dowden's devotion to the German writer[162] and of how Goethe's synthesising of classicism and romanticism reflected Shakespeare's dual debt to Greco-Roman classicism and amenability to nineteenth-century Romanticism. Shōyō's own relationship to the two traditions is also worth considering, but it is Dowden's grasp of Shakespeare's uniqueness that reverberates with the author of *Shōsetsu shinzui*:

If to lay hold of Michael Angelo and to strive with him to be the most strenuous feat achievable by the critical imagination in the world of plastic art, to deal with Shakspere requires more endurance, a firmer nerve, and a finer cunning. The great ideal artist – a Milton, a Michael Angelo, a Dante – betrays himself in spite of the haughtiest reserve. But Shakspere, if an idealist, was also above all else a realist in art, and lurks almost impregnably behind his work. "The secrets of nature have not more gift in taciturnity."[163]

Dowden adds that "Shakspere possessed that most baffling of self-defences – *humour*. Just when we have laid hold of him, he eludes us, and we hear only distant ironical laughter."[164] Shōyō himself seems touched by "ironical laughter" in the hyperbole of his account of his own efforts to lay hold of Shakespeare's genius:

From the point of view of his freedom of expression, Shakespeare is like the ancient goddess Marishiten [the female bodhisattva Marīcī in Sanskrit]. His style is like that female buddha in its solemnity and subtlety. Its divine power has a mysterious sacred virtue that can take many forms. Neither sun, moon, nor heaven can see it, nor can any man ever do so. Sometimes it has three faces, sometimes six or eight pairs of hands; it can fight with many weapons at once; it can hunt the boar, joust with sword, pike, bar, and mallet, unleash the bow from its quiver, start a fire, flail a rope. Against this monster, we Japanese are armed only with our classical language of old.[165]

Shōyō's colourful comparison of Shakespeare to a female deity is not as transgressive (and "unsexing") as it might seem since Marishiten was venerated as early as the ninth century by the samurai class as a model of self-mastery and by the merchant class in the late Edo era as a goddess of wealth and prosperity. She would have therefore been well-known to Shōyō's family, as his father was a samurai and his mother from a merchant family.

Dowden's particular contribution to Shakespeare criticism (and one that enables him to view Shakespearean elusiveness objectively) is his periodic theory of

Shakespeare's development.[166] Foreshadowing A. C. Bradley's forensic analysis of tragic "flaws" in his more influential *Shakespearean Tragedy* (1904), Dowden's periodic theory is rooted in Victorian character formation. Shōyō summarises Dowden's periodic grouping in the opening paragraph of the *Macbeth* preface:

> There are four main periods in his career according to the development of his techniques, dramatic structures and ideas. The first period comprises his formative years, the tragedy of *Romeo and Juliet*, and a number of what we might call light-hearted satirical comedies. The second period gives us his more spirited comedies and the history plays, the third his profound tragedies and the tragicomedies (cheerful on the surface and pitiless underneath), while the fourth is one of quiet dignity, characterised by a graceful and animating blend of tragic and comic elements.[167]

Dowden's conclusions resulted from careful analysis of the evidence of Shakespeare's corpus. His inductive reasoning, which was expounded more thoroughly by Moulton, appealed to Shōyō who, detached even more completely from Shakespeare's world than was Dowden, had few grounds for asserting general premises of his own. Dowden's distance from Shakespeare's world was that of his Victorian Protestantism, and (as I have mentioned) this association takes Shōyō back to Samuel Smiles and the self-made man of Shakespeare's initial reception in Japan, for even if Meiji writers could not hope to imitate Shakespeare's creativity they might at least succeed *like* Shakespeare.

For Dowden, it turns out that the secret of Shakespeare's success is that he does not change, that *pace* Polonius's "truth to self": "Shakspere in 1590, Shakspere in 1600, and Shakspere in 1610, was one and the same living entity,"[168] and usefully for Shōyō Dowden bases his assumption on the evolutionist Spencerian biology that Shōyō had imbibed at the Imperial University.[169] Shakespeare nourishes his imagination with an appetite for experience and "information" that Dowden compares to "the Arctic whale" which "gulps whole shoals of acalephæ and molluscs,"[170] while the individual remains the same. The growth in Shakespeare's intellect

> implies the avoidance of injuries which interfere with growth, escape from enemies which bring sudden end; and therefore strength, and skill, and prudence in dealing with the world. It implies a power in the organism of fitting its movements to meet numerous external co-existences and sequences. In a word, we are brought back once again to Shakespeare's resolute fidelity to the fact.[171]

It is presumably Shōyō's own "fidelity to the fact" that will bring him close to Shakespeare and enable him to succeed as a scholar and translator.

This "fidelity to the fact" imposes an aesthetic discipline which is stricter than conventional morality but which will enable the poet to achieve the mimetic ability that Shōyō praises. The rules of writing, in Shakespeare's case of structure and versification, represent an order or what Dowden calls "ideality" that is "somewhat higher than the common life of vulgar accident," and it is through a rigorous devotion to such "a system of rules and precepts"[172] that in time

> A deeper order takes authority over our being, and resumes in itself the narrower order [of "rules and precepts"]; the rhythm of our life acquires a larger harmony, a movement free and yet seen as that of nature.[173]

This is the stylistic freedom that Shōyō will endeavour to imitate, as the potential not only of Shakespeare but of all writers is arguably even more relevant to the Meiji *bundan* than Shakespearean realism. In Shakespeare's early plays, as Dowden explains, "structure determines function" while "in the later plays organization is preceded by life."[174] For Shōyō, the distinction is between the late Edo fiction of Bakin and Ryūtei Tanehiko that emphasised situation rather than character and a modern, advanced category towards which contemporaries such as Ozaki Kōyō were aspiring that was based firmly in character, and in which event and situation arose from character rather than the other way round.[175]

A final context for Dowden's thesis of character formation is Shōyō's ideas on Japanese historical drama, which he criticises for its general lack of historical perspective and detachment of historical figures from any believable context: these plays lack Dowden's sense that people become who they are through a process of interaction with that context. Shakespeare, on the other hand, creates

> a semblance of the people of past times that, deftly interspersed with details from the amateur historical accounts, succeeds in conveying a highly believable image of actual human beings dressed in the garb of history from out of the deserts of eternity, in other words of the course of cause and effect in human affairs.[176]

While "Waga kuni no shigeki" was mainly addressed at the *katsureki* "living history" plays of his contemporary Fukuchi Ōchi, Shōyō was also critical of Chikamatsu's characterisations of historical figures who, "blessed with supernatural strength and courage, divine powers, or unreasonably sharp intellect," appear as "inhuman" as "their physical attributes are superhuman."[177]

Dowden and Moulton have nothing in return to say about Japanese literature, but Shōyō's sense of cultural inferiority is echoed by H. M. Possnett's foundational *Comparative Literature* (1886), which (with Dryden and Johnson) was a major reference for a series of lectures he gave on comparative literature at Waseda between 1891 and 1892.[178] Possnett for his part had read Basil Hall Chamberlain's pioneering Noh translations of 1880, commenting that

> The characters and names of the Japanese plays translated by Mr. Chamberlain, in his *Classical Poetry of the Japanese*, show want of individual characterisation, and predominance of allegorical or abstract ideas and natural description.[179]

Possnett's book is to do with the proper balance of the group and individual in the development of national literatures, arguing for example that "excessive individualism is almost as fatal to dramatic progress as a corporate life in which all differences of personality are lost."[180] Comparing Wordsworth's poem "To the Cuckoo" with Indian and Chinese (and, by implication, Japanese) nature poetry, the latter would definitely fall on the side of the corporate and social:

> Only as a representative of his species does the Indian poet describe the seasons, only as such does the Chinese poet or philosopher describe or speculate. The Oriental knows not that concentrated personal being which looks on Nature as peculiarly connected with itself alone, and is for ever pacing round the haunts of its childhood, "seeking in vain to find the old familiar faces."[181]

This submersion of individuality is probably not conducive to Shakespeare's dramatic realism which, as Possnett argues, requires

> personal freedom from communal restraints, various types of personality, and, coexisting with this freedom and variety, a fund of social sympathies and a belief in the dignity and mysterious greatness of individual being.[182]

Shōyō's greatest challenge as a writer himself, and one that draws him to Shakespearean drama, is to grasp the universal dimensions of individual character, which is Dr. Johnson's view that "in the writings of other poets a character is too often an individual; in those of Shakespeare it is commonly a species."[183]

Johnson was constrained from making excessive judgements by his neoclassical decorum, but for Shōyō there is the opposite concern, aptly described by Possnett, that

> nothing is more difficult than to see an ideal without expanding it into universality even in the prosaic accuracy of scientific reasoning, how much more in works peculiarly belonging to the imagination.[184]

There is, as I have argued,[185] a Romantic side to Shōyō as he loses himself in his Shakespeare and Chikamatsu studies of the 1890s, culminating in his Wagnerian musical drama, *Shinkyoku Urashima*; Tsubouchi Shikō recalls that his adoptive father once told him, perhaps at the time that he was writing *Shinkyoku Urashima*, "Through my gestation in the works of Chikamatsu and Shakespeare, I should be considered a 'New Romantic.'"[186] Shōyō must be able to state his own Romantic proclivities in order then to step away from them; perhaps even more than Dowden, whose theories were founded on a Hegelian idealism that Shōyō did not necessarily understand, it is Moulton's inductive criticism that enables him to find the objectivity he desires, and so project him towards the Shakespeareans of the early twentieth century.

Moulton's particular argument was against a judicial type of criticism that evaluated rather than analysed, and (as I have mentioned) could be highly "retributive" in its judgements; he comments tartly that

in traditional philosophy wise men have sought to make the whole moral government of the universe synonymous with the judgement on the sinner.[187]

Moulton's approach favours accident over fate, redemption over retribution, and above all the autonomy of individual character. He writes that

a man's character is the momentum of his past: new influences may change the character, but in the absence of these the character acquired in the past is a real force carrying the individual in definite directions.[188]

Moulton's modern scientific criticism (which anticipates the archetypal criticism of Northrop Frye) enables Shōyō to develop the arguments of *Shōsetsu shinzui* and, in his 1890 essay "Shōsetsu sanpa" (Three Schools of Fiction),[189] apply generic categories to his contemporary fiction, above all to see how in both Shakespeare and Chikamatsu it is character that creates situation and not the other way around.[190] Moulton's grasp of the complex relationship between plot and character in Shakespearean drama represents a distinct break from the arbitrary moralism of *kanzen chōaku*:

Shakespeare in his handling of story gives recognition to accident as well as retribution; the interest of plot at one point is the moral satisfaction of nemesis, where we watch the sinner found out by his sin; it changes at another point to the not less moral sensation of pathos, our sympathy going out to the suffering which is independent of wrongdoing.[191]

Moulton is of course critical of biblical assertions of retribution as "an invariable principle,"[192] and this willingness to give "chance" a chance sits well with Shōyō's anti-didacticism and awareness of cause and effect as explanatory rather than retributive. Moreover, inductivism does not have to imply commitment to the individual object (and the implied threat of "retribution" if that commitment is withdrawn) but rather a Shakespearean sympathy that through the act of translation may transform an unknown and potentially threatening foreign text into an object of beauty in the target culture. There is a moral dimension to Shōyō's Shakespeare, but it is at one remove from the city hall bureaucrats who could tolerate kabuki only so long as it imparted a wholesome moral message: Meiji kabuki, and Shōyō's own trajectory of reform, can be said to begin with the summoning of kabuki leaders to a meeting at the new Tokyo City Hall in 1872 at which they were "ordered to adhere strictly to historical accuracy and truth" in exchange for official patronage.[193] Shōyō's Shakespeare is closer rather to a Coleridgean nexus of the ethical and aesthetic, namely that Shakespearean drama entails a moral respect and sympathy for the otherness and uniqueness of characters and situations.

**A Note on Editions**

Shōyō's reading of Western criticism prompts and supports him in his agenda of reform, but where he garnered greatest credibility among his peers was through his knowledge of Shakespeare's texts, which began with his knowledge of the numerous English editions that appeared over his lifetime. *Shēkusupiya kenkyū shiori* does not list specific editions, presumably because Shōyō would have wanted to recommend only the latest and most authoritative one (which he does), but as a student at the Imperial University he was fortunate that his own textual studies began with the popular Cambridge and Globe Shakespeares, edited by William George Clark and William Aldis Wright, which were first published in the 1860s and were among the university library's early purchases.[194] Clark and Wright pursued a professional "critical" approach, collating a single text out of the available variants that the editors deduced to represent the "mind" of the author. That was not necessarily Shōyō's game but it did support – and possibly instil – his preference for "critical commentary" "on the meaning of words, grammar, and so on as they appear in the source" over "interpretation," which as he writes professorially

> can be an extremely profound and profitable method for the more perceptive readers, but for the less perceptive "a little learning is a dangerous thing," and for the inattentive can lead to undesirable errors.[195]

What Shōyō wanted, therefore, from a Shakespeare edition was not to be told what the play meant but primarily a gloss on the difficult language.

The Globe Shakespeare did not include notes, and Shōyō may have struggled with the small font size, but the Cambridge Shakespeares were in a friendlier format with extensive notes that were probably surplus to his needs. It is likely that he used a variety of editions for his translation work, but Toyoda comments that he consulted the Macmillan editions by Kenneth Deighton, "especially for his early translations."[196] Deighton edited all but a handful of the plays between around 1890 and 1910, with his introductions providing concise summaries of the critical and editorial histories, the texts uncluttered by footnotes, and the endnotes giving the rhetorical glosses that Shōyō needed for his work. Methuen's Arden series (1899–1924), under the general editorship of Sōseki's teacher W. J. Craig until Craig's death in 1906, surpassed both the Globe and Deighton editions on all these counts, being based on the authoritative Globe and Cambridge texts, and indeed Deighton edited three plays for Arden himself, but when Shōyō made his heavily annotated translations of the first acts only of *Macbeth* and *Hamlet* in the 1890s it is probable that he looked to Deighton for the answers. Deighton's coolly forensic verdict on Hamlet's madness, argued over several pages with reference to previous commentaries, suits Shōyō's theatrical view of the play:

> it appears that in every single instance in which Hamlet's madness is manifested, he has good reason for assuming that disguise; while, on the other

hand, wherever there was no necessity to hoodwink any one, his thought, language, and actions bear no resemblance to unsoundness of intellect.[197]

Dowden, editing the First Arden *Hamlet* in 1899, is more emphatic about the prince's mental aptitude:

> Hamlet's . . . subtlety sees every side of every question, thinks too precisely on the event, considers all things too curiously, studies anew every conviction, doubts of the past, interrogates the future; it delights in ironically adopting the mental attitudes of other minds.[198]

The one edition Shōyō does specifically recommend in *Shēkusupiya kenkyū shiori* is the New Shakespeare published under the editorship of Arthur Quiller-Couch and John Dover Wilson, beginning with *The Tempest* in 1921. It seems that the editors' innovative and rational punctuation appealed to Shōyō, enabling him both to grasp the surface meanings more easily and to adapt them to his logical reading method (*ronriteki dokuhō*), discussed in Chapter 4, since in his Shakespeare primer he translates Wilson's "Note on Punctuation" in full.[199] In his short essay, Wilson reveals himself to be a man after Shōyō's heart in his appreciation of Shakespeare's dramatic poetry, declaring that "As he wrote Shakespeare had the living voice ever sounding in his ears, the flesh and blood of his creations ever moving before his eyes."[200]

Wilson claims to have kept the original punctuation as much as possible, but to have added quite a lot of commas, and indeed the following speech by Miranda is heavily punctuated:[201]

> *Miranda* [*turning*]. If by your art – my dearest father – you have
> Put the wild waters in this roar – allay them:
> The sky, it seems, would pour down stinking pitch,
> But that the sea, mounting to th' welkin's cheek,
> Dashes the fire out . . . O! I have suffered
> With those that I saw suffer: A brave vessel,
> [*in a whisper*]
> (Who had no doubt some noble creature in her!)
> Dashed all to pieces: [*sobbing*] O the cry did knock
> Against my very heart . . . poor souls, they perished . . .
>
> (1.2.1–9)

That the two editors use dashes to indicate "special dramatic significance" and avoid exclamation marks (with which "Shakespeare was very sparing in his use") unless they have been "compelled" otherwise indicates the heightened drama with which they interpret Miranda's speech:[202] mainly out of dismay at the storm and shipwreck she has just witnessed (and knows her father to have caused) but also structurally to assert the importance of poetic phrasing to the play's dramaturgy (the Shakespearean sense that language creates situation). The punctuation further indicates that the speech is not meant to be spoken quickly by a vulnerable and momentarily traumatised Miranda, and Wilson concludes his Note helpfully that

> *The Tempest* is a particularly beautiful example of dramatic pointing; and we feel confident that if, after glancing at this brief note, the reader will turn to the second scene and follow for a moment or two the pause-effects in the exquisite dialogue between Miranda and her father, he will not only master its principles without difficulty but will become a complete convert to Shakespearian punctuation.[203]

Although this advice comes too late for Shōyō himself, since he had already translated the play and is simply recommending the New Shakespeare to Japanese readers, his translation contains frequent pauses (indicated by Japanese commas) and is emphatically dramatic in its phrasing:

> *Chichiuesama, anata no hōjutsu de mizu ga ano yō ni sawagu no nara,*
> *   dōzo are wo*
> father, – by your magic – the water – in that way – if you move, – please –
> [the water] –
> *shizumete kudasare. Nami ga ōzora no hō wo utte, ano hikatte iru hi wo*
> *   kesanakereba,*
> you calm (respectful) – waves – great sky – hit, – the shining sun – extinguish (conditional),
> *ima nimo makkurona kusai mono ga tenjō kara futte kisō*
> presently – the pitch black – stinking thing – from heaven above – looks like it will fall –
> *ja. Ā, ano kurushimu no wo mite ita node, watashi mo issho ni*
> (archaic copula) oh, – that suffering – because I was seeing, – I too – together with them –
> *kurushimimashita! Ano migotona fune . . . . . . kitto, nanika rippana mono*
> *   ga norikonde ita*
> suffered! – that splendid boat (ellipsis) – surely, – some kind of noble person was boarded –
> *de arō ni . . . . . . minna konagona ni natte shimōta! Ā, ano nakigoe de*
> (speculative tense) (ellipsis) – all – to pieces – they have become! – oh, – by those wailing
> *watashi no kono mune ga itō natta! Kawaisō ni, minna shinde shimōta*
> *   no ja!*
> voices – my – this heart – came to hurt! – how pitiful, – they all died (emphatic particles)![204]

This is a modern colloquial translation that makes full use of the punctuation marks introduced into Japanese writing through the process of Meiji language reform. What he loses in translating *The Tempest* into modern Japanese rather than kabuki style is the unique intonation of kabuki actors, but what he gains is an opportunity for modern actors to modulate their voices according to the contours of Shakespeare's dramatic poetry.

## Language Reform and the Age of Translation

Shōyō's Shakespeare translations are an outstanding product of the process of language reform known as *genbun itchi*, his particular contribution being the copula *de arimasu* in contrast to Futabatei Shimei's *da*. As Indra Levy succinctly explains, whereas the *da* copula (which has become standard usage in modern Japanese) "binds statements directly to the narrator as a speaking subject with a distinct personality," "the expository *de ar[imasu]* does not bear any kind of vocal imprint at all, instead representing protagonistic feelings as transcendental verbal truths."[205] Shōyō's preference is indicative of his argument for "hiddenness" in literature, the *de arimasu* ending being a feature of his Shakespeare criticism, and it tended to a rhythmical style that prioritised literary features above semantic content.

In the 1880s, when Shōyō made his initial experimental version of *Julius Caesar* in classical *jōruri* style, he can hardly have imagined that he would end up translating the rest of Shakespeare in the vernacular that became modern Japanese. *Genbun itchi* was still a few years off, and the two standards of the written language remained – as they had been for the previous thousand years – Chinese (*kanbun*) and classical Japanese. Prominent writers such as Akinari were praised for their skill at combining Japanese syntax with Chinese characters in the style known as *wakan konkōbun*, and this style remained the norm of Meiji literature, including Shōyō's novels of the 1880s. The time-honoured *kundoku* method of reading Chinese texts according to Japanese syntax was adapted to the translation of Western texts in the early Meiji era, although more successfully to "the sphere of narrative context"[206] than to highly metaphorical texts such as Shakespeare's poetic dramas, while the richly allusive style of classical Japanese literature (*gabuntai*) made that an awkward vehicle for Western poetics.

Native stylistic mixing was for Shōyō a familiar and compelling analogy of Shakespearean style, but the two were not the same, and by the time that Shōyō started to translate the Complete Works in 1909 the classical written style had been largely supplanted by the modern vernacular, which was after all a closer formal equivalent to the vernacular standard of Shakespeare's early modern English. While Shōyō's translating style was considered old-fashioned by the likes of Sōseki, it still followed the trend of *genbun itchi* in the sense that his translations after 1909 are written in a modern vernacular rather than strictly classical Japanese, and while archaisms lent depth and variety, he was not opposed in principle to adopting a contemporary register.

Shakespeare's language may have been "for all time," but the colloquial was not the same as the contemporary for Shōyō since it included for example the urban patter of Chikamatsu's *jōruri* scripts. More crucially, his argument for the treatment of drama as literature presupposes a translating style at one remove from everyday language. Shakespeare's literariness combined what Shōyō calls "warmth" (its metaphorical dimension) and "rhythm," and Shōyō's strategy was definitely not one of disdain for the contemporary but rather to elide contemporary with classical elements. His implied hope that his translations might themselves serve to enlarge the modern language is not as fanciful as it might seem when one considers their wide readership as bestsellers in the 1920s and the rapid pace of language change in the twentieth century. Arguing on the one hand that the contemporary language was too limited for Shakespeare, Shōyō suggests that a colloquial – rather than strictly contemporary – standard of translation allows for "a more flexible and pliant" style "than [he] had expected":

> A writer like Shakespeare, with his wealth of vocabulary and lucid style unmatched in English literature before or since, can simply not be translated into the Tokyo dialect of today, even allowing for slang. (There are two or three brave souls who have tried, but to look at their translations, Ophelia and Juliet sound like bar girls and students, and Portia, Lady Macbeth, and Gertrude like the proprietresses of a tea shop or inn. They speak a vulgar language associated with the mistresses of company men.) . . . Yet even this contemporary language has the potential to become less narrow-minded and richer in vocabulary. . . . For if one is to add to what is broadly defined as a contemporary style a language that is prescribed by the rules of the colloquial (whether in current use or not), a Japanese comprised of both the contemporary and classical alike, the vulgar and refined, having both native and foreign influences, then the vocabulary will no longer be impoverished. . . . This vocabulary may not be listed in dictionaries like *Gensen* . . . or *Daigenkai*, but it is rich and broad.[207]

Shōyō may be excusing his partiality for kabuki style, but his view that the language of Shakespeare in Japanese will be subtly but ineffably different from the contemporary norm makes complete sense.

Shōyō's translations, although coming mainly after the pioneering translations of Western fiction in the 1880s and '90s by Futabatei Shimei and others, also contribute to the Westernisation of the language that was fundamental to *genbun itchi*, such as the use of personal and impersonal pronouns and relative clauses that were largely absent from classical Japanese. As ever, Shōyō's priorities are defined by Shakespeare's rhetoric (his sense, as Nakamura puts it, that in Shakespeare "the world of feeling is always bigger than the world of ideas"),[208] and he lists five characteristics, namely (1) the wealth of vocabulary, (2) what he calls the "delicate prosody," (3) the use of repetition and juxtaposition, (4) the tendency for rhyme at the end of scenes, and (5) the proliferation of adjectives;[209] the next chapter focusses on the first three of these. Shakespeare's rhetoric called for creative solutions, and, defined as it was as much by dramatic as poetic parameters, exemplifies what another of Shōyō's pupils, the Japanese literature scholar Igarashi Chikara, regarded as "true rhetoric":

> Writing without affectation means the abolition of unnatural ornament and classical conventions; it does not mean that all stylistic devices should be regarded as unnecessary.[210]

At the same time, we can find numerous examples of archaic and obsolescent usage, some of which are listed in the next chapter and which Shōyō has his own literary reasons for deploying.

Shōyō started seriously translating Shakespeare some ten to twenty years after the great age of Meiji literary translation, when the journalist Morita Shiken in particular was prominent in establishing a conscious strategy for engaging with the "intention of the original" (*genbun no ishu*) in a way that could only extend the linguistic norms of the target language.[211] Shōyō mentions the "hybrid literary style" of Shiken (who died in 1897) in his 1907 *Hamlet* essay,[212] and although he seems to feel that it is too "hybrid" "to capture Hamlet's characteristic of detachment"[213] the new linguistic norms were basically in place by 1909, and Shōyō's Shakespeare translations by default display all the grammatical features of "European-influenced style" identified by Kisaka Motoi in his 1987 study.[214] First of all, they are usually faithful in their translation choices, "you" and "thee" of course but also the ubiquitous "it," but they also contain numerous relative clauses (a rarity in classical Japanese), they use inanimate subjects with transitive verbs (the life "that struts and frets his hour upon the stage," etc.) and inanimate subjects in the passive voice ("What's done cannot be undone"), they invert normal Japanese word order to follow Shakespeare's, and they make free use of causative constructions. Meiji translation also tended to privilege sound and pronunciation as a result of its engagement with the Roman alphabet and Western linguistic theories, as Shōyō does, although he is old-fashioned in his use of Chinese characters, which were inevitably associated with the *kundoku* method of the past.[215]

\* \* \* \* \*

Finally, Satō Isao argued for the relevance to Shōyō's project of John Dryden's model of translation as paraphrase as an effective compromise between awkward literalism (metaphrase) and creative rewriting (imitation),[216] since more than other Meiji translators Shōyō tends to domesticate while maintaining a scholarly faithfulness to the source text; the next chapter gives several examples of his paraphrases, which for example in the case of relative clauses can hardly be avoided. In 1891, Shōyō translated Dryden's ode "Alexander's Feast, or the Power of Music" (1697),[217] which tells the true story of a feast that Alexander held following the defeat of the Persian king Darius at Persepolis in 331 BC. As Alexander becomes gradually more intoxicated, his bard Timotheus sings songs on his lyre that lead the conqueror through a series of powerful emotions: first praising him as a god, then of the pleasures of wine, then of the sad death of the brave Darius, then of the beauty of Alexander's lover Thäis, and finally of anger at the deaths of Alexander's soldiers, driving Alexander to destroy the Persian palace (although without further loss of life). The final stanza invokes Saint Cecilia, the patron saint of music, concluding that while Timotheus "raised a mortal to the skies,/She drew an angel down." (ll. 169–170).[218] This act of musical exchange may be an apt analogy for what is happening in Shōyō's translations as he responds in kind to the music of the source, and which Alfredo Michel Modenessi conceives in similar terms:

> The idea that translating literature is best compared with playing music applies to Shakespeare extremely well. Regardless of the style to which the musician subscribes and the language into which the translator works, neither the creative interpreter of music nor the creative interpreter of literature will ever (seek to) play, perform, or interpret (translate) their services exactly the same as someone before. This is not (only) a matter of competition; it is how the act of interpreting occurs.[219]

This chapter has mainly explored the basis of Shōyō's Shakespeare in his native culture, but just as Shakespeare's rhetoric forces him back into his culture, that culture may exert a corresponding pressure to attain equivalence between source and target, which although – and because – illusory motivates him to translate Shakespeare to a high level of scholarship and literary accomplishment.

### Notes

1 See Tsuno Kaitarō, *Kokkeina kyojin – Tsubouchi Shōyō no yume* (Tokyo: Heibonsha, 2002), 11–14, and Tsubouchi Shikō, *Tsubouchi Shōyō kenkyū* (Tokyo: Waseda University Press, 1953), 10.
2 Tsubouchi Shōyō, "Honan ni tsukite" (1885), in *Shōyō senshū*, vol. 2 (1977), 717.
3 Ibid.
4 Tsuno, 14–15.
5 See Nishiyama Matsunosuke, *Edo Culture: Daily Life and Diversions in Urban Japan, 1600–1868*, trans. and ed. Gerald Groemer (Honolulu: University of Hawai'i Press, 1997), 49–51.
6 Tsubouchi Shōyō, "Waga kuni no shigeki" (1893–4), in *Tsubouchi Shōyō shū* (1969), 287–8.
7 Tsubouchi Shōyō, "'*Makubesu* hyōshaku' no shogen" (1891), in *Shōyō senshū*, supp. vol. 3 (1978), 165–6.
8 Ibid., 164.
9 Tsuno, 137.
10 Spencer is not mentioned by name but his evolutionism is implicit in Shōyō's statement that "It is not easy to resist . . . the process of natural selection. Macaulay once suggested that the growth of civilisation will make art redundant, and his argument was a logical one. . . . Yet it relates only to the art that originates in the past and not to the novel of today, which dates back only to the eighteenth and nineteenth centuries": Tsubouchi Shōyō, "Shōsetsu shinzui" (1884–5), in *Tsubouchi Shōyō shū* (1969), 16.
11 Ueda Atsuko, *Concealment of Politics, Politics of Concealment: The Production of "Literature" in Meiji Japan* (Stanford, CA: Stanford University Press, 2007), 29.
12 "Shōsetsu shinzui," 4.
13 Ibid., 16.
14 The so-called "sixth sense" in Buddhist teaching.
15 Ibid., 19.
16 Ibid., 45, trans. Twine.
17 Tsuno, 260.
18 "Shōsetsu shinzui," 16.
19 Sadoya Shigenobu, *Tsubouchi Shōyō – dentōshugisha no kōzu* (Tokyo: Meiji Shoin, 1983), 87.

20 "Shōsetsu shinzui," 16.
21 Ibid., 17.
22 Ibid., 3.
23 Ibid., 56.
24 Ibid.
25 Ibid., 23.
26 Ibid., 33.
27 Ibid.
28 For Shōyō, a fundamental difference between Shakespeare and his classical heritage is that whereas *ninjō* were thought ultimately to reside in the person of the Emperor, Shakespeare's "feelings" clearly belonged somewhere else, and so simply by exposing himself to Shakespeare's "feelings" through the act of translation and allowing those feelings to stimulate all the rational choices he had to make in translating Shakespeare's texts, he is able to exercise his individual feelings in Shakespeare translations independently from the assumptions of classical literature even if he was still one of the Emperor's "subjects." As a corollary of *botsurisōron*, Shakespeare translation enables Shōyō to see himself for the individual that he is. See Nakamura Kan, *Tsubouchi Shōyō ron – kindai Nihon no monogatari kūkan* (Tokyo: Yūseidō, 1986), 63–8.
29 For Shōyō, the rhythms of the source text can be articulated by the reader to manifest their essential interiority, but that interiority is likely to be obscured by literal translations made into native poetic forms, and is therefore usually better conveyed by prose translations that are rhythmical and tonally sensitive rather than strictly metrical.
30 Shōyō called the Daisō lending library in Nagoya, where as a teenager he read his way through most of Tokugawa fiction, *kokoro no furusato* (Kobayashi Yoshihito, *Tsubouchi Shōyō* [Tokyo: Shimizu Shoin, 1969], 25), and Tsubouchi Shikō uses the same phrase to describe his relationship with Shakespeare (Tsubouchi Shikō, 176). Having learnt how to read his native literature at the Daisō, Shōyō transfers that skill to the reading and translation of Shakespeare, who thereby becomes a second "spiritual hometown" (since *kokoro* can mean "soul" or "spirit" as well as "heart"), although what probably both Shōyō and Shikō mean is that it is at the Daisō and within Shakespeare that he felt most at ease.
31 "'*Makubesu* hyōshaku' no shogen," 164.
32 See Suzuki Sadami, *The Concept of Literature in Japan*, trans. Royall Tyler (Kyoto: International Research Center for Japanese Studies, 2006), 155.
33 "Shōsetsu shinzui," 17. In this section Shōyō compares human behaviour to a chess game that the novelist must describe as if watching it.
34 Suzuki, 163.
35 "Shōsetsu shinzui," 20.
36 Honma Hisao, *Tsubouchi Shōyō – hito to sono geijutsu* (Tokyo: Shōhakusha, 1959), 6, 162.
37 Ibid., 10.
38 Quoted in Suzuki, 163.
39 Ibid., 85.
40 Suzuki, 88.
41 Rebekah Clements also refers to Norinaga's foresighted approach to vernacular translation as "a more accurate means of 'seeing' the source text than commentaries, which merely tell you about it second-hand": Rebekah Clements, *A Cultural History of Translation in Early Modern Japan* (Cambridge: Cambridge University Press, 2015), 87.
42 Charles Shiro Inouye, "Promoting Virtue and Punishing Vice: Tarantino's *Kill Bill* and the Return of Bakumatsu Aesthetics," *Post Script* 28, no. 2 (2009): 92.
43 "Shōsetsu shinzui," 14.
44 The government's efforts to reform kabuki began as early as 1872 with its call to leading actors to adhere more strictly to historical accuracy and avoid immoral content that might offend foreign visitors. As a result, Ichikawa Danjūrō IX developed a realistic style of drama and acting that met with only limited success, and politician Suematsu

Kenchō's Society for Theatre Reform (founded in 1886) proposed the Westernisation of theatres with the use of actresses rather than *onnagata* impersonators in female roles and removal of the *hanamichi* platform running through the audience for the purpose of dramatic entrances and exits. The use of impersonators and the *hanamichi* were thought to invite immoral behaviour but have never been abolished, and were not opposed by Shōyō, who called instead for more realistic "Shakespearean" playwriting.

45 "'*Makubesu* hyōshaku' no shogen," 168–9.
46 Yano Hōjin, "Tsubouchi Shōyō to bungaku kyōiku," *Tsubouchi Shōyō Kenkyū Shiryō* 1 (1969): 7.
47 See Lee Yeounsuk, *The Ideology of Kokugo: Nationalizing Language in Modern Japan*, trans. Maki Hirano Hubbard (Honolulu: University of Hawai'i Press, 2010), 87–90.
48 Saeki Junko, "From *Iro* (Eros) to *Ai=Love*: The Case of Tsubouchi Shōyō," trans. Indra Levy, in *Translation in Modern Japan*, ed. Indra Levy (Abingdon: Routledge, 2011), 92.
49 Noriko T. Reider, *Tales of the Supernatural in Early Modern Japan: Kaidan, Akinari, Ugetsu Monogatari* (New York: Edwin Mellen Press, 2002), 83. Ueda was, with Bakin, the most prominent of *yomihon* writers, and is best known for his collection of supernatural tales, *Ugetsu monogatari* (Tales of Rain and the Moon, 1776), filmed as *Ugetsu* by Mizoguchi Kenji in 1953.
50 Tsubouchi Shōyō, "Kaioku mandan" (1925–6), in *Shōyō senshū*, vol. 12 (1977), 348–9.
51 The Genroku era (1688–1704) was a period of cultural flourishing in which Chikamatsu became active as a writer for the puppet theatre, and is associated with the rising – but politically impotent – merchant class in the Kamigata area around Kyoto and Osaka. Genroku style arose in reaction to the oppressive Tokugawa shogunate based in Edo (now Tokyo), being flashy and hedonistic and in Chikamatsu's case escapist.
52 "Kaioku mandan," 348–9.
53 Lawrence E. Marceau, "Cultural Developments in Tokugawa Japan," in *A Companion to Japanese History*, ed. William M. Tsutsui (Oxford: Blackwell Publishing, 2007), 130.
54 Daniel Poch, *Licentious Fictions and the Nineteenth-Century Japanese Novel* (New York: Columbia University Press, 2019), 62.
55 Ibid., 82.
56 Glynne Walley, "Translator's Introduction," in Kyokutei Bakin, *Eight Dogs, Or, "Hakkenden": An Ill-Considered Jest*, trans. Glynne Walley (Ithaca, NY: Cornell University East Asia Program, 2021), xxx. *Hakkenden* has been adapted for kabuki performance.
57 Pre-Meiji written Japanese was barely punctuated. One of the effects of *genbun itchi* was to normalise shorter, punctuated sentences in the Western style.
58 Jason Karlin, *Gender and Nation in Meiji Japan: Modernity, Loss, and the Doing of History* (Honolulu: University of Hawai'i Press, 2014), 166.
59 Ibid.
60 C. Andrew Gerstle, "Introduction to Chikamatsu," in *Early Modern Japanese Literature: An Anthology, 1600–1900*, ed. Shirane Haruo (New York: Columbia University Press, 2002), 240.
61 Tsubouchi Yūzō, "Shakespeare and Chikamatsu" (1916), in *A Book of Homage to Shakespeare*, ed. Israel Gollancz and Gordon McMullan (Oxford: Oxford University Press, 2016), 545–6.
62 Ibid., 544–55.
63 Donald Keene, *World Within Walls: Japanese Literature of the Pre-Modern Era, 1600–1867* (New York: Holt, Rinehart & Winston, 1976), 255.
64 Torigoe Bunzō, ed., *Chikamatsu Monzaemon shū*, vol. 2 (Tokyo: Shōgakukan, 1975), 497.
65 Edward Dowden, *Shakspere: A Critical Study of His Mind and Art* (London: Kegan Paul, Trench and Co., 1875), 227.
66 Norinaga writes that "If one searches the bottom of one's heart it is impossible not to find love there, especially the type of love forbidden by man. And try as one might to suppress it, there will be only melancholy and bewilderment in one's heart. As love is

thus unreasonable, the love poems which come forth on such occasions are especially touching. It is also natural that there should be many love poems that suggest impropriety and licentiousness. Be that as it may, poetry follows the principle of the sorrow of existence and attempts to express without adornment the bad as well as the good. Its aim is not to select and arrange for the heart that which is good or bad": *Sources of Japanese Tradition*, vol. 2, trans. and ed. Tsunoda Ryūsaku, Wm. Theodore de Bary, and Donald Keene (New York: Columbia University Press, 1964), 32. Norinaga is referring to classical poetry but in *Shōsetsu shinzui* a similar view is applied to drama and fiction.

67 Torigoe, 507.

68 Tsubouchi Shōyō, "Chikamatsu tai Shēkusupia tai Ipusen" (1909), in *Shōyō senshū*, vol. 10 (1977), 769–814. Trans. *"History and Characteristics of Kabuki: The Japanese Classical Drama" by Shōyō Tsubouchi and Jirō Yamamoto*, ed. Matsumoto Ryōzō (Yokohama: Heiji Yamagata, 1960), 207–39.

69 Ibid., 770–1 (Matsumoto, 208).

70 Ibid., 771–4 (Matsumoto, 209).

71 Ibid., 774–6 (Matsumoto, 211–12).

72 Ibid., 777 (Matsumoto, 212–13).

73 Ibid., 777–9 (Matsumoto, 213–14).

74 Ibid., 779–81 (Matsumoto, 214–15).

75 Ibid., 781 (Matsumoto, 215).

76 Ibid., 781–4 (Matsumoto, 215–17).

77 Ibid., 784–5 (Matsumoto, 217–18).

78 Ibid., 785–7 (Matsumoto, 218–19).

79 Ibid., 787–8 (Matsumoto, 219–20).

80 Ibid., 788–90 (Matsumoto, 220–1).

81 Ibid., 790 (Matsumoto, 221).

82 Ibid., 790–3 (Matsumoto, 221–3).

83 Ibid., 793–4 (Matsumoto, 223–4).

84 Ibid., 794–5 (Matsumoto, 224).

85 Ibid., 795 (Matsumoto, 224–5).

86 Ibid., 795–6 (Matsumoto, 225).

87 Tsubouchi Shōyō, "Nihon de enzuru *Hamuretto*" (1907), in *Sheikusupia kenkyū shiryō shūsei*, vol. 2, Sasaki Takashi (Tokyo: Nihon Tosho Centre, 1997), 199.

88 Ibid., 200.

89 "The world of the Kabuki play is not the almost limitless universe in which the characters of Shakespeare and Sophocles move. But within the limits set for them, the greatest Kabuki heroes are not merely the puppet figures of melodrama": Earle Ernst, *The Kabuki Theatre* (Honolulu: University of Hawai'i Press, 1974), 243.

90 Barbara E. Thornbury, *Sukeroku's Double Identity: The Dramatic Structure of Edo Kabuki* (Ann Arbor, MI: University of Michigan Center for Japanese Studies, 1982), 77.

91 Protagonists such as Jihei and Tokubei in another Chikamatsu *sewamono*, *Sonezaki shinjū* (1703), act against social norms. In Edo kabuki, the "spirit of resistance" is embodied in a different way by a character like the samurai Sukeroku in the 1713 drama of the same name, who – like Shōyō in the 1880s and '90s – is continually picking fights.

92 Quoted by Yamamoto Jirō, "History of *Kabuki*" (1951), in Matsumoto Ryōzō, 46.

93 "Waga kuni no shigeki," 288.

94 The Kasei culture of the Bunka and Bunsei eras (1804–29) was a townsmen's culture like Chikamatsu's Genroku but more decadent.

95 Tsubouchi Shōyō, trans., "Temupesuto," in *Shōyō senshū*, vol. 4 (1977), 42.

96 Richard Emmert and Alan Cummings, "Introduction, 'Viewing the Autumn Foliage',"
   in *Kabuki Plays on Stage: Restoration and Reform, 1872–1905*, ed. James R. Brandon and Samuel L. Leiter (Honolulu: University of Hawai'i Press, 2003), 307.

97   Tsubouchi Shōyō, *Taitasu Andoronikasu* (Tokyo: Waseda University Press, 1926), 11.
98   Ibid.
99   Ibid., 11–12.
100  Thomas S. Eliot, "Seneca in Elizabethan Translation," in *Selected Essays: 1917–1932* (New York: Harcourt, Brace & World, 1950), 67.
101  Tsubouchi Shōyō, "Shēkusupiya atto randomu" (1931), in *Shōyō senshū*, supp. vol. 5 (1978), 302. Hieronimo bites out his tongue in the final scene of Thomas Kyd's *Spanish Tragedy* (1580s).
102  Tsubouchi Shōyō, "Batsu ni kawaete" [In Place of an Epilogue], in *Makubesu* (Tokyo: Chūō Kōronsha, 1935), 3–4.
103  "'*Makubesu* hyōshaku' no shogen," 163.
104  Tsubouchi Shōyō, "Azusa miko" (1891), in *Shōyō senshū*, vol. 8 (1977), 168. Trans. Poch, 173.
105  Ishida Tadahiko, *Tsubouchi Shōyō kenkyū* (Fukuoka: Kyushu University Press, 1988), 335.
106  Nakamura, 224–6.
107  Ibid.
108  Ibid., 72.
109  Ibid., 212.
110  The traditional ideal of the cultured man praised in works such as Yoshida Kenkō's *Tsurezuregusa* (Essays in Idleness, 1330–2).
111  "Temupesuto," 30.
112  Ibid.
113  "Shōsetsu shinzui," 42. In his *Tempest* afterword, Shōyō compares Shakespeare himself to the eighteenth-century neo-Confucianists for his artistic ability to see two sides of a problem, which is his genius of concealing his personal opinions ("Temupesuto," 30).
114  Dowden (1875), 227.
115  "Temupesuto," 49.
116  Ibid., 45–6.
117  Ibid., 42–3. Shōyō does, however, suggest that while the plot has no parallel in Noh or *jōruri*, Prospero resembles two popular samurai characters in nineteenth-century kabuki, Saitō Tarōsaemon and Gorōbei Masamune (34), and also compares the role of Caliban to that of *kyogen mawashi* in kabuki as a supporting character who is essential to the development of the plot (50).
118  Ibid., 48.
119  Tsubouchi Shōyō, "Manatsu no yo no yume," in *Shōyō senshū*, vol. 4 (1977), 179.
120  Shōyō calls it *inaka shibai Chūshingura shiki* ("a Chūshingura style of country play"). Ibid., 178.
121  Ibid., 179.
122  Discussed in *Kansai no senjōteki higeki* (Tokyo: Shunjūsha, 1933).
123  "Manatsu no yo no yume," 182–6.
124  Yanagita's *Shakujin mondō* [Discourse on Stone Deities], published in 1910.
125  Tsubouchi Shōyō, "Ishaku hōshaku," in *Shōyō senshū*, vol. 5 (1977), 217.
126  In a supplementary preface written for the revised version published after *Shōyō senshū* in 1933: Tsubouchi Shōyō, *Ishaku hōshaku* (Tokyo: Chūō Kōronsha, 1933), 3. He was likely influenced in this view by Anna Jameson's comparison of the two heroines in her influential *Shakespeare's Heroines: Characteristics of Women, Moral, Poetical, and Historical* (London: Saunders and Otley, 1832), 32–3, which is one of the very few works of Shakespeare criticism by female authors listed in *Shēkusupia kenkyū shiori* (91).
127  "Ishaku hōshaku," 222.
128  Ibid.

129 Ibid., 223. In *Hachi no ki*, Tokiyori, disguised as an itinerant monk, knocks on the door of the poor Tsuneyo, begging for a place to stay for the night as it is snowing heavily outside. Tsuneyo not only grants the monk's request but burns his precious potted plum, cherry, and pine trees to keep his mysterious guest warm. The Angelo equivalent are the relatives who have cheated Tsuneyo out of his land, and it is with land that he is handsomely rewarded when Tokiyori's identity is finally revealed. The comparison may have been of more than incidental significance to Shōyō since *Hachi no ki* was known as one of the favourite plays of Tokugawa Ieyasu and remained popular as a model of samurai chivalry (*bushidō*).

130 Ibid.

131 Tsubouchi Shōyō, "Antonī to Kureopatora," in *Shōyō senshū*, vol. 5 (1977), 3.

132 Ibid., 8–9.

133 Ibid., 9.

134 Ibid.; Dowden (1875), 306–07.

135 Tsubouchi Shōyō, "Henrī yonsei dainibu," in *Shōyō senshū*, vol. 4 (1977), 484–5.

136 Tsubouchi Shōyō, "Jajauma narashi," in *Shōyō senshū*, vol. 4 (1977), 663.

137 Ibid., 664.

138 Tsuno, 27.

139 Quoted in Kawatake Shigetoshi and Yanagida Izumi, *Tsubouchi Shōyō* (1939; repr., Tokyo: Daiichi Shobō, 1988), 740. Bunzaemon Kinokuniya (Kibun) made a fortune in the early eighteenth century exporting *mikan* tangerines from his native Wakayama to the capital at Edo, and one year risked storms in the Pacific to ensure that the fruit reached Edo in time for an annual festival; he later supplied the people of Osaka with salted salmon when they were threatened by an epidemic. Gohei Zeniya followed the call for the liberalisation of Japanese trade in the early nineteenth century at a time when such trade was still strictly forbidden, and may have taken his boats as far as Tasmania. Nagamasa Yamada is the best known of these three for his involvement with the Red Seal ships (*shuinsen*) during the early seventeenth century, a system established under the warlord Hideyoshi Toyotomi in 1592 to advance Japanese trade in south-east Asia and protect it from piracy but soon after abolished by the Tokugawa shogun out of fear of European influence in the Philippines and elsewhere.

140 Tsuno, 36–7. Tsuno also mentions Shōyō's commitment to "outdoor drama" (pageants).

141 Ibid., 147.

142 Moriya Sasaburō, *Nihon ni okeru Sheikusupia* (Tokyo: Yasshio Shuppan, 1986), 143.

143 The Naturalists eschewed "unnatural" theatricality (Tsuno, 31).

144 Moriya, 124.

145 Natsume Kinnosuke, *Sōseki zenshū*, vol. 16 (Tokyo: Iwanami Shoten, 2019, facsimile ed.), 27.

146 Leo Tolstoy, *Tolstoy on Shakespeare: A Critical Essay on Shakespeare*, trans. Vladimir Tchertkoff (1906; Glasgow: Good Press, 2022), 14.

147 Ibid., 32.

148 Tsubouchi Shōyō, "Torusutoi tai Shēkusupiya" (1907), in *Sheikusupia kenkyū shiryō shūsei*, vol. 2, ed. Sasaki Takashi (Tokyo: Nihon Tosho Centre, 1997), 239.

149 Ibid., 243.

150 Kang Jungki, "Shō," in *Tsubouchi Shōyō jiten* (1986), 179–80.

151 Tsubouchi Shōyō, "Iwayuru atarashii onna" (1912), in *Shōyō senshū*, vol. 8 (1977), 211–372. See Kang Jungki, "Iwayuru atarashii onna," in *Tsubouchi Shōyō jiten* (1986), 38.

152 George Orwell, "Lear, Tolstoy and the Fool" (1947), in *George Orwell: Selected Essays*, ed. Stefan Collini (Oxford: Oxford University Press, 2021), 273. Orwell pinpoints Shakespeare's likely appeal to Shōyō with his view that "Shakespeare was not a philosopher or a scientist, but he did have curiosity, he loved the surface of the earth

and the process of life – which, it should be repealed, is *not* the same thing as wanting to have a good time and stay alive as long as possible" (ibid.).

153   "Chikamatsu tai Shēkusupia tai Ipusen," 798–9 (Matsumoto Ryōzō, 228).
154   "'*Makubesu* hyōshaku' no shogen," 166.
155   Richard G. Moulton, *Shakespeare as a Dramatic Thinker* (London: Macmillan & Co., 1907), 49. Moulton was English, born in 1849 into a distinguished Methodist family, and appointed professor of English literature at the University of Chicago in 1892.
156   Ibid., 167.
157   Tsubouchi Shōyō, "Shēkusupiya kenkyū shiori" (1928), in *Shōyō senshū*, supp. vol. 5 (1977), 50.
158   Sadoya, 44.
159   Matsumoto Shinko, "Botsurisō to Edwādo Dauden," *Tsubouchi Shōyō Kenkyū Shiryō* 9 (1980): 1–12.
160   Dowden, 35.
161   Tsubouchi Shōyō, "Soko shirazu no mizuumi" (1891), in *Tsubouchi Shōyō shū* (1969), 282.
162   Dowden was elected president of the English Goethe Society in 1888.
163   Dowden, 6.
164   Ibid.
165   Tsubouchi Shōyō, "Jibun no honyaku ni tsuite" (1928), in *Shōyō senshū*, supp. vol. 5 (1977), 267.
166   Edward Dowden, *Shakespere* (London: Macmillan & Co., 1877), 47–56.
167   "'*Makubesu* hyōshaku' no shogen," 161–2.
168   Dowden (1875), 42.
169   Ibid., 46.
170   Ibid., 44.
171   Ibid., 46.
172   Ibid., 62.
173   Ibid.
174   Ibid.
175   The urban *gesaku* novels of Tanehiko, who died in 1842, remained popular until well into the Meiji era. His name is mentioned eight times in *Shōsetsu shinzui* as a stereotype of late Edo fiction that Shōyō urged his contemporaries to avoid. The novels of Kōyō, who died in 1903 at the age of thirty-five, are comparable to Thackeray rather than to Henry Fielding (or George Eliot) (Sadoya, 20).
176   "Waga kuni no shigeki," 291.
177   Ibid., 288.
178   Satō Isao, "Hishō bungaku," in *Tsubouchi Shōyō jiten* (1986), 305. Possnett was also influenced by Spencer's Social Darwinism.
179   Hutcheson M. Possnett, *Comparative Literature* (London: Kegan Paul, Trench & Co., 1886), 325.
180   Ibid., 362.
181   Ibid., 366.
182   Ibid., 357–8.
183   Henry R. Woudhuysen, ed., *Samuel Johnson on Shakespeare* (London: Penguin Books, 1989), 122. Norinaga's aesthetic of *mono no aware* asserts that the particular glimpses the universal through the force of feeling, but he was writing mainly about classical *waka* poetry.
184   Possnett, 12.
185   Daniel Gallimore, "Of Ponds, Lakes, and the Sea: Shōyō, Shakespeare, and Romanticism," in *British Romanticism in Asia: The Reception, Translation, and Transformation of Romantic Literature in East Asia and India*, ed. Alex Watson and Laurence Williams (London: Palgrave Macmillan, 2019), 273–92.

186 This comment (Tsubouchi Shikō, 127) was surely in jest since Shōyō can hardly be considered to belong to the New Romantic school of his rival Mori Ōgai, but there is a serious point that Shōyō may have been making about the permeability of generic styles.
187 Moulton, 40.
188 Ibid., 244.
189 See Ishimaru Hisashi, "Shōsetsu sanpa," in *Tsubouchi Shōyō jiten* (1986), 182.
190 Michael C. Brownstein, "Tsubouchi Shōyō on Chikamatsu and Drama," in *Currents in Japanese Culture: Translations and Transformations*, ed. Amy Vladeck (New York: Columbia University Press, 1997), 286.
191 Moulton, 50.
192 Ibid., 46.
193 Jean-Jacques Tschudin, "Danjūrō's *Katsureki-Geki* (Realistic Theatre) and the Meiji 'Theatre Reform' Movement," *Japan Forum* 11, no. 1 (1999): 83.
194 The library's purchase of Shakespeare editions dates from 1876 (Kawato Michiaki, *Meiji no Sheikusupia* (Tokyo: Ōzorasha, 2004), 251–2).
195 "'*Makubesu* hyōshaku' no shogen," 163.
196 Toyoda Minoru, *Shakespeare in Japan: An Historical Survey* (Tokyo: Iwanami Shoten, 1940), 136.
197 Kenneth Deighton, ed., *Hamlet, Prince of Denmark* (London: Macmillan & Co., 1891), xxiv.
198 Edward Dowden, ed., *The Tragedy of Hamlet* (London: Methuen & Co., 1899), xxvi.
199 "Shēkusupiya kenkyū shiori," 224–9.
200 Sir Arthur Quiller-Couch and John Dover Wilson, eds., *The Tempest* (1921; Cambridge: Cambridge University Press, 1969), lvii.
201 Ibid., 6.
202 Ibid., lviii–lix.
203 Ibid., lix–lx. Shōyō does not include this part in *Shēkusupiya kenkyū shiori*.
204 "Temupesuto," 60.
205 Indra A. Levy, *Sirens of the Western Shore: The Westernesque Femme Fatale, Translation, and Vernacular Style in Modern Japanese Literature* (New York: Columbia University Press, 2010), 39.
206 Ibid., 30.
207 "Jibun no honyaku ni tsuite," 267–8. On the Japanese dictionaries, see Note 92 in Chapter 3.
208 Nakamura, 68.
209 Moriya, 52–3.
210 Quoted in Massimiliano Tomasi, *Rhetoric in Modern Japan: Western Influences on the Development of Narrative and Oratorical Style* (Honolulu: University of Hawai'i Press, 2004), 128.
211 Saitō Mino, "Morita Shiken," in *Nihon no honyakuron – ansorojī to kaidai*, ed. Yanabu Akira, Naganuma Mikako, and Mizuno Akira (Tokyo: Hōsei University Press, 2010), 89. Shiken's strategy was more consciously focused on the target audience than what had come before.
212 "Nihon de enzuru *Hamuretto*," 196.
213 Ibid., 200.
214 Kisaka Motoi, "Gendai ōbunmyaku no hirogari", *Kokubungaku: Kaishaku to Kyōzai no Kenkyū* 32, no. 4 (1987): 124–8; Akira Mizuno, "Stylistic Norms in the Early Meiji Period: From Chinese Influences to European Influences," in *Translation and Translation Studies in the Japanese Context*, ed. Nana Sato-Rossberg and Judy Wakabayashi (London: Continuum, 2012), 96.
215 Atsuko Ueda, "Sounds, Scripts, and Styles: *Kanbun Kundokutai* and the National Language Reforms of 1880s Japan," in *Translation in Modern Japan*, ed. Indra Levy (Abingdon: Routledge, 2016), 147.

216  Satō Isao, *Tsubouchi Shōyō ni okeru Doraiden juyō no kenkyū – tōyō to seiyō ni okeru hikaku bungaku no genten* (Tokyo: Hokuseidō Shoten, 1981).
217  Tsubouchi Yūzō, *Eishibun hyōshaku* (Tokyo: Waseda University Press, 1902), 137–9.
218  Keith Walker, ed., *John Dryden: The Major Works* (Oxford: Oxford University Press, 2003), 549.
219  Alfredo Michel Modenessi, "'Dost Dialogue with Thy Shadow?': Translating Shakespeare and Stage Business," *Shakespeare Studies* 46 (2018): 71.

## References

Brownstein, Michael C. "Tsubouchi Shōyō on Chikamatsu and Drama." In *Currents in Japanese Culture: Translations and Transformations*, edited by Amy Vladeck, 279–89. New York: Columbia University Press, 1997.
Clements, Rebekah. *A Cultural History of Translation in Early Modern Japan*. Cambridge: Cambridge University Press, 2015.
Deighton, Kenneth, ed. *Hamlet, Prince of Denmark*. London: Macmillan & Co., 1891.
Dowden, Edward. *Shakespeare*. London: Macmillan & Co., 1877.
———. *Shakspere: A Critical Study of His Mind and Art*. London: Kegan Paul, Trench and Co., 1875.
———, ed. *The Tragedy of Hamlet*. London: Methuen & Co., 1899.
Eliot, Thomas S. "Seneca in Elizabethan Translation." In *Selected Essays: 1917–1932*, 65–106. New York: Harcourt, Brace & World, 1950.
Emmert, Richard and Alan Cummings. "Introduction, 'Viewing the Autumn Foliage'." In *Kabuki Plays on Stage: Restoration and Reform, 1872–1905*, edited by James R. Brandon and Samuel L. Leiter, 304–8. Honolulu: University of Hawai'i Press, 2003, https://doi.org/10.1515/9780824845919.
Ernst, Earle. *The Kabuki Theatre*. Honolulu: University of Hawai'i Press, 1974, https://doi.org/10.1515/9780824846060.
Fukuda Kiyoto and Kobayashi Yoshihito. *Tsubouchi Shōyō*. Tokyo: Shimizu Shoin, 1969.
Gallimore, Daniel. "Of Ponds, Lakes, and the Sea: Shōyō, Shakespeare, and Romanticism." In *British Romanticism in Asia: The Reception, Translation, and Transformation of Romantic Literature in East Asia and India*, edited by Alex Watson and Laurence Williams, 273–92. London: Palgrave Macmillan, 2019, https://doi.org/10.1007/978-981-13-3001-8_11.
Gerstle, C. Andrew. "Introduction to Chikamatsu." In *Early Modern Japanese Literature: An Anthology, 1600–1900*, edited by Shirane Haruo, 233–42. New York: Columbia University Press, 2002.
Honma Hisao. *Tsubouchi Shōyō – hito to sono geijutsu* [Tsubouchi Shōyō, the Person and His Art]. Tokyo: Shōhakusha, 1959.
Inagaki Tatsurō, ed. *Tsubouchi Shōyō shū* [Works of Tsubouchi Shōyō]. Tokyo: Chikuma Shobō, 1969.
Inouye, Charles Shiro. "Promoting Virtue and Punishing Vice: Tarantino's *Kill Bill* and the Return of Bakumatsu Aesthetics." *Post Script: Essays in Film and the Humanities* 28, no. 2 (Spring 2009): 92–100.
Ishida Tadahiko. *Tsubouchi Shōyō kenkyū* [Theories of Tsubouchi Shōyō]. Fukuoka: Kyushu University Press, 1988.
Ishimaru Hisashi. "'Shōsetsu sanpa'" ["Three Types of Novel"]. In *Tsubouchi Shōyō jiten* (1986), 182.
Jameson, Anna. *Shakespeare's Heroines: Characteristics of Women, Moral, Poetical, and Historical*. London: Saunders and Otley, 1832.
Kang Jungki. "Iwayuru atarashii onna" [The So-Called New Woman]. In *Tsubouchi Shōyō jiten* (1986), 38.
———. "Shō" [George Bernard Shaw]. In *Tsubouchi Shōyō jiten* (1985), 179–80.

Karlin, Jason. *Gender and Nation in Meiji Japan: Modernity, Loss, and the Doing of History*. Honolulu: University of Hawai'i Press, 2014, https://doi.org/10.21313/haw aii/9780824838263.001.0001.

Kawatake Shigetoshi and Yanagida Izumi. *Tsubouchi Shōyō*. 1939. Reprint, Tokyo: Daiichi Shobō, 1988.

Kawato Michiaki. *Meiji no Sheikusupia* [Shakespeare's Reception in the Meiji Era]. Tokyo: Ōzorasha, 2004.

Keene, Donald. *World Within Walls: Japanese Literature of the Pre-Modern Era, 1600–1867*. New York: Holt, Rinehart & Winston, 1976.

Kisaka Motoi. "Gendai ōbunmyaku no hirogari" [The Extent of Modern European-Influenced Style]. *Kokubungaku: Kaishaku to Kyōzai no Kenkyū* 32, no. 14 (November 1987): 124–8.

Lee Yeounsuk. *The Ideology of* Kokugo: *Nationalizing Language in Modern Japan*. translated by Maki Hirano Hubbard. Honolulu: University of Hawai'i Press, 2010. Originally published as *"Kokugo" to iu shisō*. Tokyo: Iwanami Shoten, 1996, https://doi.org/10.21313/hawaii/9780824833053.001.0001.

Levy, Indra A. *Sirens of the Western Shore: The Westernesque Femme Fatale, Translation, and Vernacular Style in Modern Japanese Literature*. New York: Columbia University Press, 2010, https://doi.org/10.7312/levy13786.

Marceau, Lawrence E. "Cultural Developments in Tokugawa Japan." In *A Companion to Japanese History*, edited by William M. Tsutsui, 117–35. Oxford: Blackwell Publishing, 2007, https://doi.org/10.1002/9780470751398.ch8.

Matsumoto Ryōzō, trans. and ed. *"History and Characteristics of Kabuki: The Japanese Classical Drama" by Shōyō Tsubouchi and Jirō Yamamoto*. Yokohama: Heiji Yamagata, 1960.

Matsumoto Shinko. "Botsurisō to Edwādo Dauden" [Edward Dowden and "The Hidden Ideals Debate"]. *Tsubouchi Shōyō Kenkyū Shiryō* 9 (March 1980): 1–12.

Mizuno Akira. "Stylistic Norms in the Early Meiji Period: From Chinese Influences to European Influences." In *Translation and Translation Studies in the Japanese Context*, edited by Nana Sato-Rossberg and Judy Wakabayashi, 92–114. London: Continuum, 2012.

Modenessi, Alfredo Michel. "'Dost Dialogue With Thy Shadow?': Translating Shakespeare and Stage Business." *Shakespeare Studies* 46 (2018): 70–83.

Moriya Sasaburō. *Nihon ni okeru Sheikusupia* [Shakespeare in Japan]. Tokyo: Yasshio Shuppan, 1986.

Motoori Norinaga. "Love and Poetry." In *Sources of Japanese Tradition*, vol. 2, translated and edited by Tsunoda Ryūsaku, Wm. Theodore de Bary, and Donald Keene, 30–5. New York: Columbia University Press, 1964. Originally published in *Iso no kami no sasamegoto* (1763).

Moulton, Richard G. *Shakespeare as a Dramatic Thinker*. London: Macmillan & Co., 1907.

Nakamura Kan. *Tsubouchi Shōyō ron – kindai Nihon no monogatari kūkan* [Tsubouchi Shōyō and the Space of Modern Japanese Narrative]. Tokyo: Yūseidō, 1986.

Natsume Kinnosuke. *Sōseki zenshū* [Collected Works of Natsume Sōseki], vol. 16. Tokyo: Iwanami Shoten, 2019, facsimile edition.

Nishiyama Matsunosuke. *Edo Culture: Daily Life and Diversions in Urban Japan, 1600–1868*. translated and edited by Gerald Groemer. Honolulu: University of Hawai'i Press, 1997, https://doi.org/10.1515/9780824862299.

Orwell, George. "Lear, Tolstoy and the Fool." 1947. In *George Orwell: Selected Essays*, edited by Stefan Collini, 260–75. Oxford: Oxford University Press, 2021.

Poch, Daniel. *Licentious Fictions and the Nineteenth-Century Japanese Novel*. New York: Columbia University Press, 2019, https://doi.org/10.7312/poch19370.

Possnett, Hutcheson M. *Comparative Literature*. London: Kegan Paul, Trench & Co., 1886.

Quiller-Couch, Sir Arthur, and John Dover Wilson, eds. *The New Shakespeare: The Tempest*. 1921. Cambridge: Cambridge University Press, 1969.

Reider, Noriko T. *Tales of the Supernatural in Early Modern Japan: Kaidan, Akinari, Ugetsu Monogatari*. New York: Edwin Mellen Press, 2002.

Sadoya Shigenobu. *Tsubouchi Shōyō – dentōshugisha no kōzu* [Tsubouchi Shōyō: The Making of a Traditionalist]. Tokyo: Meiji Shoin, 1983.

Saeki Junko. "From *Iro* (Eros) to *Ai=Love*: The Case of Tsubouchi Shōyō." In *Translation in Modern Japan*, translated and edited by Indra Levy, 73–101. Abingdon, Oxon: Routledge, 2016, https://doi.org/10.4324/9781315084602-5.

Saitō Mino. "Morita Shiken." In *Nihon no honyaku ron: ansorojī to kaidai* [An Anthology of Japanese Translation Studies], edited by Yanabu Akira, Naganuma Mikako, and Mizuno Akira, 89–90. Tokyo: Hōsei University Press, 2010.

Satō Isao. "Hishō bungaku" [Comparative Literature]. In *Tsubouchi Shōyō jiten* (1986), 305.

———. *Tsubouchi Shōyō ni okeru Doraiden juyō no kenkyū – tōyō to seiyō ni okeru hikaku bungaku no genten* [Shōyō and Dryden: A Focus for Literary Comparison between East and West]. Tokyo: Hokuseidō Shoten, 1981.

Shōyō Kyōkai, ed. *Shōyō senshū* [Selected Works of Tsubouchi Shōyō], 17 vols. (1927–8; reprinted with 5 supplementary volumes). Tokyo: Daiichi Shobō, 1977–8.

———, ed. *Tsubouchi Shōyō jiten* [Dictionary of Tsubouchi Shōyō Studies]. Tokyo: Heibonsha, 1986.

Suzuki Sadami. *The Concept of Literature in Japan*. translated by Royall Tyler. Kyoto: International Research Center for Japanese Studies, 2006. Originally published as *Nihon no "bungaku" gainen*. Tokyo: Sakuhinsha, 1998.

Thornbury, Barbara E. *Sukeroku's Double Identity: The Dramatic Structure of Edo Kabuki*. Ann Arbor: University of Michigan Center for Japanese Studies, 1982.

Tolstoy, Leo. *Tolstoy on Shakespeare: A Critical Essay on Shakespeare*. 1906. translated by Vladimir Tchertkoff. Glasgow: Good Press, 2022.

Tomasi, Massimiliano. *Rhetoric in Modern Japan: Western Influences on the Development of Narrative and Oratorical Style*. Honolulu: University of Hawai'i Press, 2004, https://doi.org/10.1515/9780824840570.

Torigoe Bunzō, ed. *Chikamatsu Monzaemon shū* [Works of Chikamatsu Monzaemon], vol. 2. Tokyo: Shōgakukan, 1975.

Toyoda Minoru. *Shakespeare in Japan: An Historical Survey*. Tokyo: Iwanami Shoten, 1940.

Tschudin, Jean-Jacques. "Danjūrō's *Katsureki-Geki* (Realistic Theatre) and the Meiji 'Theatre Reform' Movement." *Japan Forum* 11, no. 1 (1999): 83–94, https://doi.org/10.1080/09555809908721623.

Tsubouchi Shikō. *Tsubouchi Shōyō kenkyū* [Studies in Tsubouchi Shōyō]. Tokyo: Waseda University Press, 1953.

Tsubouchi Shōyō, trans. "Antonī to Kureopatora" [Antony and Cleopatra]. 1915. In *Shōyō senshū*, vol. 5, 1–213, 1977.

———. "Azusa miko" [The Catalpa Bow Shaman]. 1891. In *Shōyō senshū*, vol. 8, 143–82, 1977.

———. "Chikamatsu tai Shēkusupia tai Ipusen" [Chikamatsu as Compared with Shakespeare and Ibsen]. 1909. In *Shōyō senshū*, vol. 10, 769–813. translated by Matsumoto Ryōzō in Matsumoto Ryōzō, 207–39, 1977.

———, trans. "Henrī yonsei dainibu" [King Henry IV, Part 2]. 1919. In *Shōyō senshū*, vol. 4, 477–659, 1977.

———. "Honan ni tsukite" [On Adaptation]. 1885. In *Shōyō senshū*, vol. 2, 717–8, 1977.

———, trans. "Ishaku hōshaku" [Measure for Measure]. 1918. In *Shōyō senshū*, vol. 5, 215–393, 1977.

———, trans. *Ishaku hōshaku* [Measure for Measure]. Tokyo: Chūō Kōronsha, 1933.

———. "Iwayuru atarashii onna" [The So-Called "New Woman"]. 1912. In *Shōyō senshū*, vol. 8, 211–372, 1977.

———, trans. "Jajauma narashi" [The Taming of the Shrew]. 1920. In *Shōyō senshū*, vol. 4, 661–824, 1977.

———. "Jibun no honyaku ni tsuite" [About My Shakespeare Translations]. 1928. In *Shōyō senshū*, supplementary vol. 5, 254–77, 1977.

————. "Kaioku mandan" [Recollections]. 1925–6. In *Shōyō senshū*, vol. 12, 341–72, 1977.

————. *Kansai no senjōteki higeki* [Sensational Tragedies of Kansai]. Tokyo: Shunjūsha, 1933.

————, trans. *Makubesu* [Macbeth]. Tokyo: Chūō Kōronsha, 1935.

————. "'*Makubesu* hyōshaku' no shogen" [Preface to a Commentary on *Macbeth*]. 1891. In *Shōyō senshū*, supplementary vol. 3, 161–9, 1978.

————, trans. "*Manatsu no yo no yume*" [A Midsummer Night's Dream]. 1915. In *Shōyō senshū*, vol. 4, 171–304.

————. "Nihon de enzuru *Hamuretto*" [Performing *Hamlet* in Japan]. 1907. In *Sheikusupia kenkyū shiryō shūsei* [Research Materials on the Reception of Shakespeare in Japan], vol. 2, edited by Sasaki Takashi, 196–202. Tokyo: Nihon Tosho Centre, 1997.

————. "Shēkusupiya atto randamu" [Shakespeare at Random]. 1931. In *Shōyō senshū*, supplementary vol. 5, 279–373, 1978.

————. "Shēkusupiya kenkyū shiori" [A Companion to Shakespeare Studies]. 1928. In *Shōyō senshū*, supplementary vol. 5, 1–277, 1977.

————. "Shōsetsu shinzui" [The Essence of the Novel]. 1885–6. In *Tsubouchi Shōyō shū* (1969), 3–58. translated by Nanette Twine, *Occasional Papers* 11 (Department of Japanese, University of Queensland, 1981), electronic edition, accessed 23 October 2023, http://archive.nyu.edu/html.2451/14945/shoyo.htm.

————. "Soko shirazu no mizuumi" [The Bottomless Lake]. 1891. In *Tsubouchi Shōyō shū*, 279–82, 1969.

————, trans. *Taitasu Andoronikasu* [Titus Andronicus]. Tokyo: Waseda University Press, 1926.

————, trans. "Temupesuto" [The Tempest]. 1915. In *Shōyō senshū*, vol. 4, 1–169, 1977.

————. "Torusutoi tai Shēkusupiya" [Tolstoy contra Shakespeare]. 1907. In *Sheikusupia kenkyū shiryō shūsei* [Research Materials on the Reception of Shakespeare in Japan], vol. 2, edited by Sasaki Takashi, 238–46. Tokyo: Nihon Tosho Centre, 1997.

————. "Waga kuni no shigeki" [Historical Drama of Japan]. 1893–4. In *Tsubouchi Shōyō shū*, 287–315, 1969.

Tsubouchi Yūzō [Shōyō]. *Eishibun hyōshaku* [Introduction to English Poetry]. Tokyo: Waseda University Press, 1902.

————. "Shakespeare and Chikamatsu." 1916. In *A Book of Homage to Shakespeare*, edited by Israel Gollancz and Gordon McMullan, 543–6. Oxford: Oxford University Press, 2016.

Tsuno Kaitarō. *Kokkeina kyojin – Tsubouchi Shōyō no yume* [Comic Giant: The Dream of Tsubouchi Shōyō]. Tokyo: Heibonsha, 2002.

Ueda Atsuko. *Concealment of Politics, Politics of Concealment: The Production of "Literature" in Meiji Japan*. Stanford, CA: Stanford University Press, 2007, https://doi.org/10.1515/9781503626898.

————. "Sounds, Scripts, and Styles: *Kanbun Kundokutai* and the National Language Reforms of 1880s Japan." In *Translation in Modern Japan*, edited by Indra Levy, 141–64. Abingdon, Oxon: Routledge, 2016, https://doi.org/10.4324/9781315084602-9.

Walker, Keith, ed. *John Dryden: The Major Works*. Oxford: Oxford University Press, 2003.

Walley, Glynne. "Translator's Introduction." In Kyokutei [Takizawa] Bakin, *Eight Dogs, Or, "Hakkenden": An Ill-Considered Jest*, translated by Glynne Walley, xi–xlv. Ithaca, NY: Cornell University East Asia Program, 2021, https://doi.org/10.1515/9781501755194-003.

Woudhuysen, Henry R., ed. *Samuel Johnson on Shakespeare*. London: Penguin Books, 1989.

Yano Hōjin. "Tsubouchi Shōyō to bungaku kyōiku" [Tsubouchi Shōyō and Literary Education]. *Tsubouchi Shōyō Kenkyū Shiryō* 1 (September 1969): 1–12.

# 3 A Voice for Shakespeare in Modern Japan

The presence of Shōyō's "voice" in his Shakespeare translations is defined by what he calls the "two poles" of his translating style, namely the "rhythm" (*chōshi*) and "warmth" (*jōmi*) of Shakespeare's language from which they are derived.[1] Shōyō understands the importance of rhythm from his native literature in generating momentum across the line and creating meaningful patterns and correspondences that can extend across a whole play. It also carries considerable cultural capital, being associated with particular genres and writers and promoting communication within a society. He refers, for example, to Bakin-*chō*, namely the rhythmic style and prosody of the early nineteenth-century novelist Takizawa Bakin, as a rhythm that he might imitate in his translations, but at the same time is bound to consider how audiences will respond to such a style and what its usage will say about the original texts. For the same reason, he is concerned that the use of *shichigochō*, the seven-five syllabic meter common to kabuki, may support a misleading equivalence between Shakespeare and kabuki.

Warmth is a more nebulous concept than rhythm. As I have suggested, Shōyō may sometimes confuse his personal response with Shakespeare's rhetoric, but warmth is a trope for the power of that rhetoric to provoke in him a heightened awareness of the flux of his individual reality, and together with rhythm is therefore a basic emanation of what he regards as Shakespeare's "hiddenness," and resonates as such through his translation choices. He is drawn to any kind of stylistic diversity that expresses that flux and to striking words and turns of phrase that assert the uniqueness and individuality of another's character or situation. He writes that

> language corresponds to every type of class and character of man. The same content may vary in style of expression according to person, time, situation, and temperament. How Shakespeare's characters speak depends on class, character, occupation, upbringing, locality, gender, and age. He can be both fearfully funny and fearfully direct. He has a courteous side to him as well, and an artlessness. He can be both articulate and inarticulate, gentle yet intrusive, noble yet intimate, valiant, magnanimous, flippant, sincere, and natural. Shakespeare's pen delves into the heart of all things, and yet he is also skilled at mixing these styles, at weaving them together poetically, musically, and mellifluously, in a way that is pleasing to be heard.[2]

DOI: 10.4324/9781003293774-3

Translation is always to some extent an abasement of the source, whether by exaggeration or reduction, especially if the source is Shakespeare.[3] However hard Shōyō may try to reproduce Shakespeare's stylistic diversity and felicity, he must also respect his modernising culture's demand for communicative and narrative flow, since to deny the latter risks both compromising Shakespeare's realism and reverting to the hierarchy of *ga* and *zoku*, i.e. "refined" and "vulgar" (even if that hierarchy is sometimes present in Shakespeare). Within this matrix of a metaphorical warmth that may tend to obscurity and a metonymic rhythm that risks glibness, this chapter surveys a range of techniques characteristic of Shōyō's translating style.

### The Potential of Seven-Five Syllabic Meter

Shōyō's use of syllabic meter is central, for example, to the argument about kabuki stylisation in his Shakespeare translations, because it is the meter of the narrative sections of kabuki and *jōruri* drama and is frequently heard in dialogue and chanted sections as well. Yet quite apart from his wish to create out of Shakespeare translation a drama that is distinct from native genres, Shōyō also wants to avoid a naïve correlation of *shichigochō* with iambic pentameter and other Shakespearean meters, writing that "the limp rhythms of seven-five meter are quite incapable of conveying the energy and crackle of the original text," that "the narrative style [of *jōruri* and kabuki] is too verbose," and more generally that

> the rhythms of Shakespeare are considerably loftier than those of Chikamatsu, more diverse and profound, and thus the language of Chikamatsu is insufficient in itself for translating Shakespeare.[4]

We need to examine the function of *shichigochō* in kabuki texts as Shōyō's main point of reference, the extent to which he actually does use the meter in his translations, and the extent to which it is empty and redundant or else an active and meaningful ingredient in shaping and interpreting the line, even in the way that Shakespeare's meters work.

Fives and sevens are used in a limited number of combinations, usually five-seven, seven-five, and seven-seven, and are said to sound poetic because of their historical normative function in Japanese poetry and drama and their natural frequency in the spoken language; a distinction is made between the more forceful, rising poetic of five-seven meter (*goshichichō*) and the softer, more graceful quality of seven-fives. Similar to stress-based meter in English, the repetitive use of this meter generates a sense of momentum, regularity, and expectation, with one phrase leading into the next, while the contrast between long and short creates various opportunities for semantic contrasts. Against the tendency of Shakespeare's prosody to establish connections between ideas and images, syllabic meter is less associative, serving more to articulate the inner qualities of what is being said.[5]

Chikamatsu offers numerous examples of the potential of *shichigochō* for refined dramatic effects. The consistent use of the meter in the following excerpt, which is the opening of the final scene of *Sonezaki shinjū* in which the lovers Tokubei and Ohatsu make their final journey towards their double suicide, contrasts heightened feelings of dramatic excitement and poetic remorse.[6] The tolling of the temple bell sets the tone of a scene in which every moment and every syllable count:

NARRATOR.

Kono yo no nagori. [7] Yoru mo nagori. [6 with pause]
*Farewell to this world, and to the night farewell.*
Shini ni yuku mi wo [7] tatoureba [7]
*We who walk the road to death, to what shall we be likened?*
adashi ga hara no [7] michi no shimo. [5]
*To the frost by the road that leads to the graveyard,*
Hitoashi zutsu ni [7] kiete yuku. [5]
*Vanishing with each step we take ahead:*
Yume no yume koso [7] awarenare. [5]
*How sad is this dream of a dream!*

TOKUBEI.

Are kazoereba [7] akatsuki no. [5]
*Ah, did you count the bell? Of the seven strokes*
Nanatsu no toki ga [7] muttsu narite [5]
*That mark the dawn, six have sounded.*
nokoru hitotsu ga [7] konjō no. [5]
*The remaining one will be the last echo*
Kane no hibiki no [7] kiki osame. [5]
*We shall hear in this life.*

OHATSU.

Jakumetsu iraku [7]

OHATSU./TOKUBEI.

to hibiku nari. [6 with pause]
*It will echo the bliss of nirvana.*

The energy of the meter comes from the alternation of the sevens and fives and continuation of each seven into a five to complete the phrase. The metrical perfection of this particular excerpt makes it a fine example of the heightened romantic style of Chikamatsu *jōruri* and kabuki that Shōyō found attractive, ending on a harmonious double seven. Chikamatsu's romanticism is primarily his idealisation of love in death through the totality of his literary and dramatic technique, including the use of chant and *shamisen* accompaniment, but quite apart from his dramatic skill (and possibly influenced by his reading of English poetry) Shōyō regards Chikamatsu as a fine lyrical poet who appeals to sight and sound. The challenge of translating Shakespeare in the style of Chikamatsu is mainly that of transposing Shakespeare's often long and complex phrases and sentences into shorter, if musically denser, syllabic groupings.[7] Yet *shichigochō* is not only the prosody of classical drama but also the meter Shōyō adopts in some of his own dramatic writing; for example, the mellifluous opening chant of *Shinkyoku Urashima* (New Musical Drama Urashima, 1904),[8] which Ueda Bin praised for its poetic beauty:[9]

> Yose kaeru [5] kamiyo nagara no [7] oto no nami, [5] chiri ni yō toki [7] shirabe kana. [5]
> *Oh, the divine melody the waves sing, rising and falling unceasingly since the age of the gods.*

This first line is in the style of Noh *utai*, but most of the ensuing lines are either spoken or chanted in the typical styles of kabuki or *jōruri*, most commonly the operatic *nagauta* style in kabuki dance drama,[10] and these are consistently in seven-five meter. As in Chikamatsu, even quite ordinary dialogue can be written in this meter, as when Urashima's parents worry where their son has got to:[11]

> Ano yūgetsu no [7] honomeku kage no [7] nokoru uchi, [5] kaeraba [4] koko ni machi [5] tomokaku mo [5] ima ichido [5] satoite miru me [7] hana saku ka. [5] Tada uki miru ka. [7] Kari no yo wa [5] oyako no enishi [7] usu akari. [5]

FATHER.
I'll wait until the moon sets, and if he returns then because of you, I shall see him one more time.
MOTHER.
Just one last time . . .
FATHER.
I will tell him what I have to say, and we shall see if that has any effect.
BOTH.
We cannot tell.
CHANT (*takemoto*).[12]
The line connecting sons with their parents in this ephemeral world is a feeble one indeed.

In this example, we see how the longer seven syllabic suits the parents' heightened angry tone, but that it subsides sadly into a five as the father admits – *usu akari* – their lack of actual control over their son.

Syllabic meter comes naturally to a musical drama like *Shinkyoku Urashima* where most of the lines are chanted, and the musical styles borrowed from kabuki determine how the language is to be spoken and chanted. It is also a feature of *kōdan*, the traditional genre of oral storytelling that was revived in the Meiji era and relevant both to Shōyō's rather cerebral style of reciting Shakespearean texts (discussed at the beginning of Chapter 4) and to his style of lecturing on Shakespeare in which he quoted liberally from his own translations.[13] While the normative matrix of kabuki and *kōdan* is lacking in Shakespeare, *shichigochō* has a clear potential for expressing the shifting moods of Shakespeare's poetic drama, especially those written before 1914 as Shōyō was finding his way towards a more contemporary, less classical style. He uses the meter to translate the opening line of Hamlet's fourth soliloquy, "To be, or not to be," in both the 1909 version and 1933 revision cited here before shifting into a looser medley of syllabics that could nevertheless be elided to sound like *shichigochō* through the actor's vocal modulations (3.1.55–63);[14] this latter possibility (for example, that *aruiwa* could be pronounced *arwiwa*) is indicated with oblique strokes in the square brackets:

> To be, or not to be – that is the question;
> 世に在る、世に在らぬ、それが疑問ぢゃ。
> *Yo ni aru,* [4 with pause] *yo ni aranu,* [5] *sore ga gimon ja.* [7]

> Whether 'tis nobler in the mind to suffer
> The slings and arrows of outrageous fortune
> 残忍な運命の矢や石投を、只菅堪へ忍んでをるが男子の本意か、
> *Zanninna* [5] *unmei no* [5] *ya ya ishinage wo,* [7] *hitasura tae* [6/7] *shi-nonde oru ga* [7] *danshi no hon'i ka,* [8 with pause/7]

> Or to take arms against a sea of troubles
> 或は海なす艱難を逆へ撃って、
> *aruiwa umi nasu* [8/7] *kannan wo* [5] *mukaeutte,*[15] [6 with pause]

> And by opposing end them; to die: to sleep –
> 戦うて根を絶つが大丈夫の志か？死は . . . ねむり . . .
> *tatakaute* [5] *ne wo tatsu ga* [5] *daijōbu no* [6/5] *kokorozashi ka?* [six with question mark] *Shi wa . . .* [2] *nemuri . . .* [3]

> No more, and by a sleep to say we end
> に過ぎぬ。眠って心の痛みが去り、
> *ni suginu.* [4 with pause] *Nemutte kokoro no* [8/7] *itami ga sari,* [6 with pause]

> The heartache and the thousand natural shocks
> That flesh is heir to: 'tis a consummation
> Devoutly to be wished.
> 此肉に附纏うてをる千百の苦が除かるゝものならば . . . それこそ
>    上もなう願はしい大終焉ぢゃが。
> *kono niku ni* [5] *tsukimatoute oru* [8/7] *senbyaku no* [5] *kurushimi ga* [5] *nozokaruru* [5] *mono naraba* [5] . . . *Sore koso ue mo* [7] *nō nega-washii* [7] *daishūen ja ga.* [8/7] . . . .

Reading Shōyō's translation, we sense (as I have suggested) that Shakespeare's sentences are simply too long and expansive to support a strict use of the meter. The first line is like the lines in the Chikamatsu excerpt, setting one idea or image against another – "To be, or not to be"/"Farewell to this night, and to the night fare-well." – but it is clear from the rising syllabic of two fives leading to a seven and for the emphasis the rise places on *sore* ("that") that the syllabic will occur just the once and instead function as a metonym for rising emotion (the emotion that arises from indecision), and that this rising movement will recur throughout the speech, as in *Sore koso ue mo naru negawashii daishūen ja ga*, "a consummation devoutly to be wished." Moreover, the conventional syllabic at the beginning creates an expectation that Hamlet is about to say something of great significance, and this expectation is sustained through the movement of phrases towards choice rhythmical expressions such as *ya ya ishinage* ("slings and arrows"), *negawashii daishūen*, *Sore ga kokorogakari ja* ("there's the rub," 64), *shinonde orō zo* ("who would bear," 69), *Yo no ryōgyaku* ("whips . . . of time"), *nukoi no setsunasa* ("pangs of . . . love," 71), *saiban no modokashisa* ("the law's delay"), and *kono iyana yo ni, ase wo nagashite* ("sweat under a weary life," 76).[16]

In Shōyō's translations generally, the preponderance of final particles such as *ja* and *zo* and auxiliary verbs like *oru* can seem surplus to the line; there are plenty of those in this speech too, but they are effectively contained by the diction and metrical shifts. The diction is shaped by Hamlet's imaginative trajectory (life's "calamities" leading into the prospect of life after death), which in the translation is shaped by a repetitive series of noun phrases, for example *ryōshin ga* ("conscience," 82) and *hito wo okubyō mono ni* ("cowards of us all"). Repetition also generates rhythm in the phrase *ogoru yatsubara no ōhei* ("the arrogance of arrogant people") for "the proud man's contumely" (70), and Shōyō takes a liberty translating "time" in "whips . . . of time" (69) as *yo*, where *yo* literally means "world" echoing the *yo* in the first line.

Shōyō comments that a literary style is appropriate where "Shakespeare's structures are controlled more by grammar," implying that such a style will inevitably foreground the formal features of the line.[17] Hamlet's soliloquy is figurative but not grammatically complex; the feeling of control comes not so much from the language as from the dilemma in which the protagonist finds himself. Shōyō's use of syllabic meter is mainly a stylistic choice, but it may also be a metonym for a recognisable conflict between tradition and modernity in which Hamlet's rather wayward use of sevens and fives reflect a reluctant acceptance of a code (or "grammar") of honourable revenge and suicide associated with that meter in kabuki. It initiates a conversation among Shōyō's late Meiji audiences just as it does in Hamlet's mind.

A more strictly conventional use of *shichigochō* occurs in Shōyō's version of Ariel's song "Full fathom five" in *The Tempest* (1.2.397–405):[18]

> Full fathom five thy father lies,
> Of his bones are coral made;
> Those are pearls that were his eyes,
> Nothing of him that doth fade
> But doth suffer a sea-change
> Into something rich and strange.

Sea-nymphs hourly ring his knell.
Ding dong.
Hark, now I hear them.
Ding dong bell.

五尋深き水底に、
　御父上は臥したまふ。
　御骨は珊瑚、眞珠こそ
　その以前君が御龍眼。
　御體の一切朽ちもせて、
　寶と化しぬ海に入りて。
聞かずや海の女神等が
　　　ディーン・ドーン！
あれ々、君を弔ふ鐘！
　　ディーン・ドーン、ベルゝ！

*Itsuhiro fukaki* [7] *minazoko ni,* [5]
*Onchichiue wa* [7] *fushi tamau.* [5]
*Mihone wa sango,* [7] *shinju koso* [5]
*Sono kami kimi ga* [7] *onmanako.* [5]
*Gyotai no nabete* [7] *kuchi mosete,* [5]
*Takara to kashinu* [7] *umi ni irite.* [7]
*Kikazu ya umi no* [7] *megamira ga* [5]
*Dīn dōn!*
*Are are, kimi wo tomurau kane!*
*Dīn dōn, beruru!*

This is a more classical style of syllabic that loosely contrasts sevens to do with scale and authority with more subordinate fives: "five fathoms" (*itsuhiro*) with the "bottom of the sea" (*minazoko*), "respected father" (*onchichiue*) with "lying prone" (*fushi tamau*), "bones" (*mihone*) and "coral" (*sango*) with "pearls" (*shinju*), and so on. As the meter of classical Japanese poetry as well as drama, the syllabic suits the remarkable lyricism of Ariel's song, and with its imagery of nymphs, treasure, and plunging into the sea hints erotically at the meeting between Ferdinand and Miranda that is to follow.[19] As in Hamlet's soliloquy, the syllabic frames the more emotional and disordered dialogue between the two young people in which Ferdinand finds another kind of treasure.

Another model mentioned by Shōyō is that of Bakin-*chō*, the pacey syllabic style associated with the novelist Takizawa Bakin that was in popular use up to the 1880s. In the following example from Bakin's most famous work, *Nansō Satomi hakkenden* (The Eight Dog Chronicles, 1814–42), the syllabic meter is light in tone, supporting a rapid accumulation of narrative details and the inclusion of speech, dialogue, and quotation:[20]

Ori kara tsuguru [7] yakoe no [4/5] niwatori ni, [5] Shino wa kokoro, wo [7]
"Oku no ma naru, [6/7] nishin mezamashi [7] tamawanan. [5] Toku toku."

[4/5] To isogashi [5] tatsureba, [5] Hamaji wa yōyaku [8/7] tachiagari, [5] "Yo mo akeba [6/7] kitsu ni hamenan [7] kudakake no, [5] madaki nakite [6/7] sena wo yaritsutsu." [7] Sore wa koi seshi [7] kusamakura, [5] sore wa tabi yuku [7] imose no wakare, [7] tori mo nakazu wa [7] yo mo akeji, [5] yakezu wa hito no [7] me mo sameji. [5] Urameshi no [5] tori no ne ya. [5] Yo ni Ausaka no [7] afu yoi wa ara de, [8/7] yurusanu seki wa [7] waga ue ni, [5] ariake no tsuki zo [8/7] haka naki.' [4/5]

*Outside, roosters began to crow, and Shino grew anxious. "Your parents in the back room," he said, "they'll be waking up any moment. Hurry! Hurry!"*
    *At last Hamaji stood up. As she did, she recited a poem:*

*When dawn comes*
*I'll feed them to a fox,*
*the damn roosters –*
*though it's still dark,*
*they've made my lover leave.*

*"If the roosters hadn't crowed, dawn wouldn't have come. And if dawn hadn't come, people wouldn't be waking up. I hate the sound of their crowing. No night will ever hide us and allow us to meet again."*

This is a lively, resourceful prosody that moves easily between the pragmatism of the narrative (the couple's rude awakening) and the *ga* aesthetic of the moon at dawn, and the rhythmic momentum of the syllabic can be said to embody a remorseless logic of cause and effect. Shōyō admits to having been "intoxicated" with Bakin's writing as a youth,[21] and its restlessness suggests a parallel with Shakespeare's history plays, since in comparing the history plays to Bakin and Bakin's contemporary, the comic novelist Shikitei Sanba, in the preface to his translation of *Henry IV*, Part 2, Shōyō finds the former "strangely close in spirit" to his Meiji sensibility: Shakespeare's historical characters have a "self-awareness" lacking in a work like *Hakkenden* where, if anything, the characters are in constant retreat from their selves.[22] Yet one reason for avoiding Bakin-*chō* in his translations is that as poetic prose the continuous feeling of tension imposed by the syllabic meter projects onto readers a simultaneous struggle with inner passions and desires – what Daniel Poch calls "their inner dog,"[23] or the reality that "desire continually resurges from within a sphere of benevolence"[24] – that is not necessarily the effect of Shakespearean prosody, whose momentum is orchestrated across the line as an imitation of internal thought processes. This possibility may be more subliminal than overt: Glynne Walley mentions Bakin's relatively "unobtrusive" use of *shichigochō*, arguing that "for the reader unconcerned with such things, the metrical sections are experienced merely as passages of particularly intense or lovely (and perhaps difficult to parse) description."[25] Shōyō may hear all kinds of echoes of that style in Shakespearean drama; his problem is more the didactic ends to which Bakin's seductive language is heading.

Shōyō contrasts Bakin's "fluid" usage of *shichigochō* with Chikamatsu's "neutral" style,[26] implying that Bakin lacks the Shakespearean impartiality he finds in Chikamatsu's *sewamono*, but Shōyō's own style is always mixed, relying on multiple literary models, and the relative freedom of Bakin's syllabic (his frequent use of eight and six pairings as well as traditional sevens and fives) makes it an attractive resource. One straightforward parallel with the prior excerpt presents itself in the scene from *Romeo and Juliet* where the lovers are separated by the dawn after their marriage night (3.5.1–16):[27]

> JULIET.
>> Wilt thou be gone? It is not yet near day.
>> It was the nightingale, and not the lark,
>> That pierced the fearful hollow of thine ear.
>> Nightly she sings on yond pomegranate tree.
>> Believe me, love, it was the nightingale.

> 逝うとや？夜はまだ明きやせぬのに、怖つてござるお前の耳に
> 聞えたは雲雀ではなうてナイチンゲールであつたもの。夜毎に
> 彼處の柘榴へ來てあのやうに囀りをる。なあ、今のは一定ナイ
> チンゲールであらうぞ。

> *Inou to ya?* [5] *Yo wa mada* [4] *akyasenu no ni.* [6/7] *Kowagatte* [5] *gozaru omae no* [7] *mimi ni kikoeta wa* [8/7] *hibari dewa nōte* [8/7] *naichingēru* [7] *de atta mono.* [6/7] *Yogoto ni asoko no* [8] *jakuro e kite,* [6] *ano yō ni* [5] *saezuri oru.* [6/7]. *Nā, ima no wa kitto* [7] *naichingēru* [7] *de arou zo.* [5]

> ROMEO.
>> It was the lark, the herald of the morn,
>> No nightingale. Look, love, what envious streaks
>> Do lace the severing clouds in yonder east.
>> Night's candles are burnt out, and jocund day
>> Stands tiptoe on the misty mountain tops.
>> I must be gone and live, or stay and die.

> いやいや、且を知らする雲雀ぢや、ナイチンゲールの聲ではな
> い。戀人よ、あれ、お見やれ、意地の惡い横縞めが東の空の雲
> の裂目にあのやうな縁附けをる。夜の燭火は燃え盡きて、嬉し
> げな且めが霧立つ山の巓に足を爪立てゝ立つてゐる。速う往ね
> ば命助かり、停まれば死なねばならぬ。

> *Iya iya,* [4/5] *asa wo shirasuru* [7] *hibari ja,* [4/5] *naichingēru* [7] *no koe dewa nai.* [7] *Koibito yo,* [5] *are miyare,* [5] *iji no warui* [6] *yoko-jimame ga* [6] *higashi no sora no* [7] *sakeme ni ano yōna* [8] *heri wo tsuke oru.* [7] *Yoru no tomoshibi wa* [8] *moetsukite,* [6/7] *ureshigena*

[5] *ashitame ga* [5] *kiri tatsu yama no* [7] *itadaki ni* [5] *mō ashi wo*
[5] *tsuma datete* [5] *tatte iru.* [5] *Hayō inureba* [7] *inochi tasukari,* [7]
*todomareba* [5] *shinaneba naranu.* [7]

JULIET.
    Yond light is not daylight; I know it, I.
    It is some meteor that the sun exhales
    To be to thee this night a torchbearer
    And light thee on thy way to Mantua.
    Therefore stay yet; thou need'st not to be gone.

あの光明は朝ぢやない、いえいえ、朝日ではないわいの。あり
や太陽がお前の爲に、今宵マンチュアへの道案内に炬火持の役
さしよとて、急に呼出いた光り物ぢや。ぢやによつて大事な
い、まだ逝しやるには及ばぬわいの。

*Ano hikari wa* [6/7] *asa ja nai,* [5] *ie ie,* [4/5] *asahi dewa* [5] *nai wai*
*no.* [5] *Arya taiyō ga* [7] *omae no tame ni,* [7] *koyoi Manchua e* [8/7]
*no michishirabe ni* [7] *taimatsumochi no* [7] *yaku sasho tote,* [6/7] *kyu*
*ni yobidashita* [7] *hikarimono ja.* [6/7] *Ja ni yotte,* [5] *daiji nai,* [5]
*mada inasharu ni wa* [7] *oyobanu wai no.* [7]

This is a heightened style that matches the couple's vitality with the movement of the Bakin line: read syllabically, more melancholy expressions such as *Inou to ya?* ("Wilt thou be gone?") seem like natural fives, and brighter phrasings such as *asa wo shirasuru* ("the herald of the morn") are sevens. Juliet is also strikingly assertive in her use of the masculine particles *wai* and *zo*, and the classical *nu* negative characteristic of Shōyō's style with which Romeo and Juliet end the second and third speeches (each saying "no" for their different reasons) carries an erotic frisson.

## The Shōyō Line

What might be called the "Shōyō line" is not the seven-five prosody of Chikamatsu or Bakin but is more loosely based on syllabic meter in the way that its energy comes from syllabic breaks and the contrast of shorter phrases with longer ones. In Shakespeare, the emphasis is usually on thematic content rather than narrative detail, and likewise Shōyō tends to emphasise significant words (often nouns) in a sentence and phrase. One example is that of Prospero's soliloquy on "the great globe itself" (4.1.146–58) in his *Tempest* translation.[28]

    Shōyō's is not conventionally syllabic, and the positions of syllabic breaks between phrases may be difficult to justify, but as indicated in the first three blocks of the transcript the prosody hovers around the seven grouping, and may sometimes be exactly seven-five or five-seven; this technique can be tentatively described as an abstraction of *shichigochō*. The words are not stressed in the manner of Shakespeare's English, but what Shōyō calls the "musicality" of the lines arises noticeably from tensions between short vowels and double vowels, diphthongs and double consonants, as in *kono daichikyū sono mono mo* ("the great globe itself"), where the diphthong and double vowel in *daichikyū* ("great globe") create a slight hiatus that is met by the rush of short *o* morae in the next three words, *sono mono mo* (the "thing itself"). The likely emphases in phrases within the last three blocks are also indicated:

You do look, my son, in a moved sort,
As if you were dismayed. Be cheerful, sir.
ああ、婿どの、きつう駭いて氣を揉んでゐなさるやうぢゃが、
　　何も心配には及ばん。
*Ā*, [3] *muko dono, kitsū* [7] *odoroite ki wo* [7] *monde inasaru* [7] *yō ja ga,*
　　[5] *nanimo shinpai* [7] *ni wa oyoban.* [7]

Our revels now are ended.
餘興はもう濟んだのぢゃ。
*Nagusami wa* [5] *mō sunda no ja.* [7]

These our actors,
As I foretold you, were all spirits and
Are melted into air, into thin air;
あの俳優共は、豫て話しておいた通り、みんな精靈ぢゃによって、
　　空氣の中へ、薄い空氣の中へ、溶け込んでしまうた。
*Ano yakushadomo wa,* [9] *kanete hanashite* [7] *oita tōri,* [7] *minna seirei*
　　[7] *ja ni yotte,* [5] *kūki no naka e,* [7] *usui* [3] *kūki no naka e,* [7] *toke-*
　　*konde* [5] *shimouta.* [5]

And – like the baseless fabric of this vision –
ああ、此幻影の、礎もない假建物と同じやうに、
*Ā, kono maboroshi no, ishizue mo nai karidatemono to onaji yō ni,*

The cloud-capped towers, the gorgeous palaces,
The solemn temples, the great globe itself,
あの雲に沖る棲臺も、あの輪奐たる宮殿も、あの莊嚴なる堂塔も、
　　此大地球其者も、
*ano kumo ni hiiru rōdai mo, ano rinkantaru kyūden mo, ano sōgon naru*
　　*dōtō mo, kono daichikyū sono mono mo,*

Yea, all which it inherit, shall dissolve,
いや、此地上に有りとあらゆる物一切が、やがては悉く溶解して、
*iya, kono chijō ni ari to arayuru mono issai ga, yagate wa kotogotoku*
　　*yōkai shite,*

And like this insubstantial pageant faded,
Leave not a rack behind.

今消え去った彼の幻影と同様に、後には泡沫をも殘さぬのぢゃ。
*ima kiesatta ano maboroshi to dōyō ni, ato ni wa hōmatsu wo mo nokos-anu no ja.*

> We are such stuff
> As dreams are made on, and our little life
> Is rounded with a sleep.

吾々は夢と同じ品柄で出來てゐる、吾々の瑣小な一生は、眠りに
始まって眠りに終る。
*Wareware wa yume to onaji shinagara de dekite iru, wareware no sasaya-kana isshō wa, nemuri ni hajimatte nemuri ni owaru.*

Shōyō's line is essentially an imitation of the flow or continuity of the Shake-spearean line, in this case between the materiality of objects (e.g., buildings) and the reality of change that is represented by verbs such as "end" and "melt." He deploys a range of techniques, including contrasts between long and short phrases and syllables, euphony, flexible word order, deixis (the pronouns *kono* and *ano*, "this" and "that"), and the use of particles. Since there are no definite or indefinite articles in Japanese and even demonstrative pronouns such as *kono* and *ano* are avoided, Shōyō's use of *kono* and *ano* eight times in this short speech gives it a highly theatrical flavour, taking its cue from the phrase "These our actors." The phrase *nanimo shinpai ni wa oyoban* is an elaborate rendition of a phrase mean-ing "Don't worry" (with *nanimo* reassuringly emphatic, "no need to worry"); the particle *wa* is not grammatically essential but allows the phrase to flow, and the negative construction also makes it sound more detached and poetic. The series of short *a* vowels in *wareware no sasayakana isshō* ("our little life") can sug-gest the congruence of a shared experience, while the diversity of vowels in *ima kiesatta ano maboroshi to dōyō ni* ("like this insubstantial pageant faded") tropes the diversity Shōyō claims to find in Shakespeare. One poetic addition is the verb *hiiru*, written with a character meaning "open sea" (*oki*) as an image of the tow-ers "at sea" among the clouds. One mistake is *shinagara de dekite iru*, where *de* means that human life is made from the same "stuff" as "dreams" rather than generating its content.

What might seem like Chikamatsu about this illustration of Shōyō's style is its sustained musicality; what might seem like Bakin is the accumulation of phrases in the prose medium. There is little wasted, and Shōyō was perhaps thinking of this speech in particular when he wrote in his afterword to the translation that

> Shakespeare's uniqueness lies in his language rather than what he actually says. In the case of *The Tempest* which is half like a musical drama in its style, to disregard its musical qualities would be just as good as killing it. That is the difficulty of translating Shakespearean drama.[29]

Like "To be, or not to be," Prospero's soliloquy is a speech one would expect Shōyō to have wanted to translate with special care. Both speeches are metonyms for the plays in which they are found, the first about the dilemma of action and the second about the theatre of life, and they are also metonyms of Shōyō's broader appreciation of the playwright; Prospero's meditation asserts an ideal of Shakespeare's art that Shōyō probably learnt from Dowden.[30] Whether the relative sonority of these two examples will stand out from their context because Shōyō is less competent at – or less interested in – translating other Shakespearean styles (the prose banter of Stephano and Trinculo, for example) or because they stand out already in the source is a question beyond the scope of this study, but one can certainly examine how the rhetorical techniques discussed earlier are carried over into the translation of dialogue, prose, and so on. In his review of the 1911 *Hamlet*, Sōseki sets his unfavourable view of Shōyō's style against his view that

> Shakespeare's lines, just like Noh and *utai*, have this peculiar rhythm and timbre that must be decisively grasped if one is to sustain an audience's interest. Neglect this point, and one ends up losing both the poetry in a phrase like *seiran kozue wo fukiharatte* ["brushing the treetops with mountain mist"] and the colloquial force of a phrase like *Oi chotto kite kure* ["come here a moment"].[31]

It is unclear whether Sōseki is implying that Shakespeare's language is better suited to translation or adaptation in the Noh genre than the kind of complete translation that Shōyō had attempted as an imitation of kabuki's diversity, or whether he felt that Shōyō had simply not tried hard enough in doing what he did do, but it is a point that Shōyō appears to take seriously as he seeks a more integrated translating style in his final, fifth period.

Caliban's speech to Stephano and Trinculo, "Be not afeard" (3.2.133–45), is a memorable speech that Shōyō translates in a distinctly colloquial and unsonorous style:[32]

CALIBAN.      Art thou afeard?
　　　　　　おのし怖ってるのかい？
　　　　　　*Onoshi kowagatteru no ka?*
STEPHANO.   No, monster, not I.
　　　　　　うんにゃ、俺ァ怖っちゃァゐない。
　　　　　　*Un nya, oreya kowagaccha inai.*
CALIBAN.      Be not afeard.
　　　　　　怖らなくても可いよ。
　　　　　　*Kowagaranakute mo ii yo.*

　　　　　　　The isle is full of noises,
　　　　Sounds and sweet airs that give delight and hurt not.
　　此島にゃァ、常任、音がしてゐて、いろんな聲や美い音色がするけれ
　　　ども、どうもしやァしないや、只面白いばかりだ。
*Kono shima nya, shocchū, oto ga shite ite, ironna koe ya ii neiro ga suru kere-domo, dōmo shā shinai ya, tada omoshiroi bakari da.*

Sometimes a thousand twangling instruments
Will hum about mine ears;
どうかすると、幾つとも知れない道具の音が、俺の耳の傍で、ツワン
ツワンと鳴らァ。

*Dō ka suru to, ikutsu tomo shirenai dōgu no oto ga, ore no mimi no soba de, tsuwan tsuwan to narā.*

      and sometimes voices,
That if I then had waked after long sleep,
Will make me sleep again;
かと思ふと、長ァく眠て起きた後でさへも、又眠たくなるやうな人の
聲が聞えることもあらァ。

*Ka to omou to, nagāku nete okita ato de sae mo, mata nemutaku naru yōna hito no koe ga kikoeru koto mo arā.*

      and then in dreaming,
The clouds, methought, would open and show riches
Ready to drop upon me, that when I waked
I cried to dream again.
さうしていつの間にか夢を見てゐると、空の雲が漸々に開いて、い
ろんな寶物が今にも頭の上へ堕落ちかかるやうになるんだ、で、
俺、目が覺めると、嗚呼、もう一度夢が見たいッて叫くんだ。

*Sōshite itsu no ma ni ka yume wo mite iru to, sora no kumo ga dandan ni aite, ironna takaramono ga ima ni mo atama no ue e okkochi kakaru yō ni narun da, de oreme ga sameru to, ā mō ichido yume ga mitaitte wamekun da.*

STEPHANO.  This will prove a brave kingdom to me, where
I shall have my music for nothing.
*Koitsa sutekina ōkoku da wai, ōsama wa tadamonme de motte ongaku ga kikareru.*
こいつァ素的な王國だわい、王さまは無代で以て音學が聞かれる。

Shōyō chooses to depart from the source in which Caliban, having "learnt" Prospero's language, utters the speech in a version of blank verse, but instead of rendering it in anything like Prospero's elegant style it is in the inflected vernacular that Shōyō adopts for lowlife characters throughout his translations. In the source, each of Caliban's lines except the second ("Sometimes a thousand twangling instruments") contains eleven syllables rather than the ten of iambic pentameter. This extra syllable, which noticeably disrupts the iambic rhythm in lines such as "The clouds, methought, would open and show riches," gives the speech a hybrid texture of poetry and prose that subtly defines Caliban's relationship with the other characters. Caliban stands apart from the symmetries of Prospero's Renaissance world view and finds his being in the natural environment that Prospero has tamed. He is excited by this environment and feels some pride in his role as a teacher of the island's "qualities" (1.2.403), first to Prospero and here to Stephano and Trinculo, from whom his manner of speaking hardly differs in Shōyō's translation. The vernacular is heard in the endings *arā*, *narā*, and *wai*, and there is a touch of excess in the long sentence *Sōshite itsu no ma ni ka* as he struggles to contain his wonder. More than in the source, Caliban cannot control his feelings with the structured repetitions that Prospero uses, but relies on affective expressions like *dō ka suru to* ("sometimes") and *ka to omou to* ("if I think about it," again for "sometimes"). His identification with the island is heard in the assonance of the second sentence where the *sh-* in *shima* ("island") is repeated in *shocchū* ("constantly"), *shite* ("does"), *shā shinai* (meaning "does not make an ugly noise"), and *omoshiroi* ("pleasant"). Caliban may not, therefore, sound as sonorous as Prospero in Shōyō's translation, but this colloquial style is nevertheless rhythmical and musical, contrasting phrases and segments of varying length in an abstraction of syllabic meter, and also self-aware and intentional. Lacking the connotations of Shakespeare's blank verse, Shōyō seems concerned that Caliban will end up sounding too much like Prospero, and thus seems more emphatic of Caliban's subaltern role.

For a third example, Portia's speech on "The quality of mercy" (4.1.180–201) would have been well known to Shōyō's Taishō audience as the central speech of *The Merchant of Venice* and was included in the gramophone record he made for Nippon Columbia Records in 1933.[33] Shōyō's Portia effects her disguise as a male lawyer with her use of the masculine particles *ja* and *wai* and authoritative tone. As with the previous examples, the lack of stressed syllables and unbroken length of the sentences gives the speech a distinctly syllabic feel:[34]

> The quality of mercy is not strained:
> 慈悲は據ろなく施すべきものではない。
> *Jihi wa yondokoro naku hodokosubeki mono de wa nai.*

> It droppeth as the gentle rain from heaven
> Upon the place beneath.
> 慈悲は、春の小雨の自からにして地を潤すが如くに、降るものぢゃ。
> *Jihi wa, haru no kosame no onozukara ni shite chi wo uruosu ga gotoku ni, kudaru mono ja.*

> It is twice blest:
> 其徳澤は二重である。
> *Sono tokutaku wa nijū de aru.*

> It blesseth him that gives and him that takes.
> 慈悲は、之を興ふる者に取っても幸福であれば、受ける者に取っても幸福なのぢゃ。
> *Jihi wa, kore wo ataeru mono ni totte mo kōfuku de areba, ukeru mono ni totte mo kōfuku na no ja.*

> 'Tis mightiest in the mightiest; it becomes
> The throned monarch better than his crown.

慈悲は最も偉いなる人に在って、更に最も偉いなる美徳となる。
此徳が君主の胸に在れば、其光は金の冠にも幾倍する。

*Jihi wa mottomo ōi naru hito ni atte, sara ni mottomo ōi naru bitoku to
naru. Kono toku ga kunshu no mune ni areba, sono hikari wa kin no
kanmuri ni mo ikubai suru.*

His sceptre shows the force of temporal power,
The attribute to awe and majesty,
Wherein doth sit the dread and fear of kings.

彼の國王が手に持たせらるゝ笏は、彼の俗界に於ける威力や□嚴
の標章たるに過ぎないが

*Kano kokuō ga te ni motaseraruru shaku wa, hon no zokkai ni okeru
iryoku ya songen no mejirushi taru ni suginai ga*

Just as "mercy" is "twice blest," Shōyō benefits from both the shape of the Shake-spearean line and the force of his native syllabics to give the speech a remarkably bal-anced and centred quality. The series of short *o* vowels – nine in the first line – seem to imitate the patter of "the gentle rain from heaven," while the regular disruption to the vowel sequences by words containing double consonants, such as *yondokoro* ("forcibly") and *mottomo* ("most"), and to a lesser extent the double vowels in words such as *kōfuku* ("happiness"), can be said to frame the speech's rhetorical purpose, which is to extol the "quality of mercy." Shōyō omits "quality" from the first line, probably because a literal rendering such as *jihi no tokushitsu* would sound abstract and unpoetic, but as I have suggested compensates for that omission with the syllabic patter of the rainfall. Similarly, he omits the abstract "dread and fear of kings," and compensates for that omission with a dramatic gloss on "scepter" as that which an enthroned monarch might "hold in his hand" (*te ni motaseraruru shaku*). As a more general illustration of Shōyō's translating style the successive rhythms (or syllabic patter) of the phrases works to channel their momentum towards the end of the line, which in Japanese word order is usually a verb and in Shōyō's case often the expres-sive copula *ja* or a strong final particle such as *ga*.

The word *nijū* meaning "double" in "twice blest" may be a deliberate pun on "Jew" to suggest that temporal mercy is worth twice that of Shylock's demand for justice because (as Portia argues) of the former's deference to divine judgement: "We do pray for mercy,/And that same prayer doth teach us all to render/The deeds of mercy." (4.1.196–8). In both the 1914 translation and 1933 revision, Portia's "There-fore, Jew" (193) is translated *Dakara, Jiu yo*, using a now archaic character for Jewry 猶 meaning "still" or "yet." This may be echoed in the 1933 revision (although not in 1914, where *mōsu* is used for "say") in Shōyō's rendering of Portia's line as she comes down on Antonio's side, "Tarry a little. There is something else" (301), *Iya, choto mate. Mada iu koto ga aru.* (literally, "Stop it and wait a moment. There is still another thing to say." where *iu* is another word for "say"). In seeming to ignore the possibility of divine judgement, Shylock exposes himself to Portia's judgement.

One final point to be made about the Shōyō line is that especially in the case of set speeches such as "The quality of mercy" and "To be, or not to be," he will incline to translate their first lines with particular care, establishing basic phonic patterns and a syllabic rhythm that will shape the speech as a whole. We can look, for example, at how Shōyō translates the opening lines of not just "To be, or not to be," but of all seven of Hamlet's soliloquies in the 1933 revision:

1. O that this too too solid[35] flesh would melt,
   Thaw and resolve itself into a dew (1.2.129–30)

   おゝ、此硬き剛き肉が、何とて溶け融解けて露ともならぬぞ！
   *Ō, kono kataki kowaki niku ga, nani tote toke torokete tsuyu to mo naranu zo!*[36]

The intense alliteration underscores Hamlet's frustration at his limitations.

2. O all you host of heaven, O earth – what else? (1.5.92)

   おゝ、ありとある天の神々！下界にありとあらゆる神！
   *Ō, ari to aru ten no kamigami! Gekai ni ari to arayuru kami!*[37]

A repeated word play on *ari* emphasises the feeling of alarm in Hamlet's expression.

3. O, what a rogue and peasant slave am I! (2.2.485)

   おゝ、何たる無頼漢の土百姓ぞ俺は！
   *Ō, nantaru narazumono no tsuchihozeri zo ore wa!*[38]

Again alliterative, with a Shakespearean inversion at the end, *zo ore wa*, "am I."

4. To be, or not to be – that is the question (3.1.55)

   世に在る、世に在らぬ、それが疑問ぢゃ。
   *Yo ni aru, yo ni aranu, sore ga gimon ja.*[39]

A perfect five-seven-seven syllabic.

5. 'Tis now the very witching time of night
   When churchyards yawn and hell itself breathes out
   Contagion to this world. (3.2.378–80)

   今こそ夜の丑三つ時、墓は口を開き、地獄よりは毒気を送る。
   *Ima koso yoru no ushi mitsudoki, haka wa kuchi wo hiraki, jigoku yori wa dokuki wo okuru.*[40]

The lack of stressed double consonants in this line gives it a crisp syllabic quality.

6. Now might I do it. But now 'a is a-praying.
   And now I'll do't (3.3.73–4)

   今こそ遂げう、恰どよい、祈の最中。いで、怨を。
   *Ima koso togō, chōdo yoi, inori no saichū. Ide, urami wo.*[41]

The word *ima* for "now" is foregrounded by the sound plays in Shōyō's distinctly breathy rendition.

7.  How all occasions do inform against me
    And spur my dull revenge. (4.4.31–2)

    見る事、聞く事が俺を譴めて鈍った宿志を勵ましをる！
    *Miru koto, kiku koto ga ore wo semete nibutta kokorozashi wo hagemashi oru!*[42]

A typical Shōyō paraphrase with the phrase *miru koto, kiku koto* ("seeing and hearing") explaining that Hamlet is spurred to revenge by everything that he sees (and hears) going on at Elsinore.

A conspicuous feature of this selection is the prevalence of the short *o* vowel in comparison with the other four vowels:[43]

*a* ~ 38 occurrences (excluding with separate vowels such as in *ai*)
*i* ~ 33
*u* ~ 26 (including 1 double vowel)
*e* ~ 14
*o* ~ 60 (including 3 double vowels)

In all but the second soliloquy, and enhanced by items like *kono, koso* and *koto*,[44] the profusion of *o* sounds gives the speeches a focussed, urgent quality that is appropriate to Hamlet's state of mind, and with the near lack of double consonants, also sounds regularly syllabic; the lines roll off the tip of the tongue. In all but the sixth, the lines are also unified by striking repetitions and internal rhymes, notably the crisp *k* and *t* alliterations in the first soliloquy and the phonic connection between *mitsudoki* (the "witching hour") and *dokuki* ("poisonous air") in the fifth. Here as elsewhere, euphony is a feature of the Shōyō line.

## Repetition and Keywording

The previous section outlined some basic characteristics of Shōyō's translating style, above all the attention to rhythm and musicality. What I have been calling the Shōyō line is more expansive than the prosodies of post-war translators, and although still readable adopts numerous usages that are nowadays seldom heard. It may therefore "sound" unique to contemporary ears, but that uniqueness is not necessarily equivalent to Shakespearean uniqueness and works with other devices such as repetition to convey the diversity (and indeed uniqueness) that Shōyō values about Shakespeare. Prosody is mainly focussed on the individual phrase and speech. This section looks at the repetition of words across translations as a whole (keywording) in what may have been a deliberate strategy on Shōyō's part. Shōyō hints as follows at the potential of keywording in his 1928 essay on Shakespeare translation:

The same thought or feeling may be subject to diverse interpretations. When Japanese scholars first translated Shakespeare they were surprised to discover this diverse style occurring so frequently. It seemed that Shakespeare created texts rich with feeling, stridently saying the same thing again and again. That is how it seemed to them, although in the end it is a technique born from the necessity of drama. Lines which are written to be heard rather than read need to be repeated, so that skilled reciters and experienced actors will be able to agree on their meaning without being able to explain them. Composers such as Wagner work out their logic through the methodical repetition of lyrics. If you translate the same thing without varying your expression, then you may naturally feel you are wasting something and thereby harming the original. This is a particularly important point when translating Shakespeare with his rich vocabulary and universal rhetoric.[45]

Shōyō, as a translator and a dramatist himself, understands the necessity of repeating words and motifs as a strategy for conveying the source texts' thematic coherence.

Friederike von Schwerin-High offers several examples of keywords that recur in Shōyō's *Tempest* translation,[46] and seem both to have a metonymic function and – as relatively commonplace items that are easily repeated and remembered by audiences – to contrast with more distinctive phrasings. The main example she gives is the verb *oboeru*, "to remember," which (in all except the following first example) he writes with a character meaning "written record" (*ki*) rather than the two usual characters meaning "remember." Schwerin-High comments that this unusual choice of character "invests the act of remembering with both consistency and depth."[47] Almost all the examples occur in Prospero's long conversation with Miranda in 1.2, where aside from the narrative function of recalling what has brought the two to the island, they emphasise the importance of memory to the formation of Miranda's character and Prospero's plan of achieving reconciliation.

Shōyō is translating Shakespeare's play, where we find that the word "remember" and related forms such as "remember'st" occur six times in 1.2 out of a total thirteen in the play as a whole, and likewise the noun "remembrance" three out of six times. Shakespeare too presumably would wish to establish memory as a thematic and narrative device in this long opening scene, and Shōyō's unusual choice of character and the fact that all but one of his thirteen uses of *oboeru* occur in 1.2 of the translation are evidence of a possible deliberate keywording.[48] Moreover, since all these twelve instances involve Miranda, it seems no coincidence that the character *ki* shares a *kanji* radical (*bushu*) with the word Shōyō uses for "princess," *kisaki*, as follows:[49]

覚 standard usage for *oboeru*
記 Shōyō's variation for *oboeru*
妃 "princess"

The thirteen instances are listed as follows, with only the first one using the standard character:

1. The direful spectacle of the wreck which touched
   The very virtue of compassion in thee
   (Prospero, 1.2.26–7)

   あの怖ろしげな難船の有様に、深い惻隠を覚えたのも道理ぢやが
   *Ano osoroshigena nansen no arisama ni, fukai awaremi wo oboeta no mo mot-tomo ja ga*[50]

2. Canst thou remember
   A time before we came unto this cell?
   I do not think thou canst
   (Prospero, 1.2.38–40)

   其方は此窟へ来た前の事を記えてゐるか？よもや記えてはゐまいなう
   *Sonata wa kono iwaya e kita mae no koto wo oboete iru ka? Yomoya oboete wa imai nou.*[51]

4. Certainly, sir, I can.
   (Miranda, 1.2.41)

   いゝえ、ちやんと記えてをります。
   *Iie, chanto oboete orimasu.*[52]

6. By what? By any other house or person?
   Of any thing the image, tell me, that
   Hath kept with thy remembrance.
   (Prospero, 1.2.42–4)

   どうして？家か人かに記憶があるか？何でも可い、記えてゐるものをば言つて見なさい。
   *Dōshite? Ie ka hito ka ni oboe ga aru ka? Nandemo ii, oboete iru mono wo ba itte minasai.*[53]

8. ’Tis far off,
   And rather like a dream than an assurance
   That my remembrance warrants.
   (Miranda, 1.2.44–6)

   遠い前に . . . . . . 分明とは記えてはゐませぬけれど . . . . . .
   夢のやうに。
   *Tōi mae ni . . . . . . Hakkiri to wa oboete wa imasenu keredo . . . . . . yume no yō ni.*[54]

9. But how is it
   That this lives in thy mind? What see’st thou else
   In the dark backward and abysm of time?
   If thou rememb’rest aught ere thou can’st here,
   How thou cam’st here thou mayst.
   (Prospero, 1.2.48–52)

どうしてそれを記えてゐるぞ？何かまだ他に、深い昏い来し方に見え
るものは無いか？こゝへ来ぬ前の事を記えてゐるなら、どうして爰へ
来たかも記えてゐさうなものぢや。

*Dōshite sore wo oboete iru zo? Nanika mada hoka ni, fukai kurai koshikata ni
mieru mono wa nai ka? Koko e konu mae no koto wo oboete iru nara, dōshite
koko e kita kamo oboete isōna mono ja.*[55]

12. But that I do not.
    (Miranda, 1.2.52)

それは記えてをりませぬ。
*Sore wa oboete orimasenu.*[56]

13. To think o'th' teen that I have turned you to,
    Which is from my remembrance.
    (Miranda, 1.2.64–5)

記えてはゐぬけれども、嘸其時父様に御苦労をかけたであらうと思
ふと！
*Oboete wa inu keredomo, sazo sono toki totosama ni gokurō wo kaketate arou
to omou to!*[57]

A feature of most of these examples is for either the short *o* vowels in the *oboe*
stem to be echoed in contingent words like *yomoya* ("surely not") and *orimasenu* or
else to precede distinctly literary constructions like the insertion of the particle *wa*
before a classically inflected form of the present progressive like *inu* or *imasenu*.
In other words, not only may *oboeru* be a metonym for memory but it is supported
by a trope for the cultural authority Prospero has been instilling in his daughter.

Memory – along with invention, arrangement, style, and delivery – was one of
the five canons of classical rhetoric. Prospero does not teach his daughter how to
make a speech but does instil in her a sense of identity that can begin only with the
memories that regimes such as his usurping brother Antonio's find it convenient
to erase; the mixture of compassion and impatience with which she responds to
her father will soon lead her into the arms of Ferdinand, heir to Prospero's enemy
Alonso, and is thus part of Prospero's plan of revenge. Prospero's mastery of the
elements (his "rough magic") can be considered a trope for the rhetorical argument
of his revenge, and exercises of mind over matter, rhetoric, and magic are related
to each other in the Renaissance epistemology, as they were for Shōyō and his contemporaries when they appropriated rhetoric together with the "magic" of Western
science and technology in the era of modernisation. The initial interest was mainly
in eighteenth-century rhetoricians such as Hugh Blair, whose seminal *Lectures
on Rhetoric and Belles Lettres* (1783) was published in a Japanese translation
in 1880. One text that focussed specifically on literary composition rather than
oratory was Alexander Bain's *English Composition and Rhetoric* (1867), whose
translation by Kikuchi Dairoku in his *Shūji oyobi kabun* (Rhetoric and Belles
Lettres, 1879) Shōyō later acknowledged as an influence on *Shōsetsu shinzui*.[58]
Shōyō's particular contribution was his *Biji ronkō* (Theory of Rhetoric, 1893) in

which he distinguishes between what he calls the "emotional style" and "feeling power" (*jō*) of literature and the "knowing power" (*chi*) and "willing power" (*i*) of non-literary texts.[59]

Devices such as keywording serve to enhance the emotional power or warmth of a translation by developing motifs repetitively in a range of literary and dramatic contexts, but they are not didactic, and in the case of Shōyō's *Tempest* translation can even be said to enhance the sense of wonder that is intrinsic to his theory of "hidden ideals." Repetition implies consistency (or faithfulness to an idea), and rhetoric's reward for its consistency is a heightened awareness of human diversity as in what may be regarded as the play's most memorable speech, when Miranda encounters the wider world for the first time (5.1.181–4). This is a quotation with which Shōyō's readers in 1915 would probably have not been familiar but which he might, as it were, have wanted to teach them:

> O wonder!
> How many goodly creatures are there here!
> How beauteous mankind is! O brave new world
> That has such people in't.

The world may no longer be "brave" or "new" for Prospero, but for all his faults Prospero's revenge is ultimately benevolent, forestalling the murder of Alonso and Gonzalo by Antonio and Sebastian in 2.1 and freeing Ariel and Caliban at the end of the play. Moreover, just as Shōyō is unable to explain Shakespearean creativity in his theory of "hidden ideals," neither can Prospero rationalise the mystery of human personality, and this sense of mystery or wonder is verbalized in Shōyō's translation through the repetition of a word, *fushigi*, that means just that: "strange," "mysterious," or "wonderful"; it was originally a Buddhist term dating back to the ninth century connoting experience that transcended rational explanation.[60] As an everyday word in the Meiji era, its usage can be said to mirror the frequency of "strange" in particular in the Shakespearean corpus (348 times in total, compared with 394 times of "nature"), not to mention "strangeness" as a commonplace of Shakespeare criticism. *Fushigi* occurs twenty-six times in Shōyō's translation, which is the same number of occurrences as "strange" (with the related "strangely," "strangeness" and "stranger") in the source text,[61] and is given especial prominence in Miranda's speech:[62]

> まア！不思議な！おゝ、まア多数の立派な生類！人間といふ
> 者は、まア、何たる美しいものぢや！かういふ人達の住んで
> いる處は、まア、何という見事な、新奇しい世界であらう！
>> *Mā! Fushigi na! Ō, mā ōzei no rippana seirui! Ningen to iu mono*
>> *wa, mā, nantaru utsukushii mono ja! Kō iu hitotachi no sunde iru tokoro*
>> *wa, mā, nan to iu migotona, mezurashii sekai de arou!*

This is not necessarily a literary translation, serving more as an approximation of Taishō schoolgirl speech – the colloquial *rippa* ("good") and *migoto* ("great") also occur frequently in Shōyō's translations – but the context is highly dramatic, and it comes as the culmination of a string of more literary usages, of which nine are cited as follows:

1. my zenith doth depend upon
   A most auspicious star
   (Prospero, 1.2.181–2)

   予の栄枯盛衰は不思議な一つの瑞星に懸つてゐる
   *washi no eiko seisui wa fushigina hitotsu no zuisei ni kakatte iru*[63]

*Fushigi* here is a weak equivalent of "most auspicious," and instead the sense of wonder is transferred to the parallel (and slightly unusual) phrases *eiko seisui* (for "zenith") and *hitotsu no zuisei* (meaning "lucky star"). At the same time, *fushigina* gives a rhythmic focus to the sentence.

2. The strangeness of your story put
   Heaviness in me.
   (Miranda, 1.2.307–8)

   父様のお話が、あんまり不思議なので、つい眠たうなつた。
   *Totosama no ohanashi ga, anmari fushigi na no de, tsui nemutō natta.*[64]

The compact structure of the source is considerably expanded,[65] with "strangeness" becoming an adjectival phrase meaning "rather strange."

3. No wonder, sir,
   But certainly a maid.
   (Miranda, 1.2.428–9)

   おゝ、不思議な者ではない。わたしは處女ぢや。
   *Iie, fushigina mono de wa nai. Watashi wa musume ja.*[66]

The translation crisply captures the self-control of Miranda's response to Ferdinand's inquiry of the previous line as to whether she "be maid [i.e., unmarried virgin] or no."

4. But for the miracle,
   I mean our preservation
   (Gonzalo, 2.1.6–7)

   併しながら、吾々のやうに不思議の冥助を得るものは
   *Shikashi nagara, wareware no yō ni fushigi no myōjo wo eru mono wa*[67]

*Myōjo* connotes protection by the Japanese gods and Buddha. The paraphrase conveys Gonzalo's religious awe at the party's preservation, with a hiatus after *shikashi nagara* leading into an expansive structure of twenty-one morae.

5. Misery acquaints a man with/strange bedfellows!
   (Trinculo, 2.2.38–39)

窮すりやとんだ不思議な相方と同衾をするものだなァ。
*Kyū surya tonda fushigina aikata to dōkin wo suru mono da nā.*[68]

The use of *fushigi* captures the humour of Trinculo's aphorism, even if it is not exactly what he means by strangers lying with each other.

6. but follow thee,
   Thou wondrous man.
   (Caliban, 2.2.160–1)

俺はおのしに従ふよ、おのし偉い偉い不思議な人！
*Ore wa onoshi ni shitagau yo, onoshi erai erai fushigina hito!*[69]

The duplication of adjectives such as in *erai erai* is typical of Shōyō's style, and combines here with *fushigi* to convey the vulnerability of Caliban's situation and with the repetition of the archaic pronoun *onoshi* to generate a dynamic rhythmical expression.

7. They vanished strangely!
   (Francisco, 3.3.40)

奇怪な塩梅に消えてなくなりました。
*Fushigina anbai ni kiete nakunarimashita.*[70]

The translator adopts Shakespeare's technique of juxtaposing two words of similar meaning to convey the drama of Francisco's expression.

8. who most strangely
   Upon this shore where you were wrecked, was landed
   (Prospero, 5.1.160–1)

不思議にもお前さんがたが難船せられた其同じ岸邊に上陸して
*Fushigi nimo omaesangata ga nansen serareta sono onaji kishibe ni jōriku shite*[71]

As in the source, *fushigi* is well positioned to introduce the compressed structure of Prospero's explanation.

9. This is as strange a maze as e'er men trod
   (Alonso, 5.1.242)
   人間のつひぞ辿つたこともない實に不思議な八重襷路とも評すべきぢや。
   *Ningen no tsui zo tadotta koto mo nai jitsu ni fushigina yae dazukimichi tomo hyō subeki ja.*[72]

This considerable expansion gives weight to the key word *fushigi*.

An even more audible nexus occurs in the contrast between the word *baka*, meaning "foolish," "stupid," or "idiotic," and *bakemono*, meaning "spirit" or "monster," which is heard particularly in the scenes with Caliban, Stephano, and Trinculo, for example in 3.2.27–32:[73]

TRINCULO.    Wilt thou tell a monstrous lie,/being but half a fish and half a monster?
CALIBAN.     Lo, how he mocks me! Wilt thou let him, my lord?
TRINCULO.    'Lord', quoth he! That a monster should be/such a natural!
CALIBAN.     Lo, lo, again!

トリン　半分は化者で、半分は魚の癖に、人間並に人様の悪口なんか吐きやアがるない！

カリバ　あれ！あいつめ、あんなに俺を馬鹿にするだに！おのし、あれを放任ツとくか、殿さま？

トリン　殿さまだと言やアがる！あいつはお化ではなくッて大馬鹿だ！

カリバ　あれ！また俺を馬鹿にしてる！

T:    *Hanbun wa bakemono de, hanbun wa sakana no kuse ni, ningen nami ni hitosama no akkō nanka hozasayāgaru nai!*

C:    *Are! Aitsume, anna ni ore wo baka ni suru da ni! Onoshi, are wo ucchattoku ka, tonosama?*

T:    *Tonosama da to iyagaru! Aitsu wa obake dewa nakutte ōbaka da!*

C:    *Are! Mata ore wo baka ni shiteru!*

In this excerpt, we see that while the dictionary definition of *baka* meaning "foolish" is absent from the source, the word occurs three times in the translation, meaning respectively "to mock" (*baka ni suru*), "a natural idiot" (*ōbaka*), and to render the subtext in Caliban's interjection. "Fool" is a common Shakespearian item in its various forms ("foolish," "fools," etc.), occurring almost seven hundred times in the Complete Works and nine times in *The Tempest*, but remarkably Shōyō's *baka* occurs a total of eighteen times in the translation (common though as it is as an insult in modern Japanese). On the other hand, "monster" occurs thirty-eight times in the source against only twenty-five times in the translation. *Bakemono* usefully echoes *baka*, but since its basic meaning is "ghost" or "phantasm," Shōyō might want to avoid that nuance. As Schwerin-High comments, while compared with other Japanese translations, "Shōyō's realism does not seem to magnify the [play's] magical aspects," it does heighten "the general strangeness and complexity of the text . . . through his provision of new keywords and through his multi-dimensional *furigana* glossing."[74]

The following selection indicates the versatility of Shōyō's usage. In 3, *baka* substitutes for "Fie" to reinforce a tone of reproach in Antonio's backbiting, and in 10, meaning "stupid wild geese," it explicates the source's reference to barnacle geese, while the repetitions in 6, 7, and 11 may even develop the common Shakespearean theme of folly. Shōyō four times adopts the equivalent *ahō* from Kansai dialect, although not as one might expect to mark a difference between a *baka*-speaking ruling class of Prospero and the mainland aristocracy and an *ahō*-speaking subaltern class of natives and servants, but rather probably because *ahō* sounds even more offensive in a context where the standard *baka* is the norm. Prospero calls his daughter *ahō* ("Foolish wench"), and in 8 *baka* and *ahō* are juxtaposed in an ingenious (if not exactly precise) rendering of Stephano's jingle "Flout 'em and scout 'em."

1. Dull thing, I say so
   (Prospero to Ariel, 1.2.285)

   馬鹿、さう言うてをるわい。
   *Baka, sō iute oru wai.*[75]

2. Foolish wench
   (Prospero, 1.2.480)

   阿呆めが！
   *Ahōme ga!*[76]

3. Fie, what a spendthrift is he of his tongue!
   (Antonio referring to Gonzalo, 2.1.26)

   馬鹿な無駄口を利きたがる男もあつたものだ！
   *Bakana mudaguchi wo kikitagaru otoko mo atta mono da!*[77]

4. not a holiday/fool there would give a piece of silver.
   (Trinculo referring to England, 2.2.25)

   お祭日のお馬鹿さん
   *osaijitsu no obakasan*[78]

5. A most poor credulous monster! Well/drawn, monster, in good sooth.
   (Trinculo to Caliban, 2.2.112–113)

   馬鹿正直に、虚誇を眞に信けやがる化もの！
   *Baka shōjiki ni, hora wo ma ni ukeyagaru bakemono!*[79]

6. A most ridiculous monster
   (Trinculo, 2.2.162)

   馬鹿々々しい化者もあつたものだ。
   *Bakabakashii bakemono atta mono da.*[80]

7. Servant monster? The folly of this island!
   (Trinculo, 3.2.4)

   化奴だ！此島の馬鹿々々しサッたら無いや！
   *Bakeyakko da! Kono shima no bakabaka shisattara nai ya!*[81]

8. Flout 'em and scout 'em,
   And scout 'em and flout 'em
   (Stephano, 3.2.121–2)

   奴等を馬鹿に爲う。奴等を阿呆に爲う。
   *Yatsura wo baka ni shiyō. Yatsura wo ahō ni shiyō.*[82]

9. Though fools at home condemn 'em.
   (Antonio referring to travellers, 3.3.27)

   井内の蛙だけが疑つて彼れ此れ言ふのです。
   *I no uchi no kawazu dake ga utagatte kare kore iu no desu.*[83]

10. We shall lose our time,
    And all be turned to barnacles
    (Caliban, 4.1.247–8)

    今に皆な馬鹿ァな雁の鳥にされッちまふ
    *ima ni minna bakāna gan no tori ni sarecchimau*[84]

11. What a thrice-double ass
    Was I to take this drunkard for a god,
    And worship this dull fool!
    (Caliban, 5.1.296–8)

    俺まァ何で馬鹿だつたか、あんな酔ひどれを神様だと思つて、あんな
    馬鹿者を拝んだりなんかしてゐた！
    *Ore mā nande baka datta ka, anna yoidore wo kamisama da to omotte, anna
    bakamono wo ogandari nanka shite ita!*[85]

The qualities of wonder and strangeness schematised here are relevant to the aspect
of mystery or hiddenness in Shōyō's Shakespeare, and folly to a negative trait of
incoherence for which he berates so-called lesser writers. Moreover, and as Shōyō
well knows, just as stylistic diversity tends to support thematic development in
Shakespeare's plays, the repetition of commonplace items such as *fushigi* and *baka*
in the translations can be seen to accompany literary inflexions and more unique
lexical choices. To the extent that Shōyō is able to compensate lexical ordinari-
ness with literary sophistication, what is reductive about his translations is not so
much the choice of words like *fushigi* and *baka* but the assumption that his stylistic
mixing will be equivalent to Shakespeare's. The assimilative qualities of Shakespeare's style may for some Japanese readers seem unbalanced and disjointed in
Shōyō's translations with their different ranges of linguistic and cultural reference,
but this is not to deny the openness of Shakespeare's texts to interpretation and
Shōyō's role in interpreting them, nor the openness of the translations themselves
to interpretation.


## Phonetic Glossing

Keywording acts metonymically to enhance the interpretive potential of a translation. Shōyō's technique of inserting *furigana* symbols (*rubi*)[86] to indicate phonetic
readings of *kanji* and *kanji* compounds is more metaphorical in effect, serving to
reproduce an illusory depth within the line or phrase. This convention dates from
the early seventeenth century, and became widespread in the Meiji era as literacy

rates grew with the introduction of compulsory primary education and a reading public established itself. Since the use of *kanji* was not fully standardised until after 1945, and writers such as Shōyō would often use characters that exceeded the knowledge of readers educated even to high school level, *rubi* were clearly helpful to both writers and readers. Shōyō may have had a pedagogic purpose of promoting literacy through his translations, since he contrasts the breadth and diversity of Shakespeare's vocabulary with the Yamanote dialect that emerged as standard Japanese in the 1920s,[87] but his purpose is mainly literary in the way that *rubi* often indicate alternatives to the standard, expected reading.

These alternatives are usually more rhythmical and speakable than the standard readings, and (like Shakespeare's tropes of juxtaposition and repetition) can function metaphorically to defer meaning. The technique was commonly used in literary texts by Shōyō's contemporaries (although more sparingly),[88] but even when (as is usually the case, even in Shōyō's translations) there is no deviation, the use of *rubi* creates a visual rhetorical impression by default. Shōyō avoids the wholesale rendition of Shakespeare's language in classical style for the same reason as the Meiji novelists, namely that it was too allusive and suggestive for the pace of a modern narrative, but by way of compensation he finds in *rubi* a means of asserting the symbolic richness and strangeness of Shakespeare's poetic drama.

A striking example of the technique comes in the opening shots of the quarrel between Oberon and Titania in *A Midsummer Night's Dream* (2.1.46–50) as Shōyō translated it in 1915:[89]

OBERON.  Ill met by moonlight, proud Titania.
TITANIA.  What jealous Oberon? Fairies, skip hence.
          I have foresworn his bed and company.
OBERON.  Tarry, rash wanton. Am not I thy lord?
TITANIA.  Then I must be thy lady.

オビロ　　尊大家さん、わるい處で逢ったねえ月夜に。
　　　　　*Kenshikiyasan, warui tokoro de atta nē tsukiyo ni.*

チテー　　何ですッて、嫉妬家さん！．．．．．妖精ら、サッさとお跳び。わたしゃァあの人とは
　　　　　決して一しょに臥たり遊んだりはしない筈だから。
　　　　　*Nan desutte, yakkamiya-san! ... Sudamara, sassato otobi, watashā ano hito to wa kesshite issho ni netari asondari wa shinai hazu dakara.*

オビロ　　待ちな、向う見ずの淫蕩者。予は汝の殿さまぢゃァないか？
　　　　　*Machi na, mukōmizu no itazuramono. Ware wa omae no tonosama jā nai ka?*
チテー　　ぢゃ、わたしは汝の奥様でなくッちゃならない譯だ。
　　　　　*Ja, watashi wa omae no okusama de nakuccha naranai wake da.*

The *kanji* for "proud" is written *sondai*, one of several collocations for "pride," but the phonetic reading is *kenshikiya*, which besides sounding more acerbic than *sondaiya* means something slightly different, "an opinionated person." In reply, Titania calls her husband *yakkamiya* (written *shittoya*), which echoes a popular expression for jealousy, *yakimochi*, literally "a roasted rice cake." The translation characterises Titania as a type of modern woman speaking above her station, even if in *kyōgen* comedy it is usually the wife who is jealous of the husband, and yet the tone is set for the dialogue that follows. "Fairies" is written *yōsei* but pronounced *sudama*, which is a type of shape-shifting mountain and river spirit from Chinese mythology and Japanese folklore; the word is both more mellifluous than *yōsei* and more specific to its Japanese context. Likewise, Oberon's "rash wanton" (2.1.64) is translated *mukōmizu itazuramono*: *mukōmizu* means "not looking where you are going" and *itazura*, "mischief maker," is written *intō*, meaning "degenerate" or "debauched." The two characters in this compound each contain the radical for "water" that would also place Titania in the category of river spirits, as well as expressing her mutable nature.

Through this differentiation of the two writing systems (*kanji* and *kana*), readers become involved in the association of sound and image and rewarded for recognising discrepancies between given and expected readings when they arise. *Rubi* is, therefore, a technique that privileges readers' subordinate status as language learners, and (like keywording) may even support links or patterns made across a text, transferring to readers something of the translator's rhetorical interest in what I have been calling the strangeness of the source. In a tribute published a few months after Shōyō's death, Hattori Yoshika comments that

> The frequent use of *furigana* is a preferred technique of Dr. Tsubouchi, and may as such seem a little eccentric as a response to the nuances of Shakespeare's vocabulary. In my own view of the Japanese language I prefer to write without *furigana*, and yet Dr. Tsubouchi's translations would have been impossible without their use, which is a point borne out by Dr. Ōtsuki in his note on *furigana* in the *Daigenkai* dictionary, and the *furigana* add depth and colour to the vocabulary.[90]

Hattori next quotes a string of *kanji* compounds from the translations, each one glossed prodigiously with its *rubi*, and states that

> Their application is not only interesting in their context, but through their expressiveness and by dint of necessity make the translations even more readable than the original text. Of course in actual performance this rhetorical purpose will be completely lost in many cases and as a result, as has been commented, will gradually lose their stylistic purpose as directions for reading, and yet they remain a major feature of Dr. Tsubouchi's Shakespeare translations.[91]

Hattori had studied English literature at Waseda under Shōyō, later becoming a leader of Japan's free verse movement. His teacher's *rubi* must have seemed to him a striking innovation, because in his article he places it first among a roster of the translator's stylistic techniques. In contrast to a view of Shōyō's translations as being overly theatrical and lacking in poetic depth, Hattori suggests that *rubi* made both the translation and the original text easier to understand, referring here to Ōtsuki Fumihiko, the pioneer of Japanese lexicography,[92] and he makes the subtle point that, far from imposing on readers a way of reading the text, the technique is in any case obsolescent.

Shōyō's *rubi* are mainly intended to make the translations more readable but, for example, in his 1919 translation of 2.4 of *Henry IV*, Part 1, the purpose is clearly rhetorical as well. This is one of the play's memorable lowlife scenes in which Falstaff boasts to the young Prince Hal about being attacked and robbed on the highway earlier in the day, and Hal knows that Falstaff is exaggerating events because he was one of the robbers. The mood changes towards the end of the scene when news arrives of rebellion, and Hal prepares for his summons the next day before his father the king by role-playing the meeting with Falstaff. This scene epitomises the tension between poetic licence and historical veracity, and indeed the potential of poetic drama to speak the truth of history that Shōyō found fascinating in Shakespeare's history plays, and like many Japanese Shakespeareans since, he was attracted by the character of Falstaff. In his preface to the translation, Shōyō describes Falstaff as a greater "natural" even than Hamlet and Cleopatra, labelling him *goraku tonbō* ("pleasure dragonfly"), which was Shōyō's own nickname as a student.[93]

Like most of the *Falstaff* scenes, this one is written in prose rather than blank verse, and its poetic values are expressed through word play and a lively turn of phrase rather than meter; *rubi* also may compensate for the absence of poetic form. The translation provides various examples of the technique, starting with the first line, where Hal asks Poins, "Ned, prithee come out of that fat room" (2.4.1), "fat" meaning "stuffy" or "full of stale air."

ネッド、おい、頼む、その脂肪臭い室から出て来て
*Neddo, oi, tanomu, sono abura kusai heya kara dete kite*[94]

"[F]at" is written *shibō* but pronounced *abura kusai* ("stinking of fat"), which is more speakable, eliding with *heya* for "room." Shōyō supposes that this stuffy room is one smelling of old food and cooking oil, and thus makes a link with Falstaff's main physical characteristic. Falstaff dominates the scene, its Rabelaisian detail an extension of the grossness (or fatness) of his imagination. In Hal's speech that follows (3–5), "hogsheads" is read *bōdara*, a dried cod, which is a visual equivalent of the sound play on "loggerheads" and "hogsheads." Yet *bōdara* is written as *donkan*, a collocation for "dull brute," and given a further twist with the substitution of *kan*, meaning "guy," for *kan* "feeling," as *donkan* usually means "dull" or "insensitive":

POINS.    Where hast been, Hal?
PRINCE.   With three or four loggerheads, amongst three or/fourscore hogsheads.

大樽が六七十、鈍漢が三四頭といふ處にゐた。
*Ōdaru ga rokunanajū, bōdara ga sanyonhiki to iu toko ni ita.*[95]

Within the rest of Hal's long speech, there are a couple more notable examples: *donten-kan* (written *ikakeya*, "tinker"),[96] for "I can/drink with any tinker in his own language" (17–8), and *nobetsu ni* (written *renzokuteki ni*, "continually"),[97] in "do thou never leave calling 'Francis!'" (30). *Dontenkan* echoes *donkan* ("dull brute") and may also pun with *tenkan* ("epileptic"), besides suiting the phonological context in *mō donna don-tenkan to demo* ("with any tinker"). *Nobetsu ni* also suits its context, *sono aida onoshi wa nobetsu ni* ("you never stop"), and through the repetition of the *no* phoneme imitates the rhetorical emphasis made by inverting the verb in the source. In short, the tonal value of these *rubi* is Hal's humorous contempt for Falstaff's lowlife companions.

Shōyō frequently uses the character *nanji* for the Shakespearean "thou" but with two or more different readings depending on context, for example *kisama* in "Wilt thou rob this leathern jerkin, crystal-/button, not-pated" Falstaff (68–9), where *kisama* has the derogatory sense of "rogue." Shōyō handles this convoluted insult by putting the verbal structure at the beginning:

ぢや、汝（きさま）はいよいよ引剥（ひっぱ）いでしまはうてのか？あの柔革胴衣（なめしらよつき）の、水晶（すゐしやう）
鈕（ぼたん）の、五分刈頭（ふがりあたま）の、瑪瑙指輪（めなうゆびわ）の、鼠股引（ねずみももひき）の、毛絲紐（けいとひも）の、辯口（くちまへ）の好（い）い、
西班牙囊（スペインぶくろ）の . . . . . .

*Ja, kisama wa iyoiyo hippaide shimaoute no ka? Ano nameshira yokki no, suishō botan no, gobu gariatama no, menō yubiwa no, nezumi momohiki no, keito himo no, kuchimae no ii, Supein bukuro no . . . . . .*[98]

Shōyō translates Poins' "cunning match" ("what/cunning match have you made with this jest of the/drawer?," 87–9) with the word *ganrōmono*, "plaything" or "mockery," but spoken *chōsaibō*, literally "dandy roving."[99] He usually writes foreign words like the names of characters in *katakana*, having abandoned the early Meiji practice of rendering foreign names in *kanji*, but makes an exception for Harry Percy's nickname, Hotspur, which he writes *Atsuhakusha*, combining *atsu* for "hot" and *hakusha* for "spur," but the pronunciation indicated as *Hottosupā*.[100] Hotspur becomes a legend of time and place, and the nickname is developed in the caricature, "he that kills me some six or seven dozens of/Scots at a breakfast" (100–1); *Sukottorandojin* ("Scots") is written with the Meiji compound for the country rather than in *katakana*.[101]

At the end of Hal's prelude, just before Falstaff enters, "says" in "'Rivo!' says the drunkard" (108) is written with the character for *sakebu* ("shout") but pronounced *ganaru* ("yell," "scream").[102] Thus, Shōyō combines the simplicity of "says" with the obscurity of the drinking cry "Rivo!" (which he writes with the original Roman letters). Shōyō often gives *katakana* readings for classical gods such as Jupiter and Mars, but in Hal's rhetorical question, "Didst thou never see Titan kiss a dish a butter" (115), "Titan" (the red-faced Roman sun god, nodding at Falstaff) is simply *taiyō* (the sun, with the first character *tai*, "fat"), and "butter" is written *gyūraku* ("cow's ferment") but read *batā*, the modern word.[103] When the butter melts in "the sweet tale of/the sun" (116–7), "tale" meaning "persuasive speech" is translated *benkō* but read *kuchimae*. They both mean "manner of speaking," but *kuchimae* is softer and more humorous than *benkō*, comprising two native words, *kuchi* and *mae*.

The choice between *benkō* and *kuchimae* amounts to two basic tropes available to Shōyō in his translations, namely the cultural distinction between native Japanese words (*wago*) inherited from Old Japanese and *kango* (words borrowed originally from Chinese), and secondly, the orthographic similarities between different *kanji*; *wago* are usually more colloquial, and *kango* (like *rubi*) add stylistic flourish, even more so in Shōyō's time when the number of *kango* in common use was much lower than it is today.[104] One example of orthographic similarity is found in the translation of Hal's rhetorical question cited earlier, where *suishō botan* ("crystal-button") and *keito himo* ("caddis-garter") end with characters containing the same element, 鈕 (*botan*, "button") and 紐 (*himo*, "string"); the character 丑 (*ushi*) by itself means "Ox" in the Chinese zodiac, 金 "gold" or "metal," and 糸 "thread." This connection can be said to articulate the nature of Hal's (and Shakespeare's) rhetoric as being at once both pointed and regular ("buttoned") and "stringed" or connective.

In the examples I have been discussing, Shōyō's *rubi* work to lighten the tone of the dialogue. Other typical *rubi* readings with the purpose of speakability are *wake* for *riyū* ("reason") and *kecchi* for *rettō* ("inferior"). Falstaff's "Zounds" (229, "God's wounds") is written *seigon* ("solemn oath") but pronounced *Zaunzu*.[105] The scene includes numerous more distinct usages, such as when Falstaff suggests that "If reasons were as plentiful as blackberries" (232–3), and "plentiful" is translated literally *kata* but the reading *fundan* ("abundant") sounds more lavish.[106] Another example of matching *rubi* to the prosody, and in this case to the pithiness of the source, is heard when Hal reveals that he and Poins were the robbers all along:

We two saw you four set on four, and bound/them, and were masters of their wealth. (246–7)

おまえ
お前たち四人が四人の者を襲つて、それを絞つておいて、物を奪つ
たのを、おれたち二人は、ちやァんと見てゐたんだよ。

*Omaetachi yottari ga yottari no mono wo osotte, sore wo shibotte oite, mono wo totta no wo, oretachi futāri wa, chanto mite itan da yo.*[107]

*Yottari* ("four people") is the less usual reading than *yonin*, and introduces the string of rhymes on *ott-*.

When Falstaff tells Hal, "I knew ye as well as he that made/ye." (259–60), the verb for "make" is *tsukuru* ("create") but read *koshiraemasutta*, which has the rhetorical nuance of "fashioned" and is in a polite register.[108] In this speech, Falstaff uses the word "instinct" three times in succession (262–4):

but/beware instinct. The lion will not touch the true prince;/instinct is a great matter. I was now a coward on instinct.

けれども本能は恐ろしいもんだ。獅子は眞の王の子にァ歯を觸れな
いといふが、成程本能は偉いもんだ。おれァ其本能の故で臆しッ
ちまつたんだ。

> *Keredomo insuchinkuto wa osoroshii mon da. Shishi wa honto no ō nya*
> *ha wo furenai to iu ga, naruhodo, insuchinkuto wa erai mon da. Orea sono*
> *insuchinkuto no sei de oku shicchimattan da.*[109]

"Instinct" is rendered with the standard collocation *honnō*, but because Falstaff is talking about something rather different from the usual run of human and animal instincts, the reading in all three cases is the Japanese pronunciation of the English, *insuchinkuto*. Falstaff tries to recover his honour by claiming that even if he did not recognise Hal he knew "instinctively" who he was, and "The lion will not touch the true prince" (263). Tsubouchi may be foreignising this type of instinct as a myth of kingship unfamiliar to Japanese readers, but it is significant that *honnō* (while unspoken) is echoed by the word *hontō* for "true" in "true prince" (263 and 266), implying that a Japanese audience hearing the word *insuchinkuto* for the first time might guess "instinctively" that that is what Falstaff was talking about.

A few final examples illustrate the value of *rubi* for enhancing the speakability and textuality of Shōyō's translations, and in these cases the gist is towards domestication. Just as English *insuchinkuto* hints at the potential alienation of Falstaff from the prince, in other words to a time when Hal will have a royal body of his own and thus no need of Falstaff's corporeality, their present relationship is grounded pragmatically in a shared cultural context. It is this context of shared jokes and drinking words that makes the scene a challenge to translate and for Japanese readers to grasp, and so a few choice *rubi* can only serve to point the way. For example, Hal jokes that with the storm clouds of war approaching, women's virtue will soon become as cheap as the studs or hobnails on soldiers' boots (352–4):

> Why then, it is like if there come a hot June and/this civil buffeting hold, we
> shall buy maidenheads as/they buy hobnails: by the hundreds.
>
> ぢや、何だね、此盛暑になつて、尚此内亂が續いてるやうだと、
> 沓の鋲を買ふぐらゐの散財で、幾らも破瓜が出来るなう。
>
> *Ja, nan da ne, kono doyō ni natte, nao kono nairan ga tsuzuiteru yō da to,*
> *kutsu no byō wo kau gurai no sanzai de, ikura mo mizuage ga dekiru nō.*[110]

The summer heat is rendered with the word *seisho* ("height of summer"), but since June is still the rainy season in Japan, where the summer does not begin until the end of July, the reference to June is dropped, and the word is read *doyō*, the so-called "dog days" when the rains stop and traditionally braised eel (*unagi*) is eaten to store energy for the scorching heat. *Mizuage* (here written *haka*, "defloration") is the coming-of-age ceremony for apprentice geisha that was sometimes a sexual initiation as the patron sponsoring the teenage girl had the right to take her virginity. Hal's joke is prompted by Falstaff's that "You may buy land now as/cheap as stinking mackerel" (350–1), and Shōyō may be registering the connection with fish, since written differently (but pronounced the same), *mizuage* can mean "gross profits" or a "haul of fish."

Shōyō's solution might be criticised for lack of subtlety, but is arguably no less subtle than the source, and affirms a dichotomy between the foreignised and in that sense mystical instincts of the crown and the popular culture that Hal has absorbed under Falstaff's tutelage. In *Shōsetsu shinzui*, Shōyō had criticised the *gesakubon* novels of the late Edo era for being short on psychological depth and high on local, often lurid detail,[111] and this is a similar dichotomy to the one confronting Hal around a popular culture that is sensually gratifying but that he must eventually master if he is to acquire the mystical authority (or, as it were, psychological astuteness) of kingship. This tension is inscribed in the *rubi*.

In the vignette that follows, where Falstaff is pretending to be Hal's father, Hostess Quickly exclaims, "O the father, how he holds his countenance!" (382):

おやまァ！ほんとに、下等芝居そつくらだわねえ。はゝゝゝ！

*Oyamā! Honto ni, odeko shibai sokkura da wa nē. Ha ha ha ha ha!*[112]

*Odeko* means "forehead," a cue for Falstaff to mimic the king with comically raised eyebrows, but written *katō*, "inferior" or "low class," the phrase means "just like in an inferior play." Shakespeare's Quickly praises Falstaff's ability to keep a straight face, whereas the comparison Shōyō makes with a particular dramatic genre may be meant as a cultural pointer for readers wondering whether Falstaff is being serious or not.

In conclusion to this battle of wits, Falstaff boasts that "If I become not a cart as/well as another man, a plague on my bringing up" (483–4), referring to the carts that were used for transporting condemned men to the gallows, adding that "I hope I shall/as soon be strangled with a halter as another" (484–5).

すると、おれも同じ因果車のお相伴だ！お多分に洩れないで、此首根ッ子を縊られッちまふだらう。

*Suru to, ore mo onaji ingaguruma no oshōban da! Otabun ni morenaide, kono kubinekko wo kubirarecchimau darou.*[113]

literally, "If you let him in, I too will partake of my destiny, and be hanged by the scruff of my neck like all the others."

This is an idiomatic translation in which *ingaguruma* means "wheel of fortune" (the Buddhist chain of cause and effect), connecting with the pun on "major" (the major premise or logic of Hal's argument) made at the beginning of the speech with the town "mayor" or sheriff who would accompany the condemned man to the gallows. In other words, by rejecting Hal's premise that he is a coward, he admits his own premise, which is that he is not, and that he is honourable enough to accept the consequences, or effect, of his self-belief and be hanged for it. Shōyō's rhythmical translation, with the half rhyme on *oshōban* ("partaker") and *otabun* ("majority" or "others") and *k* alliteration in the final phrase, bypasses the obscure reference to the hangman's cart and so keeps the humour at the audience's level.[114]

These examples exhibit a rhetoric of translation that post-war translators have manipulated by more covert means. The pre-war convention of *rubi* comes between the elaborate woodblock technology of pre-modern Japan, in which the insertion of *furigana* was often as much decorative as functional, and the imported technology of modern movable type that together with the efficiencies engineered by mass education enabled a gradual internalisation of the reading process that rendered *rubi* largely redundant. This is a transition that Shōyō could have perhaps foretold from his role in the development of modern Japanese drama, which replaced the elaborate gestures of kabuki drama with the more discrete styles of Western acting. In this respect, his *rubi* glossings may be seen as further evidence of the histrionic quality of his translating style.

**Archaism**

Archaism is a powerful norm in Shōyō's Shakespeare translations and in literary translation in general. In a recent study, Krzysztof Filip Rudolf asserts that

> archaization, far from being merely an idle ornament, serves as a powerful vehicle for frequently suppressed emotions, doubtless constituting the very core of human experiences. The yearning for stability, the innocence embodied in culturally conditioned images of the prelapsarian bliss, the simplicity of the bygone existence, and the sepia-tinged visions of Arcadian harmony – all these subtly intertwined pictures and mental constructs constitute, to a variable degree, the very core of the archaizing motion.[115]

Shōyō's style is noticeably more archaic than that of post-war Shakespeare translators and contemporary writers who sought to develop their ideas through an integrated modern style. Although there is an inevitable crossover in his era between Edo Japanese and the modern language that resulted from language reform, Shōyō's approach to reform was gradualist, guided (as Seth Jacobowitz suggests) by aesthetic concerns, above all "his desire to read literary texts as invested or encoded with illusory depth."[116] The question then becomes whether Shōyō's archaisms can indeed recreate this illusion of depth, and if they can, whether they release those "suppressed emotions" that are central to Rudolf's description, and whether those come from Shakespeare, from his native culture and experience or somewhere more universal.

The strategy of archaism serves ideally to reproduce this illusion of depth rather than a more superficial equivalence of Shakespeare and Japanese drama, and yet to start with one wonders whether the nostalgia Rudolf regards as "inseparable" from archaism[117] is compatible with Shōyō's apparently modern view of Shakespeare's realism; in other words, whether a heavily archaistic translation can succeed in heightening readers' awareness of their lived reality or simply leave them yearning for the past. Yet, as Rudolf argues, archaism is subtly different from nostalgia, being a conscious strategy (rather than emotion) that manipulates nostalgic feelings for purposes that may in fact have little to do with hierarchies of past and present:

"Archaization is always creative, never recreative, since one is incapable of bring-ing the past, as it once was, back to life."[118]

One such creative purpose is that of defamiliarisation, which by extending the perceptual distance between reader and source may suit Shōyō's agenda of "hid-den ideals," or the illusion that Shakespeare's creative source is remote to the point of being impenetrable. Archaism may also reproduce Shakespeare's own archaising tendency, not to mention the inherent conservatism of his vision that goes beyond a divisive obsession with causes to allow readers to experience their reality for themselves,[119] and for Shōyō it relates to the basic kabuki device of setting plot innovations (*shukō*) against traditional narrative frameworks (*sekai*). Calling the latter "vertical" and the former "horizontal," Barbara E. Thornbury explains that

> The vertical represented the past in its complete and unchanging form and the horizontal represented the present in its unfolding and ever-changing form. Although the so-called vertical plot gave primary definition to a play, the horizontal plot was needed to bring a work out of the past into the present.[120]

As an example of this intersection, Watanabe Tamotsu discusses the technique of *jitsu wa*, meaning "actually" or "as a matter of fact," whereby in Mokuami's *Miya-kodori nagare no shiranami* (The Great Thief of the Miyakodori Brothel, 1854), the bandit Tengū Kozō Kiritarō disguises himself as a courtesan, Hanako, but is in actual fact a young nobleman and fugitive called Yoshida Matsuwakamaru;[121] these three personae represent the different "worlds" (*sekai*) of the outlaw, brothel, and court nobility. Hanako becomes credible as a courtesan because she is already disguising another self, and with Matsuwakamaru an innocent victim of family rivalries the technique of *jitsu wa* is characteristic of Mokuami's dramaturgy in questioning conventional roles, particularly his sympathy for tragic rogues (*shiran-ami*) which attracted the young Shōyō at around the same time as he was encoun-tering Shakespearian sympathy. As a narrative technique, Watanabe comments that the main purpose

> of interposing different worlds is to lend depth to the space of the narrative. The layering of three worlds on top of each other gives that space a historical credibility that cannot be achieved within a single world alone.[122]

These techniques resemble Shakespeare's techniques for generating multiple per-spectives, starting with the many cases of mistaken identity in the comedies. Just as kabuki characters are made meaningful by existing in a historical continuum, techniques such as disguise and cross-dressing liberate characters from the trans-fixing gaze of their immediate environment and enable them more fully to inhabit the past that created them.

In his *Measure for Measure* translation, Shōyō even makes a keyword of the *jitsu* in *jitsu wa*; *jitsu* occurs – mainly in *kanji* compounds such as *jijitsu* ("fact") and *shinjitsu* ("truth") – some sixty-nine times in the translation in contrast to just forty-three occurrences of "true," "truly," and "truth" in the source.[123] Shōyō's repetitions foreground a theme and narrative device of truth in the play, namely the Duke's kabuki-like disguise as Friar Lodowick, the unmasking of the hypocritical Angelo, and Isabella's relentless honesty, which is related to the psychological realism that Shōyō admires about the play's characterisations. The translation is not in fact notably archaic, and *jitsu* is a modern word.

Shōyō's archaisms should not be considered as ends in themselves but, as I have suggested, as one of a range of devices that give his translations their essential "warmth." Shakespeare himself is arguably most archaic in his use of classical allusions, in particular to the Ovidian mythology that represents the topos of natural desire without Christian guilt. The kabuki tradition may have seemed too close in time to Shōyō's audience, too fraught with cultural capital, for it to serve an identical purpose, but like the way that classical references in Shakespeare opened up a possibility that early modern audiences were not bound by their contemporary post-Reformation culture, so too for Shōyō's audience that – *jitsu wa* – a foreign writer like Shakespeare might have something to say to them. Moreover, since in Shōyō's theory his response to Shakespeare is to some extent shaped by the eighteenth-century *mono no aware* aesthetic of Motoori Norinaga discussed in the previous chapter, Shōyō may hope quite simply that by infusing his translations with a little of the same pathos, he might arouse an awareness that Shakespeare resounds in his readers' cultural context as well.

This chapter has already illustrated the archaic feel of Shōyō's translations with regard to their use of syllabic meter and particles such as *ja* and *wai*. Shōyō's style, by his own admission, becomes considerably more contemporary and less archaic in the fifth period (1914–28) in which he translated the majority of the plays, and therefore demands contextualisation. For sheer audibility, Shōyō sounds most consistently archaic in his choice of honorific forms, particles, and verbal inflexions, which usually come at the ends of sentences and occur with far greater frequency than archaic noun and verb choices. After 1914, Shōyō tends to opt for modern forms such as the copulas *da* and *de aru*, but even the later translations include archaisms such as *ja* and the honorific copula *gozarimasuru*, which nowadays is heard only in kabuki and samurai television dramas. Shōyō usually uses *ja* as a contraction of the copula *de aru*. In the late Edo and Meiji eras, this usage would have been associated with the Kamigata dialect of western Japan, but since Shōyō translates Shakespeare into standard Japanese rather than into any local dialect his frequent usage of the *ja* copula functions rather as an archaic alternative to the modern copulas (and possibly as an echo of Kamigata kabuki). It also sounds more dramatic and assertive than the modern copulas, and even nowadays can be used in that way.[124] Shōyō does use dialectal variations for lower-class characters in his translations, for example the mechanicals in *A Midsummer Night's Dream*, but *ja* is used by a broad section of characters: Claudius and Ophelia as well as Hamlet. As for *gozarimasuru*, it had already been replaced by *gozaimasu* as the standard usage by the end of the Edo era.

Shōyō's translations from late Meiji, notably the 1909 *Hamlet*, provide a fuller range of examples of what may be meant by archaism in Shōyō's style. As a cross-section, the following archaisms occur – and modern usages do not occur – in Act 3 of the 1909 translation.[125] These usages can be contrasted with a majority of inflexions and particles that are commonly used in modern colloquial Japanese:

| Modern usages | 64.4% | Archaisms | 35.6% |
|---|---|---|---|
| modern dictionary verb form | 151 | *-masuru* inflexion | 63 |
| connective *te/de* verb form | 190 | *gozarimasuru* (archaic copula) | 41 |
| plain past (*ta/da*) | 159 | archaic sound changes (e.g. *omoute* and *kurushimuru*)[126] | 91 |
| conditional *-ba* | 77 | *ja* (archaic copula) | 97 |
| negative copula *nai* | 33 | *nari* (archaic copula) | 11 |
| *-nu* negative | 80 | *ba* particle ("if") | 33 |
| *-zu* negative | 23 | *wai* particle (emotive) | 33 |
| *-mai* negative | 12 | *zo* particle (emotive) | 17 |
| *da*, *desu* and *de aru* (modern copulas) | 0 | *nou*, *gana*, and *zoi* particles[127] | 15 |

These figures are impressionistic, excluding common particles such as *ga* and *no* that occur in both pre-Meiji and reformed Japanese, but become meaningful when compared with Shōyō's Taishō translations, for example in the opening scenes of *Richard III* (1918) and *The Two Gentlemen of Verona* (1926), where he has all but abandoned archaic grammar:[128]

| | 1918 | 1926 |
|---|---|---|
| modern *da* and *desu* copulas | 49 | 63 |
| connective *te/de* verb form | 85 | 62 |
| plain past (*ta/da*) | 33 | 47 |
| modern dictionary verb form (including *iru*) | 80 | 40 |
| plain present negative (including *nai*) | 20 | 37 |
| polite affirmative *masu* form | 8 | 13 |
| *de gozaimasu* (polite copula) | 2 | 13 |
| *to iu* construction ("which means") | 12 | 2 |
| *– rya* (conditional) and *-cha* contractions | 12 | 8 |
| archaic particles (*ja*, *wai*, *ze*, and *zo*) | 1 | 15 |

The main deviations are that Richard sometimes uses the casual *rya* contraction and Speed, Valentine's clownish servant in *The Two Gentleman of Verona*, three times uses the dialectal *gozansu* form for the polite copula *gozaimasu*.[129] Tozawa and Asano's translation of *Julius Caesar*, published two years before the 1909 *Hamlet*, is also more noticeably modern. The following figures are for their translation of 3.2 of the source, comprising 287 lines, in which, following Caesar's assassination, Brutus and then Antony make funeral orations, each competing for the support of the Plebeians:[130]

| | | |
|---|---|---|
| modern verb inflexions | 410 | |
| – *nu* negative | 15 | |
| *zo* particle | 10 | |
| – *mai* negative | 6 | 73.2% |
| classical verb inflexions | 130 | |
| *ja* (archaic copula) | 20 | |
| *nari* (archaic copula) | 6 | |
| other archaic particles (*ba, nou, wai,* and *yai*) | 5 | 26.7% |

Shōyō's 1909 *Hamlet* is a recognisably modern text in terms of its sentence structures and inflexions, since it was after all the translation of foreign writers such as Shakespeare that spurred the modernisation of Japanese, but the preponderance of archaisms such as the *-masuru* inflexion further distinguishes it from the early postwar translation of the same play by Fukuda Tsuneari. In 3.1 (which includes the "To be, or not to be" soliloquy), Fukuda is more likely to follow the grammatical standard of ending sentences with an inflected verb phrase, and (apart from the object particle *wo*) is slightly less likely to end with a particle. Shōyō also uses longer sentences:[131]

| *Shōyō (1909)* | *(221)* | *Fukuda (1955)* | *(278)* |
|---|---|---|---|
| verb phrase | 87 | verb phrase | 153 |
| noun phrase | 34 | noun phrase | 34 |
| modern particles (*e, ka, kai, mo, mono, na, ni, no, wa, wo, ya,* and *yo*) | 54 | modern particles (*e, ga, hazu, ka, koso, na, ni, to, mo, wa,* and *wo*) | 80 |
| archaic particles and particle combinations (*ba, degana, ja, ja wae/wai, ja zo, wai, wai no, wai yai, yai, zo, zoi,* and *zo ya*) | 42 | archaic particles (*zo*) | 5 |
| other | 4 | other | 6 |

The difference can be further illustrated by a brief comparison of the two's translations of Claudius' speech as follows (3.1.161–6):

> Love! His affections do not that way tend.
> Nor what he spake, though it lacked form a little,
> Was not like madness. There's something in his soul
> O'er which his melancholy sits on brood
> And I do doubt the hatch and the disclose
> Will be some danger

Shōyō (1909)[132]

戀ぢや？いやいや戀ではないわい。只今彼れが言うたことは、聊か條理を缺いてをれど、

*Koi ja? Iyaiya koi dewa nai wai. Tadaima kare ga iuta koto wa, isasaka
kotowari wo kaite oredo,*

狂人のやうでもない。何か心中に欝々と孕み育つるものがある
わい、

*kyōjin no yō demo nai. Nanika shinchū ni utsuutsu to hagukumi sodatsuru
mono ga aru wai.*

自然それが孵つたなら容易ならぬことが出來う。

*shizen sore ga kaetta nara yōi naranu koto ga dekiu*

Fukuda (1955)[133]

恋！いや、そうとは思えぬ。いささか脈絡を欠いてはいるが、言
葉の節々、どうして

*Koi! Iya, sō to wa omoenu. Isasaka myakuraku wo kaite wa iru ga, kotoba
no fushibushi, dōshite*

狂人などであるものか―腹になにかある。あいつはそれを欝々と
してはぐくんでいる。

*kyōjin nado de aru mono ka – koshi ni nanika aru. Aitsu wa sore wo utsu-
utsu toshite hagukunde iru.*

孵ったら、取返しのつかぬことにもなろう。

*Kaettara, torikaeshi no tsukanu koto ni mo narou.*

Shōyō's version, comprising seven units, leans heavily on the emotive particle *wai*
rhyming with the negative *nai*, with both repeated; the expression *Koi ja?* and
double verb *hagukumi sodatsuru* for "hatch" are also quite consciously theatrical.
Fukuda's version of ten units runs more easily into verbal constructions such as
*kaite wa iru* and *nanika aru*, and sounds altogether lighter and more detached.

The actual modernity of Shōyō's early twentieth-century translations is also worth
emphasising in contrast to the unreformed language of his 1884 *Julius Caesar*. Translating Antony's eulogy over the slain body of Brutus (5.5.69–73),[134] Shōyō uses classical inflexions like the obligatory *beshi* that occur sparingly in the 1909 *Hamlet*, and
unlike his modern translations the text is not organised into regular Shakespearean
sentences with periods but rather as phrasal sequences that make little clear distinction between one sentence and the next. In other words, it is in the style of classical
*jōruri* (*inpontai*), which none of his later translations will resemble:

This was the noblest Roman of them all:
All the conspirators save only he
Did that they did in envy of great Caesar.
He only, in a general honest thought
And common good to all, made one of them.

アッこれぞ誠に羅馬國の、賢士の賢士、

*Atsu kore zo makoto ni Rōma koku no, kenshi no kenshi,*

well – this one – (particle) – truly – the Roman state – wise among the wise –

義人の義人、たぐひ稀なる蓋世の、英傑なりしを惜しむべし、
*gijin no gijin, tagui mare naru gaisei no, eiketsu narishi wo oshimubeshi,*
righteous among the righteous – without parallel and peerless – the
   great man (i.e., Caesar) –

敢なく黄泉の鬼となりしか、往る日獅威差殿下
*aenaku yomiji no oni to narishi ka, inuru hi Shīzaru denka*
begrudgingly – tragically – a soul in Hades – he became – of past
   times – his majesty Caesar –

をば、陰かに謀つて刺殺なせし、三十餘名の徒黨の
*wo ba, hisoka ni hakatte sekisatsu naseshi, sanjū yomei no totō no*
(emphatic particles) – secretly – conspiring – his assassination – having
   done – around thirty conspirators

中にて、誠と國家の利福の爲に、只々全般の自由の爲めに、
*uchi nite, makoto kokka no rifuku no tame ni, tadatada zenpan no jiyū
   no tame ni,*
– among – truly – the state – for the common good – only – the general
   freedom – for the sake of –

身を犧牲にして企に、興せし者は只一人、
*mi wo gisei ni shite kuwadate ni, kumi seshi mono wa tada hitori,*
his body – sacrifice – meaning to – together with – that person – only
   one of them –

此マアカス舞婁多須あるのみ
*kono Mākasu Burutasu aru nomi*
this Marcus Brutus – it is – only

The 1913 translation, by contrast, is a model of modern clarity, with the repetitions
of the *ta no da* construction for "he was" underscoring Octavius' charitable view
of "honourable" Brutus:[135]

これは徒黨中の最も高潔な羅馬人であつたのだ。此男一人の他は、
*Kore wa totō chū no mottomo kōketsuna Rōmajin de atta no da. Kono
   otoko ichinin no hoka wa,*
this one – among the conspirators – the most noble – Roman – he was –
   this one man – apart from –

何れも大シーザーを嫉み憎むの餘りにしたのだ。此男のみが、
*izuremo dai Shīzā wo sonemi nikumu no amari ni shita no da. Kono
   otoko nomi ga,*
each of them – great Caesar – jealous of – and hating – too much – they
   were – this man – only –

全く公共の爲に、一般の利福の爲に、正しい考で
*mattaku kōkyō no tame ni, ippan no rifuku no tame ni, tadashii kangae de*
entirely – for the public good – for the general benefit – in his honest
  thoughts –

其仲間に加はつたゐたのだ。
*sono nakama ni kuwatte ita no da.*
his companions – was joining with

Written for stylised declamation by a bunraku or kabuki narrator, the 1884 version
is considerably more grandiloquent than Antony's terse tribute in the source, with
which Shakespeare surprises us after the doubts Antony has previously raised about
Brutus' honour in his speech to the crowd in 3.2 ("For Brutus is an honorable man,"
91). The 1884 version combines the descriptive and speech (*serifu*) modes of *jōruri*
to maximise the pathos of Brutus' death, sounding inevitably like the finale to some
bunraku play on the theme of honour. Shōyō adds a lot to the source: Kishi Tetsuo
and Graham Bradshaw comment that his adaptation "contains both descriptions of
what is not necessarily visible, like the characters' inner feelings, and rather coer-
cive comments on the dramatic significance of a particular situation."[136]

The 1909 *Hamlet* has the advantage of regularly lineated sentences and speeches
but was still too fussily classical for the likes of Kawatake Shigetoshi.[137] In this
translation but to a markedly lesser extent in his fifth stage, Shōyō appropriates
archaism to his twin poles of rhythm and warmth, but seldom to the extent that it
becomes kabuki language. We can look at a specific example, namely the interjection *hate* (pronounced with two short vowels unlike the English "hate"), which
Shōyō uses throughout his translations and which occurs in 5.1 of the 1909 *Hamlet*
(the Gravediggers' scene) a striking fourteen times: this works out at once every
twenty-one lines of the three hundred lines of source text compared with a total
fifty-four times over the remaining 3,400 lines. *Hate* expresses surprise and even
wonder, meaning something like "Well!" or "Why!" and although it is not entirely
obsolete, it is a typical kabuki expression. In Chikamatsu's *Sonezaki shinjū*, the
courtesan Ohatsu says to Tokubei as they make their final journey: *Hate shinuru
kakugo ga kikitai* ("Well, I am prepared to die").[138]

In most of the following examples, *hate* is clearly an addition to the source.
Shōyō uses the word to frame the Gravedigger's storytelling, in particular relating
to Yorick's skull; the Gravedigger with his humour and long view enables Hamlet
to embrace his own narrative and so carry on his struggle. This is a scene in which
the separate worlds of the Renaissance prince and the clown who lives by his wits
coincide to state the play's central theme of mortality:

1. About Adam's profession, the Gravedigger says that "'A was the first that ever
   bore arms" (5.1.33), *Hāte, icchi hajime ni gojōmon wo tsuke sasshita hito ja.*[139]
   Shōyō's *hate* is inserted as a prefix to his answer to the 2nd Man's question
   "Was he a gentleman?", and inflected with a long vowel to denote the Gravedigger's status. This example connects the Gravedigger's narrative with the play's

broader narrative of sin and redemption, specifically the original sin of Old Hamlet's murder.

2. The Gravedigger answers the riddle with which he has pestered his companion: "The houses [a grave-maker] makes lasts till doomsday" (55), *Hate hakahori ga tsukuru sumai, ōsabaki no hi made mo tsuzuku wa sa*.[140] With the alliteration in the first two words, the Gravedigger comically relishes his profession's authority that stretches to the crack of doom, and hints at the deaths in the final act for which his services will likely be once more requested.

3. The Gravedigger makes a grotesque ballad of his profession: "But age with two stealing steps/Hath clawed me in his clutch/And hath shipped me into the land/ As I had never been such" (67–70), *Itsu no ma ni yara to shinami ya yosete,/ ora ga kubitama shikka to tsukama./Hate wa shimane ni nageagerarete,/kawari hateta yo konna mono ni*.[141] These two instances are different from the others because the *kanji* form is used, meaning "in conclusion" rather than "well," but they still hint at the play's overall narrative framework.

4. Now Hamlet uses the word, shifting the focus from the Gravedigger's comic detachment to the physical reality of the skulls: "Why, e'en so" (83), *Hate, masa ni sō ja*.[142]

5. Hamlet realises that the grave the Gravedigger is digging might be for a woman: "What woman then?" (124), *Hate, doko no hito no tame ni kiku no ja*.[143] This usage leads on to Hamlet's discovery of the awful truth that Ophelia has committed suicide. Shōyō heightens this dramatic revelation by reconfiguring the gender difference as the biblical difference between "man" and "wo-man" ("female man"), perhaps in allusion to Adam and to Hamlet's earlier quibble on "body" and "thing" in 4.2.[144] It is not until the Gravedigger's "One that was a woman" that *onna* ("woman") is used: before the words are *mono* and *hito* for "person," with the Gravedigger comically mistaking Hamlet's *mono* in *nani mono no tame ni* ("What man dost thou dig it for?", 122) for the other meaning of *mono* as concrete "thing," written with a different character.

6. This example is also humorous, as the Gravedigger declares what everyone believes to be the reason Hamlet was sent to England: "Why, because 'a was mad" (142), *Hate, ki no chigatta ni yotte*.[145]

7. As is this one: "Why, here in Denmark" (152), *Hate, moto wa ōjisama ja ga na, kono Denmāku koku no*.[146]

8. In the next example, as the Gravedigger rehearses his expertise in practised phrases, *hate* is again literal: "Why, sir, his hide is so tanned with his/trade that 'a will keep out water a great while" (160–1), *Hāte, omaesama, shōbaigara de kawa ga nameite oru ni yotte, daibun no aida mizu wo hajikimasuru*.[147]

9. In a final dramatic revelation, the Gravedigger appears to boast of his royal connections, with the archaic *gozarimasu* copula adding flourish: "This/same skull, sir, was, sir, Yorick's skull, the king's jester" (170–1), *Hate, kono sharekotsu wa Yorikku no dokuro de gozarimasu, ōsama no odōbō de gozarimashita wai*.[148]

The last four examples are all spoken by Hamlet and relatively straightforward, as he has subsumed the Gravedigger's comic narrative into his tragicomic viewpoint: "Why, I will fight with him upon this theme" (255), *Hate, kono koto dake wa;*[149]

as Hamlet challenges Laertes, he says "I'll do't" (266), *Hate, ore mo shite mishō wa,*[150] and "And if thou prate of mountains let them throw/Millions of acres on us till our ground" (269–70), *Nan ja, issho ni umeraretai, hate, ore mo issho ni umeraryō wai;*[151] and finally over Ophelia's body, "I loved you ever – but it is no matter" (279), *Yo wa onushi wo ai shite otta ni . . . . Hate, kamau koto wa nai.*[152]

Shōyō clearly liked the word, because when he came to revise the play in 1933 all but one of the *hate*s remained.[153] Only half of the previous examples are formal equivalents of source words, with the others rendering the subtext, and even more than the previous examples of keywording, *hate* resounds throughout the scene. Moreover, in Shōyō's dichotomy of *ninjō* and *fūzoku*, this kabuki archaism associates the Gravedigger with the latter, making him comically accepting of his role in a hierarchy that Hamlet challenges, and to the extent that the Gravedigger and his assistant do accept their role they also take pride in their occupation, as when the Gravedigger questions the right of Ophelia as a suicide to Christian burial (5.1.6–8):

GRAVEDIGGER.   How can that be, unless she [Ophelia] drowned
                           herself in her own defense?
OTHER.            Why, 'tis found so.

Professional pride develops into quite a heated argument that foreshadows the fight between Hamlet and Laertes over who has loved Ophelia the most. In this dialogue at least, the earthiness of their speech is conveyed through the heavy use of final particles:[154]

Kō.     *Waga mi wo kabaute mi wo nageta no demo nai ni, honshiki to iu koto ga aru kai yai?*
          her body – defending – body – threw (into the water) – unless – a proper burial – can it be? – bah! (particle)
OTSU.   *Demo, sore ga oyakunin sa ano iiwatashi ja wai no.*
          but – that – the official – his judgment – it is – (double emphatic particles)

The archaic *hate* is supported by an undercurrent of archaism in particles such as *ja* and *wai*, which is solely emphatic in purpose and occurs fifteen times in the scene and *ja* thirty-three times. Nor is it necessarily fanciful to suggest that *wai* echoes phonically the repetition of the interrogative "why," which occurs eighteen times in the scene out of a total fifty-five instances in the play as a whole. By way of parallel, Shōyō translates the first word in the first sentence of *A Midsummer Night's Dream,* "Now, fair Hippolyta, our nuptial hour/Draws on apace" (1.1.1–2), with the archaic *nau,* although the word is pronounced *nō* with the sense of "Listen to me!" rather than the temporal "now."[155]

One theme of this book has been Shōyō's comic acceptance of the impossibility of his task. Shōyō's archaisms are primarily creative interpretation, but just as Hamlet's nostalgia is for the lost innocence of his childhood, they may also embody a nostalgia for the relatively fixed roles of feudal society (of his samurai father, for example) that, ironically, is affirmed through the challenge of Shakespeare translation. Shōyō finds his response to Shakespeare in his native culture, but for all the real and imagined similarities his nativism exposes him to Shakespeare's ultimate foreignness.

## Lexical Diversity

Shōyō's archaising tendency comes across not so much as an end in itself but as an inevitable outcome of his engagement with Shakespeare's texts, and is therefore only one dimension of his broader appreciation of Shakespeare's lexical variety. What he notices first and foremost about Shakespearean drama is "the remarkable wealth of its vocabulary, its diversity, and the freedom with which the writer deploys it."[156] Shōyō slightly underestimates the size of Shakespeare's vocabulary at fifteen thousand words,[157] but the point for him is the breadth of Shakespeare's usage which

> includes everything from classical archaisms to the popular language of the Elizabethan age, slang, dialect, foreign words and neologisms. His language corresponds to every social class and human character type, and the same content may vary in style of expression according to the individual, period, situation, and the mood and temperament.[158]

Shōyō's priority, therefore, is to find fitting equivalents for the range of Shakespeare's lexicon. One historical advantage he has is the considerable growth in Japanese vocabulary and native literacy rates over the course of his career, evidenced and advanced by Ōtsuki Fumihiko's modern Japanese dictionaries and the influx of *kango* (Sino-Japanese words and character compounds), many of them neologisms resulting from the new terminologies and fields of knowledge introduced through the Meiji goals of modernisation and Westernisation. Shōyō had himself popularised the word *shakai* ("society") in his early novel of social mores, *Tōsei shosei katagi*.

Between 1869 and 1915, the proportion of *kango* to native Japanese words (*wago*) listed in Japanese dictionaries is estimated to have shifted from a ratio of 21.5% to 35.4% in 1869 to 55.0% to 22.6% in 1915.[159] The feudal society into which Shōyō had been born was predominantly local and agricultural, with a majority peasant class speaking local dialects and having limited reading ability; economic development in Meiji and Taishō Japan and the growth in literacy rates were facilitated by a corpus of old and new Sino-Japanese words with fixed meanings that could be learnt at school. When Sōseki complains of the difficulty of Shōyō's Japanese in his *Hamlet* translation, he may from his own teaching experience have been referring to the limited *kanji* knowledge of a semi-educated majority, but (as the drama critic Atsumi Seitarō was to comment) the literacy divide had become somewhat less of an issue by the time of the translator's death in 1935,[160] and Shōyō may have contributed to this developmental process through the repeated use in his translations of modern *kango* and phonetic *furigana* readings. This final section looks first at how Shōyō's translation of a single word, the keyword "nature" in *King Lear*, employs a range of collocations that is certainly as diverse as what Shakespeare meant by the word, and then at a selection of personal pronouns as a further example of the translator's lexical diversity.

The word "nature" occurs thirty-eight times in *King Lear*, and has been a key topic in the play's critical history, with John F. Danby arguing in his *Shakespeare's Doctrine of Nature: A Study of "King Lear"* (1948) that Shakespeare's tragedy dramatises this single word as a defining theme of early modern English discourse. As I explained in Chapter 2, "nature" also relates to Shōyō's realism. It is translated by Shōyō in order of occurrence as follows:

1. Lear asks his eldest daughter Goneril to tell him how much she loves him "That we our largest bounty may extend/Where nature doth with merit challenge." (1.1.52–3) "Nature," meaning "natural affection," is translated here *kōkō* 孝行 "filial duty,"[161] the Confucian notion of the obligation that children must naturally feel for their parents.
2. Lear is furious with Cordelia for refusing to flatter him, behaviour "Which nor our nature, nor our place can bear" (172). This "nature" contrasts Lear's individual temperament with his "place" or rank (*mibun*), and is translated simply as *sei* 性,[162] "temperament." That the basic meaning of *sei* is "sexuality" suggests how deeply Lear's pride has been rattled.
3. When Lear condemns Cordelia as "a wretch whom nature is ashamed/Almost t'acknowledge hers" (213–4), Shōyō expands the sense of "nature" here to mean literally her "present parent," *genzai no oya* 現在の親,[163] Lear himself.
4. France defends his future wife Cordelia's self-restraint as no more than "a tardiness in nature" (237), which Shōyō calls *mochimae* 持前,[164] a person's inherent characteristics.
5. In his self-introductory soliloquy, the bastard Edmund declares that "Thou, Nature, art my goddess" (1.2.1). Shōyō uses what is now the most familiar collocation, and a Meiji coinage, *daishizen* ("great nature") 大自然.[165] *Shizen*, like *fushigi*, is an old Buddhist word denoting things that exist in and of themselves, but with modernisation gained wider usage as a scientific term and in contexts such as literary naturalism.
6. In the same speech, Edmund describes the illicit sexual activity that begot him as "the lusty stealth of nature" (11). Shōyō omits this one and paraphrases the sense with a candid phrase meaning "avoiding inquisitive looks and taking [sexual] pleasure in procreation."[166]
7/8. Edmund's father, Gloucester, contrasts the rational explanation of natural occurrences such as "eclipses in the sun and moon" (103) with a political truth that human behaviour is often swayed by irrational superstitions: "Though the wisdom of Nature/can reason it thus and thus, yet nature finds itself/scourged by the sequent effects. Love cools, friendship/falls off, brothers divide" (103–7). Shōyō paraphrases the first "nature" as "scientists," *rigakushadomo*, where *ri* 理 has the traditional meaning of "the laws of nature," and the second is translated *shizenkai* 自然界, "the natural world,"[167] and therefore one that encompasses human behaviour as well.
9. Shōyō paraphrases the third instance in Gloucester's speech, "The King falls from bias of nature" (111), with a phrase meaning that the king has betrayed his natural instincts or tendencies. Shōyō here juxtaposes two words for "nature,"

*sei no shizen* 性の自然,[168] literally the "nature of his temperament," to suggest that more than lesser mortals the king's "nature" is bound symbiotically to the natural world to which all are subject.

10. When Edmund describes his legitimate half-brother Edgar's "nature" as "so far from doing harms/That he suspects none" (178–9), and Shōyō for the first time uses *seishitsu* 性質,[169] meaning "character," for "nature."

11. Confronted by Goneril's unkindness, Lear begins to regret his earlier rejection of Cordelia, "Which like an engine wrenched my frame of nature/From the fixed place" (1.4.280–1). Shōyō translates "frame of nature" literally as *hongu no seijō* 本具の性情,[170] the "main tool of my disposition," where *seijō* is a less common collocation than *seishitsu*.

12. Echoing Edmund's previous soliloquy, Lear prays to the gods to avenge Goneril's apparent ingratitude: "Hear, Nature, hear, dear goddess, hear" (289). Shōyō translates this "nature" as "the Creator," *zōka no ongami* 造化の御神,[171] in an introduction to the curse that follows ("Into her womb convey fertility" etc., 292).

13. In another outburst of *amour propre*, Lear declares to the Fool that "I will forget my nature: so kind a father!" (1.5.31). Shōyō translates "nature" here as *jō* 情,[172] "warmth" or "feeling."

14. When Kent hits back at Oswald with the words "nature disclaims in thee" (2.2.53), Shōyō again uses *zōka* in a phrase that means "nature has no memory of having made you."[173]

15. Cornwall vents his rage at Kent as an uncouth man who is unable – unlike Goneril and Regan – to conceal his true feelings with flattery: Kent "constrains the garb/Quite from his nature" (95–6). This nature becomes *mochimae*, Kent's basic temperament.[174]

16. In a moment of insight, Lear declares that "We are not ourselves/When nature, being oppressed, commands the mind/To suffer with the body" (2.2.296–8). Shōyō here omits "nature" in a considerable paraphrase that uses the *zaru wo enai* construction, meaning "have no choice but to be," in this case "have no choice but to suffer."[175] *Kokoro* 心 for "mind," but literally meaning "heart," is a powerful word in the Japanese lexicon that may also connote this hidden nature.

17. Regan bluntly reminds her father: "O sir, you are old:/Nature in you stands on the very verge/Of her confine" (335–6). "Nature" is again omitted in the translation in a paraphrase that means "your life expectancy has reached a dead end [*yukidomari*]."[176]

18./19. Lear for the time being does not doubt the integrity of his second daughter's "nature," using the word twice in the same speech: "Thy tender-hefted nature shall not give/Thee o'er to harshness" (360–1), and "Thou better know'st/The offices of nature, bond of childhood,/Effects of courtesy, dues of gratitude" (366–8). In the first instance, we hear *kidate* for the first time, although written and meaning the same as *seishitsu* 性質, probably so as to elide with the phrase as a whole, *sonata wa yasashii kidate ja ni yotte* ("because you have a gentle nature"),[177] but perhaps also as a nod to Shakespeare's unusual usage, "tender-hefted"; "heft" means "weight" or "importance," and this sense of intrinsic rather than superficial gentleness is conveyed by Shōyō's mellifluous construction. In the second instance, "nature" is *mochimae*.[178]

20./21./22. "Nature" occurs three times in rapid succession in Lear's parting shot to Goneril and Regan as he defends his requirement of a full posse of knights to serve him: "Allow not nature more than nature needs" (455) and "nature needs not what thou gorgeous wear'st" (458). In the first case, Shōyō contrasts *shizen* with *ningen* ("human beings") to explain that human beings need no more than their natural requirements for warmth, dignity, and so on demand, and in the second case the modern word *shizen* is also used.[179]

23. Running mad on the heath at night, Lear howls at the storm to "Crack nature's molds, all germens spill at one/That makes ingrateful man!" (3.2.10–11). "Nature" is again "creation," the "creative force of nature," *zōka*.[180]

24. A little later in the scene, Kent declares of the storm that "Man's nature cannot carry/Th' affliction, nor the fear" (50–1). "Nature" here becomes "man's body," *karada* 体.[181]

25. Almost the same word, *ningen no karada* 身体 ("human body"),[182] is used when Kent again complains that "The tyranny of the open night's too rough/For nature to endure" (3.4.2–3).

26. When Lear once again fumes at Goneril and Regan, "Nothing could have subdued nature/To such a lowness but his unkind daughters" (76–7), Shōyō uses *arisama* 有様, meaning "state" or "condition" (literally, "the way things are").[183]

27. As Edmund callously justifies his betrayal of his father Gloucester with the words "nature/thus gives way to loyalty" (3.5.2–3), "nature" is rendered *ko no michi* 子の道, "the way of the child."[184]

28. In the mock trial scene, Lear asks of his daughters whether there is "any cause in nature that make/these hard hearts?" (3.6.74–5). "Nature" is omitted but paraphrased with a phrase meaning "something or other that was there in the first place."[185]

29. As Gloucester arrives to warn of the plot against his master Lear, Kent reassures him that "Oppressed nature sleeps" (94). "Nature" is again omitted, and the sense paraphrased with a phrase meaning "he can sleep now he is exhausted":[186] sleep is a healthy and natural response to what he has endured.

30. The blinded Gloucester, unaware that it is Edmund's treachery that has led to his eyes being cut out, urges Edmund to "enkindle all the sparks of nature/To quit this horrid act" (3.7.85–6). Shōyō renders the sense of filial love with *kōshi no jō* 孝子の情,[187] the feeling of a dutiful child for its parent.

31. Albany expresses his disgust at his wife Goneril's inhuman conduct: "I fear your disposition;/That nature which contemns its origin/Cannot be bordered certain in itself" (4.2.32–4). Both "disposition" and "nature" are rendered as *kidate* 気立 ("temperament"),[188] which this time is pronounced as it is written.

32. Over the sleeping Lear, the Doctor tells Cordelia that "Our foster nurse of nature is repose" (4.4.12). "Nature" becomes *jintai* 人体, the "human body."[189]

33. Gloucester believes his life to have come to an end: "My snuff and loathed part of nature should/Burn itself out" (4.6.39–40). "Nature" is again rendered as "body," *karada*.[190]

34. Lear presents his fallen state as a model of the integrity that once eluded him: "Nature's above art in that respect" (86). This "nature" is *shizen*, and "art" is *jinkō*, or "artifice."[191]

35. When Gloucester is reunited with Lear, calling him "O ruined piece of nature" (130), "nature" is *daishizen,* connecting with "This great world [*daisekai*]/ Shall so wear out to naught" (130–1) in the next line.[192]
36. The Gentleman hopes Lear will calm down if he sees Cordelia again, for she is a "daughter/Who redeems nature from the general curse/Which twain have brought her to" (201–3). Shōyō expands the sense of "nature" with a phrase meaning the "bad reputation" that women in general have acquired due to her elder sisters' behaviour, contrasting that with Cordelia's "pious heart" (*gokōshin* 御孝心).[193]
37. Reunited with her father, Cordelia prays to the "kind gods" to "Cure this great breach in his abused nature" (4.7.15–6), and Shōyō expands the sense with a sonorous phrase that does indeed sound like a prayer: *gyakutai no tame ni osoroshū sokonawaremashita shintai ya seishin* ("the body and soul that have been horribly hurt by abuse").[194]
38. Edmund, mortally wounded by Edgar in combat, makes contrition for the evil he has done: "Some good I mean to do,/Despite of mine own nature" (5.3.241–2). In Shōyō's translation, *honjō* 本性 is Edmund's original but not irredeemable nature.[195]

Within this list the collocations that are repeated are *shizen* (5 times), *karada* (4), *mochimae* (3), *zōka* (3), *kidate* (2), and *jō* (also read *nasake*) (2). The character *sei* also acquires currency, and typically for Shōyō, almost all the examples involve some degree of paraphrase. Although it is clearly impossible for Shōyō to use a single word for Shakespeare's "nature," it is significant given the anti-Platonic undercurrent of his theory of "hidden ideals" that "nature" as a word that opens on to a complex historical discourse behind the play and encompasses so many meanings that it is almost a Platonic symbol in itself, should lose that symbolic power through the range of Shōyō's collocations. That is by force of necessity, but it does suggest, at least at the linguistic level, the difficulty Shōyō has from his cultural background of reaching into the "hidden ideals," Platonic or otherwise, that drive Shakespeare's creativity. The difference with Shōyō's keywording is that words such as *fushigi,* in addition to developing themes and motifs, may have a numinous quality in his native culture that corresponds with that of Platonic symbolism in Shakespeare's culture.

Reviewing the revised translations (*shinshūbon*) shortly after the translator's death, Hattori Yoshika lists a number of examples of how he feels Shōyō's lexical choices "enrich the meaning and texture" of his translations,[196] which is what Shōyō means by *jōmi.* One striking example is Shōyō's use of personal pronouns, where he goes beyond the familiar Shakespearean distinction between "you" and "thou" to express nuances of meaning. Hattori lists seventeen words for "you" and eighteen for "I" that Shōyō uses.[197] The following selection from his *Othello* revision (which had just been released at the time of Hattori's article and which Hattori singles out for praise) gives an indication of the diversity of Shōyō's usage.

Personal pronouns are often avoided in Japanese where they are not required to make sense, which makes their appearance in Shōyō's translations all the more striking. As Othello's paranoia starts to take hold in 3.3, and Desdemona innocently asks him, "How now, my dear Othello?" (283), the question becomes *Nē, anata, dō nasutta no?*,[198] where *anata* is commonly used by wives to address their husbands and expresses the affection implied by the English question. Personal pronouns occur seven times over the next seven lines, as when Othello complains "I have a pain upon my forehead, here" (288), and yet only once is a pronoun used in the Japanese, when Desdemona offers to treat her husband's headache, "Let me but bind it hard, within this hour/It will be well" (290–1), which Shōyō translates correctly with a conditional construction, *Watashi ga kittsūku yuwaeta nara*, literally "If I [*watashi*] bind it hard."[199] *Watashi* is not strictly necessary here, but like the *anata* it dramatises the couple's relationship from Desdemona's point of view as one founded on mutual trust and love, and she uses *watashi* (and the softer *watasha*) and *anata* throughout the translation in this way. The two pronouns are always written in the feminine *hiragana* in Desdemona's case rather than the more formal and masculine *kanji*, except for a few instances in the last two acts as Othello becomes more openly aggressive. In 4.2, when Desdemona implores her husband on her knees to explain "what doth [his] speech import?" (31), and he brusquely retorts "Why, what art thou?" (34), Shōyō uses both *hiragana* and *kanji* to assert her fidelity when Shakespeare uses only "your":

> Your wife, my lord: your true and loyal wife. (35)
> *Anata* 貴郎 *no tsuma desu, anata* あなた *no teijitsuna tsuma desu.*[200]

The first *anata* is archaic, used to address husbands and lovers, and contrasts with Othello's *kisama* for "thou," which is also archaic and written with a *kanji* 汝 that bluntly denotes his male superiority in the relationship. Other readings of *anata* (and the more informal *anta*) include 貴君 by the Duke and Othello, where *kimi* 君 can be used for both equals and inferiors, and 閣下, which is normally read *kakka*, meaning "your lordship," and used by Othello as he calmly defends his suit against Desdemona's father Brabantio, who is indignant that his daughter wants to marry a black man; this *anata* translates Othello's "Good signior" (1.2.60).[201] Where other male characters use the informal masculine *ore* and the more polite *boku*, Iago frequently calls himself *temae* (although read *watashi*), which sounds aggressive and even rude, and Cassio uses *unu* for "you," which is positively insulting.

Emilia, who is Iago's wife and Desdemona's confidante, also uses *watashi* (written in *hiragana* rather than *kanji*) to refer to herself, but twice uses *onoshi*, which is an archaic "you" or "thou" that by the time of the late Edo era was used mainly towards servants and other subordinates. This is shortly after Othello has strangled Desdemona, and she tells him "thou hast killed the sweetest innocent/That e'er did lift up eye" (5.2.197–8):

> *onoshi wa kono yo no naka ni ikite ite ittō kawairashii, nan no tsumi mo nai ohitori wo koroshagattan da.*[202]

The archaism contrasts with the otherwise contemporary register of the sentence, and Emilia next uses *onoshi* when she once again accuses Othello, "O thou dull

Moor, that handkerchief thou speak'st of" (223): *Ō, onore, Mūa no ōbakarōme! Onoshi ga ima itta hankachi tei no wa.*[203] With the first sentence meaning "Oh, you [pejorative], you stupid great Moor!", Emilia clearly submits to her husband's early modern racism, but Shōyō's is a warm translation that suits the warmth of Emilia's loyalty to Desdemona.[204]

* * * * *

This chapter has taken a broad look inside Shōyō's Shakespeare translations in an endeavour to understand how he recreates the rhythm, warmth, and diversity that he valued in Shakespeare. Two general points are the attention Shōyō pays to the sound of the language and the extent to which his translating style becomes more contemporary after the 1911 "kabuki *Hamlet*" (even if we find him still using *hate* and *kisama* in his 1935 *Othello* revision). A third and more covert point concerns his use of paraphrase.

The rhythmicality of Shōyō's style is based in the seven-five syllabic meter of his native drama, and even as an abstraction of that meter often has a sustained syllabic quality that is supported by phonic harmonies. Its warmth is evident more from readerly techniques such as keywording, phonetic glossing, and archaism. Although the translations may sometimes sound like kabuki, I have tried to avoid a blank equivalence with kabuki since, apart from his early *Julius Caesar* adaptation, Shōyō is always translating rather than adapting Shakespeare as a preliminary to performance by modern Japanese actors, and I am mainly interested in how he rises to the line-by-line challenges posed by Shakespeare's language. Shōyō's approach is as much scholarly and critical as it is artistic, and especially given his belief in Shakespeare's "hiddenness," his translations are unlikely to amount to anything like a coherent interpretation, kabuki or otherwise, even if he does use cohesive effects. Shōyō tries, in other words, to leave his translations open to interpretation, and similarly I hope that my analysis will encourage further study, for example of a wider and more generically balanced selection of the translations and in his use of substantives and local dialect.

## Notes

1 Tsubouchi Shōyō, "Jibun no honyaku ni tsuite," in *Shōyō senshū*, supp. vol. 5 (1977), 257. *Jōmi* 情味 (literally "emotional flavour") is defined as "emotional depth" or "appeal to human feelings"; *chōshi* is written 調子.

2 Ibid., 260.

3 See, for example, Antoine Berman's influential thesis, "Translation and the Trials of the Foreign" (1995), in *The Translation Studies Reader*, ed. Lawrence Venuti (London: Routledge, 2021), 247–260, where Berman lists twelve "deforming tendencies" found in translations, among which "clarification," "ennoblement," and "expansion" are relevant to Shōyō's tendency to paraphrase.

4 Tsubouchi Shōyō, "Nihon de enzuru *Hamuretto*" (1907), in *Sheikusupia kenkyū shiryō shūsei*, vol. 2, ed. Sasaki Takashi (Tokyo: Nihon Tosho Centre, 1997), 200–1.

5 Resonance is also an important concept in Japanese poetics, whether *hibiki* ("echo") or *nioi* ("odour"), albeit usually too subtle for the dramatic flow of the Shakespearean line.

6 Mori Shū, Torigoe Bunzō, and Nagatomo Chiyoji, eds., *Chikamatsu Monzaemon shū*, vol. 1 (Tokyo: Shōgakukan, 1974), 77. Trans. Donald Keene, *Four Major Plays of Chikamatsu* (New York: Columbia University Press, 1998), 51–2.

7 Tsubouchi Shōyō, "Chikamatsu no *jōruri*" (1890), in *Shōyō senshū*, vol. 8 (1977), 669–70. The same argument can be made about imitating the syllabic style of Shōyō's kabuki mentor Kawatake Mokuami, whose mastery of *shichigochō* was if anything greater than Chikamatsu's.

8 Tsubouchi Shōyō, "Shinkyoku Urashima" (1904), in *Shōyō senshū*, vol. 3 (1977), 2.

9 Ueda Bin, "*Shingakugekiron* narabi ni *Shinkyoku Urashima*," *Kabuki* 56 (1904): 1. Ueda's translation of European symbolist poetry, *Kaichōon* (The Sound of the Tide, 1905), is considered the outstanding literary translation of the late Meiji era.

10 Like an operatic aria in the way that a single dancer dances a set piece at the front of the stage, and therefore representing a parallel with Shakespearean soliloquy. There also seems to me a parallel between the transition from Noh *utai* to kabuki style and Shakespeare's mixing of classical and more modern modes of expression.

11 "Shinkyoku Urashima," 21–2.

12 An intense style of *shamisen* accompaniment that contrasts with the lighter tone of *nagauta*.

13 *Kōdan* reciters are usually seated at a desk or lectern.

14 Tsubouchi Shōyō, *Hamuretto* (Tokyo: Chūō Kōronsha, 1933), 114.

15 As an example of Shōyō's technique of phonetic glossing discussed later in this chapter, *mukae* is written with a character that means to "fight back" when *mukaeru* means to "welcome," suggesting that Hamlet in a sense "welcomes" his fate.

16 *Hamuretto* (1933), 115.

17 "Jibun no honyaku ni tsuite," 256.

18 Tsubouchi Shōyō, "Temupesuto" (1915), in *Shōyō senshū*, vol. 4 (1977), 78–9.

19 The sea has a range of erotic connotations in Japanese culture that Shōyō had previously explored in *Shinkyoku Urashima*, where the princess Otohime in the disguise of a turtle gives the poor fisher boy Urashima Tarō a ride on her back to her father the Dragon King in his palace at the bottom of the sea.

20 Nakamura Yukihiko and Mizuno Minoru, eds., *Akinari/Bakin: kanshō koten Nihon bungaku*, vol. 35 (Tokyo: Kadokawa Shoten, 1977), 275. Trans. Chris Drake, in Shirane Haruo, ed., *Early Modern Japanese Literature: An Anthology, 1600–1900* (New York: Columbia University Press, 2002), 908.

21 Tsubouchi Shōyō, "Kyokutei Bakin" (1920), in *Shōyō senshū*, vol. 12 (1977), 297.

22 Tsubouchi Shōyō, "Henrī yonsei dainibu" (1919), in *Shōyō senshū*, vol. 4 (1977), 484.

23 Daniel Poch, *Licentious Fictions and the Nineteenth-Century Japanese Novel* (New York: Columbia University Press, 2019), 81.

24 Ibid., 62.

25 Glynne Walley, "Translator's Introduction," in Kyokutei Bakin, *Eight Dogs, Or, "Hakkenden": An Ill-Considered Jest*, trans. Glynne Walley (Ithaca, NY: Cornell University East Asia Program, 2021), xxx. Walley further comments on the text's linguistic sophistication (xxix).

26 "Temupesuto," 45.

27 Tsubouchi Shōyō, *Romio to Jurietto* (Tokyo: Waseda University Press, 1910), 142–3.

28 "Temupesuto," 145.

29 Ibid., 46.

30 Ibid., 44, where Shōyō expounds (but does not quote) Dowden's influential view that "we identify Prospero in some measure with Shakspere himself. It is rather because the temper of Prospero, the grave harmony of his character, his self-mastery, his calm validity of will, his sensitiveness to wrong, his unfaltering justice, and with these, a certain abandonment, a remoteness from the common joys and sorrows of the world, are characteristic of Shakspere as discovered to us in all his latest plays. Prospero is a harmonious and fully developed *will*" (Edward Dowden, *Shakspere: A Critical Study of His Mind and Art* (London: Kegan Paul, Trench and Co., 1875), 417).

31  Natsume Kinnosuke, "Tsubouchi-hakase to *Hamuretto*" (1911), in *Sōseki zenshū*, vol. 16 (Tokyo: Iwanami Shoten, 2019, facsimile ed.), 397.

32  "Temupesuto," 128–9.

33  The recording is available in two parts on YouTube at www.youtube.com/watch?v= Zu4gNuQwjf8 and www.youtube.com/watch?v=4zjMLYWilUw&t=25s (hatayaen), accessed 16 November 2023.

34  Tsubouchi Shōyō, *Venisu no shōnin* (Tokyo: Chūō Kōronsha, 1933), 163–4.

35  "Sallied" ("assailed") in the First Quarto reading adopted in the Arden Third Shakespeare edition rather than the First Folio reading "solid" in the late Victorian editions (e.g. Dowden's Arden) available to Shōyō.

36  *Hamuretto* (1933), 20.

37  Ibid., 49.

38  Ibid., 106.

39  Ibid., 114.

40  Ibid., 151.

41  Ibid., 156.

42  Ibid., 188.

43  According to one recent analysis, *o* occurs slightly less in everyday Japanese than other vowels (Tamaoka Katsuo and Makioka Shōgo, "Frequency of Occurrence for Units of Phonemes, Morae, and Syllables Appearing in a Lexical Corpus of a Japanese Newspaper," *Behavior Research Methods, Instruments, & Computers* 36, no. 3 [2004]: 531–47), which from a present perspective would make Shōyō's usage of it all the more distinctive.

44  In Japanese poetics, the consonant *k* is said to have a bright, clear quality.

45  "Jibun no honyaku ni tsuite," 261.

46  Friederike von Schwerin-High, *Shakespeare, Reception and Translation: Germany and Japan* (New York: Continuum, 2004), 180.

47  Ibid.

48  Shōyō's reason for not using *oboeru* is likely to be stylistic. For example, Gonzalo's "remember whom thou hast aboard" (1.1.19) becomes "you must not forget" (*wasurechai ikan zo*).

49  The *bushu* (or *kanji* radical) which often indicate the meaning and reading of characters.

50  "Temupesuto," 61.

51  Ibid.

52  Ibid.

53  Ibid., 62. In this line, the topic of "remembrance" is rendered initially with a noun, *kioku* (memory) that contains the *ki* character, but is read with the softer *oboe* (the noun form of *oboeru*).

54  Ibid.

55  Ibid.

56  Ibid.

57  Ibid., 63.

58  See Massimiliano Tomasi, *Rhetoric in Modern Japan: Western Influences on the Development of Narrative and Oratorical Style* (Honolulu: University of Hawaii Press, 2004), 65–6.

59  Tsubouchi Shōyō, "Biji ronkō" (1893), in *Shōyō senshū*, vol. 11 (1977), 30.

60  An earlier version of my discussion of Shōyō's repetition of *fushigi* appeared in my article, "Tsubouchi Shōyō to Sheikusupia no 'fushigi'," Society of Humanities, Kwansei Gakuin University, *Jinbun Ronkyū* 72, no. 3 (2022): 65–90.

61  Shōyō's reason for not using *fushigi* more than twenty-six times in his translation is, as ever, semantic. For example, Prospero's "to my state grew stranger" (1.2.76) becomes *dandan kokuji ni tōzakatte* ("gradually distanced from affairs of state") ("Temupesuto," 63) and in Ariel's song "something rich and strange" (402) becomes *takara to keshinu* ("changing into treasure") (ibid., 79); the latter usage evokes the beauty of coral and pearls rather than the subjective state implied by *fushigi*.

62  Ibid., 161.

63  Ibid., 68.
64  Ibid., 73.
65  See Note 3.
66  Ibid., 80.
67  Ibid., 85.
68  Ibid., 106.
69  Ibid., 113.
70  Ibid., 132.
71  Ibid., 160.
72  Ibid., 164.
73  Ibid., 122–3.
74  Schwerin-High, 200.
75  "Temupesuto," 72.
76  Ibid., 83.
77  Ibid., 86.
78  Ibid., 105.
79  Ibid., 112.
80  Ibid., 113.
81  Ibid., 121.
82  Ibid., 127.
83  Ibid., 131.
84  Ibid., 151.
85  Ibid., 167.
86  *Kana* symbols (also called *yomigana* or *rubi*) printed above or to the right of *kanji* characters to indicate their intended pronunciation. When modern printing technology was imported from Britain in the early Meiji era, the type size adopted for *furigana* was equivalent to what British printers of the time called "ruby" type.
87  "Jibun no Shēkusupiya honyaku ni tsuite," 263. Shōyō does not use *rubi* in the Japanese readers he wrote for primary school pupils in the 1900s for the obvious reason that these were meant to test and develop pupils' knowledge of *kanji*.
88  The inclusion of *rubi* depended on the educational level of the target readership. The anthology *Kindai gikyoku shū*, ed. Sofue Shōji (Tokyo: Kadokawa Shoten, 1974), indicates its use in a selection of popular plays from the Meiji and Taishō eras. Most of the writers anthologised use *rubi* sparingly, while the literary translations of ten Shakespeare plays by Tozawa Koya and Asano Hyōkyo (1905–9) were published almost entirely without *rubi*.
89  Tsubouchi Shōyō, "Manatsu no yo no yume" (1915), in *Shōyō senshū*, vol. 4 (1977), 211.
90  Hattori Yoshika, "Shinshūbon to Tsubouchi-hakase," *Saō Fukkō* 20 (1935): 3.
91  Ibid., 3–4.
92  Ōtsuki's *Genkai* [Sea of Words] dictionary, considered the first modern Japanese-language dictionary and modelled on *Webster's Dictionary*, was published in 1889–91, and his posthumous *Daigenkai* [Great Sea of Words] in 1932–7.
93  Tsubouchi Shōyō, "Henrī yonsei daiichibu" (1919), in *Shōyō senshū*, vol. 4 (1977), 309.
94  Ibid., 368.
95  Ibid.
96  Ibid., 369.
97  Ibid.
98  Ibid., 371. The full speech reads: "Wilt thou rob this leathern-jerkin, crystal-/button, not-pated, agate-ring, puke-stocking, caddis-/garter, smooth-tongue, Spanish-pouch?" (2.4.68–70).
99  Ibid., 373.
100  Ibid.

101  Ibid. 蘇國人.
102  Ibid., 374.
103  Ibid.
104  This is described by Yanabu Akira's "cassette effect" (or "jewel box") theory of Japanese translation, namely that the use of *kanji* in translations of foreign texts, whether from Chinese in pre-modern times or from European languages since the Meiji era, conveys to Japanese readers an expectation of significance even when the source meaning is unfamiliar to them; for Shōyō, this trope may be sufficient in itself to connote Shakespeare's illusory depth. See Yanabu Akira, "Translation in Japan: The Cassette Effect," *TTR: traduction, terminologie, redaction* 22, no. 1 (2009): 19–28.
105  "Henrī yonsei daiichibu," 380.
106  Ibid.
107  Ibid., 381.
108  Ibid., 382. Falstaff is referring to Hal's father, the king.
109  Ibid.
110  Ibid., 387.
111  "Novels in Japan have traditionally been regarded as tools for education, with their main purpose typically being to promote virtuous behaviour and condemn wickedness. The reality, however, is that the only stories people actually want to read have been those containing luridly violent or obscene material": Tsubouchi Shōyō, "Shōsetsu shinzui" (1884–5), in *Tsubouchi Shōyō shū* (1969), 3.
112  "Henrī yonsei daiichibu, 389.
113  Ibid., 394.
114  Apart from "major" which is written *daiteian* ("major premise") and read *mējoa*, and "sheriff," which is also written in *kanji* and read *mēyoa*, there are no divergencies between *kanji* and *rubi* in this speech.
115  Krzysztof Filip Rudolf, *Archaization in Literary Translation as Nostalgic Pastiche* (New York: Peter Lang, 2019), 7–8.
116  Seth Jacobowitz, *Writing Technology in Meiji Japan: A Media History of Modern Japanese Literature and Visual Culture* (Boston, MA: Harvard University Asia Center, 2014), 221.
117  Rudolf, 151.
118  Ibid.
119  The Shakespeare translator learns to distinguish between words Shakespeare uses that were not archaic in his time but are considered so nowadays (e.g. "forsooth," "perchance") and medievalisms that would have been considered archaic, such as "eyne" ("eyes") and "hight" ("be called").
120  Barbara E. Thornbury, *Sukeroku's Double Identity: The Structure of Edo Kabuki* (Ann Arbor: Michigan Papers in Japanese Studies, 1982), 21.
121  Watanabe Tamotsu, *Kabuki no kotoba* (Tokyo: Taishūkan Shoten, 2004), 226–31.
122  Ibid., 230.
123  I examine this keywording in my article "Shōyō's Realism and Shakespeare's Real Women: The Case of Isabella," Kwansei Gakuin University, *Journal of the Society of English and American Literature* 67 (2023): 1–24.
124  *Ja* is still common in western Japan, although less so in Kansai where it was replaced by *ya* in the late Edo era, and more generally characterises the speech of old men. It is also heard in the standard negative colloquial *ja nai* ("is not").
125  Tsubouchi Shōyō, *Hamuretto* (Tokyo: Waseda University Press, 1909), 106–66.
126  In modern Japanese, written and pronounced *omotte* and *kurushimeru*. Up to and including his Shakespeare revisions of the early 1930s, Shōyō's preference is for classical orthography, for example *kefu* for *kyō* ("today"), and old-style *kanji*, neither of which was officially reformed or standardised until after 1945.
127  *Nō* solicits either attention or agreement (equivalent to the modern *ne* particle), *zoi* indicates mild emphasis, and *gana* unfulfilled hope or uncertainty.

128 Tsubouchi Shōyō, *Richādo sansei* (Tokyo: Waseda University Press, 1918), 1–14, and Tsubouchi Shōyō, *Verōna no futashinshi* (Tokyo: Waseda University Press, 1926), 1–13.

129 For example, *sorya* short for *sore wa* ("that is") and *kerya* for the conditional inflexion *kereba*. *Gozansu* is still used in the eastern Kantō region, but to Shōyō's readers would have probably sounded like a kabuki usage.

130 Tozawa Koya and Asano Wasaburō, trans., *Juriasu Shīzā* (Tokyo: Dai Nihon Tosho, 1907), 128–53.

131 *Hamuretto* (1909), 106–18, and Fukuda Tsuneari, trans., *Hamuretto* (Tokyo: Shinchōsha, 1988), 81–90.

132 *Hamuretto* (1909), 117. The 1933 revision differs only in two small details.

133 Fukuda, 89.

134 Tsubouchi Shōyō, "Shīzaru kidan: jiyū no tachi nagori no kireaji" (1884), in *Shōyō senshū*, supp. vol. 2 (1977), 437–8.

135 Tsubouchi Shōyō, *Jūriyasu Shīzā* (Tokyo: Waseda University Press, 1914), 221.

136 Tetsuo Kishi and Graham Bradshaw, *Shakespeare in Japan* (London: Continuum, 2005), 7.

137 A twenty-two-year-old Kawatake played Voltimand in the 1911 Bungei Kyōkai production, and later commented that Shōyō's "translation was heavy in formal traditional language, which was hard to follow when presented on stage." Quoted in Fujikura Takeo, "Child Drama for Domestic Presentation: The First Known Japanese Concept of Child Drama," *Youth Theatre Journal* 18 (2004): 117.

138 *Chikamatsu Monzaemon shū*, vol. 1 (1974), 74.

139 *Hamuretto* (1909), 216.

140 Ibid., 217–18.

141 Ibid., 219.

142 Ibid., 220.

143 Ibid., 223.

144 "The body is with the King, but the King is not/with the body. The King is a thing" (4.2.25–6): Hamlet's taunting of Rosencrantz and Guildenstern that a king can assert his authority in name as well as person. The opening line of the play, spoken by Barnardo, is "Who's there?" (1.1.1), which Shōyō translates *Nani mono ja?* (ibid., 1), literally "What person is it?"

145 Ibid., 224.

146 Ibid., 225.

147 Ibid., 226.

148 Ibid., 227.

149 Ibid., 234.

150 Ibid.

151 Ibid.

152 Ibid., 235.

153 Iago uses *hate* throughout both the 1911 *Othello* translation and its 1935 revision.

154 *Hamuretto* (1909), 214.

155 "Manatsu no yo no yume, 191.

156 "Jibun no honyaku ni tsuite," 259.

157 Nowadays estimated at over twenty thousand words, with some 1,700 words being the first recorded use.

158 "Jibun no honyaku ni tsuite," 259.

159 Akamatsu Nobuhiko, "Literary Acquisitions in Japanese-English Bilinguals," in *Handbook of Orthography and Literacy*, ed. R. Malatesha Joshi and P. G. Aaron (New York: Routledge, 2005), 481.

160 Atsumi Seitarō, "Nihon in okeru *Hamuretto* jōenshi," *Saō Fukkō* 1 (1933): 33.

161 Tsubouchi Shōyō, *Riya ō* (Tokyo: Waseda University Press, 1912), 5.

162 Ibid., 13.

163  Ibid., 16.
164  Ibid., 17.
165  Ibid., 24.
166  Ibid., 25.
167  Ibid., 32.
168  Ibid.
169  Ibid., 37.
170  Ibid., 61.
171  Ibid., 62.
172  Ibid., 70.
173  Ibid., 88.
174  Ibid., 91.
175  Ibid., 106.
176  Ibid., 109.
177  Ibid., 112.
178  Ibid.
179  Ibid., 119.
180  Ibid., 128.
181  Ibid., 132.
182  Ibid., 139.
183  Ibid., 144.
184  Ibid., 153.
185  Ibid., 162.
186  Ibid., 163.
187  Ibid., 174.
188  Ibid., 187.
189  Ibid., 198.
190  Ibid., 206.
191  Ibid., 210.
192  Ibid., 214.
193  Ibid., 219.
194  Ibid., 228.
195  Ibid., 265.
196  Hattori, 3.
197  Ibid., 5–6.
198  *Oserō* (1935), 139.
199  Ibid., 140. *Kittsūku* ("tightly") is conventionally written *kitsuku* but as *kittsūku* nicely physicalises Desdemona's binding her husband's head.
200  Ibid., 206.
201  Ibid., 21.
202  Ibid., 270–1.
203  Ibid., 273.
204  Emilia's expression may echo the racism of Desdemona's father Brabantio in 1.2 when he asks Othello, "O, thou foul thief, where hast thou stowed my daughter?" (62), the first part of which Shōyō translates *Ō, onore, kegawashii tōzokume* (ibid., 21).

## References

Akamatsu Nobuhiko. "Literary Acquisitions in Japanese-English Bilinguals." In *Handbook of Orthography and Literacy*, edited by R. Malatesha Joshi and P. G. Aaron, 481–96. New York: Routledge, 2005, https://doi.org/10.4324/9780203448526.

Atsumi Seitarō. "Nihon in okeru *Hamuretto* jōenshi" [Productions of *Hamlet* in Japan]. *Saō Fukkō* 1 (October 1933): 30–6.

Berman, Antoine. "Translation and the Trials of the Foreign." 1995. In *The Translation Studies Reader*, edited by Lawrence Venuti, 247–60. London: Routledge, 2021, https://doi.org/10.4324/9780429280641-28.

Danby, John F. *Shakespeare's Doctrine of Nature: A Study of "King Lear"*. London: Faber & Faber, 1948.

Dowden, Edward. *Shakspere: A Critical Study of His Mind and Art*. London: Kegan Paul, Trench and Co., 1875.

Fujikura Takeo. "Child Drama for Domestic Presentation: The First Known Japanese Concept of Child Drama." *Youth Theatre Journal* 18 (May 2004): 107–21, https://doi.org/10.1080/08929092.2004.10012567.

Fukuda Tsuneari, trans. *Hamuretto* [Hamlet]. 1967. Tokyo: Shinchōsha, 1988.

Gallimore, Daniel. "Shōyō's Realism and Shakespeare's Real Women: The Case of Isabella." Kwansei Gakuin University, *Journal of the Society of English and American Literature* 67 (March 2023): 1–24.

———. "Tsubouchi Shōyō to Sheikusupia no 'fushigi'" [Strangeness in the Shakespeare Translations of Tsubouchi Shōyō]. Society of Humanities, Kwansei Gakuin University, *Jinbun Ronkyū* 72, no. 3 (December 2022): 65–90.

Hattori Yoshika. "Shinshūbon to Tsubouchi-hakase" [The Revised Shakespeare Translations of Dr Tsubouchi]. *Saō Fukkō* 20 (May 1935): 2–10.

Inagaki Tatsurō, ed. *Tsubouchi Shōyō shū* [Works of Tsubouchi Shōyō]. Tokyo: Chikuma Shobō, 1969.

Jacobowitz, Seth. *Writing Technology in Meiji Japan: A Media History of Modern Japanese Literature and Visual Culture*. Boston, MA: Harvard University Asia Center, 2014, https://doi.org/10.1163/9781684175628.

Keene, Donald, trans. and ed. *Four Major Plays of Chikamatsu*. New York: Columbia University Press, 1998.

Kishi Tetsuo and Graham Bradshaw. *Shakespeare in Japan*. London: Continuum, 2005.

Mori Shū, Torigoe Bunzō, and Nagatomo Chiyoji, eds. *Chikamatsu Monzaemon shū* [Works of Chikamatsu Monzaemon], vol. 1. Tokyo: Shōgakukan, 1974.

Nakamura Yukihiko and Mizuno Minoru, eds. *Akinari/Bakin: kanshō koten Nihon bungaku* [Anthology of Classical Japanese Literature: Akinari and Bakin], vol. 35. Tokyo: Kadokawa Shoten, 1977.

Natsume Kinnosuke. "Tsubouchi-hakase to *Hamuretto*" [Dr. Tsubouchi's *Hamlet*]. 1911. In *Sōseki zenshū* [Complete Works of Natsume Sōseki], vol. 16, 393–8. Tokyo: Iwanami Shoten, 2019.

Poch, Daniel. *Licentious Fictions and the Nineteenth-Century Japanese Novel*. New York: Columbia University Press, 2019, https://doi.org/10.7312/poch19370.

Proudfoot, Richard, Ann Thompson, David Scott Kastan, and Henry R. Woudhuysen, eds. *The Arden Shakespeare Third Series: Complete Works*. London: Bloomsbury Arden, 2020.

Rudolf, Krzysztof Filip. *Archaization in Literary Translation as Nostalgic Pastiche*. New York: Peter Lang, 2019, https://doi.org/10.3726/b15408.

Schwerin-High, Friederike von. *Shakespeare, Reception and Translation: Germany and Japan*. New York: Continuum, 2004, https://doi.org/10.5040/9781472555489.

Shirane Haruo, ed. *Early Modern Japanese Literature: An Anthology, 1600–1900*. New York: Columbia University Press, 2002.

Shōyō Kyōkai, ed. *Shōyō senshū* [Selected Works of Tsubouchi Shōyō], 17 vols. (1927–8; reprinted with 5 supplementary volumes). Tokyo: Daiichi Shobō, 1977–8.

Sofue Shōji, ed. *Kindai gikyoku shū* [Anthology of Modern Japanese Plays]. Tokyo: Kadokawa Shoten, 1974.

Tamaoka Katsuo and Makioka Shōgo. "Frequency of Occurrence for Units of Phonemes, Morae, and Syllables Appearing in a Lexical Corpus of a Japanese Newspaper." *Behavior*

*Research Methods, Instruments, & Computers* 36, no. 3 (May 2004): 531–47, https://doi. org/10.3758/bf03195600.

Thornbury, Barbara E. *Sukeroku's Double Identity: The Structure of Edo Kabuki*. Ann Arbor: Michigan Papers in Japanese Studies, 1982.

Tomasi, Massimiliano. *Rhetoric in Modern Japan: Western Influences on the Development of Narrative and Oratorical Style*. Honolulu: University of Hawai'i Press, 2004, https:// doi.org/10.1515/9780824840570.

Tozawa Koya and Asano Wasaburō, trans. *Juriasu Shīzā* [Julius Caesar]. Tokyo: Dai Nihon Tosho, 1907.

Tsubouchi Shōyō. "Biji ronkō" [Theory of Rhetoric]. 1893. In *Shōyō senshū*, vol. 11, 1–155, 1977.

———. "Chikamatsu no *jōruri*" [Chikamatsu's Puppet Plays]. 1890. In *Shōyō senshū*, supplementary vol. 3, 161–9, 1978.

———, trans. *Hamuretto* [Hamlet]. Tokyo: Waseda University Press, 1909.

———, trans. *Hamuretto* [Hamlet]. Tokyo: Chūō Kōronsha, 1933.

———, trans. "Henrī yonsei daiichibu" [King Henry IV, Part 1]. 1919. In *Shōyō senshū*, vol. 4, 305–475, 1977.

———, trans. "Henrī yonsei dainibu" [King Henry IV, Part 2]. 1919. In *Shōyō senshū*, vol. 4, 477–659, 1977.

———. "Jibun no honyaku ni tsuite" [About My Shakespeare Translations]. 1928. In *Shōyō senshū*, supplementary vol. 5, 254–77, 1977.

———, trans. *Jūriyasu Shīzā* [Julius Caesar]. Tokyo: Waseda University Press, 1914.

———. "Kyokutei Bakin" [Kyokutei Bakin]. 1920. In *Shōyō senshū*, vol. 12, 295–317, 1977.

———, trans. "Manatsu no yo no yume" [A Midsummer Night's Dream]. 1915. In *Shōyō senshū*, vol. 4, 171–304.

———. "Nihon de enzuru *Hamuretto*" [Performing *Hamlet* in Japan]. 1907. In *Sheikusupia kenkyū shiryō shūsei* [Research Materials on the Reception of Shakespeare in Japan], vol. 2, edited by Sasaki Takashi, 196–202. Tokyo: Nihon Tosho Centre, 1997.

———, trans. *Oserō* [Othello]. Tokyo: Waseda University Press, 1911.

———, trans. *Oserō* [Othello]. Tokyo: Chūō Kōronsha, 1935.

———, trans. *Richādo sansei* [King Richard III]. Tokyo: Waseda University Press, 1918.

———, trans. *Riya ō* [King Lear]. Tokyo: Waseda University Press, 1912.

———, trans. *Romio to Jurietto* [Romeo and Juliet]. Tokyo: Waseda University Press, 1910.

———, trans. "Shīzaru kidan – jiyū no tachi nagori no kireaji" [Amazing Tale of Caesar: The Lingering Sharpness of the Sword of Freedom]. 1884. In *Shōyō senshū*, supplementary vol. 2, 293–439, 1977.

———. "Shinkyoku Urashima" [New Musical Drama Urashima]. 1904. In *Shōyō senshū*, vol. 3, 1–99, 1977.

———. "Shōsetsu shinzui" [The Essence of the Novel]. 1885–6. In *Tsubouchi Shōyō shū*, 3–58, 1969.

———, trans. "Temupesuto" [The Tempest]. 1915. In *Shōyō senshū*, vol. 4, 1–169, 1977.

———, trans. *Venisu no shōnin* [The Merchant of Venice]. Tokyo: Chūō Kōronsha, 1933.

———, trans. *Verōna no futashinshi* [The Two Gentlemen of Verona]. Tokyo: Waseda University Press, 1926.

Ueda Bin. "*Shingakugekiron* narabi ni *Shinkyoku Urashima*" [Review of Tsubouchi Shōyō's *Theory of Musical Drama* and *Shinkyoku Urashima*]. *Kabuki* 56 (December 1904): 1–8.

Walley, Glynne. "Translator's Introduction." In *Kyokutei [Takizawa] Bakin, Eight Dogs, Or, "Hakkenden": An Ill-Considered Jest*, translated by Glynne Walley, xi–xlv. Ithaca, NY: Cornell University East Asia Program, 2021, https://doi.org/10.1515/9781501755194-003.

Watanabe Tamotsu. *Kabuki no kotoba* [Kabuki Words]. Tokyo: Taishūkan Shoten, 2004.

Yanabu Akira. "Translation in Japan: The Cassette Effect." *TTR: Traduction, Terminologie, Redaction* 22, no. 1 (January 2009): 19–28, https://doi.org/10.7202/044780ar.

# 4 Staging Shōyō

The previous chapter identified several characteristics of Shōyō's translating style that may amount to a distinctive sound or "voice" of Shōyō that is recognised as forceful and melodic, a model indeed of how Shakespeare might sound in any language. Shōyō's formative experience of how Shakespeare sounded in English was of the touring production by the Miln Company in 1891, and as Kobayashi Kaori argues, it was Miln's Victorian declamatory style that influenced him when he came to direct *Hamlet* with the Bungei Kyōkai in 1911.[1] Another way of putting this is that since Shōyō believed Shakespeare to delineate individual characters more clearly than they were in his native traditions, while being bound historically to translate Shakespeare in a style close to the declamatory styles of *kōdan* and *jōruri* narrative, it was inevitable that his translations would stand out all the more for their musical, even "romantic" qualities.

The Miln Company's productions coincided fortuitously with Shōyō's views on reading as they emerged from the broader views on fiction and drama he had expounded over the previous decade. Shōyō conceives of drama in more purely abstract terms than the concrete practices of his native theatre, regarding Shakespeare's plays as "ideal examples" of the integration of plot and character that he desired for Meiji fiction.[2] Having little opportunity to see Shakespeare performed in either English or Japanese until the late Meiji era, Shōyō was reading the plays as he did novels, and since an implied but essential purpose of the modernisation of his native fiction and drama was as a "defence of the inner life" against the onset of modernity,[3] the rich interiority of Shakespearean drama was readily appropriated to that project.

In the same year as his outing to the Gaiety Theatre, Shōyō outlined a new "logical reading method" (*ronriteki dokuhō*) which rejected the recitative reading style of past convention that tended to ignore inner meaning in favour of a more theatrical or performative style that was better able to excavate the "deep significance of the text,"[4] and (in the words of Maeda Ai) demanded

> sensitivity to a tonality that [could] express emotions ranging from inspiration to sorrow, attentiveness to shifts in cadence and intonation for conveying proper emphases, and care in expressing required tempo and pauses appropriate to the feelings conveyed by the writing.[5]

DOI: 10.4324/9781003293774-4

In the same year in the "hidden ideals" debate, Shōyō warned against the dangers of all but the "more perceptive readers" engaging in subjective interpretation of Shakespeare's texts, but in expounding his reading method he seems strikingly confident in his own capacity to grasp an author's "true will."[6] His point, therefore, is that through sensitive reading any reader can grasp a text's inner significance without having to say what it means, and in that sense his reading method corresponds to the glossing – rather than critical interpretation – of "words, grammar, and so on" as a principle for effective Shakespeare commentary.[7]

Shōyō is of course himself a reader, and his translations can be considered exercises in "sensitivity" to the contours of Shakespeare's texts. He will put his reading method to good use with the play reading group he founded in 1890 for his Waseda students, which read aloud Shakespeare as well as kabuki scripts, and both his founding of the Bungei Kyōkai in 1906 and his project of translating the Complete Works benefit from that experience. Shōyō's reading method makes for a markedly "speaker-bound" style of translation in which "exteriority is heightened,"[8] and coupled with the premium he attaches to an idealised "natural" interiority, his dramaturgy puts great pressure on his actors both to honour that interiority and enunciate a text that is not in fact Shakespeare's but Shōyō's reading of Shakespeare; as Kano Ayako puts it, Shōyō "wants both *makoto* ['sincerity'] and *nasake* ['feeling']" from his actors.[9]

While Shōyō's high expectations may indeed explain the breakup of the Bungei Kyōkai in 1913 and the negative response of Natsume Sōseki and others, this chapter focusses first on how Shōyō seeks to make his translations dramatic and actable and secondly on how they were staged through to the 1960s, when they were supplanted by the more modern versions of Fukuda Tsuneari and others. Comparing Shōyō and Fukuda, Anzai Tetsuo observes that while Shōyō stresses the amount of breath needed to deliver lines, Fukuda tends to emphasise the integration of line and gesture.[10] In other words, even as performance texts Shōyō's translations will always start with the voice and – as was palpably the case with the 1911 *Hamlet* – this practice will be to the likely detriment of the rest of the actor's body. Sōseki's albeit undeveloped argument for Noh adaptation was for a dramaturgy in which Shakespeare's text would be reduced to an aesthetically pleasing minimum and the textual loss recompensed by the integrated gestures of Noh actors.[11]

Shōyō's preference for translation over adaptation was frustrating both for kabuki actors such as Matsumoto Kōshirō VII (who played Othello in Shōyō's translation in 1925), who were forced to sacrifice their freedom "to improvise and act spontaneously" to the structural demands of Shakespeare's integrated text,[12] and for the amateurs of the Bungei Kyōkai who were caught between Shōyō's kabuki inflexions and the promise of a Western dramaturgy that was modern to the extent that even if Shōyō's translations did sometimes sound like kabuki his template was modern rather than classical Japanese.

That Shōyō's sonorous language, especially when supported by wooden acting, could tend to monotony is suggested by his debate of the late 1890s with Takayama Chogyū. Against Shōyō's subordination of poetry to history, Chogyū preferred Romantic individualists like Hamlet who resisted the forces of history with their

memorable rhetoric and proved the greater ontological significance of the "problems of the human heart" than whatever history had to teach.[13] Shōyō's fascination with Shakespearean individuality is always, therefore, tempered by whatever
moral lesson (or consequence of the chain of cause and effect) the drama is meant
to impart so that no character – not even Hamlet – can be allowed to dominate
the drama as a whole. This latter point is the point that T. S. Eliot will make in his
influential analysis of "Hamlet and His Problems" (1919).[14] Shōyō shares with
Eliot a dissatisfaction with Romantic subjectivity, and although he is unable to find
his way through Shakespeare to any singular ideal outside of his own individual
and moral response there is a sense in which the "big idea" for Shōyō is no less
than drama itself.

Shōyō's theatricality is something of a double-edged sword. In 1939, the distinguished Shakespearean Alwin Thaler, reporting a letter received from a friend
teaching at a university in Kyushu and the friend's Japanese colleague, tells the
world that Shōyō's

> method of approach is to appreciate Shakespeare from a purely dramatic or
> theatrical point of view. In this respect he is quite removed from [the] philo-
> sophical-idealistic criticism of Bradley or Dowden. He has the histrionic or
> realistic attitude of the playwright.[15]

Shōyō's achievement was widely praised in the final years of his life and at the
time of his death, especially among his Waseda coterie who honoured his passing in 1935 with an official citation in the National Diet,[16] but writing in 1934
one Tsuji Hisaichi despairs of the difficulty of persuading a modern audience that
Shōyō's Shakespeares were something other than the kabuki of old, and blames
audience disinterest on the "chaotic state of modern Japanese drama."[17] Shōyō
himself never claimed to have the final word, since he both acknowledged rival
translations published during his lifetime as welcome contributions to the "cult" of
Japanese Shakespeare and intended his own translations as no more than scripts for
interpretation by other hands, whether by actors or later translators; one indication
of the amenability of his revised versions at least to actors' pockets was the adoption of the compact A6 *bunkōbon* format introduced by publishers in the 1920s in
preference to the larger *tankōbon* format in which the original translations had been
published. Moreover, if Shōyō's translations were amenable to the "idea" of drama
then they could also be amenable, at least in theory, to the modernist ideas of Stanislavsky and Edward Gordon Craig, as these figures were appropriated by Osanai
Kaoru, who directed Shōyō's *Julius Caesar* and *A Midsummer Night's Dream* in
1925 and 1928, respectively. Osanai admired the modern psychological depth of
Shōyō's *En no gyōja* (Hermit En, 1916) when he came to direct it for the Tsukiji
Little Theatre in 1926,[18] and it is within this framework of the emerging modern
Japanese theatre (*shingeki*) that his translations should be discussed.

Finally, while the histrionic "attitude" mentioned by Thaler relates to kabuki as
a pre-modern or early modern presentational type of drama, the actual drama of his
translations may also be discretely present within a more modern, representational

strand, such as the metonymies discussed in the previous chapter. This strand can be said to represent Shōyō's individual response, but (as von Schwerin-High suggests) it would be a response derived from the sheer heterogeneity of Shakespeare's style, its capacity to be at once "extremely economical and extremely lavish."[19] Prospero's speech on "the great globe itself" is an example of Shakespearean lavishness that Shōyō translates with appropriate sonority, but the extent to which his translations are truly theatrical will arise from his engagement with more discrete and incidental details.

## Stage Directions

Shōyō's stage directions go somewhat beyond the entrances and exits of English editions to indicate dramatic pauses and the tone of voice and emotional response of characters. For example, at the end of Hamlet's fourth soliloquy, when Hamlet realises the presence of Ophelia (3.1.85–9), Shōyō adds two directions that are absent from both Deighton's Macmillan (1890) and Dowden's Arden (1899) editions (the two editions that he probably consulted)[20] to reinforce the speech's theatrical gist:

> And enterprises of great pitch and moment
> With this regard their currents turn away
> And lose the name of action. Soft you now,
> The fair Ophelia! Nymph, in thy orisons
> Be all my sins remembered.
> *ikana daiji no kuwadate mo, kono yue ni sore,*
> *hate wa jikkō no na wo ushinau . . .* (*Ofiriya ni me wo tsukete*)
>     ["He notices Ophelia."]
> *Ya, mate shibashi! Ofiriya ja na! . . .* (*Ofiriya ni tai shi*) ["To Ophelia."]
>     *Nau, himegimi,*
> *yo ga tsumi no shōmetsu wo mo inori soeteta morei.*[21]

In Shakespeare's blank verse, Hamlet's recognition of Ophelia is subsumed into the discourse of the preceding soliloquy on suicide, with a slight awkwardness registered with the extra two syllables in line 88. The ellipses and stage directions in Shōyō's prose translation make more of the drama of the moment and change of pace necessary to diffuse the pressing cumulative rhythms of the Japanese soliloquy. The brusque masculine tone of *Ya, mate shibashi! Ofiriya ja na!* renders the familiarity implicit in "fair" and "nymph," while the actual omission of "fair" is compensated with a noun *shōmetsu* that has the religious connotation of "expiation" but can also mean "extinction," and therefore makes the connection made by Shakespeare's blank verse with the soliloquy.

The insertion of ellipses and stage directions in this example is clearly theatrical in intent. Shōyō's Hamlet is actively engaging with others and reflecting on his situation rather than merely reciting prepared speeches; the dramatic pauses give him time to realise that prayer is another type of "extinction" whose religious context is enough to deter him from killing himself. A similar direction Shōyō uses throughout his translations, although noticeably more in his early ones of the 1890s and 1900s, is the *omoiire*, or stylised meditative pose associated with kabuki. *Omoiire* are not only stylised but particularly associated with dramatic entrances and exits along the *hanamichi* platform that connects the stage right side of the main stage with the rear of the auditorium; in other words, a place of maximum audience impact, which is an aspect of kabuki stagecraft that Shōyō's translations cannot imitate.

The *omoiire* direction is given no less than twenty-five times in Shōyō's initial 1906 version of the trial scene in *The Merchant of Venice*, with the most striking sequence occurring in the following dialogue (4.1.236–45), where each of the interjections are followed by *omoiire*:[22]

SHYLOCK.

By my soul I swear,
There is no power in the tongue of man
To alter me. I stay here on my bond.
>*Hearing this Antonio makes an omoiire pose.*

ANTONIO.

Most heartily I do beseech the court
To give the judgement.
>*Portia also makes an omoiire pose.*

PORTIA.    Why then, thus it is:
You must prepare your bosom for his knife.
>*Portia makes an omoiire pose at Antonio.*

SHYLOCK.

O noble judge! O excellent young man!
>*Shylock makes a delighted omoiire pose.*

PORTIA.

For the intent and purpose of the law
Hath full relation to the penalty
Which here appeareth due upon the bond.
>*Hearing this, Shylock examines the faces of the Duke*
>*and the others, and strikes a triumphant omoiire pose.*

These gestures rebound on Shylock as the judgement goes against him, so that twice consecutively he has the special direction *mokuzen omoiire*, or "silent pose."[23] Together with numerous conventional directions detailing steps back, pace of speech, and so on, the overall impression is highly melodramatic; every emotional twist and turn is made to count, as in a scene from kabuki.

When Shōyō came to translate the play in full in 1914, all of the *omoiire* were cut, and then in 1933 when he revised his translation, he inserted a number of more modern directions, intended mainly for Shylock's opponents. The first occurs in Bassanio's initial exchange with Shylock, when Bassanio asks the Jew, "Do all men kill the things they do not love?" (65). Shōyō's direction is *yaya hageshiku*, "somewhat passionately,"[24] indicating that the question is more rhetorical than philosophical, and Shylock replies "indifferently" – *reizen toshite* – "Hates any man the thing he would not kill?" (66).[25] Two lines later his attitude "becomes decisive" (*kitto natte*) when he asks "What, wouldst thou have a serpent sting thee twice?" (68),[26] and this dramatic tension sets the tone for the rest of the scene which Shōyō shapes with a few more emotional indicators of a similar vein. When Portia seems at first to support Shylock's suit, and he cries out "A Daniel come to judgement" (219), he does so *kanshin shite*, "admiringly."[27] Shōyō picks up the bitter pun in Antonio's lament that "if the Jew do cut but deep enough/I'll pay it instantly with all my heart" (276–7), adding the direction *warai wo fukumite* ("with a laugh") and a play on words in the speech, *shin ni "zenshin,"* "truly with all my heart."[28] This direction is repeated ironically when Bassanio and Gratiano profess they would rather their wives suffer at the hands of Shylock than their friend Antonio. Portia and Nerissa speak their protests ("Your wife would give you little thanks for that," 284) not as asides but *dokugo no yō ni*, "like a soliloquy,"[29] and when at the end of the scene Portia asks Bassanio for his ring in lieu of payment he is "worried" (*komatte*).[30] Finally, in lieu of *omoiire*, the three directions that describe Shylock's retreat from the stage parallel the three earlier directions that describe his rising excitement. "Nay, take my life and all" (370) is uttered "in a state of desperation" (*yake ni natte*).[31] When Portia asks him "Art thou contented, Jew?" (400), Shōyō hints at the agonised double meaning in Shylock's reply "I am content" (401) with the direction *Genki mattaku sosō shite*, "Completely dispirited,"[32] and then "staggers off stage," *yoromeki yoromeki hairu*.[33]

Shōyō's directions are remarkable for being there at all: Asano Hyōkyo's translation of the play, also published in 1906 although not intended for stage performance, contains no directions of the kind that Shōyō uses. In 1914, he replaces the constructed pose of the *omoiire* with the controlled environment of a Western-style courtroom and Shakespeare's dramaturgy, and his directions are interpretive, indicating for example that Shylock's "What, wouldst thou have a serpent sting thee twice?" is a statement of will rather than a casual insult, and that Antonio's bitter laugh may be a prompt to both actor and audience to register Shōyō's wordplay. If the scene contains any *omoiire* it is the soliloquised complaints of Portia and Nerissa, "Your wife would give you little thanks for that." Given what he has said in a previous scene about his own humanity ("Hath not a Jew eyes?"), Shylock's most bitter realisation may be that his opponents are "human" as well.

The slightness of these directions makes them all the more effective. The unlineated prose format leaves Shōyō no space for the footnotes used in contemporary translations, and instead he sometimes explains obscurities in parentheses or else indents them in a smaller font. These glosses are more common in translations of plays with many cultural references, such as *The Merry Wives of Windsor*, where the lowlife Nym's opening sally, "Slice, I say! *Pauca, pauca*, slice, that's my humour" (1.1.124), elicits a lengthy note on humour in which the translator explains that although collocations such as *iki* ("spirit") and *share* ("joke") do not connote the Elizabethan physiological four humours, Nym himself is misusing the word.[34]

Plays such as *Henry V* would have been less familiar to Shōyō's readership. At the beginning of the English lesson scene in the latter play (3.4), where Alice teaches the French princess Katherine the English names of parts of the body, Shōyō explains that

> The scene is written entirely in French. In a military play like *Henry V* that is generally lacking in erotic interest, this rather comical scene represents a deliberate change of mood, and for the boy actors who played female roles in Shakespeare's time an opportunity for them to speak a language different from English pronunciation.[35]

Shōyō glosses "boy actors" as *oyama*, or kabuki actors who specialise in female roles, and in the 1934 revision adds that the scene's effectiveness depends "of course" on the actors' skills.[36]

Noting also the proximity of French to English pronunciation (e.g., *fingres*), Shōyō's strategy is to write the English parts of the body in both *katakana* and *rōmaji* and their French equivalents in Japanese (*te* for *main*/"hand," etc.). Shōyō does not explain either in parentheses or through his translation that "foot" might sound like *foutre*, "to fuck," and "count" like *con*, "cunt," although there might be an oblique wordplay on the Japanese equivalents *futto* meaning "abruptly" and *kaun* meaning either "family fortunes" or "summer clouds"; the repetition of the bright *k* consonant captures the princess's spirit of mock outrage. In any case, it was a play Shōyō apparently enjoyed translating,[37] and the joke for his Japanese readers was that, like French, Japanese consonants (except for the single consonant *n*) always precede a vowel:

KATHERINE.  De foot *et* de coun? *O Seigneur Dieu, ils sont les mots de son mauvais, corruptible, gros, et impudique, et non pour les dames d'honneur d'user. Je ne voudrais prononcer ces mots devant les seigneurs de France, pour tout le monde. Foh!* De foot *et* de coun! *Néanmoins, je réciterai une autre fois ma leçon ensemble:* d'hand, de fingres, de nails, d'arm, d'elbow, de nick, de sin, de foot, de coun. (3.4.47–54)

> *De futto ni de kaun. Mā? Nan to iu iya na, midarana, kikigurushii, kegarawashii hatsuon no kotoba darō. Kifujin ni wa ieyashinai wa nē. Furansu no kizokutachi no mae de wa dō shitatte iwarenai kotoba desu. Mā! De futto da no, de kaun da no. Demo, mō ichido hajime-kkara naraimashō. De hando, de fingurusu, de nēruzu, de āmu, de erubō, de nikku, de shin, de futto, de kaun.*[38]

While Shōyō's gloss and his modern translation may seem to sell the scene to his Japanese actors, these would have been adult females rather than adolescent boys, although the translation has never been staged.

Hasegawa Tenkei recalled of Shōyō's lecturing on *King Lear* that his teacher's lively explanations enabled him to "visualise people of whom he had never heard" and that his stage directions seemed "almost to come from Shakespeare himself."[39] This aptitude is also evident in a silent film made of Shōyō's final lecture at Waseda in 1928, also on *King Lear*, in which he theatrically clasps the sides of his head, no doubt quoting the king in his madness. Shōyō's stage directions in the published version are not excessive, mainly entrances, exits, and asides (when those are not clear from the text), but he also includes several emotional markers similar to those in the *Merchant* translations, and usually at the beginning of speeches. Some of these, especially in Lear's dialogue with the Fool in 1.5, indicate emotional subtexts, in the case of the dialogue that Lear is genuinely remorseful at his earlier treatment of Cordelia, but most of them serve to shape the translator's interpretation in a way similar to the keywords examined in the previous chapter. Shōyō's interpretation is centred on Lear, who has twenty-one of the thirty-seven directions (against only about a fifth of the number of words in the play). The repeated use of *hanmon* ("anguish") in 1.5 is especially notable for expressing Lear's rising anger, and the concentration of emotional markers in the first two acts suggests that having gone truly mad in Act 3 Lear is no longer "acting" as such, and thus his mood changes no longer need to be indicated with stage directions.

*sokke naku* "curtly"[40]
CORDELIA.   Nothing, my lord. (1.1.87)

*me ni kado tatete* "glaring"[41]
LEAR.        Nothing will come of nothing. Speak again. (90)

*odoroki ahorete* "astounded"[42]
LEAR.        But goes thy heart with this? (105)

*kakukaku to natte* "brilliantly" (i.e. "regally," as Lear is about to condemn Cordelia)[43]
LEAR.        Let it be so. (109)

*reisei wo yosootte* "acting dispassionately"[44]
LEAR.        My lord of Burgundy (190)

*iyoiyo okotte* "getting more and more angry"[45]
LEAR.        Better thou/Hadst not been born (235–6)

*kiwamete hiniku ni* "with extreme sarcasm"[46]
LEAR.        Are you our daughter? (to Goneril, 1.4.209)

*to goku hiniku ni* "very sarcastically"[47]
LEAR.        I should be false persuaded I/had daughters. (224–5)

*iyoiyo hiniku ni* "with renewed sarcasm"[48]
LEAR.        Your name, fair gentlewoman? (227)

*kiwamete hiyaka ni, bujaku no chōshi de* "extremely coldly and in a contemptuous tone"[49]
GONERIL.   This admiration, sir, is much o'the savour/Of other your new pranks. (228–9)

*kaku to natte* "regally" (again)[50]
LEAR.        Darkness and devils! (243)

*to niwaka ni hizamazuite, ten wo aoide, ikari takeritsutsu norou*
"He kneels abruptly, looks up to the heavens, and curses with extreme ferocity."[51]
LEAR.      Hear, Nature, hear, dear goddess, hear (267)

*hanmon no omoiire* "anguished pose"[52]
LEAR.      I did her [i.e., Cordelia] wrong. (1.5.24)

*hanmon shite* "with anguish"[53]
LEAR.      I will forget my nature (31)

*mata hanmon shite* "anguished again"[54]
LEAR.      To take't again perforce – monster ingratitude! (37)

*mata hanmon shite* "anguished again"[55]
LEAR.      O let me not be mad, not mad, sweet heaven! (43)

*hanmon shite* "in anguish"[56]
LEAR.      O, how this mother swells up toward my heart! (2.2.246)

*yatto kigen wo naoshite* "finally cheering up"[57]
LEAR.      Good morrow to you both. (to Cornwall and Regan, 2.4.316)

*hiyaka ni* "coldly"[58]
REGAN.      I pray you, sir, take patience. (327)

*to Riya wa hizamazuite, goku hinikuna kofun de, Gonariru ni shazai suru mane wo suru*
"Lear kneels, and in a very sarcastic way of speaking pretends to apologize to Goneril."[59]
LEAR.      Dear daughter, I confess that I am old (343)

*gōzen to* "haughtily"[60]
CORNWALL. I set him there, sir [i.e., Kent in the stocks] (388)

*odoroki ahorete* "astonished"[61]
LEAR.      Those wicked creatures yet do look well favoured (445)

*fungeki shite* "exploding with anger"[62]
LEAR.      To have a thousand with red burning spits/Come hissing in upon 'em!
          [i.e., Goneril and Regan] (3.6.15–6)

*fushinsō ni* "distrustfully"[63]
LEAR.      I'll see that straight. (to Kent, 5.3.285)

This final direction indicates on the one hand that the grieving Lear does not immediately acknowledge Kent and Caius as being one and the same, but it also hints that Lear has acquired a wisdom to distinguish between appearance and reality that he tragically lacked in the opening division scene.

Shōyō's stage directions are more explicatory than those of post-war translators –
Fukuda Tsuneari's 1967 translation of the play contains none of Shōyō's explicatory
direction – but his readers were encountering a play that was less known in Taishō
Japan than *Hamlet*. The anguish that seeps from his interpretive directions indicates
that for Shōyō Lear's suffering is every bit as real as that of the more innocent Ophelia.
Lear's rising passion erupts in his crazed raging against the elements when he goes out
into the storm in the middle of the night, and at that point the directions almost stop.

### Shōyō's Revisions

As I mentioned in Chapter 2, *Macbeth* is the play whose initial translation seems
to have caused Shōyō particular embarrassment. Repenting of basic errors and
phrasings that were either "inappropriate," "excessively literal," or "exaggerated,"
Shōyō claims to have altered some 60% of the 1916 version,[64] and indeed parts of
his revised version, such as the second half of Macbeth's soliloquy in 1.7.12–28,
were substantially rewritten:[65]

1. He's here in double trust:
   First, as I am his kinsman and his subject –
   Strong both against the deed

   *Nijū ni shinrai suru riyū ga atte, kare wa koko e kite iru no da. Mazu ore wa kare
   no kinshin demo ari, shinka demo aru kara, kesshite sō iu akuji wo okonaubeki
   de nai.* (1916)

   *Kare wa nijū ni shinrai suru riyū ga atte, koko e kite iru no da. Mazu, ore wa
   kare no kinshin demo ari, shinka de mo aru, dakara, kesshite sō iu akuji nazo
   wo shisō ni nai to omotte iru.* (1935)

Shōyō puts "he" (*kare*) in the middle of the sentence to emphasize that Duncan,
rather than Macbeth, is the person "here in double trust,"[66] and replaces a phrase
meaning "I ought not to do the deed" (*akuji wo okonaubeki de nai*) with one meaning "I think it is unlikely I would do such a thing" (*akuji nazo wo shisō ni nai to
omotte iru*) to generate a more theatrical nuance.[67]

2. then, as his host,
   Who should against the murderer shut the door,
   Not bear the knife myself.

   *Tsugi ni ore wa, tsutomete gyakui aru mono no chikayoran yō ni mamorubeki
   hazu no aruji na no dakara, jibun de yaiba wo furuu nazo to iu koto wa aruma-
   jiki koto da.* (1916)

   *Tsugi ni, ore wa aruji da, kari nimo gyakui aru mono wo shite chikayorashime-
   nai yō wa mamoru no ga tōzen da no ni, jishin de yaiba wo furuu nazo wa motte
   no hoka da.* (1935)

This revision too is more straightforwardly theatrical in the way that Macbeth's role
as "host" (*aruji*) is emphasised in the word order and the possible wordplay on *aru-
majiki* ("unbecoming") replaced with a phrase meaning "out of the question" (*motte
no hoka*).

3. Besides, this Duncan
   Hath borne his faculties so meek, hath been
   So clear in his great office, that his virtues
   Will bleed like angels, trumpet-tongued, against
   The deep damnation of his taking off;

   *Iwanya ano Dankan wa, ano tōri onwa ni, kanjin ni, nanra no ketten mo naku, yoku kokukun toshite no shokuseki wo tsukushite kite iru no da kara, kare wo shii suru to iu yō na daigyaku wo okonatta jibun ni wa, ano otoko no heiso no toku ga, rappazetsu no tenshi no yō ni, tsumi nakushite gai sareta urami wo nobetateru de arou.* (1916)

   *Nominarazu, ano Dankan wa, onwa, kanjin ni, jūrai dō iu ketten mo naku, kokukun toshite no shokuseki wo tsukushite kite iru. Dakara, kare wo korosu yōna daihidō wo okonatta jibun nyā, kare no heiso no shukutoku ga, rappazetsu no tenshi no gotoku, tsumi nakute zetsugai sareta fujōri wo nobetateru de arou.* (1935)

This revision slightly objectifies Macbeth's position; for example, with a phrase implying that although Duncan has been a virtuous king "up to now" (*jūrai*) he too is only human, and also by replacing *daigyaku* ("great treason") with *daihidō* ("great atrocity") to emphasise how the murder will appear at the moment of its discovery rather than self-incriminating Macbeth as the killer. The nuance of "feminine virtue" in *shukutoku* may imply contempt for Duncan's character, which would also make for a colder, more calculated tone.

4. And pity, like a naked new-born babe,
   Striding the blast, or heaven's cherubin, horsed
   Upon the sightless couriers of the air,
   Shall blow the horrid deed in every eye,
   That tears shall drown the wind.

   *Sōshite seken no dōjō wa, umaretate no akago ga kaze ni notta yō ni itaitashigari, mata wa me ni mien sora no hayauma ni notta tendō no yō ni, meireiteki ni, kono osoroshii akugyō wo jinjin no me e fukikonde, sono kaze mo nagu hodo no namida no ame wo moyōsaseru de arou.* (1916)

   *Sōshite seken no dōjō wa, reppū ni notta umaretate no akago ka, me ni wa mienu, sora no hayauma ni matagatta tendō ka no yō ni, kono osoroshii akugyō wo hitobito no me e fukikomi, sono reppū mo nagu hodo no namida no ame wo moyōsaseru de arou.* (1935)

This revision shifts the emphasis from the "babe" (who is described as "pitiful" in the 1916 version) to the drama of the elements, replacing *kaze* for "wind" with a more expressive word, *reppū*, meaning "fierce wind," and foregrounding *reppū* in the word order.

5. I have no spur
   To prick the sides of my intent, but only
   Vaulting ambition, which o'er-leaps itself,
   And falls on thither.

   *Ore ga nokkatte iru kono kuwadate wo shigeki suru hakusha wa, hitotsu mo nai, tada haneagaru daiyashinme ga, ono ga bunzai wo tobikoshite, tonde mo nai hō e okkochiyō toshite iru.* (1916)

*Ore ga nokkatte iru kono kuwadate wo shigeki subeki hakusha wa, hitotsu mo nai, tada haneagaru yashinme ga, tsui haneagari sugite, tonde mo nai hō e okkochiyō toshite iru bakari da.* (1935)

The change from *shigeki suru* ("stimulate" for "spur") to *shigeki subeki* ("ought to stimulate") implies in the revision that if Macbeth had any other reason than his own ambition to kill Duncan it would be a legitimate one, and it also opens up a rhyme with *sugite* ("too much") in a phrase meaning "to leap too high" (*hane-gari sugite*). By omitting a redundant reference to social position (*ono ga bunzai*), Shōyō is better able to dramatise the equine imagery.

In the prior excerpt Shōyō is seen to be working towards a more performable text that, for example, clarifies the dramatic relationship between Macbeth and Duncan, but given that Shōyō was already a few years into his final stage of translating Shakespeare in a contemporary colloquial style when he came to translate *Macbeth*, his 1933 revision of the 1909 "kabuki *Hamlet*" promises an even more dramatic rewriting.

The most famous revision was that of the classical-sounding *Nagarauru ka, nagaraunu ka?* for "To be, or not to be" to the more contemporary *Yo ni aru, yo ni aranu?*,[68] but the revised translation is far from being a complete rewrite, and the changes are superficial. It was clearly important for Shōyō to preserve the courtly Renaissance style of the source text, and in revising the following dialogue of Hamlet and Ophelia (3.2.121–32)[69] his intent seems mainly to make it less fussily classical and more speakable for modern actors:[70]

HAMLET.    Lady, shall I lie in your lap?

>  *Shibaraku onmo wo kasasemasei.* (1909)
>  for a moment – your skirt (polite) – please lend (archaic imperative)
>  *Hīsan, shibaraku onmo wo karimashō ze.* (1934)
>  lady shall I borrow – (male particle, menacing in tone)

OPHELIA.    No, my lord.

>  *Amoshi, gozen.* (1909)
>  oh (archaic) – my lord
>  *A, moshi, . . .* (1934)
>  oh – I suppose (vague)

HAMLET.    I mean, my head upon your lap?

>  *Hate, mo no suso e choto kashira wo noseru bakari ja.* (1909)
>  well – hem of skirt – a little – whether – I can rest – only – (archaic particle)
>  [Unchanged. (1934)]

OPHELIA.    Ay, my lord.

>  *Yoroshū gozarimasu.* (1909)
>  fine – that is (archaic copula)
>  *Hai, dōzo.* (1934)
>  yes – go ahead

HAMLET.    Do you think I meant country matters?

> *Hinabiiza demo suru tobashi omoyatta ka?* (1909)
> rural matters – even – I suppose (with archaic particles) – did you think?
> *Midarana koto demo suru to omou te?* (1934)
> obscene things – even – I suppose – do you think?

OPHELIA.    I think nothing, my lord.

> *Iie, nantomo omoimasenu.* (1909)
> no – nothing – I think (archaic negative)
> *Ie, ano, nantomo . . .* (1934)
> no – well – nothing

HAMLET.    That's a fair thought to lie between maids' legs.

> *Hate, bijin no kyakukan ni makura nado to wa ei omoitsuki ja wai.* (1909)
> well – beautiful woman's – between her legs – pillow and so on –
> (particles) – nice
> (colloquial) – idea – is – (emotional male particle)
> [Unchanged. (1934)]

OPHELIA.    What is, my lord?

> *E, nan to gyoi nasaremasuru?* (1909)
> what – what – your will – to do (archaic and respectful)
> *E, nan to gyoi asobasu?* (1934)
>                                          to do (respectful and slightly archaic)

HAMLET.    Nothing.

> *Nani sa.* (1909)
> i.e. nothing (colloquial)
> [Unchanged. (1934)]

OPHELIA.    You are merry, my lord.

> *Ikō ukarete oide isaseraremasu.* (1909)
> extremely – merry – you are (archaic, polite inflexion)
> *Ikō ukarete oide asobasu.* (1934)
>                                          (slightly less archaic)

HAMLET.    Who, I?

> *Tare ga, yo ga?* (1909)
> who – I? (both old-fashioned usages)
> *Dare ga, washi ga?* (1934)
> who – I? (more modern)

OPHELIA.    Ay, my lord.

> *Gyoi ni gozarimasu.* (1909)
> *Gyoi.* (1934)

Shōyō's revision makes for a tenser, more aggressive tone. The use of *midara*, meaning "lewd" or "obscene" for "country matters," is more explicit than the source, and in losing elegant inflexions such as *isaseraremasu* and *omoimasenu* (and in two instances being apparently too nervous to finish her sentence) the 1933 Ophelia seems more threatened by Hamlet's madness. As for Ophelia's madness in the next act, Shōyō's version of her song ("Tomorrow is Saint Valentine's day") is generally considered less poetic than the twenty-seven-year-old Mori Ōgai's version of 1889, and in the wake of the 1911 *Hamlet* staging was criticised by a colleague of Shōyō at Waseda, Kimura Takatarō, for being both inaccurate and uninspired:

> Mr. Tsubouchi's translation contains mistakes and mistranslations, and several lines are omitted (perhaps deliberately), so that as a whole it comes across as extremely inaccurate and imprecise as well as lacking the poetic intent of the original, which ultimately makes it unsuited as a tool of scholarly research.[71]

Kimura's quibbles seem pedantic, for example that Shōyō translates Ophelia's line "Tomorrow is Saint Valentine's day" as *Asu wa jūyokka Barenchin-sama yo* ("Tomorrow's the fourteenth, St. Valentine's"),[72] when Shakespeare was writing 150 years before the adoption of the Gregorian calendar in Britain (and would therefore have been ten days later). Yet it was clearly good enough for Shōyō. In 1933 the only change he makes is to translate an extra two lines (4.5.62–3) that he had inexplicably omitted from the 1909 version:[73]

> Quoth she, 'Before you tumbled me
> You promised me to wed.'
> *Washi wo korobasu tsui mae made wa*
> *kitto meoto to iuta ja nai ka,*
> *to uramu onago ni tsurenai otoko.*

The verb *korobasu* (literally "to trip someone up") has the same sexual nuance as "tumbled," and being the crudest expression in the song may have given Shōyō reason to make the previous dialogue in 3.2 more overtly sexual as well. The section of 4.5 that Shōyō revises most extensively is the ensuing dialogue when Laertes bursts on the scene demanding vengeance for his father's death.[74] These revisions serve mainly to inject a little urgency into this dramatic scene, as when Gertrude rushes to protect her husband from the threat of physical attack by Laertes:

> But not by him. (4.5.128)
> *Saritote ō no toga dewa nashi.* (1909)
> *To iute, sore wa ō no sei dewa nai.* (1933)

Likewise, when Claudius tries to reason with Laertes:

Who shall stay you? (135)

*Nani to seba onushi wo osae todomubeki zo?* (1909)

*Taga chikara wo kariraba, onushi wo toriosaeru koto ga dekiru de arou
    ka?* (1933)

## Organisation of Speech and Dialogue

Shōyō's revisions relate to his broader appreciation of what he calls the "care with
which [Shakespeare] arranges dialogue for the stage,"[75] and while he cannot imitate the blank verse that drives so much Shakespearian dialogue, what Shōyō can
imitate is a tension between metrical continuity and the breaks that occur within
and across the line. For Shōyō's way with words, we can start with his translation
of the first part of Macbeth's soliloquy discussed in the previous section (1.7.1–7),
in which monosyllabic Anglo-Saxon words work with longer words of Romance
origin in a style that exemplifies Shakespeare's rhetorical diversity:[76]

> If it were done when, 'tis done, then 'twere well
> It were done quickly. If th'assassination
> Could trammel up the consequence, and catch
> With his surcease, success: that but this blow
> Might be the be-all and the end-all, here,
> But here, upon this bank and shoal of time,
> We'd jump the life to come.

> *Yatte shimaeba, sore de koto ga sumu mono nara, hayaku yatte shimatta
>     hō ga ii. Ansatsu*
> if I do it – then – the thing – will finish (conditional) – quickly done – would
>     be better – assassination –
> *to iu hitoami wo kudashi sae sureba, issai no kekka wo rashi tsukushite
>     shimaeru mono nara,*
> (which is) a single net – is dropped – even if – a single result – thin
>     gauze – do everything to –
> *mono nara, kono hitogeki de motte banji shūkyoku suru mono nara, sore
>     ga kono yo de no, "toki" no*
> (conditional) – by this single blow – all things – would end (conditional) –
>     that – in this world – "time" –
> *kochira gishi, kono asase de no shūkyoku de aru no nara, mirai nanka
>     kamatta koto wa nain da.*
> this bank – these shallows – of the end – if they are – future – something
>     like – trouble – there is no

Shōyō's paraphrase is both modern and speakable, imitating the rhetorical movement of Macbeth's soliloquy from condition to consequence through the rhythmic
repetition of a modal verb, *shimau*, that expresses finality. The dynamic tension
of the Shakespearean line is reproduced through the contrast between words with

double consonants (*yatte, shimatta*, etc.) and sequences of short vowels, notably in the opening phrase *sore de koto ga sumu mono nara* ("and if it is finished"). Shōyō's *banji shūkyoku* ("end of everything") is a satisfying equivalent for "be-all and end-all": a typical four-character idiom (*yoji jukugo*) used in Japanese to convey idiomatic or rhetorical flair, *banji* meaning ten thousand things and *ban* (or *man*) having this sense of a large or even infinite number. The addition of *nanka* ("something or other") conveys the villain's casual disregard for the consequences of his actions, and the three-times repetition of the deictic *kono* ("this") also adds to the speech's drama, emphasising that Macbeth's image of transcending his human fate belongs to his own imaginary world rather than to a more generalised or universal sphere. While Macbeth's disregard for consequences makes him an anti-hero of Shōyō's realism, it also makes him theatrically fascinating as he sacrifices his autonomy to forces beyond his control, appeals constantly to the audience through his rhetoric, and opens a window onto an eternity from which he is tragically separated, which is the "eternity" Shōyō recognises in the play: "Those with a universal way of thinking will find the world, and those with their eyes on eternity will find eternity."[77] *Macbeth* was one of Shōyō's translations to be staged during his lifetime, initially in part in 1916 and finally in full in 1923.

Two examples of wordplay from *The Taming of the Shrew* and *The Tempest*, which were also staged during Shōyō's lifetime, offer evidence of how Shōyō responds both overtly and more covertly to Shakespeare's skill at arranging dialogue. In the wooing scene of the former, as Kate rebuffs Petruchio's advances (2.1.193–9),[78] we see how Shōyō transfers the rhythmic stress on "moved" to the volitional form of the verb *morau*, which literally means to "receive" but is commonly used as here with a preceding verb as a causative construction meaning to get somebody to do something for you. The volitional *moraō* comprises three consecutive vowels (pronounced *moraou*), which contrast rhythmically with the *te* and *ta* connective and past verb forms, for example in *omotte yatte kitatte*, "you say you've come here thinking [to make me your wife]," a highly colloquial expression whose bluster compensates for the almost untranslatable "in good time":

> Myself am moved to woo thee for my wife.
> *Kimi wo toite sai ni natte moraō to omotte yatte kitan da yo.*

KATHERINE.
> 'Moved'. In good time, let him that moved you hither
> Remove you hence. I knew you at the first
> You were a movable.
> (*Tsukkendon ni*) ["Brusquely"] *Moraō to omotte yatte kitatte? Watashi wa mata sono yatte kita hito ni, sugu kaette moraō to omotterun desu. Anata wa, mita tokoro kara, sugu ni hanekaerisōna kagu ni nitete yo.*

PETRUCHIO.
> Why, what's a movable?
> *Hanekaeru kagu ni? To iu no wa?*

KATHERINE.  A joint-stool.
>  *Anata wa tatami isu yo.*

PETRUCHIO.
>  Thou hast hit it: come, sit on me.
>  *Kekkō . . . . Sa, okakenasai.*
>  (*To hiza wo sashidashite, gozaregoshi ni naru.*)
>  ["Extending one knee, he makes himself into a footstool."]

Shōyō conveys the likely unfamiliarity of "moveable" in the way that Japanese read-ers also might be wondering what is meant by "rebounding furniture" (*hanekaeru kagu*) until Kate explains what she means. Translating the following dialogue from *The Tempest* (2.1.10–26), Shōyō uses a paronomasia typical of Japanese poetry[79] to articulate a tension between the faithful counsellor Gonzalo and the Machiavellian courtiers Antonio and Sebastian as, washed up on Prospero's island, they negotiate their unfamiliar surroundings:[80]

SEBASTIAN.  He receives comfort like cold/porridge.
>  (*Bōhaku*) ["Aside."] *Sekkaku no goimon mo, hiya zōsui atsukai to kite iru.*
ANTONIO.  The visitor will not give him/o'er so.
>  (*Sebasuchiyan ni*) ["To Sebastian."] *Tokoro ga, goimon gakari wa, sonna koto de hekomu yōna oshōsan ja arimasen.*
SEBASTIAN.  Look, he's winding up the watch of his wit;
>  By and by it will strike –
>  (*Antoniō ni*) *Gorannasai, taishō shikiri ni chie no tokei wo maite iru. Ima ni chīn to kuru darō.*
GONZALO.  (*to Alonso*) Sir –
>  (*Ō ni*) *Ee, moshi . . . . .*
SEBASTIAN.  One. Tell.
>  (*Antoniō ni*) *Hitotsu . . . . . Kazoetamae.*

This dialogue depends for its dramatic effect on Antonio and Sebastian being able to express their irritation with Gonzalo without openly insulting him. Thus, the first "he" is not explicitly named as Antonio as he resents Gonzalo's efforts to cheer everyone up, nor the second "he" ("winding up the watch of his wit") as Gonzalo. Shōyō respects this lacuna, although he does add a couple of pejorative labels for Gonzalo, *oshōsan* (a "non-Christian priest") and *taishō* ("old man"), to convey the courtiers' sarcasm; without these labels, the sense that Gonzalo is offering consola-tion to Alonzo might be taken more literally. "Wit" too is difficult to translate with its layers of meaning (eight in Dr. Johnson's Dictionary), but by translating it as "wisdom" (*chie*) Shōyō makes it a kind of pivot word through the phonic echo in *chin* (onomatopoeic "ting") and *chinkyaku* ("grief" personified as a guest). The continuing dialogue develops this discourse on wisdom, with Antonio concluding that Gonzalo is *bakana mudaguchi* (literally, "stupid prattler" for "spendthrift") while being "wise" enough to hide his own intentions. The use of phonic echo may also alert audiences to Shōyō's treatment of the wordplay on "dolour" (the consequence of self-pity) and "dollar" (the entertainer's fee) through the repetition of *kan* in *kanashimi* ("grief"), *kantai* ("entertainment"), *kane* ("money"), and *kannen* ("resignation"); this Japanese Gonzalo is clearly meant to mishear Sebastian's *kane* for *kannen* in the same way that in the source Gonzalo mishears "dollar" for "dolour":[81]

GONZALO.

When every grief is entertained that's offered,/comes to th'entertainer –
(*Kakugen rashiku*) ["Spoken like an adage."] *Ee, kanashimi kuru toki wa, kore wo chinkyaku no gotoku kantai seyo, shikaran ni wa onozukara ni shite . . . . .*

SEBASTIAN.    A dollar.
(*Waza to kikoeru yō ni*) ["As if meaning to be heard."] *Kane ga mōkaru.*

GONZALO.

Dolour comes to him indeed. You have/spoken truer than you purposed.
(*Sebasuchiyan wo mikaerite*) ["Looking round at Sebastian."] *Ika nimo. Kannen ga dekiru, akirame ga tsuku . . . . . Iwau to omotte oide nasareta yori mo, seitōna koto wo oii nasareta no ja.*

SEBASTIAN.

You have taken it wiselier than I meant you/should.
(*Gonzarō ni*) *Iya, kocchi ga omotte ita yori mo socchi ga rikō ni toita no da.*

GONZALO. *(to Alonso)* Therefore, my lord –
(*Ō ni*) *De gozarimasuru kara . . . . .*

ANTONIO. Fie, what a spendthrift is he of his tongue.
(*Bōhaku*) *Bakana mudaguchi wo kikitagaru otoko mo atta mono da.*

What Shōyō cannot do, because it would undermine the naturalised register of the dialogue, is to render Gonzalo's lines in a purely classical style and the lines of Antonio and Sebastian in modern Japanese. There may be a generation gap between the two sides but not of a thousand years, and it is probably more significant for Shōyō that the differing attitudes reflect a similar dichotomy in the history of drama, where (as he observes in *Shōsetsu shinzui*) styles of expression have tended to become more subtle and restrained, and therefore less like Gonzalo, as societies have evolved.[82] This dichotomy relates to Shōyō's generic sense of what he describes with regard to *The Tempest* as "the delicate transitions from the historical to the contemporary."[83] These are the kabuki genres (*jidaimono* and *sewamono*), but applied to Shakespeare it refers among other things to the artful juxtaposition of the private and familial with the public and political, Prospero as both father and duke. By way of reference, the reason *Kanadehon Chūshingura* has been compared to *Hamlet* is surely not only because they are both revenge tragedies but also because realistic domestic – and, as in *Hamlet*, often humorous – scenes are skilfully woven into the revenge plot.

As a dialectical tension, juxtapositions are arguably nowhere more apparent than in *King Lear* where, having renounced his political role, the old king is unable to find a personal mode of existence and descends into madness. As the most exhaustively demanding of the tragedies, *King Lear* probably meant more to Shōyō as an academic rather than performance text, but he translated the play in 1912, and his translation was staged in 1919. The following final example of how Shōyō handles Shakespeare's organisation of speech (2.4.236–248) juxtaposes a song in which the Fool satirises Lear's folly for having given away his kingdom, and the first rumblings of Lear's insanity prior to his flight into the storm, which although not in dialogue with the Fool do seem to be pricked by the Fool's satire. Shōyō's version seems typical of his translating style as a whole in the way that it contrasts a dialectal register for the Fool (for example, the colloquial *nya*)[84] with the loftier rhythms of the king; it uses the same pun on "dolour" as in the scene from *The Tempest* discussed earlier:[85]

FOOL. Winter's not gone yet, if the wild geese fly that way.
*Fuyu wa mada icchi mawanai nā, gan ga socchi e tobu yō jā.*

Fathers that bear rags
Do make their children blind,
(*Fushi wo tsukete*) ["As a song."] *Oyaji tsuzure kirya ko wa mina mekura,*

But fathers that bear bags
Shall see their children kind.
*oyaji saifu mocha ko wa mina kōkō.*

Fortune, that arrant whore,
Ne'er turns the key to the poor.
*Un no megami wa naute no baita,*
*zeni no nai hō nya me mo kurenu.*

But, for all this, thou shalt have as many do dolours for thy/daughters as thou canst tell in a year.
*Da keredo, omae wa, musumesan no okage de, nenjū "kannen"* [pun on *kane*, "money"][86] *nya fujiyū shinai ya.*

LEAR. O, how this mother swells up toward my heart!
(*Hanmon shite*) ["In anguish."] *Ō, shaku ga, kono munasaki e!*

*Hysterica passio*, down, thou climbing sorrow,
*Hisuteriya passhō me, sagare, onore,*

Thy element's below. Where is this daughter?
*wakinoboru mune no nayami, onore no idokoro wa shita ja wai! . . . . .*
*Musume wa doko ni oru?*

Lear's first line is a perfect five-seven. As in the source, where Lear's blank verse overflows into lines of eleven, thirteen, and eleven syllables respectively, the use of the syllabic suggests a personality pushed into an extremity with which he is mentally unable to cope but for which only he can be held responsible. In Noh drama, the figure of the mad mother is commonly associated with separation from children (rather than fathers or husbands): the Noh sub-genre called *kyōjomono*, or "madwoman's Noh," the most famous example being the fifteenth-century *Sumidagawa*. Yet although Shōyō omits any specific reference to mothers, he does insinuate the unwanted feminine through the internal rhyme on *idokoro* ("whereabouts" or "residence") and *doko* ("where"). In fact, the use of an unfamiliar foreign expression (*hysterica passio*) and an archaic word for "self" (*onore*)[87] imply an othering of insanity not in the maternal but in the foreign and the past, with a possible pun on *Ō, shaku* (where *shaku* is literally an abdominal spasm or convulsion) and *ōshaku*, or "king's sceptre," with that *shaku* being an item of Japanese regalia dating back to the eighth century.[88] In this reading, Lear fears both the foreign, as his third daughter Cordelia is wed to the King of France, and his own past mistakes; one can further imagine a symbolic sceptre that Lear is unwilling to relinquish but having had to do so now wanders uncomfortably within his psyche.

### Kabuki Shōyō

In a tribute to Shōyō published shortly after his death in 1935, playwright Nagata Hideo contrasts what he sees as the "extremely dialectical tendency of the *shingeki* drama as it has lately become" with the more professional basis of the Bungei Kyōkai and its heirs; in other words, their determination to make professional actors out of amateurs.[89] Nagata was personally grateful to Shōyō for helping him at the beginning of his writing career twenty years earlier, but he had never been part of the Bungei Kyōkai and admits that in 1914 he had been drawn instead to the literary idealism (*bungakutsū*) of Mori Ōgai and the Jiyū Gekijō (Free Theatre), which was founded in 1909. Over the ten years of its operations it concentrated on staging modern European plays, beginning with Ōgai's translation of Ibsen's *John Gabriel Borkman*. The Jiyū Gekijō was "free" (and therefore appealing to a university graduate like Nagata) because of its focus on literary and dramatic content rather than the audience appeal of individual actors or even a single theatrical base, whereas for Nagata the Shōyō school was focussed on "human feelings" (being *ninjōtsū*) rather than ideas, and committed to nurturing a generation of actors capable of exploiting those feelings to theatrical effect.[90]

The considerable irony of Nagata's distinction is that whereas Jiyū Gekijō was co-founded by a university-educated director and playwright, Osanai Kaoru, and a kabuki actor and impresario, Ichikawa Sadanji II, and relied exclusively on Sadanji's troupe of kabuki actors to render modern European Naturalism on a Japanese stage (in which effort they struggled), the Bungei Kyōkai employed amateurs from outside the kabuki world to stage a playwright whom Shōyō insisted had more in common with classical kabuki than any modern literary school. The Bungei Kyōkai was founded a few years before the Jiyū Gekijō and, unlike the latter, employed female as well as male actors. Yet Shōyō's inculcation of professional skills such as the appropriate delivery of lines was not dissimilar from the previous three hundred years of kabuki tradition, in which actors had always identified themselves with role types in which they could apply their skills – for example as female impersonators – rather than the literary value of individual plays. In this regard, Nagata sees its role as essentially precursory, commenting of Shōyō's Shakespeare translations that

> Considered as a necessary preliminary to the development of modern Japanese drama and through their use of the language of kabuki and *kyōgen* rather than contemporary Japanese, they revealed a profound sensitivity to the artistic tastes [*shukō*] of the Japanese people.[91]

Nagata's is not a negative assessment, but he is repeating a common view of Shōyō's Shakespeares that they warmed people up to the idea of modern drama by speaking a language that the audience already knew, and he qualifies this opinion by implying that audience distaste for Shōyō's so-called "kabuki Shakespeares" was a denial of their own cultural instincts.

The previous chapter identified aspects of kabuki style in Shōyō's Shakespeare translations, such as the use of seven-five syllabic meter and of archaism, and yet it is remarkable that out of the roughly fifty productions of his translations staged up to the time of his death, only five featured professional kabuki actors and, whether they starred kabuki actors or not, Shakespeare productions of this period were largely free of the techniques traditionally associated with kabuki, such as offstage shamisen accompaniment (*geza*), spectacular *kumadori* makeup, choreographed dance items, and the *hanamichi* stage.[92] This section therefore looks briefly at how Shōyō's translations, without exactly being kabuki scripts, seem to offer themselves up for performance by prewar Japanese actors who could be expected to speak the "language of kabuki."

Shōyō's *Othello* translation of 1911 is one of his translations that was performed specifically by kabuki actors, with Matsumoto Kōshirō VII acting the protagonist in 1917, but as a translation represented a departure from the 1903 adaptation by Emi Suiin (set in recently colonised Formosa). Along with *Hamlet* and *Romeo and Juliet*, the translation mixes classical and colloquial styles (*gazoku setchū*) as a template from which Shōyō was gradually to depart after 1913, but this reliance on the classical does not necessarily make it any more or less like kabuki, which depends rather on the foregrounding of theatrical effects.

The final scene of the original play is strikingly akin to kabuki, comprising a desperate soliloquy (5.2.1–22) similar to kabuki narrative, although spoken by Othello rather than by a separate narrator as he approaches his victim, a sublime dialogue as Othello sets about smothering Desdemona (23–123) that recalls any number of sacrificial victims in kabuki as she asserts her innocence, a dramatic discovery scene (164–335) as Iago's treachery is revealed, and then Othello's final speech as he is allowed to assert his "service to the state" before committing suicide (336–357), which recalls the honourable suicides of kabuki tradition (although unlike the

revenge plots in *Hamlet* and *Kanadehon Chūshingura*, there are no kabuki plays
in which husbands are tricked into murdering their wives). A translation in kabuki
style will assert each of these four stages as great theatrical moments but are arguably less Shakespearean to the extent that Othello's interiority is subordinated to
a kabuki code of duty and feeling. Elements of Shōyō's 1911 translation, starting
with the opening soliloquy (1–7), suggest just such an indulgence of feeling rather
than anything more internalised:[93]

> It is the cause, it is the cause, my soul!
> Let me not name it to you, you chaste stars.
> It is the cause. Yet I'll not shed her blood
> Nor scar that whiter skin of hers than snow
> And smooth as monumental alabaster:
> Yet she must die, else she'll betray more men.
> Put out the light, and then put out the light!

> *Kore ga tame ja wai, kore ga tame ja wai . . . . . Nanji, kiyoki hoshi yo,*
> *kono koto wo iwasete kureru na! . . . . . Kore ga tame ja wai. To wa ie*
> *are no chi wa nagasumai zo, matta yuki yori mo shiroi, sekka seki yori*
> *mo namerakana are no hada ni wa kizu wo tsukemai. To wa ie ikaite wa*
> *okarenu wai, ikaite oita nara, mata mo otoko wo otoshiire oru de arou.*
> *Tomoshibi wo kiyaite, sore kara kono tomoshibi wo kiyasu no ja.*

At a literary level, this is an example of Shōyō at his best; the rhythm is shaped
by the kind of sound plays and sequences we have come to associate with Shōyō,
such as *sekka seki yori mo nameraka* (for "smooth as monumental alabaster") and
*mata mo otoko wo otoshiire oru de arou* ("else she'll betray more men"). It is also
highly emotional in the style of a kabuki hero, the speech of a man at the end of
his tether, although a possible deliberate mistake with the comparative *yori mo* to
state that Desdemona is smoother "even than" (rather than as "smooth as") alabaster suggests that Shōyō's Othello idealises his young wife even more than in the
original. Shōyō's hyperbole may be in response to the contradiction in Othello's
argument, namely that while he is convinced of his wife's infidelity the comparisons with snow and alabaster insist on her purity. Finally, the lack of a comma and
of any double consonants after *sore kara* give the expression a strongly syllabic
feel, similar to kabuki.

When Shōyō came to revise his translation in the final months of his life this
was one of many parts that he radically rewrote.[94] Reproductions of pages from the
printed version of the original translation bespattered with Shōyō's red-pencilled
corrections appeared soon after his death, for example in black and white in Chūō
Kōron's promotional monthly *Saō Fukkō*.[95]

> *(Nasakenage ni)* ["With pathos."] *Kore ga tame nan ja, kore ga tame nan*
> *ja, mattaku . . . . . Ā, kiyorakana hoshitachi yo, dō ka, kuchi ni dasasenaide*
> *kure! . . . . . Kore ga tame nan ja mattaku. Demo, are no chi wa nagasumai.*

*Yuki yori mo shiroi, sekka seki yori mo subekkoi are no hada nya kizu wa tsukemai. Demo, ikashichā okaren, ikashite okya, kono ue mata, nandomo otoko wo otoshiire oru jarō kara. Tomoshibi wo keshite, sore kara, kono tomoshibi wo kesun ja.*

This is a modernised version, with the direction *nasakenage ni* shifting the focus from the sonority of the language to how the actor chooses to speak the lines, since Shōyō is aware that a modern actor – being freed from the stylised delivery of kabuki speech – could deliver even a mundane expression such as *Kore ga tame nan ja* with great emotive force. This version is shaped not so much by sound sequences and inflexions but by the blunt connective *demo* (for "but"), which has none of the elusive quality of *to wa ie* but does serve to make the speech more of a reasoned justification for what Othello is about to do. That also is the point made by the change from *tame ja wai* to *tame nan ja*, which has the less histrionic but more discursive nuance of a man who has finally realized what he has to do. The use of the assertively male particle *wai* in the 1911 translation makes it more an embodiment of sexual revenge, but Othello's sexualised otherness in the revision is expressed more through colloquial inflexions such as *subekkoi* ("purer") and *ikashichā okaren* ("must not live"). The inclusion of *subekkoi* meaning "slippery" connotes Desdemona's alleged infidelity, but this is less strongly implied in the 1911 translation.

This shift from kabuki to modern style is also apparent in how Shōyō translates the ensuing dialogue with Desdemona (23–32):[96]

DESDEMONA.   Who's there? Othello?
             *Tare ja? Oserō dono ka?* (1911)
             *Dāre? . . . . Oserō dono desu ka?* (1935)

OTHELLO.     Ay, Desdemona.
             *Sō ja, Dezudemōna.* (1911)
             *Un, ore ja.* (1935)

DESDEMONA.   Will you come to bed, my lord?
             *Mada oyorimasenu kae?* (1911)
             *Mada oyoranain desu ka?* (1935)

OTHELLO.     Have you prayed tonight, Desdemon?
             *Dezudemōna, konya no kitō wa sunda ka?* (1911)
             *Dezudemōna, konya no kitō ni sunda ka?* (1935)

DESDEMONA.   Ay, my lord.
             *Hai, sumaita wai na.* (1911)
             *Hai, sumashimashita.* (1935)

OTHELLO.     If you bethink yourself of any crime
             Unreconciled as yet to heaven and grace,
             Solicit for it straight.

> *Moshi ten no ojihi ga mada yō kōte nai tsumi ga aru nara, isoide negauta ga ii.* (1911)
> *Ten no ojihi wo mada yō negaute oran warui koto ga aru nara, ima no uchi ni, isoide negau ga ei.* (1935)

DESDEMONA.   Alack, my lord, what may you mean by that?
　　　　　　　*Haremā, nande sono yōna koto wo?* (1911)
　　　　　　　*Ara, mā, naze? Naze sonna koto wo ossharu?* (1935)

OTHELLO.   Well, do it, and be brief; I will walk by.
　　　　　　I would not kill thy unprepared spirit,
　　　　　　No, heaven forfend! I would not kill thy soul.
　　　　　　*Hate, hayō sore wo sei. Ore wa aruite iyō. Kakugo no dekite inu mono wo koroshita unai. Iya iya, kesshite! Sochi no tamashii wo ba koroshita unai.* (1911)
　　　　　　*Sa, hayō sei. Ore wa sokoira wo aruitoru kara. Kakugo no deki toran mono wo koroshitakunai. Iya, kesshite! Tamashii wo koroshitaku wa nai.* (1935)

Shōyō's *Othello* revision exemplifies not only his trajectory towards a more modern and speakable style and format of Shakespeare translation but also the dangers of a classical style that seemed to revel too much in the sounds of the language at the expense of the underlying logic of the lines.

## Performance History

### *Theatrical Models*

Brian Powell observes separately that Japanese theatre in the twentieth century "was to some extent shaped by the interaction between *shingeki* and *kabuki*"[97] and that "Japanese Shakespeare" was not taken seriously by foreign audiences until the tours by Ninagawa and Suzuki Tadashi to Britain and the United States in the 1980s.[98] The latter achieved an integration of text and performance of which Shōyō could only have dreamt, while Shōyō was faced with the conundrum of developing a modern style of producing Shakespeare in Japanese when his personal notion of theatrical practice was basically derived from kabuki. Nevertheless, Shōyō's Shakespeares were staged mainly in modern Western-style theatres such as Tokyo's Imperial Theatre, which allowed for a non-traditional representation of Shakespeare's dramaturgy, and were performed mainly by actors from outside the kabuki tradition, such as Doi Shunsho and Matsui Sumako who, schooled by Shōyō in the Western heritage, sought to adapt Shakespeare's texts to their Japanese bodies. Having looked at how Shōyō endeavours to make his translations performable, this second half of the chapter surveys the substantial performance history of his translations that has continued even into the twenty-first century, with as much emphasis as possible on the problems posed by Shōyō's language.

Shōyō never saw Shakespeare staged in the English theatre, but many of his acolytes did, and sources such as *Saō Fukkō* contain numerous reviews of what they saw there. His *Sheikusupiya kenkyū shiori* includes a chapter on modern directing styles,[99] and his prefaces refer frequently to English actors and directors of the previous 150 years, in the 1912 *Lear* preface, for example, where he is interested in the nineteenth-century reversion from the Nahum Tate adaptation (previously favoured by David Garrick, Edmund Kean, and John Philip Kemble, as he mentions) to Shakespeare's original version with the deaths of Lear and Cordelia that was revived by William Macready in 1838 and more completely by Henry Irving in 1892, with Ellen Terry as Cordelia.[100] Irving, who died in 1905, was the outstanding Shakespeare actor at the time Shōyō started to translate the plays, but Shōyō's distaste for Irving's rather feminised Shylock reflects a difficulty he had with any kind of theatre that seemed to put contemporary fashion before the seriousness of dramatic literature, especially Shakespeare. In the latter case, Shōyō's impression was derived mainly from Sadanji's performance of the role, which was known to imitate Irving's, in the 1913 production directed by Matsui Shōyō.[101] Shōyō did not mean to condemn Irving's acting outright, but he was uncomfortable with male acting that reminded him of kabuki *onnagata*, and seems generally to have preferred a manly style of acting for male roles.

Shōyō is critical of Harley Granville-Barker's view of Shakespeare as a writer who subscribes to a "rich naturalism" (and disliked Granville-Barker's controversial *Dream* production of 1914 in which the fairies were portrayed as Cambodian idols),[102] regarding naturalism – along with romanticism, symbolism, and even realism – as modern labels that obfuscated the essential "impartiality" (*fusoku furi*) of Shakespeare's vision.[103] Shōyō insists that modern realism is not the same as Shakespeare's realism and, glancing at his own kabuki tradition which had always eschewed both modern dress and a more modern pace of delivery, is puzzled by the high speed, modern-dress productions of Granville-Barker and Barry Jackson. His pupil Honma Hisao had seen Jackson's *Macbeth* at the Royal Court Theatre in 1928 in which Macbeth appeared in military khaki and his wife in a 1920s party frock, and in a carefully argued review for *Saō Fukkō* that included two stills from the production was unable finally to come down on either side of the opposing views that modern dress enhanced or obscured the play's "poetic vision."[104]

Shōyō only ever directed *Hamlet* and *The Merchant of Venice*, and especially with the 1911 *Hamlet* was concerned with ensuring that his actors understood the lines and that the lines were delivered audibly and in an appropriate manner. Actors were dressed in the kind of traditional garb familiar to Shōyō from Victorian Shakespeare editions, and framed pictorially in the nineteenth-century style within the proscenium arch of the Imperial Theatre. A full-page reproduction of Irving's Hamlet – relaxed and in control – in the frontispiece of the 1909 translation[105] suggests more than a debt to the Victorian character acting of Irving and Herbert Beerbohm Tree, and Shōyō's personal understanding of Shakespearean character could only have been informed by the introductions and notes in the Victorian Shakespeares, including Irving's own edition of 1889–90 co-edited with Frank Marshall, which was the first performance-oriented edition since 1773 and in Shōyō's possession.

The Bungei Kyōkai *Hamlet* came a few months before the seminal Moscow Art Theatre production of the play by Konstantin Stanislavski and Edward Gordon Craig, and Shōyō left it to the younger generation (above all Osanai Kaoru) to adopt their ideas. Stanislavski and Craig were less inimical to his project than Granville-Barker for their focus on the art of acting rather than on matters of interpretation. (As with Irving and Tree, Shōyō usually mentions Craig in tandem with the director Max Reinhardt.) Craig's mother, Ellen Terry, was already known to Shōyō as Irving's Portia (and in other roles), and Craig's reciprocal interest in the Japanese theatre was received keenly in early Taishō Japan.[106] Moreover, there was a parallel that Shōyō does not explore between Craig's disciplined Übermarionette and his own theory of "hidden ideals" (*botsurisō*), except that the genius of concealment is transferred by Craig from Shakespeare to the actor; as he writes, "the highest art is that which conceals the craft and forgets the craftsman."[107] *Botsurisō* was the term coined by Shōyō in 1891, and is borrowed by the film director and Craigean Murata Minoru in an essay of 1913 entitled "Engeki no botsurisō shugi" (The Ideology of Hiddenness in Drama) in which he argues simply that the hidden object of drama must be society rather than the individual, and that drama succeeds to the extent that it is able to conceal this motive.[108] Murata does not mention Shōyō, but likewise for Shōyō Shakespeare's appeal is his relevance to every type of person and thus to society as a whole. Shōyō had no ambition to be a modern Stanislavskian director, but Craig's origins in the theatre of Irving and Terry suggests that attention to detail was certainly the place to start,[109] and Shōyō carries over his directorial attention to detail to the stage directions and revisions in his published translations. The potential for psychological realism in Victorian character acting was germane to Shōyō's realism, but (by his own admission) his brief foray into Shakespeare directing and his overall view of Shakespeare lacked the dominant ideas associated with both modernist directing and *shingeki*, so that coupled with their sonorous, slightly old-fashioned language, his translations whether on page or stage could be seen as showy and inconsistent, like kabuki, and also amenable to kabuki actors who wanted to engage with Shakespeare's characters.

### *1901–13: Period of Experimentation*

The performance history of Shōyō's Shakespeare translations can be divided into four periods.[110] The first period (1901–13) is one of experimentation, and is characterised on the one hand by Shōyō's determination to stage the plays in complete translation rather than as adaptations and, on the other, by the Meiji preference for Japanisation, which is a feature of Sadanji's kabuki-style *Merchant* and of the Bungei Kyōkai *Hamlet*. Apart from Sadanji and the Ii Yōhō *Julius Caesar* in 1901, which was of Shōyō's early 1884 *jōruri* adaptation and done in *shinpa* style,[111] all of the following were by the Bungei Kyōkai, founded in 1906 at the initiative of Shōyō's pupil Shimamura Hōgetsu on his return from three years of study at the universities of Oxford and Berlin. Hōgetsu had been to numerous theatre performances while in Europe, and is nowadays remembered as a pioneer of the

Naturalism that was ultimately to the detriment of Shōyō's more cautiously academic approach.

The Bungei Kyōkai brought together a group of more or less gifted amateur actors, most of them former pupils of Shōyō's such as Doi Shunsho and Tōgi Tetteki, who had participated in his reading group at Waseda in the 1890s, but including a few outsiders, such as Matsui Sumako who played Ophelia in the 1911 *Hamlet*. Doi had previously acted with Kawakami Otojirō's *shinpa* troupe and Tōgi had been a court musician, but none of the Bungei Kyōkai members had been trained in kabuki and instead were subjected to an ambitious two years' programme in Western and Japanese dramatic theory and practice. Shōyō's theatrical experience was as a director rather than actor and with the modern kabuki plays (*shin kabuki*) he had been writing and staging with professional kabuki actors over the previous ten years. It is this romanticised hybridisation of East and West together with Shōyō's ideological purity that characterises the Bungei Kyōkai's achievement.

It was Shōyō's commitment to text and translation over performance and adaptation, and use of non-kabuki amateurs and female actors, that made the Bungei Kyōkai Japan's first "modern" theatre company, but it was not a commercial enterprise. The commercial input of the new *shingeki* came from kabuki actor Ichikawa Sadanji who, inheriting his father's Meijiza theatre in 1902 and sensing an opportunity for artistic and commercial novelty in the performance of translations of Western plays, in 1909 joined forces with Osanai Kaoru (who was a graduate of the Tokyo University English department) to establish the Jiyū Gekijō, the second and other of the *shingeki* pioneers. As I have mentioned, the Jiyū Gekijō staged modern European playwrights such as Ibsen and Wedekind rather than Shakespeare, but Sadanji and Osanai had (like Hōgetsu) been to Europe and knew the British and continental theatre in a way that Shōyō never could. After their company was disbanded in 1919, they were allies with Shōyō in producing Shakespeare on the modern Japanese stage, relying of course on Shōyō's translations. Another feature of this experimental period is that up to the 1911 *Hamlet* it was rare for Shakespeare plays to be staged in whole; even in early Shōwa it was usual for the trial scene only to be performed in productions of *The Merchant of Venice*.[112]

| | | |
|---|---|---|
| 1901 (July) | *Julius Caesar* | Ii Yōhō company (Meijiza) |
| 1906 (November) | *The Merchant of Venice* | Bungei Kyōkai, with Tōgi Tetteki as Shylock and Doi Shunsho as Portia (Kabukiza) |
| 1907 (November) | *Hamlet* | Bungei Kyōkai, with Doi Shunsho as Hamlet and Matsui Sumako as Ophelia (Hongōza) |
| 1908 (January) | *The Merchant of Venice* | Ichikawa Sadanji's company, with Ichikawa Sadanji II as Shylock and Ichikawa Shōchō II as Portia (Meijiza), followed by performances at Yokohamaza (February), Osaka Nakaza (May), Kyoto Minamiza (June), and Kobe Daikokuza (July) |
| 1910 (March) | *Hamlet* | Bungei Kyōkai, dir. Doi Shunsho |

| 1910 (March) | *The Merchant of Venice* | Bungei Kyōkai, dir. Tōgi Tetteki |
|---|---|---|
| 1911 (May) | *Hamlet* | Bungei Kyōkai, dir. Shōyō, with Doi Shun-sho as Hamlet, Matsui Sumako as Ophelia, Tōgi Tetteki as Claudius, Kamiyama Uraji as Gertrude, Katō Seiichi as Polonius, Hayashi Yawara as Laertes, Mori Eijirō as Horatio, and Takeda Masanori as Ghost (Imperial Theatre) |
| 1911 (July) | *Hamlet* | Bungei Kyōkai (Osaka Kadoza) |
| 1911 (November to December) | *The Merchant of Venice* | Bungei Kyōkai (Imperial Theatre), followed by performance at Osaka Nakaza (March 1912) |
| 1913 (March) | *The Merchant of Venice* | Ichikawa Sadanji company (Hongōza) |
| 1913 (June to July) | *Julius Caesar* | Bungei Kyōkai, dir. Matsui Shōyō (Imperial Theatre) |

### *1913–28: Canonisation and Consolidation*

The second period (1913–28) is one of canonisation and consolidation as Shōyō departs from active involvement in the Tokyo theatre to complete his translations, and Shakespeare production is delegated to the second generation of *shingeki* companies. The crowd-drawing staples were still *Hamlet* and *The Merchant of Venice*, but among the tragedies, *Macbeth*, *Othello*, and *Julius Caesar* and among the comedies, *A Midsummer Night's Dream*, *Twelfth Night*, and *The Taming of the Shrew* all gained acceptance.

The Kindaigeki Kyōkai (Modern Theatre Society), which staged *The Merchant of Venice* in 1913 and the first Japanese production of *King Lear* in 1919, was formed in 1912 by a Bungei Kyōkai member, Kamiyama Sōjin, and his wife Yamakawa Uraji; disbanding the company in 1919, the couple moved to California where Sōjin became famous as an actor in silent films. Both Shōyō and Mori Ōgai were appointed advisors to the Kindaigeki Kyōkai, and their staging of Ōgai's *Macbeth* translation in 1913 was the first in Japan of the tragedy. Hōgetsu and Sumako's Geijutsuza (Art Theatre) in 1914 staged a sensational adaptation of Tolstoy's *Resurrection*. Their adaptation of a work by the fiercest and most moralistic of anti-Shakespeareans was not necessarily meant to rebuff Shōyō, although it considerably exceeded the 1911 *Hamlet* as both a commercial and artistic success, but their *Antony and Cleopatra* (also in 1914) was not a success; that was Shōyō's domain.[113]

The intended inheritor of the Shōyō mantle was the Mumeikai (Anonymous Company), which was founded in 1914 by Doi, Tōgi, and kabuki actor Ikeda Daigo, and the same year staged *Macbeth* in Shōyō's translation, but the company was disbanded following Doi's untimely death the next year. Continuity of a sort came also from Katō Seiichi, Shōyō's Polonius, who in 1913 with three others founded the Butai Kyōkai (named after London's Stage Society), staging the trial scene in 1915 and 1924, but Shōyō's actual inheritors were Osanai and his adopted son Tsubouchi Shikō, who were only tangentially involved with the Bungei Kyōkai and overseas during the climactic final year of the Bungei Kyōkai's activities; Osanai ended up in Moscow, where he met with Stanislavsky, and Shikō at Harvard and Oxford, where he corresponded with Craig.[114] Their return to Japan brought new approaches to stage directing which Shōyō basically welcomed. Shikō directed Shakespeare (including *Hamlet* in his own translation) first for the Gekijutsukai (Dramatic Arts Society) before being appointed artistic director of Kobayashi Ichizō's Takarazuka Revue, near Osaka, in 1926. The Takarazuka Revue was founded as Japan's first all-female musical theatre troupe in 1913 and staged several Shakespeare adaptations in the prewar years. Shōyō welcomed this opportunity for young women to train and perform as professional artists within a very different environment both from the geisha culture of old and from kabuki, where women were forbidden from acting. That Shikō directed the first Japanese production of *The Merry Wives of Windsor* in Takarazuka (albeit for a local amateur group rather than the Revue) seems a poignant reflection on his own troubled romantic history and the patriarchal Meiji morality of "good wives and wise mothers" (*ryōsai kenbo*) inculcated by both Shōyō and the Revue. He had been forbidden by Shōyō from marrying an American actress he had met during his stay at Harvard, and in 1920 was legally disowned by Shōyō when he married a Takarazuka actress, Kumoi Namiko. Their marriage lasted until Shikō's death in 1986 at the age of ninety-eight, and produced the television actress Tsubouchi Mikiko.[115]

During this second period, kabuki actors Sadanji and Matsumoto Kōshirō VII played Mark Antony and Othello respectively, but the drift was towards the modernism of Osanai's Tsukiji Little Theatre, whose exuberant *Dream* at the Imperial Theatre in July 1928 celebrated Shōyō's recent completion of his translation of the Complete Works; the theatre had been rebuilt after suffering extensive damage in the Great Kanto Earthquake of 1923. Osanai rejected traditional kabuki, with its basis in song and dance (the *ka* and *bu* of kabuki), in favour of spoken drama and rational acting, but a problem of early *shingeki* was that it was too intellectually serious to reach a mass audience and be commercially viable.[116] A compromise was made by another Bungei Kyōkai alumnus, Sawada Shōjirō, whose *shinkokugeki* "new national theatre" movement combined modern with kabuki elements and was both prolific and successful. Sawada had stood up to the headstrong Sumako at the Bungei Kyōkai and later Geijutsuza, and for Shōyō became a model example of his philosophy of making professionals out of amateurs. Shōyō delivered a moving eulogy at Sawada's funeral following the actor's early death from meningitis in 1929, calling him "glorious in death as in life."[117] His one Shakespeare outing was as Coriolanus at the Imperial Theatre in 1926, fighting with real swords: *shinkokugeki* was in some respects the forerunner of the post-war samurai films and specialised in elaborate swordfighting scenes. Sawada's *Coriolanus* was organised to raise funds for the rebuilding of the Shakespeare Memorial Theatre in Stratford-upon-Avon after it had been gutted by fire earlier that year: an indication not only of the actor's popularity but also of how far Japanese Shakespeare production had come under Shōyō's mentorship since the adaptations of late Meiji, and Sawada was speaking Shōyō's translation in contemporary style published in 1922.

| 1913 (November) | *The Merchant of Venice* | Kindaigeki Kyōkai (Osaka Chikamatsuza) |
|---|---|---|
| 1915 (May) | *The Merchant of Venice* | Butai Kyōkai (Imperial Theatre) |
| 1916 (June) | *Macbeth* | Mumeikai, dir. Tsubouchi Shikō, with Tōgi Tetteki as Macbeth and Kagawa Tamae as Lady Macbeth (Yūrakuza) (three hundredth anniversary of Shakespeare's death), followed by performances at Osaka Nakaza and Kyoto Minamiza (July) |
| 1917 (March) | *Othello* | Kobe Jurakukan, with Matsumoto Kōshirō VII as Othello, Yamada Yoshiko as Desdemona, and Tōgi Tetteki as Iago |
| 1919 (February) | *King Lear* | Kindaigeki Kyōkai, dir. Kamiyama Shōjin, with Kamiyama as Lear (Yūrakuza) |
| 1921 (February) | *The Merchant of Venice* | Geijutsukai, dir. Furukawa Toshitaka and Katō Chōji (Marunouchi) |
| 1921 (June and October) | *Hamlet* | Geijutsukai (Kyōbashi and Totsuka Scott Hall), followed by performance at Kobe Jurakukan (June 1923) |
| 1922 (May) | *The Merchant of Venice* | Geijutsukai (Ushigome Kaikan), and outdoor performances in Koishikawa (April 1923) and in Hibiya Park (July 1923) |
| 1922 (November) | *Macbeth* | Geijutsukai (Ushigome Kaikan) and at Karui-zawa Green Hotel (August 1923) |
| 1923 (July) | *Julius Caesar* | Mumei Kyōkai (Yūrakuza) |
| 1924 (February) | *The Merchant of Venice* | Butai Kyōkai (Hōchi Kōdō), with Sasaki Tsumoru as Shylock and Natsukawa Shizue as Portia |
| 1924 (May and June) | *Hamlet* | Geijutsukai (Shibuya Jurakuza and Chiba Inohanaza) |
| 1924 (October) | *The Merchant of Venice* | Geijutsukai, dir. Tsubouchi Shikō (Osaka Chūō Kōkaikan) |
| 1925 (January) | *Julius Caesar* | Tsukiji Little Theatre, dir. Osanai Kaoru and Hijikata Yoshi |
| 1925 (March) | *Julius Caesar* | Kabukiza, with Ichikawa Sadanji II as Antony, Matsumoto Kōshirō VII as Caesar, and Ichi-kawa Shōchō II as Calpurnia |
| 1926 (July) | *The Merry Wives of Windsor* | Takarazuka Kokuminza, dir, Tsubouchi Shikō, with Furukawa Toshitaka as Falstaff |

| 1926 (August) | *Coriolanus* | Imperial Theatre, with Sawada Shōjirō as Coriolanus and Hisamatsu Kiyoko as Volumnia (Shinkokugeki) (to raise funds for Shakespeare Memorial Theatre, Stratford-on-Avon) |
| 1928 (June) | *Twelfth Night* | Ōkuma Hall, dir. Katō Chōji (Chikyūza) (to raise funds for Shōyō's Enpaku theatre museum and library at Waseda) |
| 1928 (July) | *A Midsummer Night's Dream* | Imperial Theatre, dir. Osanai Kaoru, Aoyama Sugisaku and Hijikata Yoshi (Tsukiji Little Theatre) (to commemorate Shōyō's completion of his Shakespeare translations) |

### *1928–35: Shōyō Triumphant*

Much of the activity of the third period (1928–35) was centred on Waseda, as the completion and opening of Shōyō's theatre museum and library (Enpaku) at the university in October 1928 provided a permanent base for Shakespeare and theatrical research. The museum's façade, modelled on the Elizabethan Fortune Theatre, was sometimes used for Shakespeare performances, but these were usually staged in the university's Ōkuma Hall, guaranteeing a large student audience. Shōyō himself was often ill and at home in Atami during the last seven years of his life, but the commercial publisher Chūō Kōron capitalised on the success of the first editions of his translations (issued in single volumes by Waseda University Press between 1909 and 1928) to publish his revised versions between 1933 and 1935. A publisher's blurb of 1934 calls these "the Bible of the religion of Shakespeare in the Far East that will promote many new crusades in the theatrical world."[118]

Shōyō's main aim in revising his translations was to make them more amenable for teaching and performance, and this educational motive underlies most of the productions of this period. The Shinshunza (New Year Company) was centred on two of the former Bungei Kyōkai actors, Katō Seiichi and Mori Eijirō, and with conscious mentoring from Shōyō its debut *Hamlet* production in September 1933 was praised for its distinctively contemporary language and delivery in contrast to the *Hamlet* of twenty-two years previous in which both actors had appeared.[119] Katō and Mori were established *shingeki* actors, based in Kansai, and Shinshunza closed after only three productions.

A more lasting impression was achieved by a former pupil of Shōyō named Katō Chōji, who as early as 1921 had been involved with the Geijutsukai (Arts Society), playing Bassanio and Lady Macbeth, and appeared in Shōyō's Atami pageant before being appointed director of Chikyūza (Globe Theatre) in 1927. Katō was to lead Shakespeare production in the early post-war period (also taking a position at the Enpaku), and in this third period he premiered productions in the Shōyō translations of *Twelfth Night*, *Much Ado About Nothing*, and the two parts of *Henry IV*. Osanai Kaoru died suddenly a few months after the celebratory *Dream* production, but in September 1933 the Tsukiji Little Theatre celebrated the publication of the revised translations with a *Hamlet* under the direction of one of Sōseki's former disciples, the writer Kume Masao.[120] A similar tribute was made by Ichikawa Sadanji as the same month he resurrected his 1909 *Merchant* with a forty-six-year-old Ichikawa Shōchō as Desdemona. Katō Chōji, who had a parallel career as a writer of native dance dramas, had been taken on by Onoe Kikugorō VI to teach directing at Kikugorō's new school for the children of kabuki families, and in this role he directed students in four Shakespeare productions, including of *King Lear*, which was staged at Waseda in April 1935 (together with three of Shōyō's original kabuki pieces) in honour of Shōyō, who had died on 28 February. Productions of Shōyō's translations ceased for the time being, and following the outbreak of the war with China in 1937, there were no Shakespeare productions in Japan between 1937 and June 1946.

Centred on figures such as Katō and Shōyō himself, Shakespeare production still allowed a freedom of exchange between the kabuki and modern theatres that is unusual today. In 2005, Ninagawa Yukio came to direct his kabuki *Twelfth Night* because of his personal enthusiasm for kabuki rather than any directorial experience in the genre. Ninagawa's production achieved an artistic and commercial success that Sadanji could only have dreamt of, mainly due to Ninagawa's understanding of kabuki as theatre and the collaboration of a troupe of kabuki actors led by Onoe Kikugorō VII. At the same time, Ninagawa's non-kabuki actors have grown up in a mainstream commercial theatre that the Shakespeare actors of early Shōwa helped to create. Mitsuda Ken, who played Petruchio in 1929, became well known as a film actor in the post-war era, taking roles in Mizoguchi Kenji's *Sanshō the Bailiff* in 1954 and Kurosawa Akira's *Hamlet* adaptation, *The Bad Sleep Well*, in 1960, while Susukida Kenji acted in numerous period films for the major studios through the 1950s, and the central role of Tsū, the crane, in Kinoshita Junji's long-running *Yūzuru* (Twilight Crane, 1948) was specially created for Tsukiji's Desdemona of 1934, Yamamoto Yasue. Shōyō could hardly have hoped for better.

| 1929 (March) | *The Taming of the Shrew* | Imperial Hotel theatre, dir. Katō Chōji, with Takasu Kenji (Mitsuda Ken) as Petruchio (Chikyūza) |
| 1929 (April) | *Othello* | Takarazuka Kokuminza, dir. Tsubouchi Shikō |
| 1929 (November) | *Much Ado About Nothing* | Imperial Hotel theatre (Chikyūza) |
| 1930 (March) | *The Taming of the Shrew* | Takarazuka Kokuminza, dir. Tsubouchi Shikō, with Izumo Mikiko as Katherine |
| 1930 (March) | *Twelfth Night* | Hikōkan Kōdō (Chikyūza) |
| 1931 (January) | *Henry IV, Pt. 1* | Hikōkan Kōdō, with Aoki Saburō as Falstaff (Chikyūza) |
| 1931 (April) | *Othello* | Ōkuma Hall, dir. Katō Chōji (Chikyūza) |
| 1931 (April) | *The Taming of the Shrew* | Ōkuma Hall (Chikyūza) |
| 1931 (April) | *The Tempest* | Ōkuma Hall, with Takai Yoshirō as Prospero (Chikyūza) |

| 1931 (December) | *Henry IV, Pt. 2* | Hikōkan Kōdō (Chikyūza) |
|---|---|---|
| 1932 (April) | *Macbeth* | Ōkuma Hall (Chikyūza) |
| 1932 (October) | *The Merchant of Venice* | Ōkuma Hall, dir. Katō Chōji (Waseda University fiftieth anniversary) |
| 1933 (September) | *Hamlet* | Ōkuma Hall, with Mori Eijirō as Hamlet and Katō Seiichi as Claudius (Shinshunza) |
| 1933 (September) | *Julius Caesar* | Ōkuma Hall, with Mori as Caesar and Katō as Antony (Shinshunza) |
| 1933 (October) | *Hamlet* | Tsukiji Little Theatre, dir. Kume Masao (publication of revised translations), followed by performances at Osaka Bunrakuza (June 1934) |
| 1933 (October) | *The Merchant of Venice* | Ichikawa Sadanji company, with Ichikawa Sadanji II as Shylock and Ichikawa Shōchō II as Portia (Tokyo Gekijō) |
| 1934 (January) | *The Merchant of Venice* | Nagoya Misonoza (Nihon Haiyū Gakkō) |
| 1934 (January) | *The Taming of the Shrew* | Hibiya Kōkaidō (Nihon Haiyū Gakkō) |
| 1934 (April) | *Othello* | Ōkuma Hall, with Susukida Kenji as Othello and Yamamoto Yasue as Desdemona (Tsukiji Little Theatre) |
| 1934 (August) | *A Midsummer Night's Dream* | Yokohama Ongakudō outdoor night stage, dir. Katō Chōji (Nihon Haiyū Gakkō), and at Hibiya Kōkaidō (September) |
| 1935 (April) | *King Lear* | Ōkuma Hall, with Susukida Kenji as Lear (Nihon Haiyū Gakkō) (memorial production following Shōyō's death on February 28, 1935) |

### After 1946: "Old Man Shōyō"

In the early post-war era, Shōyō both benefitted from his status as a patriarch of Japan's cultural Westernisation and suffered for what many saw as a patriarchal mindset; this mixed view continues to this day. As early as 1947, the Enpaku organised an exhibition about its founder, which was visited by the teenage Crown Prince Akihito, but the stage translations by Fukuda Tsuneari and Odashima Yūshi that succeeded Shōyō's in the 1960s and '70s were not only more contemporary in their language but clearly the products of post-war democratisation. Shōyō's educated, rhetorical style seemed to speak down to his audience, while Fukuda – although in his way as authoritarian as Shōyō – developed a communicative stage language influenced by speech act theory and his personal experience of the London theatre, and Odashima in the 1970s offered a lively, poetic Shakespeare who even seemed to speak the same language of his youthful student audience. Finally, it should be noted that neither Fukuda nor Odashima were graduates of Shōyō's Waseda but of Tokyo University, and the companies that introduced their translations had little direct connection with the Shōyō stable, either.

The touring productions by Zenshinza (Progressive Theatre Company) of *A Midsummer Night's Dream* and *Romeo and Juliet* in the immediate post-war years were highly successful in promoting interest in Shakespeare, but Zenshinza was a modern kabuki troupe founded in 1931,[121] and in the 1950s Shōyō's translations became largely the domain of Katō Chōji's Kindai Gekijō (Modern Theatre), which comprised mainly Waseda arts graduates. The company was renamed Kindaiza in 1966 under the leadership of Nemoto Yoshiya, last staged a Shōyō translation in 1977, and folded in 2012. The Kindai Gekijō's productions would seldom run for more than a few days, taking place in the public and commercial halls that sufficed for rented theatrical space before the erection of larger, purpose-built venues such as the Nissay Theatre in 1963. The so-called "lighter," less controversial plays such as *A Midsummer Night's Dream* and *The Taming of the Shrew* were regularly performed, and the Kindai Gekijō also premiered productions of *The Comedy of Errors* and *The Winter's Tale* in Shōyō's translations. It is remarkable that *Romeo and Juliet*, which has been as popular in Japan as anywhere else and was staged as an adaptation under Osanai's direction as early as 1904, had to wait until Zenshinza in 1950 before being done in Shōyō's translation, and then never again. Irrespective of the latter's strengths and weaknesses, this lacuna suggests an apprehension about setting the theme of Christianised young love within Shōyō's kabuki field, in other words that the two lovers were definitely not to be confused with the kabuki "water trade" of old. But just as Othello's dark tragedy had appealed to prewar kabuki actors, the role of Shakespeare's greatest comic villain, Richard III, was taken by two kabuki actors, first in 1964 by Nakamura Kanzaburō XVII in a production directed by Fukuda Tsuneari in Fukuda's translation for the 400th anniversary of Shakespeare's birth, and then by Onoe Tatsunosuke in a production of Shōyō's 1918 translation at Tokyo's Sunshine Theatre in 1980.[122] Wada Yutaka, who directed the Tatsunosuke production, commented that Shōyō's translations were "ideal for Shakespeare in terms of their musicality and audience appeal."[123] One might add that since the most rhetorical and therefore musical of roles in the play is Richard, and since Richard was being played by an actor skilled in the kabuki art of musical vocal delivery, that particular casting would seem to associate Shōyō's so-called kabuki style with the alienated, even manipulative traits of Richard's character.

Bungakuza (Literature Theatre) made a similar decision when they adapted the Shōyō translation for a highly innovative staging of *Richard III* by British director Leon Rubin, starring the company's principal actor, Emori Tōru (one of the outstanding Shakespeare actors of the post-war Japanese theatre),[124] as Richard. Rubin had sensed that Shōyō's old-fashioned style might be suited for "the complicated human relationships" depicted in Shakespeare's history play, but although the translation was well received by audiences, Rubin and Emori found it lacking in the humour nowadays associated with the protagonist and felt obliged to adapt it accordingly.[125] The translations have also been used by a semi-professional company, Za (literally, "Theatre Company"), founded in 1992 under the leadership of Jō Haruhiko, who had played Prospero in Ninagawa's *Tempest* the same year.[126] Jō, whose original training had been in *kyōgen* acting, has said of the Shōyō translations that "although they do contain some old words, their use of language comes closest to our Japanese DNA, being beautiful and unaffected in its power."[127]

The Za company's Shōyō Shakespeares have been performed by a group of amateur and professional actors all over the age of fifty, and are representative of the company's mission of preserving Japan's literary culture, primarily through staged readings of short stories by writers such as Izumi Kyōka from the Meiji and prewar period, in other words from Shōyō's era. Jō's comment, while representative of the anxieties of Japan's ageing society, reflects on how Shōyō himself saw his response to Shakespeare as coming from within his native aesthetics rather than the unknowable beyond of the writer's genius, and suggests that Shōyō's continued appropriation in the twenty-first century will likely also be for nostalgic purposes.[128]

A similar argument was made by Arai Yoshio, one of the original members of the Kindai Gekijō although a graduate of Gakushūin University rather than of Waseda, who between 1987 and 1992 gave a series of public recitals of Shakespeare's complete plays in Japanese to raise funds for the construction of Sam Wanamaker's Globe Theatre in London (which was finally opened in 1997).[129] Arai mainly used the post-war translations of Kinoshita Junji and others, but Kinoshita was (like Shōyō) a successful playwright who emphasised the orality of Shakespeare translation, and during the course of his recitals Arai received lessons in *kyōgen* delivery from the *kyōgen* master Izumi Motohide. This dually academic and professional approach (since Arai's career was as an English literature professor based at Gakushūin and later Komazawa universities) recalls the mixed curriculum of the Bungei Kyōkai, but given his friendship with Wanamaker and Wanamaker's commitment to "authentic" performance conditions at the Globe replica, Arai's defence of Shōyō's "archaic" translating style[130] seems to have been as much about rescuing Shōyō from cultural commodification and allowing Shōyō's translations to shine as aesthetically "beautiful" texts irrespective of their origins. For someone like Arai, Shōyō's style is not theatrical self-indulgence but a conscious exploration of Shakespeare's original meanings through the medium of a language that would detract from those meanings if it were anything *but* beautiful.

| 1946 (June and July) | *A Midsummer Night's Dream* | Imperial Theatre, dir. Mikami Isao and Hijikata Yoshi, with Mori Masayuki as Theseus (Tōhō) |
|---|---|---|
| 1947 (November) | *The Merchant of Venice* | Engeki Hakubutsukan outdoor theatre, dir. Miyagawa Masaharu (Zenshinza), followed by performance at Osaka Asahi Kaikan (January 1948) |
| 1948 (May to July) | *Much Ado About Nothing* | Hibiya Shin Ongakudō and local tour (Zenshinza) |

| | | |
|---|---|---|
| 1948 (July) | *The Merchant of Venice* | Osaka Kabukiza, with Bandō Jusaburō III as Shylock |
| 1948 (October) | *The Merchant of Venice* | Tokyo Gekijō, dir. Kawatake Shigetoshi, with Ichikawa Sarunosuke II as Shylock and Mizutani Yaeko as Portia |
| 1948 (October) | *The Merchant of Venice* | Engeki Hakubutsukan outdoor theatre (Zenshinza) |
| 1949 (May to December) | *A Midsummer Night's Dream* | Ōkuma Hall followed by national tour, dir. Miyagawa Masaharu and Hijikata Yoshi, with Kawarasaki Chōjūrō IV as Bottom (Zenshinza) |
| 1949 (October) | *The Merchant of Venice* | Yomiuri Hall (Zenshinza) |
| 1950 (May and February to December) | *Romeo and Juliet* | Kyōritsu Kōdō followed by national tour, with Segawa Tamon as Romeo and Noda Eiko as Juliet (Zenshinza) |
| 1950 (May) | *Twelfth Night* | Ōkuma Hall, dir. Katō Chōji (Kindai Gekijō) |
| 1950 (October) | *The Tempest* | Ōkuma Hall, with Hara Takayuki as Prospero (Kindai Gekijō) |
| 1951 (January) | *The Comedy of Errors* | Ōkuma Hall (Kindai Gekijō) |
| 1951 (June) | *The Taming of the Shrew* | Ōkuma Hall (Kindai Gekijō) |
| 1951 (November) | *A Midsummer Night's Dream* | Ōkuma Hall (Kindai Gekijō) |
| 1952 (May) | *The Merchant of Venice* | Ōkuma Hall (Kindai Gekijō) |
| 1952 (November) | *Much Ado About Nothing* | Ōkuma Hall (Kindai Gekijō) |
| 1953 (February) | *The Taming of the Shrew* | Asahi Shimbun, Tokyo (Kindai Gekijō) |
| 1953 (May) | *Macbeth* | Ōkuma Hall (Kindai Gekijō) |
| 1953 (October) | *The Taming of the Shrew* | Ōkuma Hall and Engeki Hakubutsukan outdoor theatre (Kindai Gekijō) (25th anniversary of Engeki Hakubutsukan) |
| 1954 (April) | *Twelfth Night* | Mitsukoshi Theatre (Kindai Gekijō) |
| 1954 (July) | *A Midsummer Night's Dream* | Mitsukoshi Theatre (Kindai Gekijō) |
| 1954 (November) | *The Comedy of Errors* | Ōkuma Hall (Kindai Gekijō) |
| 1954 (December) | *The Taming of the Shrew* | Engeki Hakubutsukan outdoor theatre, dir. Katō Chōji (Kindai Gekijō) |
| 1955 (January) | *The Tempest* | Ōkuma Hall (Kindai Gekijō) |
| 1955 (February) | *The Merchant of Venice* | Osaka Kōdō (Kindai Gekijō) |

| | | |
|---|---|---|
| 1955 (May) | *The Winter's Tale* | Ōkuma Hall (Kindai Gekijō) |
| 1955 (August) | *Much Ado About Nothing* | Engeki Hakubutsukan outdoor theatre (Kindai Gekijō) |
| 1955 (October) | *King Lear* | Hitotsubashi Kōdō (Kindai Gekijō) |
| 1956 (May) | *Othello* | Ōkuma Hall, with Hōga Takashi as Othello and Hanayagi Jusuke III as Desdemona (Bungeiza) |
| 1956 (July) | *Twelfth Night* | Chiyoda Kōkaidō, dir. Hijikata Yoshi, with Tsuki Machiko as Viola and Maki Fuyukichi as Malvolio (Bugeiza) |
| 1956 (November) | *A Midsummer Night's Dream* | Itabashi Kumin Kaikan (Kindai Gekijō) |
| 1957 (May) | *The Merchant of Venice* | Waseda lecture hall (Kindai Gekijō) |
| 1957 (July) | *Othello* | Aoyama Ohara Kaikan (Bungeiza) |
| 1957 (September) | *The Merchant of Venice* | Tōyoko Hall, dir. Katō Chōji, Ichikawa Sadanji III as Shylock and Nakamura Fukusuke VI as Portia (Onoe Kikugorō company) |
| 1957 (December) | *The Taming of the Shrew* | Chiyoda Kōkaidō (Kindai Gekijō) |
| 1958 (October) | *The Winter's Tale* | Ōkuma Hall and Engeki Hakubutsukan outdoor theatre (Kindai Gekijō) |
| 1959 (May) | *Julius Caesar* | Waseda Memorial Hall, dir. Innami Takashi and Katō Chōji, with Katō Seiichi as Caesar (broadcast on NHK television) |
| 1961 (June) | *King Lear* | Iino Hall (Kindai Gekijō) |
| 1961 (October) | *A Midsummer Night's Dream* | Kōsei Nenkin Kaikan (Kindai Gekijō) |
| 1963 (October) | *King Lear* | Ōkuma Hall and Iino Hall, dir. Innami Takashi (Kindai Gekikyōkai) (four hundredth anniversary of Shakespeare's birth) |
| 1965 (July) | *The Taming of the Shrew* | Asahi Seimei Hall and Kobe Youth Centre (Kindai Gekijō) |
| 1966 (July) | *The Taming of the Shrew* | Asahi Seimei Hall (Kindai Gekijō) |
| 1966 (October) | *Twelfth Night* | Sabo Kaikan, dir. Katō Chōji (Kindaiza) |
| 1968 (July) | *A Midsummer Night's Dream* | Daiichi Seimei Hall, dir. Nemoto Yoshiya and Katō Chōji (Kindaiza) |
| 1969 (September) | *Macbeth* | Sabo Kaikan and Saitama Kaikan, dir. Nemoto Yoshiya and Arai Yoshio (Kindaiza) |
| 1969 (December) | *The Winter's Tale* | Nōkyō Hall (Kindaiza) |

| | | |
|---|---|---|
| 1970 (November) | *Twelfth Night* | Tōjō Kaikan, dir. Arai Yoshio, with Arai as Malvolio (Kindaiza and London Shakespeare Group) |
| 1971 (September) | *The Taming of the Shrew* | Nōkyō Hall, dir. Kikuchi Akira (Kindaiza) |
| 1972 (July) | *The Comedy of Errors* | Nōkyō Hall (Kindaiza) |
| 1976 (October) | *King Lear* | Kanagawa Prefectural Youth Centre (Kindaiza) |
| 1977 (October) | *A Midsummer Night's Dream* | Kanagawa Prefectural Youth Centre (Kindaiza) |
| 1980 (November) | *Richard III* | Sunshine Theatre, dir. Wada Yutaka, with Onoe Tatsunosuke as Richard |
| 2003 (November) | *Richard III* | Setagaya Public Arts Theatre, dir. Leon Rubin, with Emiri Tōru as Richard (Bungakuza), preceded by national tour (September and October) |
| 2005 (March) | *A Midsummer Night's Dream* | Sōgetsu Hall (Engeki Club Za) |
| 2006 (March) | *Much Ado About Nothing* | Sōgetsu Hall (Za) |
| 2007 (March and April) | *The Merchant of Venice* | Sōgetsu Hall (Za) |
| 2008 (March) | *A Midsummer Night's Dream* | Sōgetsu Hall (Za) |
| 2009 (March) | *The Taming of the Shrew* | Sōgetsu Hall (Za) |
| 2010 (March) | *The Merry Wives of Windsor* | Sōgetsu Hall (Za) |
| 2011 (February) | *King Lear* | Sōgetsu Hall (Za) |
| 2014 (March) | *The Winter's Tale* | Sōgetsu Hall (Za) |
| 2016 (February) | *Much Ado About Nothing* | Sōgetsu Hall (Za) |
| 2017 (March) | *Cymbeline* | Sōgetsu Hall (Za) |

### Perspectives on the Bungei Kyōkai *Hamlet*

This next section makes a more detailed appraisal of some of the prominent productions of Shōyō's Shakespeare translations, discussing their context within the emerging modern Japanese theatre and the challenges posed to actors and audiences by their language. The most significant of these is the Bungei Kyōkai's staging of *Hamlet* at the Imperial Theatre, Tokyo, between 20 and 26 May 1911, followed by performances at Osaka's Kadoza between July 1 and 7 of that year. The immediate context for this production was a series of *Hamlet* productions that began with Kawakami Otojirō's troupe at the Hongōza in 1903, but those were melodramatic adaptations in *shinpa* and kabuki style that appropriated Shakespeare's tragedy to a native morality or political message.[131] The Bungei Kyōkai had previously staged experimental productions of the first three acts only in Shōyō's translation, the first at Hongōza in November 1907 and the second at their studio at Shōyō's home in March 1910, but in staging the complete five acts, and thus by including Ophelia's mad scenes in Act 4 and the Gravediggers' scene in 5.1 in an unadapted translation, the company was exposing its late Meiji audience to a Western dramatic text that was monumental in its ambiguities and openness to interpretation. Of course the Bungei Kyōkai was mediating Shakespeare's play through Shōyō's translation, but, as he was later to observe, he was taking on a work that somewhat exceeded his cultural horizons.[132]

Shōyō's interest in the kind of realistic theatre that *Hamlet* came to represent in twentieth-century Japan had been stirred initially not by Shakespeare but by the realistic acting style of Ichikawa Danjūrō IX, and it was with the tacit support of Danjūrō and other reform-minded kabuki actors, notably Ichikawa Sadanji I and Onoe Kikugorō V (who had been born, respectively, in 1838, 1842, and 1844), that Shōyō set about creating his own modern kabuki plays influenced by Shakespearean dramaturgy. The most successful of these, *Kiri hitoha* (A Single Paulownia Leaf, 1894–5), was finally staged at the Tokyoza in March 1904, but the deaths of Kikugorō the previous February, of Danjūrō the previous September, and then of Sadanji in August 1904 left a considerable gap in the kabuki world that Shōyō, for one, felt the younger generation of actors was unable to fill.

Shōyō, as a man of letters rather than the theatre, was also reluctant to fill the gap by becoming the leader of the reform movement, and in his initial resistance to the proposal by Hōgetsu and the others for a fully-fledged theatre company one feels something of the Danish prince's fear of committing himself, in Shōyō's case to overcoming the forces of retrogression.[133] For the time being, what Shōyō did commit himself to was his project of a new musical drama, his ambitious *Shinkyoku Urashima*, which was staged in part by the Bungei Kyōkai in November 1907, and his modern kabuki dance dramas. Both these projects were transitional to his work with Shakespeare, *Shinkyoku Urashima* in the idealisation of musicality as a unifying force that is expressed in the musicality of his translating style and his dance dramas through the parallel of *furigoto* dance solos with the Shakespearean soliloquy.[134] Yet this trajectory of dramatic reform is broken by a text, *Hamlet*, vastly more complex than he himself was capable of writing:[135] having committed himself to translating the Complete Works, Shōyō could no longer be at the centre of either modern drama or kabuki playwriting in the new Taishō era. The other modern aspect of the 1911 *Hamlet* was the use of actresses to play the two female parts, Matsui Sumako as Ophelia and Kamiyama Uraji as Gertrude, and in this aspect too Shakespeare's play is seen to take over as Ophelia's madness becomes a trope for a suppressed femaleness in Japan's theatrical culture.

The production can be said to have succeeded on account of its novelty as a complete and unadapted stage translation of a Shakespeare play (not to mention Shakespeare's iconic status) and the strong performances by Doi, Tōgi, and Sumako, but for Natsume Sōseki, who had seen Shakespeare performed in the London theatre, it was both an artistic failure (through its excruciating fidelity to the source) and an insult to the intelligence of a modern Japanese audience. He exclaims:

> I feel, indeed I would insist, that to put it around that Shakespeare is some kind of authority on reality is a considerable lie. There might be some impartial purpose in the linking of paragraphs to reveal the causes and effects of joy and anger, but for such expressions to be cloaked in joy and anger is repulsive, unnatural, outrageous. Such an idea has never been used as a vehicle of mutual understanding by either the Japanese of today or the English people of today or of Shakespeare's times.[136]

Another way of putting Sōseki's argument is that in the 1911 *Hamlet* the two aspects of Shakespearean rhetoric and archaic Japanese language and acting styles blocked each other out to become an argument for realism in the naively didactic style of popular Japanese drama, riding the waves of its emotions. This impression was confirmed by Shōyō's decision at the last moment to have the actors use kabuki-type gestures rather than the Westernised ones in which they had been coached by a couple of British instructors at Waseda who had studied drama in Britain.

As Sōseki complained, Shōyō's *Hamlet* offered little of the fascination of the "sight of ordinary human beings on a stage":[137] the Tokyo and Osaka audiences were being deprived of the opportunity of seeing the Bungei Kyōkai actors make passable and indeed "fascinate[ing]" imitations of Irving or whoever, and instead were treated to an amateur kabuki style of acting that the audience knew only too well. Nevertheless, with three months of intensive rehearsal directed by Shōyō himself, the production had great verve, and the following candid review from the relative distance of Osaka seems all the more revealing of its actual strengths:

> The feeble musical accompaniment in the first scene gave a weird impression, and the way Laertes in his first scene with Ophelia swivelled his neck from side to side in response to his sister's innocent bleatings looked somewhat pathetic. I am afraid that our fledgling Japanese actresses are lacking in vocal power. The scene when Hamlet meets with the Ghost was good, and should satisfy those people who know their Irving, although I could not help thinking it would have benefitted from a little more variety of tone. Ophelia looked extremely amateur in the fifth scene when she is with Hamlet, and made me realise from the weakness of her posture that this actress has never learnt how to dance. Claudius was an old-fashioned villain capable of flattering his subjects with the proper tone of voice. The way Gertrude spoke her lines when the court clapped on stage during the play scene sounded like a high school girl, which nevertheless suited her gentle bearing.

In the scene when he remonstrates with Hamlet, Polonius was quite energetic but his delivery was very clumsy and did not carry at all, and his physical
bearing was disagreeably lacking in power, so there was nothing to suggest
the real Polonius. Just some young guy trying to be an old guy was what
it looked like; this was especially noticeable in his first scene with Laertes.
Things warmed up with Hamlet's soliloquy and the play within the play where
Hamlet became noticeably more energetic. This kind of acting is almost
unknown to Japanese people, and therefore clashed with the rather obscure
tone of delivery. . . . The way that Hamlet and Horatio observed Claudius'
"every move" in the play scene was quite effective. In particular, the scene
when . . . Hamlet takes out his dagger to kill Claudius, who is lost in his
worldly desires as he prays to a crucifix, and then departs being unable to kill
the king (who gets up) was somehow like *kagura* drama [an ancient Shinto
ritual dance that became popular as entertainment in the Edo era]. Next to
the sword fighting scene Queen Gertrude was also good, although I wish she
could have been a bit freer with her facial expressions. It was Ophelia's mad
scene, though, that seemed most characteristic of the Bungei Kyōkai style.
The way her eyes glistened triumphantly from out of her exhausted face as
she sang her song, the mournful lilt of the lyric and of Ophelia's movements,
had a poignancy that connected the performance with one of Dr. Tsubouchi's
musical dramas, and hit the audience like the ripples of a wave.[138]

The reviewer almost ignores Hamlet's "To be, or not to be" soliloquy, and instead
focusses on Ophelia's mad scene, the subject of the production's most famous
photograph. Since Sōseki had famously referred to John Everard Millais's Pre-
Raphaelite painting of the drowned Ophelia in his novel *Kusamakura* (The Three-
Cornered World, 1906) and his own critical review of the Bungei Kyōkai *Hamlet*
had appeared in the Tokyo *Nichinichi Shimbun* a full month before, albeit without
any mention of Ophelia, the anonymous Osaka reviewer may be referring obliquely
to what Sōseki had written, but more likely it is in recognition of the psychological realism of Shōyō's project: his modern awareness that it is the innocent (and
female) who suffer.

Shōyō wanted his *Hamlet* to strike a middle path between the gaudy realism
of the Victorian theatre and the simpler, barer modern stages of Poel and Craig.
Within the experimental framework of the Bungei Kyōkai, this middle path might
even achieve that synthesis of East and West that Shōyō found so challenging,
which in practical terms was the coordination of Westernised costumes and actors'
movements with Japanese speech. These difficulties are explored in a retrospective
that appeared in *Saō Fukkō* more than twenty years later:[139]

The 1911 *Hamlet* was generally well received, with particular acclaim for
"consistency of direction," "appropriateness of venue," "ensemble work"
and "the pains that Dr. Tsubouchi ha[d] clearly taken over every aspect of the
production." Nevertheless, there was still plenty of room for improvement.
First of all, since much of the action took place in front of the curtain, there

was a tendency for lines to be swallowed up by the rear of the stage and be inaudible to the audience. As a result, all the actors sounded strained, and Doi's Hamlet even in some pain as he sought to project himself. The Doctor was much concerned on this point, and after three or four performances he was largely able to solve the problem by reinforcing the curtains with boards, even if that was a concession to the modern style of directing. Some people also commented on the unnatural tone of the translation due to its strict adherence to the original text, and on how difficult the lines were to understand, although I think those criticisms would be less of an issue today.

As for the individual performances, Doi's Hamlet was exciting and full of energy, and particularly effective in the funeral scene. Tōgi's Claudius looked the part, although his facial expressions lacked variety, and Tōgi only came into his own in his second role as the Gravedigger. Katō's Polonius was mocked by some for its ostentation and lack of style, which was a pity, since in retrospect his performance seemed entirely appropriate. Katō had done no more than was asked of the role, and considering his particular qualities as an actor . . . the criticism he received was entirely unwarranted. Mori's Horatio came across as more of a subordinate than a close friend to Hamlet, which was probably on account of his youth. Hayashi's Laertes was criticised for emotional rigidity in his scene with Ophelia [i.e., for sounding stilted and lacking vitality], so that his lines started to sound like kabuki *jidaimono*. What with his back turned frequently to the audience, he was uniformly panned by the critics, which is probably why he was soon after released from the Bungei Kyōkai. Takeda's Ghost was considered exceptional, but his Player King the opposite. Sasaki's Marcellus had dignity, and the critics agreed that Miki and Yokogawa were admirable as Rosencrantz and Guildenstern.

As for the two women, Uraji had tremendous presence as the Queen: her timing was good, and she was utterly professional in her movements and delivery. Sumako's Ophelia was also praised for her excellent timing and the quality of profound pathos she elicited from the part. And yet it seems they were somehow handicapped in their performance, which was not necessarily such a great success for the two actors. In any case, the production at the Imperial Theatre was just the first half, because starting on 1 July of the same year it was staged over seven days at the Osaka Kadoza, and proved a sensation in the Kamigata theatrical world.

Although the two critics seem to have seen completely different productions, it is telling that the Tokyo-based Atsumi should emphasise the production's energy (typical of Edo kabuki) and the *wagoto* Osaka reviewer its stylistic faults and the fate of the young woman.

### Katō Chōji's Twelfth Night

Katō Chōji was a natural heir to Shōyō in terms of his dual background in the modern and traditional theatres and his commitment to a finished, "beautiful" product;

his reluctance to write lengthy programme notes for his numerous Shakespeare productions no doubt expresses a belief that Shōyō had already said everything that needed to be said about the plays in question. Nevertheless, a reflection he wrote on directing *Twelfth Night* for Chikyūza at the Okuma Hall in June 1928 provides a relatively complete introduction to his individual approach, and since this was both Katō's first production for Chikyūza and the first of *Twelfth Night* in any translation his directing plan can be considered a basis for his next forty years of directing Shakespeare for Chikyūza and the Kindai Gekijō.

Katō begins by outlining four styles of Shakespeare production, the first being a traditional mimetic style that he identifies with the Bungei Kyōkai.[140] Quoting the views of what he calls the "twin pillars" of nineteenth-century theatrical realism, Edmund Kean and Henry Irving, on how they believed Venice in *The Merchant of Venice* should be staged as a busy panorama of nobles, citizens, merchants, "whores," and masked figures on bridges, Katō refers to a touristic Shakespeare that was of lasting appeal to Japanese audiences and could be effectively imitated through repeated experiment but which, because it was expensive to mount, risked "bankruptcy and foreclosure" (the near fate of the play's Antonio). The reference to Venice is significant not only because *The Merchant of Venice* was easily the best known in Japan of Shakespeare's plays in the prewar era but also as an image of diversity that was essential to Shōyō's view of Shakespeare.

The second, "archaic" approach of William Poel's "original practices" is relevant, for example, to the Fortune Theatre façade of the Waseda theatre museum and of an Elizabethan-style outdoor theatre in the Koishikawa district of Tokyo that Katō had himself used for a *Merchant* production in 1922 prior to the theatre's loss in the 1923 earthquake. Although he does not give any indication of what he himself may have learnt of Shakespeare's original meanings from using these spaces, the archaic approach resounds with Shōyō's reason for using archaic language in his translations, in particular his assumption that by allowing the rhetoric – which includes the theatrical infrastructure as well as the language – to speak for itself the meanings will make themselves felt as well. The third style Katō names is the expressionist, subjective approach of modern directors such as Reinhardt and Craig, which he identifies with the rising *shingeki* rather than with Kindai Gekijō. Shōyō had warned against reading too much into Shakespeare, and likewise would have agreed with Katō on the danger of modern dress productions muting Shakespeare's "true value" with their novelty.[141]

In directing *Twelfth Night*, Katō is audience-oriented, taking as his cue Orsino's line "So full of shapes is fancy/That it alone is high fantastical" (1.1.14–5). Rather than offering his own subjective interpretation, Katō sees his role as allowing the collective and individual imaginations of his audience to wander freely, which he fulfils primarily by means of a curtained upstage inner stage for Orsino's palace and a slightly narrower but also curtained downstage outer stage for Olivia's house and garden. Each of the stages is edged with doors, with Katō's notes mainly listing the series of entrances and exits out of which each scene is constructed.[142] This combination of careful stage directing with the two stages can be said to allow a continuous movement of perspective that mirrors the audience's own "fantastical" shape-making, but since this concept is originally Orsino's and Orsino is based upstage, it also creates an illusion that any movement (or exit) upstage will be towards a higher Platonic sphere that Orsino embodies and any movement downstage will be towards the more sublunary world of Olivia's household and the audience.

Katō had done his homework: in addition to his knowledge of modern British directors such as Barry Jackson, he took hints from an illustrated volume of Elizabethan costume designs published by Hodder and Stoughton, and the songs were from Edward Naylor's authoritative *Shakespeare and Music* (1896).[143] He also timed his production at 3 hours and 38 minutes, which, given that there were cuts (including, inexplicably, Feste's dialogue with Olivia in 1.5), suggests a more than leisurely pace. Shōyō's translation would have taken longer to get through than post-war versions; it was not until Fukuda in the 1950s that Japanese Shakespeare productions sought to imitate the pace of the London theatre.

All in all, Katō seems geared towards a well-spoken and tightly choreographed overall effect, and was clearly nervous about getting it right because, as he explains, Shakespeare's comedies were much less centred than the tragedies on strong individual characters who (in the hands of professional actors) could be expected to keep the performance together; he is also worried that his actors lacked the musical and dance skills of Western performers to cope with that important dimension of *Twelfth Night*.[144] The only one of his mainly amateur cast to achieve lasting success was a twenty-six-year-old Mitsuda Ken as Malvolio, but Katō's purely theatrical view of Shakespeare's comedy creates a sound basis for future developments, and was one against which the rising generation of proletarian directors such as Mikami Isao could react in Katō's words.

> *Twelfth Night* is a work that has been unanimously praised by critics for the consistent excellence of its comic elements, the thoroughness of its artistry, and the agreeable harmonisation of its characterisations. It is full of beautiful poetry from the love sentiments of the opening lines through to the Fool's song at the end, which will satisfy the poet, while its combination of scenic, choreographic, musical, and pictorial effects make it of great interest to the stage director as well, and its diversity of form and the equal interest of the different characters will surely appeal to actors. All these strengths add up to create a work that can only draw the audience's applause.[145]

### *Tsukiji* Dream

Katō's *Twelfth Night* came just a few weeks before a grander and more ambitious production of *A Midsummer Night's Dream* by Osanai's Tsukiji Little Theatre, codirected with Aoyama Sugisaku and Hijikata Yoshi and staged at the Imperial Theatre between 26 and 30 July 1928. This too was the play's premiere in the Japanese theatre and in Shōyō's translation, and was remarkable for employing Japan's first professional symphony orchestra, founded in 1926 and conducted by Konoe Hidemaro,[146] to play the complete incidental music by Mendelssohn, a full seven years before Max Reinhardt's use of the same music in his 1936 Hollywood film. Osanai had seen photographs of the original 1905 Reinhardt production with its revolving stage, and commented that against the darkness of Reinhardt's *Dream* he himself preferred a lighter overall effect that corresponded with the play's rhythms.[147] The director's express hope was that audiences would leave the theatre saying *hitoban no yume wo mita* ("I saw a dream tonight"):[148] Shakespeare had shown the "miracle of appearances" in which "nothing [was] impossible."[149]

The production clearly resonated with the sophisticated modern ambience of nearby Ginza, which was more bourgeois than feudal.[150] Osanai's disciple, the left-wing playwright Kubo Sakae, called the lovers "mechanical puppets" in contrast to the natural honesty of the actual mechanicals,[151] and another playwright, Kōri Torahiko, contrasted the play's poetry and comic realism with the dialectical tendency of modern Japanese drama ("the need to see everything in terms of conflict"),[152] observing that "if the play seems lacking in feeling, that is because we are lacking in sensibility."[153] This was Shōyō's dream come true, a tribute to his romantic spirit: it was broadcast on Japanese radio on 3 August 1928, with the programme including a tribute to Dame Ellen Terry, who had recently died.[154] Osanai's *Dream* also boasted something of a star-studded cast, or at least budding stars such as Yamamoto Yasue and Murase Sachiko, who played Puck in a leotard and who in 1991, aged eighty-six, was to act alongside Richard Gere in one of Kurosawa's last films, *Rhapsody in August*. Yoshida Kenkichi, the production's designer, recalled that by far its most memorable aspect was Murase's Puck, which "overflow[ed] with a vitality" that put even Shakespeare to shame.[155]

For all its triumphalism, the production deserves to be contrasted with the darker mood of Shōyō's *En no gyōja*, which Osanai unstintingly admired and had directed for Tsukiji two years earlier. *En no gyōja*, Shōyō's *Tempest*, is regarded as his most autobiographical work, casting the troubled mountain hermit as Shōyō and his disciple Hirotaru, who fails to "follow his teachings because of his love for a woman," as Hōgetsu,[156] but this combination reaches a happier conclusion in *Dream*, where Puck is no more than incompetent. Moreover, the play's object of marriage could only have satisfied the middle-class audience, when Shōyō was sometimes suspected of having no message at all and by this time had attained the model of marital respectability with his almost-illiterate wife, Sen. Finally, another remarkable feature of the 1928 *Dream* was the use of a revolving stage recently installed at the Imperial Theatre. The irony of this innovation was that as a technology it had originated not in Europe but in the kabuki theatre of early eighteenth-century Edo, and was introduced into European theatres only in the late nineteenth century. Tokyo's Imperial Theatre was on the European model with a proscenium arch so that with the revolving stage, the Mendelssohn accompaniment, and Shōyō's translation, the production may have had the overall effect of a being a Westernised kabuki (albeit of a very different register). This irony could not have been lost on Shōyō, who more than thirty years before had commented that Chikamatsu's *jidaimono* had about as much historical accuracy as *A Midsummer Night's Dream*:

> To read one of Chikamatsu's history plays always feels like one is reading Shakespeare's *A Midsummer Night's Dream*, by which I mean that because these plays ignore the historical aspects, even characters, in favour of the depiction of human feelings, all they are doing is borrowing the names, times and places of the past.[157]

Now, having completed his translations, he had himself "made history."

* * * * *

The critic Asano Tokiichirō thought the 1928 *Dream* the most successful of Shakespeare productions of the period, and that, contrary to the post-war era, Shakespeare's comedies were more successfully produced at this time than the tragedies.[158] While Shōyō's *Hamlet* and *Othello* struggled to distinguish themselves from kabuki *jidaimono*, Shakespearean comedy filled a gap that kabuki was generically unable to fill. Kabuki has its comic scenes, of course, but the endings are usually tragic, and kabuki audiences had always gone to kabuki to experience the gamut of emotions rather than anything as integrated as Shōyō's realism or a Shakespearean "happy end." The stage directions, revisions, and organisation of dialogue analysed in the first half of this chapter, together with Shōyō's "logical," head-down reading of the texts, imposed a kind of order on the modern Japanese theatre as it sought to align itself with modernity and its Western counterpart. This order is to some extent exemplified by the production history of his Shakespeare translations.

## Notes

1  Kobayashi Kaori, "Shakespeare and National Identity: Tsubouchi Shōyō and His Authentic Shakespeare Productions in Japan," *Shakespeare* 2, no. 1 (2006): 62–3.
2  Michael C. Brownstein, "Tsubouchi Shōyō on Chikamatsu and Drama," in *Currents in Japanese Culture: Translations and Transformations*, ed. Amy Vladeck (New York: Columbia University Press, 1997), 287.
3  Ibid., 288.
4  Maeda Ai, "From Communal Performance to Solitary Reading," trans. and ed. James A. Fujii, in Maeda Ai, *Text and the City: Essays on Japanese Modernity* (Durham, NC: Duke University Press, 1973), 235.
5  Ibid., 236.
6  Tsubouchi Shōyō, "'*Makubesu* hyōshaku' no shogen" (1891), in *Shōyō senshū*, supp. vol. 3 (1977), 163.
7  Ibid.
8  Friederike von Schwerin-High, *Shakespeare, Reception and Translation: Germany and Japan* (New York: Continuum, 2004), 214.
9  Kano Ayako, *Acting Like a Woman in Modern Japan: Theater, Gender, and Nationalism* (London: Palgrave Macmillan, 2001), 161.
10  Anzai Tetsuo, "Tsubouchi Shōyō to Fukuda Tsuneari," *Sophia* 15, no. 1 (1966): 45.

11 Natsume Kinnosuke, "Tsubouchi-hakase to *Hamuretto*" (1911), in *Sōseki zenshū*, vol. 16 (Tokyo: Iwanami Shoten, 2019, facsimile ed.), 397, where Sōseki comments that "Shakespeare's lines, just like Noh chanting [*utai*], have this peculiar rhythm and timbre that must be grasped decisively if one is to sustain an audience's interest." Given Sōseki's argument for "deep" reading and the necessity of conveying *Hamlet*'s "deep" meanings to Japanese audiences, then adaptation in Noh style must be preferable to him to the complete translation of texts practised by Shōyō.

12 James R. Brandon, "Kabuki and Shakespeare: Balancing Yin and Yang," *The Drama Review* 43, no. 2 (1999): 34.

13 Sadoya Shigenobu, *Tsubouchi Shōyō – dentōshugisha no kōzu* (Tokyo: Meiji Shoin, 1983), 114.

14 Eliot complains that "the levity of Hamlet, his repetition of phrase, his puns, are not part of a deliberate plan of dissimulation, but a form of emotional relief. In the character Hamlet it is the buffoonery of an emotion which can find no outlet in action; in the dramatist it is the buffoonery of an emotion which he cannot express in art." Thomas S. Eliot, *The Sacred Wood: Essays on Poetry and Criticism* (London: Methuen, 1960), 102.

15 Alwin Thaler, "Shakspere in Japan," *The Shakespeare Association Bulletin* 14, no. 3 (1939): 192.

16 The only other pre-war writer to have been memorialised in this way was Sōseki in 1916.

17 Tsuji Hisaichi, "Saō fukkō no ippōsaku," *Saō Fukkō* 11 (1934): 9. Tsuji, who was a twenty-year-old German literature major at Tokyo University at the time of writing and later a successful screenwriter and film producer, argues forcefully that the fact that Shōyō's translations are "Shakespeare" and stage language will inevitably differ from the everyday language should override audience scruples about them sounding old-fashioned.

18 J. Thomas Rimer, *Towards a Modern Japanese Theatre: Kishida Kunio* (Princeton, NJ: Princeton University Press, 1974), 19–20.

19 Schwerin-High, 107.

20 As I explained in Chapter 2, Shōyō seems to have favoured the Deighton Macmillan editions for their notes especially for his earlier translations, but given his longstanding influence by Dowden he may have also consulted Dowden's *Hamlet* when he translated the play in 1909. The main difference between the two is that Dowden has a question mark after "fair Ophelia" and Deighton an exclamation mark, and Dowden's more speculative punctuation is echoed in a footnote on "action" where he comments that "With the thought of action this soliloquy opens and closes" and that "suicide, indeed, is not the theme of the soliloquy, but it incidentally enters into it": Edward Dowden, ed., *The Tragedy of Hamlet* (London: Methuen & Co., 1899), 101. Deighton in his endnote merely glosses "action" without additional explanation: Kenneth Deighton, ed., *Hamlet, Prince of Denmark* (London: Macmillan & Co., 1891), 206. Shōyō opts for the exclamation mark, and while Deighton and Dowden both annotate "pitch" (and the Folio preference for "pith"), Shōyō's paraphrase of "enterprises of great pitch and moment" with a phrase meaning "such kind of important undertakings" also suggests a more straightforwardly theatrical approach.

21 Tsubouchi Shōyō, *Hamuretto* (Tokyo: Waseda University Press, 1909), 111–12. The directions are unchanged in the 1933 revision.

22 Tsubouchi Shōyō, "Venisu no shōnin" (1906), in *Meiji honyaku bungaku zenshū*, vol. 4, ed. Kawato Michiaki and Sakakibara Takanori (Tokyo: Ōzorasha, 1997), 208–9.

23 Ibid., 216.

24 Tsubouchi Shōyō, *Venisu no shōnin* (Tokyo: Chūō Kōronsha, 1933), 154.

25 Ibid.

26 Ibid.

27 Ibid., 166.

28  Ibid., 170.
29  Ibid.
30  Ibid., 182.
31  Ibid., 177.
32  Ibid., 179.
33  Ibid., 180.
34  Shōyō's solution is to translate "humour" as *kibun* ("mood," "feeling") with *iki* in small brackets: *Winzā no yōkina nyōbōtachi* (Tokyo: Waseda University Press, 1926), 12–13.
35  Tsubouchi Shōyō, *Henrī gosei* (Tokyo: Waseda University Press, 1928), 94–5.
36  Ibid., 101.
37  According to Hattori Yoshika, in *Zadankai: Tsubouchi Shōyō kenkyū*, ed. Inagaki Tatsurō and Oka Yasuo (Tokyo: Kindai Bunka Kenkyūsho, 1976), 248.
38  *Henrī gosei*, 399.
39  Hasegawa Tenkei, "Tsubouchi-sensei no *Riya ō* kōgi," *Saō Fukkō* 14 (1934): 19.
40  Tsubouchi Shōyō, *Riya ō* (Tokyo: Chūō Kōronsha, 1934), 8. Most of these directions are also given in the original 1912 translation.
41  Ibid., 9.
42  Ibid., 10.
43  Ibid.
44  Ibid., 17.
45  Ibid., 20.
46  Ibid., 62.
47  Ibid., 63.
48  Ibid., 64.
49  Ibid.
50  Ibid., 65.
51  Ibid., 67.
52  Ibid., 76.
53  Ibid.
54  Ibid., 77.
55  Ibid.
56  Ibid., 110.
57  Ibid., 116.
58  Ibid., 117.
59  Ibid., 118.
60  Ibid., 123.
61  Ibid., 127.
62  Ibid., 128.
63  Ibid., 289.
64  Tsubouchi Shōyō, "Batsu ni kawaete" [In Place of an Epilogue], in *Makubesu* (1935), 1.
65  Tsubouchi Shōyō, "Makubesu" (1916), in *Shōyō senshū*, vol. 5 (1977), 438, and Tsubouchi Shōyō, *Makubesu* (Tokyo: Chūō Kōronsha, 1935), 36–7.
66  In fact, in "treble trust" as Duncan's kinsman, subject, and host.
67  The phrase *shisō ni nai* denotes appearance, specifically "not to appear to do."
68  *Hamuretto* (1909), 110, and Tsubouchi Shōyō, *Hamuretto* (Tokyo: Chūō Kōronsha, 1933), 114.
69  In this case, the citation and line numbers are from Edward Dowden, ed., *The Tragedy of Hamlet* (London: Methuen & Co., 1899), 114, which is probably the edition that Shōyō consulted, because the two lines "I mean, my head upon your lap?/Ay, my lord" are absent from the Third Arden edition (2016, revised).
70  *Hamuretto* (1909), 125–6, and Tsubouchi Shōyō, *Hamuretto* (Tokyo: Chūō Kōronsha, 1934), 130–1.
71  Kimura Takatarō, "'Hamuretto' no tōyōteki zairyō," in *Sheikusupia kenkyū shiryō shūsei*, vol. 8, ed. Sasaki Takashi (1915; repr., Tokyo: Nihon Tosho Centre, 1997), 176.

72  Ibid., 186.

73  *Hamuretto* (1934), 195.

74  *Hamuretto* (1909), 192, and *Hamuretto* (1934), 200.

75  "Jibun no honyaku ni tsuite," 260.

76  *Makubesu* (1933), 437–8.

77  Tsubouchi Shōyō, "'*Makubesu* hyōshaku' no shogen" (1891), in *Shōyō senshū*, supp. vol. 3 (1978), 169.

78  Tsubouchi Shōyō, "Jajauma narashi" (1920), in *Shōyō senshū*, vol. 4 (1977), 728.

79  Devices such as *kakekotoba* (pivot words) in classical Japanese poetry involve the repetition of homophonic words with different meanings, the best-known example being *matsu* meaning "wait" or "pine tree" (under which lovers might "wait" for each other) depending on the *kanji* character is used. Shōyō's wordplay is at the more basic level of *goroawase* (sound play or linear rhyming); the dramatic context does not allow (or demand) the more resonant, sophisticated level of *kakekotoba*.

80  Tsubouchi Shōyō, "Temupesuto" (1915), in *Shōyō senshū*, vol. 4 (1977), 86.

81  Ibid.

82  "Shōsetsu shinzui," 15.

83  "Temupesuto," 45.

84  *Nya* is usually a negative inflexion but can be used as here as a postposition, and is characteristic of *jōruri* style.

85  Tsubouchi Shōyō, *Riya ō* (Tokyo: Waseda University Press, 1912), 102.

86  Shōyō highlights the pun by writing *kannen* in a combination of *hiragana* for *ka* and *ne* and small *katakana* for the two single consonants *n* and adding three sidemarks (*bōten*) alongside the word, the equivalent of English italics. *Kannen* is the Fool's dialectal pronunciation, and so Shōyō also gives the *kanji* compound *kannan* in small brackets to explain the meaning.

87  The unfamiliar *hysterica passio* is glossed with the single character *shaku* ("spasm") in brackets, indicating physical rather than mental trauma. The *kanji* given for self is *nanji* ("you") but the *rubi* reading is *onore*, which usually means "I" but as a label of abuse can also mean "you." Shōyō's Lear is addressing a feared dimension of his self.

88  The Japanese sceptre is an oblong wooden tablet that is held vertically in the right hand.

89  Nagata Hideo, "Tsubouchi-hakase no tsuioku," *Teatoro* 10 (1935): 8.

90  Ibid.

91  Ibid.

92  Brandon, 39.

93  Tsubouchi Shōyō, *Oserō* (Tokyo: Waseda University Press, 1911), 219.

94  Tsubouchi Shōyō, *Oserō* (Tokyo: Chūō Kōronsha, 1935), 250–1.

95  Honma Hisao, "Gendaifuku no *Makubesu*," *Saō Fukkō* 19 (1935): 10.

96  *Oserō* (1911), 220–1, and *Oserō* (1935), 252–3.

97  Brian Powell, *Japan's Modern Theatre: A Century of Change and Continuity* (Abingdon, Oxon: Routledge, 2013), xi.

98  Brian Powell, "One Man's *Hamlet* in 1911 Japan: The Bungei Kyōkai Production in the Imperial Theatre," in *Shakespeare and the Japanese Stage*, ed. Sasayama Takashi, J. R. Mulryne, and Margaret Shewring (Cambridge: Cambridge University Press, 1998), 38.

99  Tsubouchi Shōyō, "Shēkusupiya kenkyū shiori" (1928), in *Shōyō senshū*, supp. vol. 5 (1977), 212–19.

100  *Riya ō* (1912), 13–14.

101  Suzuki Yukio, "Ābingu," in *Tsubouchi Shōyō jiten*, ed. Shōyō Kyōkai (Tokyo: Heibonsha, 1986), 16.

102  "Shēkusupiya kenkyū shiori," 217.

103  Ibid., 311.

104  Hisao, 21.

105  Many (although not all) of Shōyō's translations are illustrated with unacknowledged line drawings of scenes, and all of them are fronted with full-page reproductions that

are acknowledged. The Irving Hamlet is the portrait by Edwin Long. Shōyō's *Othello* translation is fronted with a two-page colour reproduction of a painting by Karl Becker. The revisions, being in a smaller, cheaper format, contain fewer illustrations.

106 See Lee Sang Kyong, "Edward Gordon Craig and Japanese Theatre," *Asian Theatre Journal* 17, no. 2 (2000): 215–35.

107 Quoted in Christopher Innes, *Edward Gordon Craig: A Vision of Theatre* (London: Routledge, 2013), 123.

108 Murata Minoru, "Engeki no botsurisō shugi," in *Sheikusupia kenkyū shiryō shūsei*, vol. 6, ed. Sasaki Takashi (Tokyo: Nihon Tosho Centre, 1997), 189–90. The essay was published in the periodical *Toride* (no. 9, *Macbeth* special issue, September 1913). Murata is more explicitly political than Shōyō would have been with his focus on social conditions as opposed to individual morality. The immediate context of the *Toride* special issue was Mori Ōgai's translation of the play for the Kindaigeki Kyōkai, for which Shōyō wrote an appreciative preface.

109 Craig began his career as an actor in the 1890s for Irving's company before turning to stage design, and admired the director's way of eliminating superfluous movement and diction, "thus creating a true synthesis of passion with controlled expression" (Innes, 16) that Craig even likened to the Noh drama he saw performed in London in 1900.

110 The production listings are from Kikuchi Akira et al., "Honyaku geki," in *Tsubouchi Shōyō jiten* (1986), 523–30.

111 See Fuhara Yoshiaki, "The *Caesar Kidan*: The Earliest Japanese Translation of Shakespeare's *Julius Caesar* and Its Performance," *Hitotsubashi Journal of Arts and Sciences* 4, no. 1 (1964): 22–38.

112 Reflecting the kabuki practice of staging single scenes from plays as set pieces in kabuki programmes.

113 This they achieved through Hōgetsu's promotional talent and the starring role of Sumako, who was transformed from the suicidal Ophelia to a "force of nature" in her portrayal of Katyusha in the company's adaptation of Tolstoy's *Resurrection* in 1914, which ran for 444 performances and achieved further success with a gramophone record of Katyusha's song that sold twenty thousand copies. Sumako had also starred as Nora in the Bungei Kyōkai's production of Ibsen's *Doll's House* in 1911. Geijutsuza's *Resurrection* (*Fukkatsu*) appealed to a rising social awareness in early Taishō society, and established Sumako's full-blooded modern woman as an alternative to the geisha roles of Sada Yacco (Sumako's main rival) and the chauvinism of the Bungei Kyōkai. The Geijutsuza disbanded following Hōgetsu's death from Spanish flu in November 1918 and Sumako's suicide in January 1919.

114 See Yamaguchi Yōko, "Shikō Tsubouchi's Unpublished Letters to Edward Gordon Craig with an Introduction about Their Intercultural Context," *Forum Modernes Theater* 28, no. 2 (2018): 193–203. Shikō was interested in translating part of Craig's *On the Art of the Theatre* (1905).

115 Kumoi died in 2003 at the age of 102, and Shikō's American lover by suicide in 1928.

116 Osanai's ambition was also limited by his artistic limitations. See Ōya Reiko, "Kaoru Osanai and the Impact of Edward Gordon Craig's Theatrical Ideals on Japan's *Shingeki* (New Theatre) Movement," *Shakespeare* 9, no. 4 (2013): 418–27.

117 Tsubouchi Shōyō, "Sawada Shōjirō wo chō suru ji" (1929), in *Shōyō senshū*, supp. vol. 5 (1977), 551.

118 Tsubouchi Shōyō, ed., *Sheikusupiya nyūmon* (Tokyo: Chūō Kōronsha, 1934), 9.

119 Innami Takashi, "Shinshunza," in *Tsubouchi Shōyō jiten* (1986), 201.

120 Kume was a popular playwright, novelist, and haiku poet who had been interested in *Hamlet* since writing his graduation thesis on the play at the Imperial University. He was the third to make a complete translation of the play.

121 Zenshinza emerged out of the proletarian drama movement of the 1920s, and (as its name implies) was ideologically opposed to the feudal system in which kabuki originated; in 1949 its entire membership and their families joined the Japan Communist

Party. In February 1934, the company staged Shōyō's *Hototogisu kojō rakugetsu* (A Sinking Moon Over the Lonely Castle Where the Cuckoo Cries, 1897) in the writer's presence, and although Shōyō was no socialist he certainly wished to bring Shakespeare to the masses, which Zenshinza achieved with their remarkable tour of *A Midsummer Night's Dream* to schools and factories around the country in 1949; as trained kabuki actors they could have had no difficulty with Shōyō's language. In a discussion of how Zenshinza has reconciled its convictions with both a feudal art form and the commercial realities of theatrical production, Brian Powell suggests that "in a curious way, the need to reconcile an artistic belief with a political ideology has brought about a reexamination of classical *kabuki* and an attempt to rediscover the original significance of its plays as works of art": "Communist *Kabuki*: A Contradiction in Terms?," in *A Kabuki Reader: History and Performance*, ed. Samuel L. Leiter (London: M. E. Sharpe, 2002), 184. This approach may also be germane to Shōyō's determination to bypass present-day ideologies and let Shakespeare speak for himself.

122 The Fukuda production was at Tokyo's Nissay Theatre. Shōyō's translation was also preceded to the stage by the Odashima translation in 1976.

123 Quoted in Moriya Sasaburō, *Nihon ni okeru Sheikusupia* (Tokyo: Yasshio Shuppan, 1986), 9.

124 Emori has also played Hamlet, King Lear, Macbeth, and Othello.

125 Email message from Leon Rubin (7 March 2023). The production, which I saw at the Setagaya Public Arts Theatre, was also remarkable for the use of CNN-type live footage of missile attacks, which worked with Shōyō's translation to evoke the situation of a regime made redundant by the force of history.

126 Jō's background in *kyōgen* drama would have been appreciated by Shōyō, who adopted *kyōgen* style for parts of his early translations and recognised the congruity of *kyōgen* as a comic genre with the comic dimension even of Shakespearean tragedy.

127 Quoted on "Senior Engeki Web," blog.s-geki.net/?eid=1125759 (2 March 2009), accessed 15 May 2023. I saw the company's *Dream* production in 2008, and was impressed by the evident pleasure these amateur seniors took in speaking Shōyō's lines. I am grateful to the Za office for sending me copies of the posters for their ten Shōyō Shakespeares.

128 Shōyō's translations are still sometimes heard in staged readings.

129 See my article on Arai, "Speaking Shakespeare in Japanese: Some Contemporary Exponents," in *Foreign Shakespeare: Contemporary Performance in the New Asias*, ed. Dennis Kennedy and Yong Li Lan (Cambridge: Cambridge University Press, 2010), 42–56.

130 Arai Yoshio, "Shōyō to Sheikusupia," *Tsubouchi Shōyō Shiryō Kenkyū* 5 (1974): 39–51.

131 *Shinpa* ("new school") drama emerged from the political liberalism of the 1880s, and although contrasting with the "old school" (*kyūha*) of "feudal" kabuki looked and sounded a lot like kabuki because of its continued use of *onnagata* and off-stage music; Shōyō's Shakespeare-influenced "modern" kabuki plays of the late Meiji era strove for an altogether more literary and less melodramatic effect. The actress Mizutani Yaeko, who helped to keep *shinpa* alive in the post-war era through her acting skills, played Portia in 1948 in Shōyō's translation, and before that in 1935 was a sensational female Hamlet in a production by Katō Chōji of Tsubouchi Shikō's translation.

132 "Jibun no honyaku ni tsuite," 255.

133 Ōzasa Yoshio, *Nihon shingeki zenshi*, vol. 1 (Tokyo: Hakusuisha, 2001), 43–6.

134 See my chapter, "Of Ponds, Lakes, and the Sea: Shōyō, Shakespeare, and Romanticism," in *British Romanticism in Asia: The Reception, Translation, and Transformation of Romantic Literature in East Asia and India*, ed. Alex Watson and Laurence Williams (London: Palgrave Macmillan, 2019), 11.

135 Shōyō's range of cultural reference was greater than Shakespeare's, but his position on a trajectory of national reform seems to me to make him incapable of Shakespearean ambiguity.

136 Natsume, 395–6.
137 Ibid., 397–8.
138 Anonymous, "Bungei Kyōkai – Osaka Kadoza de *Hamuretto*," *Kyoto Nisshutsu Shimbun* (3 July 1911), in Hamaguchi Kuniko, ed., "Hamuretto gekihyō shū," *Tsubouchi Shōyō Kenkyū Shiryō* 15 (1997): 153–4. At the beginning of the review, the critic expresses sarcasm at Shōyō's promotional material, which he feels patronised Kansai audiences with their view of *Hamlet* as being somehow "more classical" than their own ancient culture.
139 Atsumi Seitarō, "Nihon ni okeru *Hamuretto* jōenshi," *Saō Fukkō* 1 (1933): 33–5. Atsumi was eighteen at the time of the 1911 production.
140 Katō Chōji, "*Jūniya* enshutsu nōto" (1933), in *Sheikusupia geki no honyaku to enshutsu – Tsubouchi Shōyō to Katō Chōji*, ed. Arai Yoshio (Tokyo: Eikōsha, 2010), 175–8.
141 Ibid., 176.
142 Ibid., 179–80.
143 Naylor's book is listed in *Shēkusupiya kenkyū shiori* (193, his name misspelt "Mayloer"). In 1904, Naylor was appointed lecturer in music at Emmanuel College, Cambridge, and in this capacity tutored musicologist Tokugawa Yorisada (a descendant of the Tokugawa shoguns), for whom he composed a popular overture.
144 Katō, 175.
145 Ibid.
146 A younger brother of statesman Konoe Fumimaro and a distinguished conductor and composer in pre- and post-war Japan, he founded the New Symphony Orchestra of Tokyo in 1926 (now the NHK Symphony Orchestra).
147 Osanai Kaoru, "*Manatsu no yo no yume* ni tsuite," *Tsukiji Shōgekijō* 5, no. 4 (1928): 3.
148 Ibid., 4.
149 Ibid., 5.
150 The commercial Ginza district recovered quickly from the devastating Great Kantō earthquake of 1 September 1923, with the opening of the Ginza underground line (the first in Asia) in 1927.
151 Kubo Sakae, "*Manatsu no yo no yume* no rinkaku," *Tsukiji Shōgekijō* 5, no. 4 (1928): 13.
152 Kōri Torahiko, "*Natsu no yo no yume* ni tsuite," *Teigeki* 69 (1928): 25.
153 Ibid., 27.
154 Japanese public broadcasting began in 1925.
155 Yoshida Kenkichi, *Tsukiji Shōgekijō no jidai* (Tokyo: Yaegake Shobō, 1971), 199.
156 Rimer, 19.
157 Tsubouchi Shōyō, "Waga kuni no shigeki" (1893–4), in *Tsubouchi Shōyō shū* (1969), 288.
158 Asano Tokiichirō, *Watashi no Tsukiji gekijō* (Tokyo: Shūei Shuppan, 1970), 258.

## References

Anzai Tetsuo. "Tsubouchi Shōyō to Fukuda Tsuneari" [Shōyō Tsubouchi and Tsuneari Fukuda: On the Japanese Interpretation of Shakespeare]. *Sophia* 15, no. 1 (April 1966): 42–64.
Arai Yoshio. "Shōyō no Sheikusupia" [Shōyō's Shakespeare]. *Tsubouchi Shōyō Kenkyū Shiryō* 5 (May 1974): 39–52.
Asano Tokiichirō. *Watashi no Tsukiji gekijō* [Recollections of the Tsukiji Little Theatre]. Tokyo: Shūei Shuppan, 1970.
Atsumi Seitarō. "Nihon in okeru *Hamuretto* jōenshi" [Productions of *Hamlet* in Japan]. *Saō Fukkō* 1 (October 1933): 30–6.
Brandon, James R. "Kabuki and Shakespeare: Balancing Yin and Yang." *The Drama Review* 43, no. 2 (Summer 1999): 15–53, https://doi.org/10.1162/105420499760265190.

Brownstein, Michael C. "Tsubouchi Shōyō on Chikamatsu and Drama." In *Currents in Japanese Culture: Translations and Transformations*, edited by Amy Vladeck, 279–89. New York: Columbia University Press, 1997.

Deighton, Kenneth, ed. *Hamlet, Prince of Denmark*. London: Macmillan & Co., 1891.

Dowden, Edward, ed. *The Tragedy of Hamlet*. London: Methuen & Co., 1899.

Eliot, Thomas S. *The Sacred Wood: Essays on Poetry and Criticism*. London: Methuen, 1960.

Fuhara Yoshiaki. "The *Caesar Kidan*: The Earliest Japanese Translation of Shakespeare's *Julius Caesar* and Its Performance." *Hitotsubashi Journal of Arts and Sciences* 4, no. 1 (March 1964): 22–38.

Gallimore, Daniel. "Of Ponds, Lakes, and the Sea: Shōyō, Shakespeare, and Romanticism." In *British Romanticism in Asia: The Reception, Translation, and Transformation of Romantic Literature in East Asia and India*, edited by Alex Watson and Laurence Williams, 273–92. London: Palgrave Macmillan, 2019, https://doi.org/10.1007/978-981-13-3001-8_11.

———. "Speaking Shakespeare in Japanese: Some Contemporary Exponents." In *Foreign Shakespeare: Contemporary Performance in the New Asias*, edited by Dennis Kennedy and Yong Li Lan, 42–56. Cambridge: Cambridge University Press, 2010.

Hamaguchi Kuniko, ed. "*Hamuretto* gekihyō shū" [Collected Reviews of Bungei Kyōkai *Hamlet* Production]. *Tsubouchi Shōyō Kenkyū Shiryō* 15 (August 1997): 124–70.

Hasegawa Tenkei. "Tsubouchi-sensei no *Riya ō* kōgi" [Professor Tsubouchi's *Lear* Lectures]. *Saō Fukkō* 14 (November 1934): 17–21.

Honma Hisao. "Gendaifuku no *Makubesu*" [*Macbeth* in Modern Dress]. *Saō Fukkō* 17 (February 1935): 16–21.

Inagaki Tatsurō and Oka Yasuo, eds. *Zadankai: Tsubouchi Shōyō kenkyū* [Symposia on Tsubouchi Shōyō Studies]. Tokyo: Kindai Bunka Kenkyūsho, 1976.

Innami Takashi. "Shinshunza." In *Tsubouchi Shōyō jiten* [Dictionary of Tsubouchi Shōyō Studies], edited by Shōyō Kyōkai, 201. Tokyo: Heibonsha, 1986.

Innes, Christopher. *Edward Gordon Craig: A Vision of Theatre*. London: Routledge, 2013, https://doi.org/10.4324/9781315078953.

Kano Ayako. *Acting Like a Woman in Modern Japan: Theater, Gender, and Nationalism*. London: Palgrave Macmillan, 2001, https://doi.org/10.1007/978-1-349-63315-9.

Katō Chōji. "*Jūniya* enshutsu nōto" [Notes on Directing *Twelfth Night*]. 1933. In *Sheikusupia geki no honyaku to enshutsu – Tsubouchi Shōyō to Katō Chōji* [Shakespeare in Japanese Translation and Performance: Tsubouchi Shōyō and Katō Chōji], edited by Arai Yoshio, 175–8. Tokyo: Eikōsha, 2010.

Kikuchi Akira, Matsumoto Kaoru and Ichiki Shizuko, ed. "Honyaku geki" [Productions of Translations by Tsubouchi Shōyō]. In *Tsubouchi Shōyō jiten* [Dictionary of Tsubouchi Shōyō Studies], edited by Shōyō Kyōkai, 523–30. Tokyo: Heibonsha, 1986.

Kimura Takatarō. "'Hamuretto' no tōyōteki zairyō" [Shakspere's *Hamlet* as a Mere Compilation of the Oriental Materials, Chiefly Japanese]. 1915. In *Sheikusupia kenkyū shiryō shūsei* [Research Materials on the Reception of Shakespeare in Japan], vol. 8, edited by Sasaki Takashi, 1–250. Tokyo: Nihon Tosho Centre, 1997.

Kobayashi Kaori. "Shakespeare and National Identity: Tsubouchi Shōyō and His 'Authentic' Shakespeare Productions in Japan." *Shakespeare* 2, no. 1 (June 2006): 59–76, https://doi.org/10.1080/17450910600662919.

Kōri Torahiko. "*Natsu no yo no yume* ni tsuite" [Introduction to *A Midsummer Night's Dream*]. *Teigeki* 69 (August 1928): 24–8.

Kubo Sakae. "*Manatsu no yo no yume* no rinkaku" [Outline of *A Midsummer Night's Dream*]. *Tsukiji Shōgekijō* 5, no. 4 (August 1928): 11–4.

Lee Sang Kyong. "Edward Gordon Craig and Japanese Theatre." *Asian Theatre Journal* 17, no. 2 (January 2000): 215–35, https://doi.org/10.1353/atj.2000.0018.

Maeda Ai. "From Communal Performance to Solitary Reading." 1973. In *Text and the City: Essays on Japanese Modernity*, translated and edited by James A. Fujii, 223–54. Durham, NC: Duke University Press, 2004, https://doi.org/10.1515/9780822385622-010.

Moriya Sasaburō. *Nihon ni okeru Sheikusupia* [Shakespeare in Japan]. Tokyo: Yasshio Shuppan, 1986.

Murata Minoru. "Engeki no botsurisō shugi" [The Ideology of Hiddenness in Drama]. 1913. In *Sheikusupia kenkyū shiryō shūsei* [Research Materials on the Reception of Shakespeare in Japan], vol. 6, edited by Sasaki Takashi, 189–90. Tokyo: Nihon Tosho Centre, 1997.

Nagata Hideo. "Tsubouchi-hakase no tsuioku" [Memory of Dr. Tsubouchi]. *Teatoro* 10 (April 1935): 7–8.

Natsume Kinnosuke. "Tsubouchi-hakase to *Hamuretto*" [Dr. Tsubouchi's *Hamlet*]. 1911. In *Sōseki zenshū* [Complete Works of Natsume Sōseki], vol. 16, 393–8. Tokyo: Iwanami Shoten, 2019.

Osanai Kaoru. "*Manatsu no yo no yume* ni tsuite" [Introduction to *A Midsummer Night's Dream*]. *Tsukiji Shōgekijō* 5, no. 4 (August 1928): 2–5.

Ōya Reiko. "Kaoru Osanai and the Impact of Edward Gordon Craig's Theatrical Ideals on Japan's *Shingeki* (New Theatre) Movement', *Shakespeare* 9, no. 4 (July 2013), 418–27, https://doi.org/10.1080/17450918.2013.807296.

Ōzasa Yoshio. *Nihon shingeki zenshi* [A Comprehensive History of Modern Japanese Drama], vol. 1. Tokyo: Hakusuisha, 2001.

Powell, Brian. "Communist *Kabuki*: A Contradiction in Terms?" In *A Kabuki Reader: History and Performance*, edited by Samuel L. Leiter, 167–85. London: M. E. Sharpe, 2002, https://doi.org/10.4324/9781315706832.

———. *Japan's Modern Theatre: A Century of Change and Continuity*. Abingdon, Oxon: Routledge, 2013.

———. "One Man's *Hamlet* in 1911 Japan: The Bungei Kyokai Production in the Imperial Theatre." In *Shakespeare and the Japanese Stage*, edited by Sasayama Takashi, J. R. Mulryne, and Margaret Shewring, 38–52. Cambridge: Cambridge University Press, 1998.

Proudfoot, Richard, Ann Thompson, David Scott Kastan, and Henry R. Woudhuysen, eds. *The Arden Shakespeare Third Series: Complete Works*. London: Bloomsbury Arden, 2020.

Rimer, J. Thomas. *Towards a Modern Japanese Theatre: Kishida Kunio*. Princeton, NJ: Princeton University Press, 1974, https://doi.org/10.1515/9781400870875.

Sadoya Shigenobu. *Tsubouchi Shōyō – dentōshugisha no kōzu* [Tsubouchi Shōyō: The Making of a Traditionalist]. Tokyo: Meiji Shoin, 1983.

Schwerin-High, Friederike von. *Shakespeare, Reception and Translation: Germany and Japan*. New York: Continuum, 2004, https://doi.org/10.5040/9781472555489.

Shōyō Kyōkai, ed. *Shōyō senshū* [Selected Works of Tsubouchi Shōyō], 17 vols. (1927–8; reprinted with 5 supplementary volumes). Tokyo: Daiichi Shobō, 1977–8.

Suzuki Yukio. "Ābingu" [Irving]. In *Tsubouchi Shōyō jiten* [Dictionary of Tsubouchi Shōyō Studies], edited by Shōyō Kyōkai, 16. Tokyo: Heibonsha, 1986.

Thaler, Alwin. "Shakspere in Japan." *The Shakespeare Association Bulletin* 14, no. 3 (October 1939): 192.

Tsubouchi Shōyō, trans. *Hamuretto* [Hamlet]. Tokyo: Waseda University Press, 1909.

———, trans. *Hamuretto* [Hamlet.] Tokyo: Chūō Kōronsha, 1933.

———, trans. *Henrī gosei* [King Henry V]. Tokyo: Waseda University Press, 1928.

———, trans. "Jajauma narashi" [The Taming of the Shrew]. 1920. In *Shōyō senshū*, vol. 4, 661–824, 1977.

———. "Jibun no honyaku ni tsuite" [About My Shakespeare Translations]. 1928. In *Shōyō senshū*, supplementary vol. 5, 254–77, 1977.

———, trans. "Makubesu" [Macbeth]. 1916. In *Shōyō senshū*, vol. 4, 395–541, 1977.

———, trans. *Makubesu* [Macbeth]. Tokyo: Chūō Kōronsha, 1935.

———. "'*Makubesu* hyōshaku' no shogen" [Preface to a Commentary on *Macbeth*]. 1891. In *Shōyō senshū*, supplementary vol. 3, 161–9, 1978.

———, trans. *Oserō* [Othello]. Tokyo: Waseda University Press, 1911.

———, trans. *Oserō* [Othello]. Tokyo: Chūō Kōronsha, 1935.

———, trans. *Riya ō* [King Lear]. Tokyo: Waseda University Press, 1912.

————, trans. *Riya ō* [King Lear]. Tokyo: Chūō Kōronsha, 1934.

————. "Sawada Shōjirō wo chō suru ji" [Eulogy for Sawada Shōjirō]. 1929. In *Shōyō senshū*, supplementary vol. 5, 248–51, 1977.

————. "Shēkusupiya atto randamu" [Shakespeare at Random]. 1931. In *Shōyō senshū*, supplementary vol. 5, 279–373, 1977.

————. "Shēkusupiya kenkyū shiori" [A Companion to Shakespeare Studies]. 1928. In *Shōyō senshū*, supplementary vol. 5, 1–277, 1977.

————, ed. *Sheikusupiya nyūmon* [Introduction to Shakespeare]. Tokyo: Chūō Kōronsha, 1934.

————. "Shōsetsu shinzui" [The Essence of the Novel]. 1885–6. In *Tsubouchi Shōyō shū* [Works of Tsubouchi Shōyō], edited by Inagaki Tatsurō, 3–58. Tokyo: Chikuma Shobō, 1969.

————, trans. "Temupesuto" [The Tempest]. 1915. In *Shōyō senshū*, vol. 4, 1–169, 1977.

————, trans. "Venisu no shōnin" [The Merchant of Venice]. 1906. In *Meiji honyaku bungaku zenshū* [Complete Literary Translations of the Meiji Era], vol. 4, edited by Kawato Michiaki and Sakakibara Takanori, 186–226. Tokyo: Ōzorasha, 1997.

————, trans. *Venisu no shōnin* [The Merchant of Venice]. Tokyo: Chūō Kōronsha, 1933.

————. "Waga kuni no shigeki" [Historical Drama of Japan]. 1893–4. In *Tsubouchi Shōyō shū* [Works of Tsubouchi Shōyō], edited by Inagaki Tatsurō, 287–315. Tokyo: Chikuma Shobō, 1969.

————, trans. *Winzā no yōkina nyōbō* [The Merry Wives of Windsor]. Tokyo: Waseda University Press, 1926.

Tsuji Hisaichi. "Saō fukkō no ippōsaku" [A Way Forward for the Shakespeare Renaissance]. *Saō Fukkō* 11 (August 1934): 6–11.

Yamaguchi Yōko. "Shikō Tsubouchi's Unpublished Letters to Edward Gordon Craig with an Introduction about Their Intercultural Context." *Forum Modernes Theater* 28, no. 2 (September 2018): 193–203, https://doi.org/10.1353/fmt.2013.0020.

Yoshida Kenkichi. *Tsukiji Shōgekijō no jidai* [My Days with the Tsukiji Little Theatre]. Tokyo: Yaegake Shobō, 1971.

# Conclusion
## Shōyō's Field

Shōyō's utilitarian motive for translating Shakespeare was always the reform of his national drama but it is based in a more distinctly "Oriental" frame of reference than the busy samurai Shakespeares of postwar Japan.[1] An English handbook for his Waseda theatre museum published in 1929 includes the following literal translation of a calligraphy in Shōyō's hand of a poem by the Kangxi emperor (seventeenth to eighteenth centuries):

> The sun and moon are light; the waters of sea and river, oil; wind and thunder, sounds of drum and wooden clappers; heaven, earth, and man, a huge playhouse. Yao and Shun (ancient rulers of China) are female impersonators; Tang and Wu (later rulers), old characters; Tsao and Mang (revels), clowns and knowers; men of past, present, and future, so many *dramatis personae*.[2]

While the monism of Confucian and Taoist belief implicit in the poem – the notion that heaven, earth and "man" are one – may differ from the dualism of Shakespeare's religious background, not to mention the chauvinism of his modernising society, its citation seems to position Shōyō's Shakespeare historically between the Chinese literary models that influenced the Tokugawa writers whom Shōyō had rejected in his youth and the Greater East Asian Co-Prosperity Sphere announced by Prime Minister Konoe Fumimaro in 1938.

This appropriation relates probably as much to the broader genre of drama as to Shakespeare, since at its founding in 1928 the Waseda museum held predominantly Japanese and Chinese rather than English publications and had been established by Shōyō with the purpose of promoting a "comprehensive study" of drama "in all its forms and aspects as affected by time and space";[3] Shōyō refers quite frequently to Chinese genres (in particular Peking opera) in his writings on drama. Nonetheless, the statement of a distinctly "Oriental" world view in the context of a museum modelled on the Elizabethan Fortune Playhouse can be said to echo the Meiji slogan of intercultural harmonisation that influenced Shōyō, namely the synthesis of local Japanese (*wa*), universal Chinese (*kan*), and spiritualised Western (*yō*) elements that was mentioned in Chapter 1.

As far as his translations were concerned, this synthesis had been bypassed by the achievement of Meiji language reform (*genbun itchi*) in developing a satisfactory

DOI: 10.4324/9781003293774-5

written standard that was influenced by English sentence structure and retained a central role for Sino-Japanese characters (*kanji*) in determining and clarifying meaning,[4] while their origin in Shakespeare's texts is discretely present in the poetics of translation and the translator's interpretation of the source. Shōyō's 1916 *Macbeth* translation yields the following example (5.5.23–5):[5]

> Life's but a walking shadow, a poor player,
> That struts and frets his hour upon the stage,
> And then is heard no more.

> 人生は歩いてゐる影たるに過ぎん、只一時、舞臺の上で、ぎっく
> りばったりをやって、やがて最早噂もされなくなる惨めな俳優だ

> *Jinsei wa aruite iru kage taru ni sugin, tada ichiji, butai no ue de, gikkuri battari wo yatte, yagate mō uwasa mo sarenaku naru mijimena haiyū da*

Shōyō's sentence comprises twelve single *kanji* or *kanji* compounds that state its propositional meaning, namely "life" (*jinsei*), "walk" (*aruite*), "shadow" (*kage*), "no more than" for "but" (*sugin*), "only" (*tada*), "one hour" (*ichiji*), "stage" (*butai*), "upon" (*ue*), "no more" (*mō*), "rumour" for "is heard" (*uwasa*), "wretched" for "poor" (*mijime*), and "actor" (*haiyū*). The obscurity of the native grammatical elements, such as the topic marker *wa* and the copula *da*, can be said to trope the arbitrariness of *wa* locality, and the mimetic words *gikkuri* ("with a start") and *battari* ("with a thud") the hiddenness of the native Japanese body.[6]

Shakespeare's text here is present both in the rhythm of the phrasing, which is based on native syllabics rather than iambic pentameter and enhanced by the rhyme on *yatte* and *yagate* and slight hiatus in *mō*, and in the translator's interpretation. The focus of the source is on the pitiful image of the "poor player" who seems merely to be going through the motions of his role, while Shōyō slightly emphasises the pathos of the idea of a life that is lived as action or acting (and therefore without spiritual depth) through the use of commas to delineate the three Aristotelian unities of time (*tada ichiji*, "his hour"),[7] place (*butai no ue de*, "upon the stage"), and manner (*gikkuri battari wo yatte*, "That struts and frets").

\* \* \* \* \*

This concluding chapter explores the niche, or field, that Shōyō makes for himself as a Shakespeare translator in early twentieth-century Japan. Given his beginnings as a writer and theorist of fiction, not to mention the fact that he always translated Shakespeare in prose rather than poetry, one perspective may be that for Shōyō, Shakespeare translation constitutes an ongoing narrative that is driven both thematically and stylistically by the dialectic of the particular, universal, and metaphysical of *wakanyō*. This is a journey through which Shōyō can discover and assert his identity within the two poles of the "Oriental" past and the modern West, exemplifying Judith Woodsworth's thesis that "translation is not only a mode of writing but a way of being,"[8] and he does so not only as a Japanese but as an East Asian writer and translator.

Shōyō's early trajectory was inspired in part by the medieval Chinese historical romance *Water Margin* (*Suikoden* in Japanese), which he read in his youth in the translation by Bakin that triggered a nineteenth-century Japanese craze for the work. The young Shōyō and his contemporaries were familiar with the Chinese classics in a way that is comparable with the influence of ancient Roman literature in the English Renaissance, so that when he came to establish the Department of Literature at Waseda in 1890, one of its underlying principles was the assimilation of *wakanyō* with its three constituent fields of Japanese, Chinese, and Western literature. Ōkuma Shigenobu's Waseda aimed generally to turn out patriotic, civilised youths, which for Shōyō meant exposing them to the light of literary works whose aesthetic qualities could be grasped instinctively rather than through ideological affiliation or noble birth. He memorably expresses his assimilative vision in his essay "The Bottomless Lake," discussed in Chapter 2 and published in *Yomiuri Shimbun* the first New Year's Day after the department's founding. This lake represented the creativity in all literature (but especially, as Shōyō imagined it, the fathomless genius of Shakespeare and Goethe):

> It was a bewitching lake indeed, with its sapient mountains and benevolent plum trees, gnarled pine and oak trees weathered by snows and frosts, and beyond the weaving willow trees. A single tree bespoke the virtues of moderation and discretion, while scattering maples revealed the essence of the ancient virtues, those which the heart has always treasured. Like the constant prayers of a monk on his way, the fall of the maple leaves told of the emptiness of earthly existence. The placid waters were an illusion; the abundant trees without number were comparable to the eighty-four thousand cycles of reincarnation. Here there blossomed fruits of cherry, peach and apricot, which ripened in the sun.[9]

Referencing also haiku by Matsuo Basho ("On a withered branch a crow is perched. An autumn evening.") and the Maple Bridge of Suzhou, which was built in the sixth century just as Buddhism was being introduced to Japan, Shōyō describes a Confucian father with his Christian son who admire the lake from their shared vantage point:

> The Christian assuaged my anguish at this floating world, pointing to the fruits that ripened as the blossom fell; his hope for eternity could be seen in the spring buds that succeed to the leaves of autumn just as the flowing waters of the lake intimated the limitless blue expanse of the sea. The lake was a microcosm of earthly life, the sea a boundless heaven. The Christian cried out in his dread "O Lord!," for the way to hell passes also to the gate of heaven.[10]

In his conclusion, Shōyō states that the scene's timeless beauty will be undermined by any attempts to "dive in" and rationalise its qualities.[11] In contrast to academic and political rationalisation, the main benefit for Shōyō of both fiction and drama was that it enabled readers to talk about themselves and construct their own narratives, and by sharing these narratives in a common language to foster love of country. Yet his Waseda patriotism differed subtly both from Meiji imperialism, which filtered subjective experience through the figure of the Emperor,[12] and from Shimamura Hōgetsu's late Meiji Naturalism, which tended to ignore the imperative of objective reality in favour of subjectivity.

The assimilation of *wakanyō* also stands in contrast to the policy of deAsianisation (*datsua ron*) proposed in 1885 by Fukuzawa Yukichi (the founder in 1858 of Waseda's main rival, Keio University). The abandonment of the traditional *kundoku* method for translating Chinese texts into Japanese in favour of the liberal (*iyaku*) and more literal (*chikuyaku*) translation strategies necessitated by Western texts was not necessarily Fukuzawa's concern, but there is an analogy between Fukuzawa's distaste for the rigid conservatism of Qing-dynasty China and the abandonment of the formalism of *kundoku* for the more rigorous integration of form and content practised by Meiji translators. While Shōyō is himself a Meiji translator, there is a crossover between *kundoku* as a reading method and the attention of his own "logical" reading method (discussed at the beginning of Chapter 4) to the formal features of the Shakespearean source, and his reverence for the source may even hark back to a basic Chinese Confucian ethos that, as Martha Cheung explains, "ha[s] often been used by translators . . . to describe two different, contrasting styles of translation":

> The Master [i.e., Confucius] said, "When substance outweighs attention to form and beauty, there is the coarseness of the unmannered; when attention to form and beauty outweighs substance, there is the pedantry of a scribe. Only when attention to form and beauty and substance are equally blended do we get the man of true virtue."[13]

Shōyō, who had learnt how to write his language through his schooling in the Confucian classics, pursues a similar integration of the aesthetic and ethical in his Shakespeare translations.

Chinese vocabulary (*kango*) gave Edo literature a vigour and authority that was dispersed through the process of *genbun itchi* but at the same time recovered through the rapid popularisation of *kanji* compounds in the Meiji era and twentieth century. Shōyō's Shakespeare translations can be broadly said to effect a balance of *kango* and *wago* (native Japanese words) that, for example through his technique of phonetic glossing examined in Chapter 3, serves as an interplay of the particular and general in *wakanyō* to mimic the interplay of the aesthetic and ethical that masks the sources of Shakespeare's creativity. One obvious discrepancy in this analogy, however, is that according at least to Shōyō's theory of "hidden ideals," the *yō* of *wakanyō* is rather more open to scrutiny than is the metaphysical basis of Shakespeare's imagination, and yet although his Shakespeare may ultimately be unable to say *what* it is, the act of repeated deferral generates a considerable amount of talk (or "dialogue"), which is Shōyō's skill as a writer and dramatist. In this connection, Kobayashi Yoshihito comments that while Shōyō's *Tōsei shosei katagi* was criticised for sounding too much like Bakin in its narrative and descriptive sections, its numerous dialogues were more convincingly "modern."[14] This feature reflects the performative dimension of Bakin and other Edo writers that I have mentioned, the sense that Bakin's *shichigochō* in particular is always on the verge of tumbling into performed speech.

The context of *wakanyō* also substantiates the rather unusual structure of Shōyō's field of cultural production. While his Shakespeare translations accrued considerable symbolic and economic capital in their time, Shōyō avoids (or defers) temporal erasure, first by conflating Shakespeare's "hiddenness" with his own cultural past so that obsolescence no longer matters, and secondly (and similarly) by insisting that their purpose is not in fact their survival as a new cultural field but simply to release the diverse ideals of their readers (which can be equally well released by reading other translations or indeed Shakespeare in the original). This second point explains why the discipleship that constitutes his field extends well beyond those of his Waseda students who chose to become Shakespeare scholars themselves.

Shōyō's circle is not exactly as prestigious as that of a Dr. Johnson, but among his former pupils (including a number mentioned in previous chapters) are the Japanese literary scholar Igarashi Chikara (graduated 1894), the poet and art historian Aizu Yaichi (1896), the cultural critic and Freud translator Hasegawa Tenkei (1897), the translator of French literature Yoshie Takamatsu (1906), the free verse poet Hattori Yoshika (1908), and the Meiji literary scholar Honma Hisao (1909). Shōyō's most celebrated pupils were the novelist Futabatei Shimei (who first visited Shōyō at his home in 1886 in the wake of *Shōsetsu shinzui*) and Shimamura Hōgetsu (1894). Futabatei fulfils Shōyō's realism with his view that fiction could express an idea that did not have to amount to *kanzen chōaku* didacticism and which could work with form to achieve the illusion of realism that Shōyō had largely failed to achieve in his own writing. Figures such as Aizu and Hasegawa admired Shōyō for his intellectual passion and erudition, but Hōgetsu demonstrated that Naturalism could open onto much the same vanishing perspective as his teacher's realism – in other words, that objectivity and subjectivity had a common goal – through his less histrionic and interventionist strategy of reflection and introspection. Finally, actors such as Sawada Shōjirō can only have appreciated Shōyō's leadership in enabling them to make careers in a profession that a generation before had been closed to them.

Shōyō's pedagogy inculcates a readerly "response to circumstances" out of which character is formed, while the nexus of *wakanyō* balances objective distance (and the potential evasion of responsibility) with the native (or at least Confucianist) imperative of virtue. This process plays itself out in the kabuki play Shōyō wrote in the early 1890s to illustrate his modern ideas on drama, *Kiri hitoha*, which as a tragedy of circumstance (*kankyō higeki*) about a group of strong characters raised Shakespearean questions about human motivation and the force of destiny, and contains a number of Shakespearean parallels.

The play is based on the historical episode of the Fall of Osaka Castle in 1615, which Shōyō carefully researched, when the Tokugawa shogunate forced its main rival, the Toyotomi clan in Osaka, into capitulation and thus secured its dominance through to the Meiji Restoration of 1868. The atmosphere of the play is similar to *Hamlet* in the way that the action takes place in and around a castle, where the Toyotomi clan is divided against itself, although the action remains unresolved at the end and the catastrophe that resulted in the suicides of the Toyotomi head, Hideyori, and his mother Yodogimi (the favourite concubine of the warlord and clan's founder, Hideyoshi, whose ghost appears in a central scene) is not portrayed. Shōyō's aim was to present history from the same "commoner" (*heimin*) level of his students (rather than something like the "great man theory of history"),[15] and indeed neither Hideyori nor the Tokugawa shogun Ieyasu appears in the play. Rather the plot is focused on the loyal samurai Katsumoto Katagiri, who engages with the shogun offstage in what he knows will be futile negotiations on behalf of his Toyotomi master (and is heartily distrusted by the Toyotomi family). Katsumoto is similar to Hamlet in his integrity and awareness of reality, while the play as a whole attempts an equivalence between the high-flown romanticism of Shakespeare's *Hamlet* and the rhythmic *shichigochō* of *ningyō jōruri*. Like many of Shōyō's achievements, the play (although not staged until 1904) was a critical sensation, with the novelist Uchida Roan declaring that

> At the time Tsubouchi wrote *Kiri hitoha*, the kabuki world was an autocracy, with Danjūrō its pope, Ōchi its Grand Vizier and the plays of Mokuami its written constitution, so that to go against the status quo by writing a new kind of drama required the courage of a Martin Luther burning the papal bulls. It was really most interesting, and of course quite different from *Tōsei shosei katagi*. No one but Tsubouchi could have contrived such scenes as the dream of cherry blossom viewing and the spear dance. By his efforts, he opened a gate into "the Land of *Shibai* ['plays']" that had been closed to outsiders over the previous two or more centuries.[16]

In addition, there is a scene where one of the Tokugawa supporters drowns himself in a pond like Ophelia and another where Yodogimi mistakenly kills her handmaid Chinpaku like Hamlet stabbing Polonius behind the arras, and Yodogimi's hysterical outburst in the second act has been compared to those of Lady Macbeth:[17]

> *Sakimidaretaru* [7] *yamayuri no* [5], *ano fusuma e wo* [7] *miru ni tsuke* [5],
> *omoi zo izuru* [7] *sugi koshikata* [6/7], *tokoro mo Kaga no* [7] *Hakusan naru* [6/7],
> *Senjagaike no* [7] *meisan to* [5], *yo ni kikoetaru* [7] *kuroyuri no* [5],
> *sono hana kurabe* [7] *ga moto to nari* [6/7], *Kita no Mandokoro no* [7] *nikushimi uke* [6/7]
> *hakanaku horobishi* [8] *Sassa Narimasa* [7]. *Ide sono koro wa* [7] *mizukara ga* [5],
> *sakari no hana ya* [7] *haru fukaki* [5], *Jurakuden no* [6] *eika no yume* [6/7],

> *ware hitotabi* [6] *emu toki wa* [5], *hoi yori idete* [7] *ten ga shita* [5],
> *rokujū yoshū wo* [8] *shōaku arishi* [7], *ano taikō tote* [8] *nan no eiyū* [7].

> Looking at the picture on the sliding door of wild lilies in full bloom,
> I cannot help but reflect on things past: on how the famous flower of
>    Senjagaike
> Took to the field with that black lily, Sassa Narimasa, whose transient
>    life expired,
> A victim of the bile of Hideyoshi's wife. At that time I myself
> Was in the flower of my youth, the glory of the Jurakudai.
> I smile to myself as I slip from my ordinary robe
> And remember what a hero that man was, who had the whole country in
>    his hands.

The strength of this heightened writing style is its blending of precise historic and dramatic details (the lilies on the *fusuma* sliding door) to convey the personality of a woman who has lived solely for the aphrodisiac of power. Yodogimi (a niece of the other of the three warlords, Oda Nobunaga) came to prominence in the early 1590s when Hideyoshi's principal wife (known as Mandokoro) was unable to have children, and then in 1595 Hideyoshi ordered his nephew Hidetsugu, lord of the Jurakudai castle in Kyoto, to commit *seppuku* on suspicion of treachery (along with Hidetsugu's thirty-nine wives, concubines, and children). Yodogimi, as Hideyori's mother, was a vocal supporter of the Toyotomi claim, while Mandokoro supported Ieyasu (and survived into old age). This brutal memory, recalling the tyranny of Henry VIII, lies at the heart of Shōyō's play, and "explains" (*pace* Fortinbras' entry into Elsinore at the end of *Hamlet*) why the more "rational" regime of the Tokugawas had to prevail. Its historicity represented a radical break from the *jidaimono* of the past, where often historical events would be set in previous eras to avoid censorship. Yodogimi's speech is not one to be found in Shakespeare's *Macbeth* but can be compared with Lady Macbeth's taunting of her husband's manly pride and her own sense of identity, as in the following metaphorically complex speech (1.5.40–3):

> Come, you spirits
> That tend on mortal thoughts, unsex me here,
> And fill me from the crown to the toe, top-full
> Of direst cruelty. Make thick my blood

Shōyō's later plays, such as *Hototogisu kojō rakugetsu* (A Sinking Moon over the Lonely Castle Where the Cuckoo Cries, 1897) about the eventual suicide of Katsumoto, are closer to contemporary speech and make less use of kabuki techniques such as the onstage narrator, while *En no gyōja* (Hermit En, 1917), about the seventh-century founder of the syncretic Shugendō religion, is not a kabuki play at all. The putative connection of the latter with Shakespeare's *Tempest* (which Shōyō had translated two years previous) is that En must overcome the female demon

Hitonokushi, who therefore corresponds with Caliban's mother Sycorax, to secure control of his mountain, while En's disciple Hirotaru resembles both Caliban and Ariel in his reluctance to accept En's authority. In a 1902 newspaper article, Shōyō had criticised Nietzsche's fashionable Dionysiac philosophy as little more than "amoral individualism,"[18] and so his creation of what David G. Goodman called a "transhistorical, Nietzschean Übermensch" in the character of En is at first surprising.[19] Yet as Goodman suggests, Shōyō may simply have been meaning to turn Nietzsche on his head by asserting the utility of religious values in a time of moral decadence, not to mention the power of spiritual (and artistic) discipline. In the spirit of Shōyō's anti-didacticism, it may also be seen as the dramatic portrayal of a troubled individual struggling to preserve his spiritual autonomy in the face of cultural resistance, with Hitonokushi representing the emergence of a new hedonistic culture in Taishō Japan, and as a story from Japanese legend it counters the domestic focus of much of the translated European and modern native drama of the period. Moreover, in 1917, as "superhuman" feats become more feasible with the introduction of new technologies such as the aeroplane, *En no gyōja* also hinted at the responsibility of the individual in the modern age.

In the late Meiji and early Taishō eras, Japan was starting to come to terms with its own responsibilities, as it had annexed Taiwan in 1895 and Korea in 1910, and a number of young Taiwanese and Koreans came to study at Japanese universities, including under Shōyō at Waseda. It is well known that the first Korean translations of complete Shakespeare plays, *Hamlet* in 1921 and *The Merchant of Venice* in 1924, were not made from the original texts but were influenced by Shōyō's late Meiji translations of the plays as they had been studied by Korean graduates of his university. With this context in mind, in 1965 the drama critic Ozaki Hirotsugu expressed surprise at Shōyō's apparent silence on the massacre of ethnic Koreans by vigilante groups in the chaotic aftermath of the Great Kanto Earthquake of 1 September 1923.[20]

Shōyō's silence on the atrocity is characteristic of his lifelong tendency to avoid political controversy that may even be seen as impotence. A subtext of this monograph has been that Shōyō became a Shakespeare translator because, having in the 1880s set standards for literary realism that he himself could not attain, he could at least absorb himself in the repeated act of reproducing Shakespeare's superior realism in his native language, and if that seemed inauthentic and self-serving, he was also doing it for the stimulation of the emerging modern Japanese theatre. The Shōyō of Taishō and early Shōwa can seem hopelessly at odds with the ideological commitment of the younger generation, but at the very least his Shakespeare translations introduced to the modern theatre were plays with logical motives and a beginning, a middle, and an end; if he was sometimes puritanical in his views, he had successfully diverted his former dilettantism towards a lifelong involvement with the "pleasure of the text" that in his view was morally preferable to the pleasure quarters of his youth.

The young Shōyō's *Tōsei shosei katagi* was criticised for its convoluted plot and surfeit of characters, but these generic limitations are largely irrelevant to the spheres of playwriting and Shakespeare translation, where there was less need to complicate the scene with his personal reflections and he could be guided by his visual aesthetic sense of what looked right on stage. In his middle and old age, the challenge Shōyō faces is that the role he had inherited from his upbringing in *baku-matsu* (i.e. late Edo) Japan of the literati (*bunjin*) of ancient Chinese and Japanese tradition was less acceptable to the era of "Taishō democracy,"[21] so that like Hermit En he struggles to keep his place on the mountain. Houghton had chastised him at the Imperial University for writing a didactic analysis of Gertrude's character, and although he went along with Houghton's anti-didacticism, there must have been times in this new age of shifting dialectics when he wondered why on earth he should not criticise Gertrude or anyone else for failing to set an adequate example, and in Gertrude's case the latter would have amounted to much the same "fulfill-ment of ideals" (i.e., assertion of personal opinion) that he believed Shakespearean drama to effect.

Shōyō's early reception by the Meiji *bundan* and recognition by Ōkuma more or less guaranteed his career and social status (which was an opportunity less available to the next generation), and as the "comic giant" portrayed by Tsuno Kaitarō he basically welcomed the modern age. Yet behind his comic persona lay many sadnesses, including the loss of his parents in his early twenties; the prema-ture deaths of Futabatei, Hōgetsu, and his adopted son and nephew Daizō (another nephew was killed in the Russo-Japanese War); the difficulties with Shikō; and perhaps above all the inability of his wife to bear him children of his own. Accord-ing to Tsuno, visitors to Atami in Shōyō's final years found a lonely old man:[22] one who, having achieved his life's work, may have finally welcomed that "eter-nity" he had previously suggested "those with their eyes on eternity" might find in Shakespeare.[23]

## Notes

1 The two most prominent being Kurosawa Akira's 1957 film adaptation of *Macbeth*, *Kumonosujō* (Throne of Blood), and Ninagawa Yukio's stage production of the same play (premiered in 1985), which were set respectively in medieval and sixteenth-century Japan. I use the outdated label "Oriental" to refer to East Asia in the sense that Shōyō would have understood it, and as a direct translation of the Japanese word *tōyō* ("the East").

2 Tsubouchi Shōyō, *A Handbook of the Tsubouchi Memorial Theatre Museum at Waseda University* (Tokyo: Tsubouchi Memorial Theatre Museum, 1929), 4.

3 Ibid.

4 Shōyō explains in *Shōsetsu shinzui* that the use of Chinese expressions in Japanese fic-tion imparted "vigour," which was the vigour of generalization against a native tendency for vagueness and verbosity: Tsubouchi Shōyō, "Shōsetsu shinzui" (1885–6), in *Tsub-ouchi Shōyō shū*, ed. Inagaki Tatsurō (Tokyo: Chikuma Shobō, 1969), 35.

5 Tsubouchi Shōyō, *Makubesu* (Tokyo: Chūō Kōronsha, 1935), 179.

6 Hidden in the sense that as mimetic words (*gitaigo*), which are abundant in Japanese, they imitate an action rather than expressing it overtly in the manner of onomatopoeia.

7 The initial 1916 version does not have a comma after *tada ichiji*. Its inclusion in the 1935 revision was probably intended to make the speech more speakable.

8 Judith Woodsworth, *Telling the Story of Translation: Writers Who Translate* (London: Bloomsbury, 2017), 2.

9 Tsubouchi Shōyō, "Soko shirazu no mizuumi" (1891), in Inagaki, *Tsubouchi Shōyō shū*, 279–80. Shōyō's is clearly a Japanese lake, although he does not relate it to any individual Japanese writer, and at the end of his essay he declares that the only other two places of comparable beauty are "a swamp in England called 'Shake-sphere'" [i.e., as a writer of "earth-shattering" genius] and "one in Germany called *gyōten*" [connoting Romantic "astonishment," i.e., Goethe] (282).

10 Ibid., 280.

11 Ibid., 282.

12 Irokawa Daikichi mentions the primary school textbooks Shōyō wrote between 1899 and 1901 that sold as many as one hundred thousand copies before being censored by government authorities. The passages censored were those that implicitly rejected the notion of the Meiji emperor as a living god, that praised social philanthropy above entrepreneurial gain, and which criticised racial discrimination: Irokawa Daikichi, *The Culture of the Meiji Period*, trans. and ed. Marius B. Jansen (Princeton, NJ: Princeton University Press, 1985), 308–9.

13 Martha P. Y. Cheung, ed. and trans., *An Anthology of Chinese Discourse on Translation*, vol. 1 (London: Routledge, 2014), 6.

14 Kobayashi Yoshihito, *Tsubouchi Shōyō* (Tokyo: Shimizu Shoin, 1969), 121.

15 Ibid., 141.

16 Uchida Roan, *Shinpen omoidasu hitobito* (1925), ed. Kōno Toshirō (Tokyo: Iwanami Shoten, 1994), 152.

17 Fujinami Takayuki, ed., *Kiri hitoha* (Tokyo: Hakusuisha, 1992), 74.

18 Satō Isao, "Nīche," in *Tsubouchi Shōyō jiten*, ed. Shōyō Kyōkai (Tokyo: Heibonsha, 1986), 281.

19 David G. Goodman, *Five Plays by Kishida Kunio* (Ithaca, NY: Cornell University Press, 1989), 17.

20 Ozaki Hirotsugu, *Tsubouchi Shōyō – Nihon kindaigeki no sōjishatachi* (Tokyo: Miraisha, 1965), 134. An estimated six thousand people, most of them ethnic Koreans, are alleged to have been murdered in the Tokyo area on suspicion, for example, of poisoning the water supplies. Ozaki is surprised from the point of view of Shōyō's reputation as a "Confucian-style" and therefore morally upright educationist (*kyōikuka*), and similarly questions his failure to condemn the murders by military police in September 1923 of the radical writers Ōsugi Sakae and Hirasawa Keishichi.

21 The Taishō era (1912–26) saw the introduction of representative democracy and other liberal reforms, as well as considerable economic growth.

22 Tsuno Kaitarō, *Kokkeina kyojin – Tsubouchi Shōyō no yume* (Tokyo: Heibonsha, 2002), 272–3. Tsuno discusses an unproven theory that Shōyō hastened his death from acute bronchitis by overdosing on the bromides he had been prescribed for his insomnia (290–9).

23 Tsubouchi Shōyō, "'*Makubesu* hyōshaku' no shogen" (1891), in *Shōyō senshū*, ed. Shōyō Kyōkai, supp. vol. 3 (1978), 169.

## References

Cheung, Martha P. Y., ed. and trans. *An Anthology of Chinese Discourse on Translation, Vol. 1: From Earliest Times to the Buddhist Project*. London: Routledge, 2014, https://doi.org/10.4324/9781315759470.

Fujinami Takayuki, ed. *Kiri hitoha* [A Single Paulownia Leaf]. 1894–5. Tokyo: Hakusuisha, 1992.

Goodman, David G. *Five Plays by Kishida Kunio*. Ithaca, NY: Cornell University Press, 1989.

Inagaki Tatsurō, ed. *Tsubouchi Shōyō shū* [Works of Tsubouchi Shōyō]. Tokyo: Chikuma Shobō, 1969.

Irokawa Daikichi. *The Culture of the Meiji Period*. translated and edited by Marius B. Jansen. Princeton, NJ: Princeton University Press, 1985. Originally published as *Meiji no bunka*. Tokyo: Iwanami Shoten, 1970, https://doi.org/10.2307/j.ctvx5wbxq.

Ozaki Hirotsugu. *Tsubouchi Shōyō – Nihon kindaigeki no sōjishatachi* [Tsubouchi Shōyō: Pioneer of Modern Japanese Drama]. Tokyo: Miraisha, 1965.

Satō Isao. "Nīche" [Nietzsche]. In *Tsubouchi Shōyō jiten* [Dictionary of Tsubouchi Shōyō Studies], edited by Shōyō Kyōkai, 281. Tokyo: Heibonsha, 1986.

Tsubouchi Shōyō. *A Handbook of the Tsubouchi Memorial Theatre Museum at Waseda University*. Tokyo: Tsubouchi Memorial Theatre Museum, 1929.

———. "'*Makubesu* hyōshaku' no shogen" [Preface to a Commentary on *Macbeth*]. 1891. In *Shōyō senshū*, supplementary vol. 3, edited by Shōyō Kyōkai, 161–9. Tokyo: Daiichi Shobō, 1978.

———. *Shōsetsu shinzui* [The Essence of the Novel]. 1885–6. In *Tsubouchi Shōyō shū*, edited by Inagaki, 3–58.

———. "Soko shirazu no mizuumi" [The Bottomless Lake]. 1891. In *Tsubouchi Shōyō shū*, edited by Inagaki, 279–82.

———, trans. *Makubesu* [Macbeth]. Tokyo: Chūō Kōronsha, 1935.

Tsuno Kaitarō. *Kokkeina kyojin – Tsubouchi Shōyō no yume* [Comic Giant: The Dream of Tsubouchi Shōyō]. Tokyo: Heibonsha, 2002.

Uchida Roan. *Shinpen omoidasu hitobito* [Memories of Meiji Writers]. 1925. edited by Kōno Toshirō. Tokyo: Iwanami Shoten, 1994.

Woodsworth, Judith. *Telling the Story of Translation: Writers Who Translate*. London: Bloomsbury, 2017, https://doi.org/10.5040/9781474277112.

# Index

For Product Safety Concerns and Information please contact our EU
representative  GPSR@taylorandfrancis.com
Taylor & Francis Verlag GmbH, Kaufingerstraße 24, 80331 München, Germany

www.ingramcontent.com/pod-product-compliance
Lightning Source LLC
Chambersburg PA
CBHW071605110726
47908CB00007B/2246